Helen Coursey

LABOUR MARKET POLICIES IN THE ERA OF PERVASIVE AUSTERITY
A European perspective

Edited by Sotiria Theodoropoulou

First published in Great Britain in 2018 by

Policy Press
University of Bristol
1-9 Old Park Hill
Bristol
BS2 8BB
UK
t: +44 (0)117 954 5940
pp-info@bristol.ac.uk
www.policypress.co.uk

North America office:
Policy Press
c/o The University of Chicago Press
1427 East 60th Street
Chicago, IL 60637, USA
t: +1 773 702 7700
f: +1 773-702-9756
sales@press.uchicago.edu
www.press.uchicago.edu

© Policy Press 2018

British Library Cataloguing in Publication Data
A catalogue record for this book is available from the British Library

Library of Congress Cataloging-in-Publication Data
A catalog record for this book has been requested

ISBN 978-1-4473-3586-3 hardback
ISBN 978-1-4473-3587-0 ePdf
ISBN 978-1-4473-3588-7 ePub
ISBN 978-1-4473-3589-4 Mobi

The right of Sotiria Theodoropoulou to be identified as editor of this work has been asserted by her in accordance with the Copyright, Designs and Patents Act 1988.

All rights reserved: no part of this publication may be reproduced, stored in a retrieval system, or transmitted in any form or by any means, electronic, mechanical, photocopying, recording, or otherwise without the prior permission of Policy Press.

The statements and opinions contained within this publication are solely those of the editor and contributors and not of the University of Bristol or Policy Press. The University of Bristol and Policy Press disclaim responsibility for any injury to persons or property resulting from any material published in this publication.

Policy Press works to counter discrimination on grounds of gender, race, disability, age and sexuality.

Cover design by Policy Press
Front cover image: iStock
Printed and bound in Great Britain by CPI Group (UK) Ltd, Croydon, CR0 4YY
Policy Press uses environmentally responsible print partners

Contents

List of figures and tables	vii
Notes on contributors	xiii
Acknowledgements	xix

one	**Labour market policies in the era of European pervasive austerity: a review** *Sotiria Theodoropoulou*	1
	Introduction	1
	New approaches to labour market policies under the pressures of 'permanent austerity' and the emergence of 'new' social risks	2
	Blame avoidance, credit claiming and patterns of policy change	4
	New policy agendas	5
	Is this time different?	6
	Empirical approach and organisation of the book	8
two	**Structural reforms in Europe: a comparative overview** *Chiara Agostini and David Natali*	15
	Introduction	15
	Socio-economic reforms in Europe: common path or different strategies?	16
	Structural reforms in the European Union: some conceptual clarification	18
	Structural reform trends: a cluster-by-cluster overview	20
	Concluding remarks	33
	Appendix	38
three	**Income support policies and labour market reforms under austerity in Greece** *Manos Matsaganis*	43
	Introduction	43
	Income support	45
	Active labour market policies	50
	Employment protection legislation	56
	Conclusion	60
	Appendix	65

four	The Italian labour market policy reforms and the economic crisis: coming towards the end of Italian exceptionalism? *Patrik Vesan and Emmanuele Pavoli*	69
	Introduction	69
	Main aspects of the Italian labour market before and since the onset of the crisis	70
	Changes in the traditional model: from the mid-1990s until the crisis	73
	Towards a new institutional landscape: the 'long jump' of labour market policy reforms during the economic crisis	75
	A fragile and still incomplete path towards a new labour market policy regime	84
five	French employment market policies: dualisation and destabilisation *Hélène Caune and Sotiria Theodoropoulou*	91
	Introduction	91
	Macroeconomic and labour market background	92
	Labour market policies prior to the crisis: the gradual shift towards dualisation	96
	Labour market policies since 2009: cyclical measures to support young people and flexibilisation reforms	99
	Conclusion: France under austerity and the ambiguous attempt to tackle dualisation	108
six	The German exception: welfare protectionism instead of retrenchment *Werner Eichhorst and Anke Hassel*	115
	Introduction	115
	Welfare reforms during the 2000s	117
	Germany during the crisis	120
	Welfare reforms since 2010: re-regulation rather than retrenchment policies	125
	Conclusion	137

Contents

seven	The Netherlands and the crisis: from activation to 'deficiency compensation' *Marcel Hoogenboom*	141

    Introduction 141
    The consequences of the crisis and early policy reactions 142
    Reform of the Dutch unemployment provision system 146
    and active labour market policies up to the crisis (1980s–2008)
    Emergency measures and reform plans (2008–10) 153
    The politics of reform (2010–present) 156
    Conclusion 161

eight	Dualising the Swedish model: insiders and outsiders and labour market policy reform in Sweden: an overview *Johan Bo Davidsson*	169

    Introduction 169
    Labour market policy reform from the 1990s and onwards 170
    Recent developments: labour market policy and 189
    economic crisis
    Conclusion 190

nine	No longer 'fit for purpose'? Consolidation and catch-up in Irish labour market policy *Fiona Dukelow*	197

    Introduction 197
    Setting the context: the economic crisis and its 198
    consequences for labour market policy
    Mapping key changes in labour market policy 202
    Concluding remarks 219

ten	Retrenchment, conditionality and flexibility – UK labour market policies in the era of austerity *Elke Heins and Hayley Bennett*	225

    Introduction 225
    The UK crisis context 226
    Unemployment benefits: Jobseeker's Allowance 228
    Employment protection legislation 230
    Active labour market policies 233
    Training and human capital formation 235
    Needs-based social protection for the unemployed 239
    Discussion 240
    Conclusion 244

eleven	Czechia: political experimentation or incremental reforms? *Tomáš Sirovátka*	253
	Introduction	253
	Economic development during the crisis and related European Union regulations	255
	Labour market policies	256
	Minimum income protection and activation of long-term unemployed and social assistance recipients	264
	Politics of the reforms in labour market-related policies	267
	Conclusion	270
	Appendix	274
twelve	Slovakia: perpetual austerity and growing emphasis on activation *Stefan Domonkos*	277
	Introduction	277
	Macroeconomic and macro-institutional context	278
	Labour market policies during the economic transition and beyond	283
	Conclusions: assessing the impact of EU austerity on labour market policies	298
thirteen	Slovenian labour market policies under austerity: narrowing the gap between the well- and the less well-protected in the labour market? *Miroljub Ignjatović and Maša Filipovič Hrast*	309
	Introduction	309
	Context and policy changes up to 2010	310
	Labour market policy developments and outcomes since 2010	316
	Conclusion	329
	Appendix	333
fourteen	Conclusions *Sotiria Theodoropoulou*	337
	Introduction	337
	Changes in labour market policies	338
	Increasing and divergent labour market insecurity	354
	Concluding remarks	358
Index		363

List of figures and tables

Figures

2.1	Pensions expenditure as a percentage of GDP, 1999–2012	38
2.2	Net replacement rates, pensions, 2006, 2008, 2010, 2012	38
2.3	Public expenditure on education as a percentage of GDP, 1999–2011	39
2.4	Public expenditure on education as a share of total public expenditure 1999–2011	39
2.5	Public expenditure on R&D and the public sector, 1999–2012	40
2.6	General government expenditure in the remuneration of employees as a share of GDP, 1999–2012	40
3.1	Coverage rate of unemployment benefits in Greece, 2010–16	50
5.1	Real GDP, employment (in 000s) and total average annual hours worked growth (2007=100), France, 2007–16	93
5.2	Public expenditure in different types of labour market policies as a share of GDP, France, 1998–2014	100
6.1	Employment rates as a percentage of the working-age population (age 15–64), various EU countries, 2000–15	120
6.2	Unemployment rates as a percentage of the labour force, various EU countries, 2000–15	121
6.3	Short-time workers in Germany, 2005–16	122
6.4	Minimum wage in percent of median wage of full-time workers, OECD-Europe countries and US, 2014	126
6.5	Collective bargaining coverage, as a percentage of all workers, Germany, 1998–2015	127
6.6	Unemployment and long-term unemployment in Germany as a percentage of the active population, 2000–15	130
6.7	Expenditure on active labour market policies as a percentage of GDP, selected EU member states, 2000–14	131
6.8	Expenditure on active labour market policies as a percentage of GDP, selected EU member states	131
6.9	Employment rate of workers aged 55–64 as a percentage of the total population, selected EU member states, 2000–15	132
7.1	Real GDP growth and government deficit in the Netherlands, 2005–16 (% of GDP)	144
7.2	Unemployment total labour force (15–65 years of age) and youth unemployment (15–35 years of age); and benefit recipients of unemployment insurance and social assistance, as a percentage of the labour force, 2004–16	145

7.3	Spending on active labour market policies in the Netherlands: spending per recipient (€) and total spending as percentage of real GDP, 1990–2014	150
7.4	Activation budgets of social assistance and unemployment insurance: average spending per recipient (€), 2007–15	163
8.1	Employment protection legislation – regular and temporary contracts, Sweden, 1985–2013	173
8.2	Net replacement rates in the unemployment insurance, Sweden and the EU15	178
8.3	Spending on passive and active measures, and unemployment (standard scores), Sweden, 1985–2013	179
8.4	Social assistance, spending and household recipient rates, Sweden 1990–2015	183
8.5	Labour-market programmes, spending on active measures, Sweden, EU15 and Nordic countries, 1985–2015	185
8.6	Labour market programmes, spending on training, Sweden, EU15 and Nordic countries, 1985–2015	185
8.7	Type of active labour market programme spending, Sweden, 1985–2015	186
9.1	Government deficit, government debt and GDP growth rate, Ireland, 2007–16	199
9.2	Unemployment and long-term unemployment rate, Ireland, 1990–2016	200
10.1	Unemployment rates, EU28 and UK, 2007–16	227
10.2	Real GDP growth rate (volume), EU28 and UK since 2007, percentage change on previous year	227
10.3	UK gross government debt as percentage of GDP since 2007	228
10.4	Jobseeker's Allowance expenditure, UK, 2001–17	229
10.5	Jobseeker's Allowance sanctioning trends, UK, April 2000–October 2016	241
10.6	Employment Support Allowance sanctioning trends, Great Britain, January 2008–July 2016	242
12.1	Total, youth and long-term unemployment rates in Slovakia, 1994–2015	281
12.2	Unemployment benefit recipients as a percentage of registered unemployed, Slovakia, various years 1997–2015	285
12.3	Expenditure on active labour market policies in Slovakia, Austria, France and Germany as a percentage of nominal GDP, 1991–2014	292
12.4	Participation in active labour market policies in Slovakia, 2005–14 ('000)	293

Contents

13.1	Number of unemployed registered with the employment service at the end of the year, Slovenia, 1967–2016	310
13.2	Share of unemployment benefit recipients in total registered unemployed, Slovenia, 1991–2016	311
13.3	Level of flexible employment among persons in employment, Slovenia, 2007–16	314
13.4	Consolidated gross debt and net borrowing/deficit at year-end, Slovenia, 2000–16 (% of GDP)	315
13.5	Chronological overview of the most important reforms, Slovenia, 2010–16	317
13.6	At-risk-of-poverty rates by labour market status (aged 18 years and more), Slovenia, 2005–16	323
13.7	In-work at-risk-of-poverty rates for some forms of employment in Slovenia by employment status, 2005–16	325
13.8	Number of registered unemployed and expenditure for labour market policies, Slovenia, 2008–15	328
14.1	Fiscal consolidation effort and labour market reform effort per year, selected European Union member states, 2010–14	341
14.2	Labour market reform effort per year and average annual growth of unemployed, selected European Union member states, 2010–14	341
14.3	Public expenditure in labour market services per person wanting to work, selected European Union member states, 1998–2015	342
14.4	Public expenditure in labour market policy measures per person wanting to work, selected European Union member states, 1998–2015	342
14.5	Public expenditure in labour market (financial) support policies per person wanting to work, selected European Union member states, 1998–2015	343
14.6	Long-term unemployment as share of total unemployment, selected European Union member states, 2008, 2010, 2015	344
14.7	Evolution of the OECD labour market insecurity indicator (% of previous earnings), selected European Union member states, 2007, 2010 and 2013	356
14.8	Evolution of the OECD unemployment risk indicator (% of time), selected European Union member states, 2007, 2010 and 2013	357
14.9	Evolution of the OECD effective unemployment insurance indicator (% of previous earnings), selected European Union member states, 2007, 2010 and 2013	358

Tables

2.1	A typology of structural reform trends	19
2.2	Overview of structural reforms in Europe	41
3.1	Changes in labour market policies in Greece from 2010 onwards	66
4.1	Activity rates over time, Italy and the EU15	70
4.2	Temporary employees as a percentage of the total number of employees over time, Italy and EU15	71
4.3	Main reason for temporary employment, Italy and EU15	72
4.4	Unemployment rates, Italy and EU15	72
4.5	Number of unemployed and employed and their relative variation over time, Italy and EU15	73
4.6	Industrial and post-industrial labour market policy instruments since the recent economic crisis, Italy	82
6.1	German labour market reforms, 2009–2017	123
7.1	Dutch governments, 2007–16	144
7.2	Major changes in unemployment provision, ALMP and job protection programmes in the Netherlands, 1987–present	148
8.1	Major labour market policy reforms in Sweden, 1990–2016	188
9.1	Summary of changes to benefit schemes for the unemployed, Ireland	203
9.2	Summary of changes to Jobseeker's Allowance and One-Parent Family Payment, Ireland	207
9.3	Summary of changes to existing activation programmes and payments, Ireland	212
9.4	Participant numbers, activation payments and programmes, Ireland, 2008–15	214
10.1	Social and labour market policy instruments pre-crisis and post-crisis, UK	245
11.1	Selected macroeconomic indicators, Czechia (annual averages in %)	255
11.2	Net replacement rates for unemployment benefits for two levels of wages, different household compositions and the initial phase of unemployment (no top-up benefits included)	258
11.3	Active labour market policy during 2010–14: participants and expenditure (Public Employment Service register data)	260
11.4	Employment protection legislation index in the Czech Republic (OECD methodology)	263

11.5	Net replacement rates for the total of social benefits for the long-term unemployed (60th month of unemployment), for two levels of wages and for different household composition	265
11.6	Summary of the changes to the policies for the unemployed, Czech Republic	275
12.1	The economic environment and regional disparities in Slovakia, 2004–15	282
12.2	Minimum notice period and severance pay according to the Slovak labour code, 2002–15	288
12.3	Selected active labour market policy instruments in the Slovak legislation, 1991–2015	290
12.4	Needs-based income support in Slovakia, 2004–15	296
12.5	Summarising policy trajectories from the pre-accession to post-crisis European Union in Slovakia	299
13.1	Summary of labour market policy changes in Slovenia	334
14.1	Reform effort per year, selected EU member states, 2000–14	340
14.2	Summary of labour market policy developments, selected European Union member states, 2010–16	352

Notes on contributors

Chiara Agostini, PhD in public policy analysis, is currently researcher at the 'Centro di Ricerca e Documentazione Luigi Einaudi' (Turin, Italy). She was post-doc research fellow at University of Rome (2008/09), Bologna (2011/12) and Milan (2013). In 2015, she was researcher at the European Social Observatory (Brussels). Her work mostly deals with the comparative analysis of social and education policy and European social governance in the same field.

Hayley Bennett (PhD Edinburgh) is a research fellow in the Academy of Government at the University of Edinburgh. Her research focuses on the design and delivery of policies aimed at reducing unemployment and poverty. She previously held positions as a research fellow in the departments of politics and international relations ('What Works Scotland' – ESRC project), and of social policy ('Combating Poverty in Europe' – FP7 project) in the University of Edinburgh. Her research has been published in the *Journal of Social Policy*, *Social Policy and Administration* and *Work, Employment and Society*.

Hélène Caune is senior lecturer in political science at the University of Toulouse, France. A former visiting fellow at Harvard University, she holds a PhD from Sciences Po Paris. Hélène's research deals with the definition and implementation of European employment policies and the tensions between European integration and member states' welfare systems. She has been engaged in several collective research projects, such as the Network of Excellence 'Recwowe' (Reconciling work and welfare), and the ERC-funded project 'Reconciling Economic and Social Europe' (REScEU) led by Maurizio Ferrera. Her work has been published in several peer-reviewed journals and collective book chapters.

Johan Bo Davidsson is an assistant professor at Lund University, Sweden. He holds a PhD from European University Institute, where he wrote his thesis on the politics of labour market reform in France, Sweden and the UK. He has published on this topic in journals such as *Political Studies* and the *European Journal of Political Research*. He currently works on a project on cabinet ministers and social policy reform.

Stefan Domonkos is currently a researcher at the Institute of Economic Research of the Slovak Academy of Sciences. Prior to this, he was a researcher at MZES-Mannheim, from where he also obtained his PhD, and at CELSI in Bratislava. His research focused on the political and economic aspects of pension reforms in Central and Eastern Europe, as well as public opinion on pension and taxation reforms, and has been published by Global Social Policy and the International Monetary Fund.

Fiona Dukelow is a lecturer in the School of Applied Social Studies, University College Cork, Ireland. Her research interests include critical welfare theory and various aspects of historical and contemporary Irish social policy and Irish welfare state change. Her publications include: *Defining events: Power, resistance and identity in twenty-first-century Ireland* (Manchester UP, 2015) (co-edited with Rosie Meade); *The Irish welfare state in the twenty-first century: Challenges and change* (Palgrave, 2016) (co-edited with Mary P. Murphy); and *Irish social policy: A critical introduction* (2nd edn) (Policy Press, 2017) (co-authored with Mairéad Considine).

Werner Eichhorst is head of the research group on labour market and social policies in Europe at IZA (Bonn), Germany. He has previously worked at the Max Planck Institute for Social Research (Cologne) and the Bertelsmann foundation. His research work and publications focus on international comparative analysis of institutions and the development of labour markets, the comparison of employment policy strategies and reform processes, the future of work, and change in the world of work. He frequently acts as a policy advisor.

Anke Hassel is the academic director of the Institute of Economic and Social Research (WSI) of the Hans Böckler Foundation and professor of public policy at the Hertie School of Governance in Berlin (on leave). From 2009 until 2012, she was Senior Visiting Fellow at the European Institute of the London School of Economics. Her research interest is in the interplay between modern business and social systems. She has written extensively about the transformation of the German political economy in a comparative perspective and the role of labour market institutions in the Eurozone.

Elke Heins is lecturer in social policy at the University of Edinburgh, UK. Her research mainly focuses on labour market and social policy in comparative and European perspective, with a particular interest in the politics of welfare. Recent articles dealt with the concept of flexicurity, the involvement of trade unions and third sector organisations in welfare policy delivery, and the privatisation of welfare services. Together with Caroline de la Porte, she edited the book *The sovereign debt crisis, the EU and welfare state reform* (Palgrave, 2016).

Marcel Hoogenboom is an assistant professor at the Department of Social and Behavioural Sciences at the University of Utrecht. He obtained a PhD degree in sociology at the Amsterdam Institute for Social Science Research (ASSR) of Amsterdam University after studying political science at the University of Leiden. Prior to his current post, he worked as a researcher and teacher at the University of Twente. His research interests include comparative welfare state analysis in unemployment provision and social assistance. His work has been published in, among others, the *Journal of European Social Policy* and by Oxford University Press.

Maša Filipovič Hrast is associate professor at the University of Ljubljana, Faculty of Social Sciences, and member of the Research Centre for Welfare Studies. Her research interests focus on social policy and the welfare state, as well as problems of social exclusion. She has published in national and international journals, as well as books. Her recent publications deal with the changes of the Slovenian welfare state, for example, she co-authored a chapter in Schubert et al, *Challenges to European welfare system* (Springer, 2016).

Miroljub Ignjatović is researcher and assistant professor at the University of Ljubljana, Faculty of Social Sciences, and member of the Centre for Organisational and Human Resources Research at the same faculty. His research interests focus on the labour market (especially on the consequences of labour market flexibilisation), social policy and the welfare state. He has published in national and international journals, as well as and books. A recent publication deals with the precarisation of the Slovenian labour market in the 21st century (co-authored with Aleksandra Kanjuo Mrčela).

Manos Matsaganis is associate professor of public finance at Politecnico di Milano. Trained as an economist in Greece (AUEB) and in England (MSc, York; PhD, Bristol), he has worked at the London School of Economics (1990–93), the Greek Prime Minister's Office (1997–2001), the University of Crete (1996–99 and 2001–04) and the Athens University of Economics and Business (2004–16), where he founded and coordinated the Policy Analysis Research Unit. He sits on the Board of the European Network of Social Policy Analysis (ESPAnet).

David Natali is Professor of Comparative and EU Politics at the Sant'Anna School of Advanced Studies of Pisa, and associate researcher at the European Social Observatory of Brussels. He holds a doctorate in political science at the European University Institute in Florence. He has been involved in several integrated European projects and networks of excellence. His research is mainly centred on a comparative analysis of social policy reforms, EU integration, industrial relations and the politics of welfare. He teaches on the doctorate programme of the Scuola Normale Superiore (SNS) – Institute of Humanities and Social Sciences in Florence. His most recent publications include: D. Natali (ed) *The new pension mix in Europe* (PIE-Peter Lang, 2017), B. Vanhercke, D. Bouget and D. Natali (eds) *Social policy in the European Union: state of play 2016* (ETUI/OSE, 2016) and A. Agostini, V. Lisi, D. Natali and S. Sabato, *Balancing protection and investment: Structural reforms in five countries* (ETUI, 2016).

Emmanuele Pavolini is full professor in economic sociology and social policy at the University of Macerata, Italy. His research interests are comparative social policy and family policies. He has recently published several articles and books on Southern European welfare states during the austerity and economic crisis years.

Tomáš Sirovátka is professor of social policy at the Faculty of Social Studies, Masaryk University. He carried out a number of research projects on social policy and employment policy. He publishes in international journals like *Social Policy and Administration*, *International Journal of Sociology and Social Policy*, *Journal of Comparative Policy Analysis*, *Journal of European Social Policy* and *European Journal of Social Security*. He contributed to several comparative books on employment and social policy, and co-edited *The governance of active welfare states in Europe* (Palgrave/Macmillan, 2011) and *Innovation in social services: The public–private mix in service provision, fiscal policy and employment* (Ashgate, 2014) and *Effective interventions for unemployed young people in Europe: Social innovation or paradigm shift?* (Routledge, 2017).

Sotiria Theodoropoulou is senior researcher and head of the European economic, employment and social policies unit at the European Trade Union Institute (ETUI) in Brussels, where she has been studying and publishing on the impact of fiscal austerity and EU economic governance reforms on macroeconomic performance and labour market policies in Europe. She earned her PhD in European political economy from the European Institute of the London School of Economics with a thesis on the political economy of unemployment in Europe. Her research has been published in *Comparative European Politics* and collective volumes by Oxford University Press and Palgrave MacMillan.

Patrik Vesan is associate professor in Political Science at the University of Aosta Valley. He is a member of the REScEU project and collaborates with the 'Percorsi di Secondo Welfare' laboratory (see: www.secondowelfare.it). His main areas of research are European and comparative employment policies, public administration and policy analysis, comparative local development policy, European governance, multilevel governance theory, and intergovernmental relations.

Acknowledgements

The project that has led to the publication of this book was initiated at and financed by the European Trade Union Institute (ETUI), the independent research and education institute of the European Trade Union Confederation (ETUC). The ETUI itself is financially supported by the European Union.

I am grateful to all the authors who enthusiastically accepted to participate in the project and for their feedback at various stages. Versions of the book chapters were presented and discussed at an ETUI workshop in Brussels in December 2014, the University Association for Contemporary European Studies (UACES) 2016 conference in London, the Society for the Advancement of Socio-Economics (SASE) 2017 conference in Lyon and the Council for European Studies (CES) 2017 conference in Lyon. I would like to thank the participants in these workshops and conferences, in particular, Philippe Pochet and Janine Leschke, for their useful suggestions. Last but not least, I would like to thank the three anonymous referees for their constructive comments on the proposal and the manuscript of the book. The usual disclaimer applies.

I am indebted to several of my colleagues at the ETUI for their advice at various stages of this project. In particular, I would like to thank, without implicating, Maria Jepsen for her guidance throughout, Magda Bernaciak and Martin Myant for their advice in dealing with aspects of the publication process, and Kathleen Llanwarne and James Patterson for editing early versions of the book proposal and the manuscript. I am particularly thankful to Laura Vickers from The Policy Press for her encouragement, advice and patience.

This book is dedicated with gratitude to my family: to my parents, and especially my mother, a Greek labour market 'outsider', for all the love and the early opportunities they made sure I got in the hope that I would fare better than they did; and to my husband and children, Kristian, Nicólas and Zoé, for their endless encouragement, support, patience and love.

Sotiria Theodoropoulou
August 2017, Brussels

ONE

Labour market policies in the era of European pervasive austerity: a review

Sotiria Theodoropoulou

Introduction

This edited volume investigates whether and, if so, how the patterns of change of labour market policies in European Union (EU) member states have altered since the emergence in 2010 of reinforced pressures on public spending ('fiscal austerity'). More specifically, the book explores, through national case studies: whether retrenchment or expansion has taken place; whether there has been a shift in the logic of activation policies; and how the retrenchment and expansion of protection have been distributed across the well-protected and the less well-protected labour market populations. Looking at the big European picture, do we see a convergence or a divergence in labour market policy trends and outputs? Can we identify different patterns of change across member states? Last but not least, we ask whether there has been a divergence or convergence in labour market insecurity that can be associated with the ongoing policy changes and macroeconomic conditions.

Here, labour market policies are considered a domain of social policy. We thus examine changes in government policy interventions in unemployment benefit systems (insurance and assistance), employment protection legislation (EPL) and active labour market policies (ALMPs). In that respect, this book focuses on a special case of the broad question of whether and, if so, how social policies in Europe have been changing in the context of EU-driven fiscal austerity since 2010.

The questions of whether and, if so, how social policies in general and labour market and unemployment policies in particular have been adapting under the financing pressures from 'permanent austerity' (Pierson, 1998), but also following the emergence of 'new' social risks (eg possessing low or obsolete skills, and insufficient social security coverage), have been studied extensively since the 1990s (for a sample from a very extended list, see Pierson, 1994, 1996, 2001; Clayton and Pontusson, 1998; Esping-Andersen, 1999; Esping-Andersen et al, 2002; Korpi and Palme, 2003; Hacker, 2004; Armingeon and Bonoli, 2006; Starke, 2006; Hausermann, 2010; Clasen and Clegg, 2011a; Bonoli and Natali, 2012c; Vis and Hemerijck, 2014; Huber and Stephens, 2015). Key changes identified in the literature have included, as well as questioned, retrenchment in more or less overt or politically costly forms but also the development of new policy approaches and instruments, such as activation, social investment and 'needs-based' policies, for addressing ('new') social risks (for a review, see Häusermann, 2012). Moreover, convergence has been 'contingent': while countries have not converged into a single model, there have been commonalities in the responses to the aforementioned pressures with the shift from passive to more active (ie promoting employment) social policies (Hemerijck, 2006; Bonoli and Natali, 2012b).

New approaches to labour market policies under the pressures of 'permanent austerity' and the emergence of 'new' social risks

The 1970s marked the gradual decline of the manufacturing sector as the prime locus of employment creation and its substitution by the services sector, with its inherently low potential for productivity growth. The tertiarisation of employment has been linked to the aggregate productivity slowdown in advanced economies (Baumol and Bowen, 1966; Baumol, 1967). This slowdown put a limit on the growth potential of wages, thus creating direct constraints on the financing of social policies, which has been dubbed 'permanent austerity' (Pierson, 1998).[1]

The shift of employment creation to the services sectors has created a trilemma among the goals of full employment, wage equality and (public) budgetary restraint (Appelbaum and Schettkat, 1994, 1995; Iversen and Wren, 1998): given low productivity growth, employment creation in many services sectors, especially those requiring relatively low and 'generic' skills, can take place either if labour costs (whether in the form of wages or in the form of hiring and firing costs) are allowed to fall together with wage (and/or working conditions) equality, or if the state subsidises job creation in the public sector (eg in the social services).

The realities of the tertiarisation of employment creation and the associated trilemma called for a shift from the logic of labour market policies of the industrial era. Passive income support and the provision of channels for labour market exit of the (long-term) unemployed became ineffective and expensive. Generous unemployment benefits and highly protective employment protection legislation were no longer as necessary for encouraging workers to invest in industry- or firm-specific skills useful in manufacturing sectors (compare with Estevez-Abe et al, 2001). In fact, generous unemployment benefits were likely to raise the reservation wages of former manufacturing workers, thus making their shift to less well-paid service jobs harder. Moreover, the nature of demand in services favours 'atypical' forms of employment, while women, a group more likely to be subject to 'new' social risks, are typically strongly represented in service employment. More recently, the advent of information and communication technologies and their adoption in the production of services has helped ease the low productivity growth constraint at the heart of the trilemma. However, to take advantage of this higher productivity growth potential, governments may need to invest in expanding access to higher education (Wren et al, 2013).

Thus, new approaches to labour market policies emerged. More specifically, activation strategies for both the unemployed and the non-employed were developed (further) and gained in importance, with a variety of instruments. While commonly aiming at lowering the obstacles to becoming employed, the basic elements of activation policy instruments are, on the one hand, 'demanding' from the non-employed to actively seek for and accept jobs, while, on the other, 'enabling' elements that aim at increasing the employability, productivity and ultimately attractiveness of job-seekers to employers.

Bonoli (2010) goes beyond this dichotomy to further distinguish four ideal-types, namely: incentive reinforcement measures, aiming at strengthening the work incentives for benefit recipients; employment assistance measures, aiming at removing obstacles to labour market participation; occupation measures, aiming at keeping unemployed people occupied so as to ultimately prevent the deterioration of their human capital; and, finally, vocational training or measures providing basic education, aiming at enhancing the skills of those who had not had a chance of acquiring sufficient training before or who need reskilling. Of these, incentive reinforcement and employment assistance are, in general, less costly than occupation and training measures (Bonoli, 2010), while a meta-analysis of 100 evaluation studies of ALMPs has suggested that employment assistance combined with incentive reinforcement and wage subsidies to employers in the private sector tend to be more effective than job creation in the public sector (Kluve, 2010, cited in Matsaganis, 2018). Training and, to some extent, occupation instruments are also related to strategies of 'social investment' (compare with Jenson, 2012). Further to activation measures, new policies have focused on supplementing the income of the working poor and at improving social protection, including access to unemployment benefits, for those workers under atypical contracts or career trajectories, whose contribution records would not necessarily allow them to qualify for support under the main unemployment insurance systems (Bonoli and Natali, 2012b).

In sum, a distinction can be drawn between 'old' and 'new' labour market policy instruments (Häusermann, 2012: 113–15). Old labour market policy instruments include passive benefits replacing the income of qualifying unemployed workers and employment protection legislation. On the other hand, new labour market policy instruments have developed or become more widely adopted since the 1990s and include active labour market policies, investment in training and human capital formation, and 'needs-based' income support for the long-term unemployed. Activation and social investment aim at protecting beneficiaries by helping them engage in gainful employment. On the other hand, 'needs-based' new labour market policy instruments aim at protecting those who cannot engage in gainful employment but do not qualify for unemployment insurance benefits.

Blame avoidance, credit claiming and patterns of policy change

The notions of 'blame avoidance' and 'credit claiming' by office-seeking governments have been used in the political-economy literature for predicting and explaining the direction of change in social and labour market policies (Pierson, 1994, 1996, 1998; Weaver, 1986; Bonoli, 2012). As Pierson (1998) argued, despite the significant financial pressures of 'permanent austerity' on welfare states, governments seeking re-election would be unlikely to pursue 'radical' changes in social policies in order to avoid taking the blame for rolling back policies that have become popular with their (politically powerful or veto-powered) beneficiaries. Instead, Pierson (1994) and Weaver (1986) argued that strategies involving reducing the visibility of reforms (eg through policy 'drift', layering or conversion) (Hacker, 2004; Streeck and Thelen, 2005), delaying their effects from taking place, making changes 'automatic' (eg linking retirement age to life expectancy) and dividing voters between winners and losers would be more likely (Bonoli, 2012). Arguably, however, there are circumstances that permit deviations from this principle. Fiscal crises or the pursuit of a 'superior objective' (such as membership of Economic and Monetary Union [EMU]) could mitigate the incompatibility between pursuing unpopular policies and seeking votes: governments could instead claim credit for averting worse fiscal developments or achieving the 'superior' objective (Bonoli, 2012).

Taking the 'path of least resistance' by directing the effects of policy retrenchment onto politically weak groups is also a strategy that minimises the political costs of retrenchment. In the case of labour market policies, taking the path of least resistance could involve directing cutbacks to labour market 'outsiders' instead of 'insiders', provided that the interests of the two groups are different (Rueda, 2007). The deregulation of employment protection legislation 'at the margin', that is, for 'atypical' employment contracts, is a characteristic example of taking the path of least resistance. Such a strategy could further reinforce dualisation in the labour market (Emmenegger et al, 2012). At the same time, however, there has been literature suggesting that following structural or other changes in the labour market, the division of interests between the two groups may be blurred (see, eg, Vlandas, 2013), leading to policy changes that are puzzling given the principle of 'blame avoidance'.

Last but not least, pursuing 'affordable credit claiming' by expanding pro-employment and/or social investment policies (as discussed in the previous section) has been another instance where social policy developments have countered what would have been expected in the face of permanent austerity pressures. This has been an option that has found support on both the Left and the Right, while the comparatively low level of funding for such programmes has allowed expansions to be highly visible (Bonoli, 2012).

New policy agendas

The emergence of 'new' labour market policy instruments alongside 'old' ones has allowed important changes in patterns of policy even in cases where it would have been unexpected, most notably, continental labour market regimes (Iversen and Wren, 1998; Esping-Andersen, 1999). Policy change has been multidimensional, often involving expansion and retrenchment in different policy instruments (Häusermann, 2012). Such 'mixed' strategies include 'flexicurity', whereby retrenchment in EPL for regular contracts is combined with strengthening income support and activation policies for the unemployed, with the stated purpose of protecting workers rather than jobs, as well as what Hausermann calls 'welfare readjustment' and 'welfare protectionism'. The latter two strategies are applicable in the case of dualised labour markets, whereby there is differentiation in the rules and entitlements applied to different groups, usually called 'insiders' and 'outsiders'.[2] Whereas welfare readjustment involves retrenching policy instruments benefiting insiders in order to allow expansion on policy instruments benefiting outsiders, welfare protectionism involves expanding policies benefiting insiders at the expense of outsiders (Häusermann, 2012). Welfare readjustment and flexicurity are thus 'recalibration' strategies, whereby the policy mix is adapted to meet new needs in the labour market and elsewhere. Given the increasing dualisation of labour markets, recalibration agendas gained ground in Europe (Clasen et al, 2012), at least as an intention.

Following influential recommendations for labour market deregulation in the early to mid-1990s (OECD, 1994), the promotion of flexicurity became a stated objective of the European Employment Strategy (EES) from 2005, which was later renewed with the Europe 2020 strategy, while activation was an important orientation since the launch of the EES in the mid-1990s. The launch of the Europe 2020 strategy in 2010, however, coincided with a sharp turn in fiscal policies and reforms in the EU's economic governance, which have resulted in even stricter limits on public spending, limits that, according to prominent economists (eg DeLong and Summers, 2012; Krugman, 2013; Wren-Lewis, 2015), have turned the initial sharp economic downturn from the financial crisis into the Great Recession.

Is this time different?

Given the rich existing literature on the transformation of social and labour market policies, why would the exercise undertaken in this book be a useful one at this juncture? Austerity has already been dubbed 'permanent' since the 1990s, so what should warrant considering whether there are changes in the patterns of labour market policies after 2010 in Europe?

This time, pressures to contain public spending are occurring against a background of a deep and long recession, with large and long-lasting drops in employment and increases in unemployment. The term 'permanent' austerity was used to characterise pressures for controlling public spending on welfare states at a time when European economies either grew, even if at lower rates than during the '*trente glorieuses*', or went through much shorter and shallower slowdowns in output growth. Wren-Lewis (2016: 3) defines fiscal austerity as 'fiscal consolidation which leads to a significant increase in involuntary unemployment or in the output gap' (ie in low demand).

In that sense, the recent crisis has been generating pressures both on the supply (cost) and on the demand for labour market policies, but also social policies more generally, and this is likely to have several implications on the trade-offs that policymakers have been dealing with when reforming labour market policies over the last few decades. Income support for the unemployed is likely to be more desirable both from the perspective of the beneficiaries and from a macroeconomic perspective in order to stabilise economies against the effects of recession. Activation policies are likely to be less effective in a context where jobs are scarce and job-seekers plenty, requiring more resources and more of them dedicated to more 'enabling' (and expensive) instruments in order to achieve their goals. High and rising unemployment may also alter the distinction between insiders and outsiders, with the former feeling less insulated from the risk of unemployment while the employment prospects of the latter deteriorate even further.

Membership of the EMU adds to the difference in circumstances facing policymakers in many countries in Europe compared to earlier 'permanent' austerity. On the one hand, the area's fiscal rules are now more binding and, for many economists, less sensible[3] than ever. Therefore, 'indirect' pressures on member states' social and labour market policies have increased (compare with Leibfried and Pierson, 1995; Leibfried, 2010). In some cases, the EU has even become quite intrusive in national labour policymaking through the new governance instruments that were developed as part of the provision of financial support ('bailing out') of member states that faced sovereign debt/balance of payments crises (Theodoropoulou, 2015). On the other hand, membership of the EMU has meant that fiscal pressures have, in several cases, morphed into an outright sovereign debt crisis, while the conditions under which member states have been receiving financial support have been sufficiently harsh to provide examples to avoid. The case for cost-cutting reforms that allow policymakers to claim credit for averting a public debt crisis and a bail-out under onerous conditions may have become more tempting to appeal to under current conditions. At the same time, however, one has to question the 'responsibility' of such cuts given the criticism that fiscal austerity has been subjected to by mainstream economists (Blanchard and Leigh, 2013; Krugman, 2013; Wren-Lewis, 2013; Ball, 2014).

It would not be an overstatement to argue that under the current circumstances of all the social policy domains, labour market and unemployment policies are those facing the greatest challenges in the context of EU austerity. Retrenchment and cost-cutting in social and labour market policies is an approach that has been widely expected (Armingeon, 2013), although the way in which such pressures have been distributed across policy areas, policy instruments and risk-bearers is only now starting to emerge more clearly.

Empirical approach and organisation of the book

This book aspires to provide a detailed mapping of developments in labour market policies in the context of EU fiscal austerity by comparing – in each country case study and covering a wide geographic area within the EU – developments in the field after 2010 with the earlier pattern of change (since the 1990s). The explanations of the patterns of reform are beyond the scope of this book, which is why there is no systematic examination of the politics behind the observed changes. Our aim is to provide students and researchers in the field with empirical material that will serve as a point of departure for identifying puzzles and spark further research.

In order to potentially maximise the coverage of patterns of change, country cases that have been subject to different EU fiscal austerity pressures have been selected to be studied from different welfare/labour market regimes/varieties of capitalism, including from Central and Eastern Europe (CEE). Social policies in the latter came under different pressures from the 1990s due to the transition from centrally planned to market economies. However, CEE countries are included here as their labour markets have also seen liberalisation and the rise of precarious employment, while, in several of them, policy changes have also been subject to fiscal pressures. The assumption is that pressures for austerity have, in general, been stronger within the EMU rather than outside as member states outside the EMU had more adjustment tools at their disposal to manage the impact of the financial crisis that broke out in 2008/09 and its aftermath on public finances. Austerity pressures and adjustment capacities, however, have not been uniform across the EMU either as different member states have had different revenue-raising capacities and followed different mixes of investment and consumption (Beramendi et al, 2015).

Country cases are thus selected from the Anglo-Saxon (Ireland, UK), the Nordic/Hybrid (Sweden, the Netherlands), the Continental European (Germany, France), the Southern European (Greece, Italy) and the CEE regimes (Czech Republic, Slovakia, Slovenia) (Esping-Andersen, 1999; Davidsson, 2011; Bonoli, 2013). In fact, within the CEE group, we distinguish further, using the Bohle and Greskovits (2007) scheme, into Embedded Neo-Liberal Market Economies (ENLMEs) (Czechia, Slovakia) and the Neo-Corporatist Market Economy (Slovenia).

To add some structure to the mapping of changes given the diversity of the countries examined in the volume, we principally, though not exclusively, focus on unemployment benefits (insurance and assistance), ALMPs (of all types) and EPL, but also on social assistance benefits for the non-employed of working age insofar as there have been trends of 'risk re-categorisation' (Clasen and Clegg, 2011b). In line with the change trends discussed earlier and with the observation that the patterns of welfare state change prior to the crisis had been multidimensional (Bonoli and Natali, 2012a), the contributors to the book address the following questions:

- How have policy retrenchment/expansion been distributed across the various labour market and unemployment policy instruments, namely, unemployment benefits (insurance and assistance), EPL and ALMPs? As retrenchment, we count cuts in expenditure and in entitlements (eg the tightening of eligibility criteria), but also less visible forms such as 'drift' (Hacker, 2004).
- If the 'insider–outsider' division has hitherto been relevant in the particular labour market, how have policy retrenchment/expansion been distributed between the two groups and with respect to which policy instruments? Have new 'insider–outsider' divisions emerged and, if so, along which lines?
- Has the balance in the use of activation policy instruments shifted and, if so, in favour of which type of instruments? The cheaper and arguably more 'punitive' ones, such as 'incentive reinforcement' and 'employment assistance', or the more expensive but also likely to be more 'enabling' and akin to social investment instruments, such as 'training' and 'occupation' (compare with Eichhorst and Konle-Seidl, 2008; Bonoli, 2010)?

To put developments in labour market policies during the recent recession into a broader policy and geographical context, the following chapter considers structural reforms in a number of areas in addition to labour markets, such as pension policies, research and development, education, and public administration. The authors examine changes across the EU28 by labour market regimes during the recession of

2008–12 and develop a typology of reform strategies on the basis of how countries in different regimes combine the objectives of investment for growth and protection (compare with Beramendi et al, 2015). The rest of the book consists of the national case studies ordered by regime, whereas a final chapter summarises the findings.

Notes

[1.] Other factors underpinning 'permanent austerity' have been the maturation of welfare states and the ageing of populations (Pierson, 1998).

[2.] Jessoula and colleagues (2010), in a study of the Italian labour market, distinguish an additional group, the so-called 'mid-siders'. For a similar division in the Greek labour market, see also the discussion in Chapter Three.

[3.] It is not the existence of fiscal rules per se that is questioned as some coordination of national fiscal policies is necessary in a monetary union (DeGrauwe, 2012). Rather, it is the content of the rules that only guard against too high deficits but not too high surpluses, as well as the burdening of national fiscal policies with way too many functions that constrain the stabilisation function, that is criticised (Mabbett and Schelkle, 2016).

References

Appelbaum, E. and Schettkat, R. (1994) 'The end of full employment? On economic development in industrialized countries', *Intereconomics*, 29(3): 122–30.

Appelbaum, E. and Schettkat, R. (1995) 'Employment and productivity in industrialized countries', *International Labor Review*, 134(4–5): 605–23.

Armingeon, K. (2013) 'Breaking with the past? Why the global financial crisis led to austerity policies but not to modernization of the welfare state', in C. Pierson, F.G. Castles and I.K. Naumann (eds) *The welfare state reader* (3rd edn), Cambridge: Polity Press.

Armingeon, K. and Bonoli, G. (eds) (2006) *The politics of post-industrial welfare states*, London: Routledge.

Ball, L. (2014) *Long-term damage from the Great Recession in OECD countries*, mimeo, Baltimore, MD: Johns Hopkins University.

Baumol, W.J. (1967) 'The macroeconomics of unbalanced growth', *American Economic Review*, 57(3): 415–26.

Baumol, W.J. and Bowen, W.G. (1966) *Performing arts: The economic dilemma*, New York, NY: Twentieth Century Fund.

Beramendi, P., Hausermann, S., Kitschelt, H. and Kriesi, H. (eds) (2015) *The politics of advanced capitalism*, Cambridge: Cambridge University Press.

Blanchard, O.J. and Leigh, D. (2013) *Growth forecast errors and fiscal multipliers*, IMF Working Paper WP/13/1, Washington, DC: IMF.

Bohle, D. and Greskovits, B. (2007) 'Neoliberalism, embedded neoliberalism and neocorporatism: towards transnational capitalism in Central-Eastern Europe', *West European Politics*, 30: 443–66.

Bonoli, G. (2010) *The political economy of active labour market policies*, RECWOWE Working Paper REC-WP 01/2010, Edinburgh: RECWOWE Publication, Dissemination and Dialogue Center.

Bonoli, G. (2012) 'Blame avoidance and credit claiming revisited', in G. Bonoli and D. Natali (eds) *The politics of the 'new' welfare state*, Oxford: Oxford University Press.

Bonoli, G. (2013) *The origins of active social policy. Labour market and childcare policies in a comparative perspective*, Oxford: Oxford University Press.

Bonoli, G. and Natali, D. (2012a) 'Multidimensional transformations in the early 21st century welfare states', in G. Bonoli and D. Natali (eds) *The politics of the new welfare state*, Oxford: Oxford University Press.

Bonoli, G. and Natali, D. (2012b) 'The politics of the "new" welfare state: analysing reforms in Western Europe', in G. Bonoli and D. Natali (eds) *The politics of the new welfare state*, Oxford: Oxford University Press.

Bonoli, G. and Natali, D. (eds) (2012c) *The politics of the new welfare state*, Oxford: Oxford University Press.

Clasen, J. and Clegg, D. (eds) (2011a) *Regulating the risk of unemployment: National adaptations to post-industrial labour markets in Europe*, Oxford: Oxford University Press.

Clasen, J. and Clegg, D. (2011b) 'Unemployment protection and labour market change in Europe: towards "triple integration"?', in J. Clasen and D. Clegg (eds) *Regulating the risk of unemployment: National adaptations to post-industrial labour markets in Europe*, Oxford: Oxford University Press.

Clasen, J., Clegg, D. and Kvist, J. (2012) *European labour market policies in (the) crisis*, ETUI Working Paper 2012.12, Brussels: ETUI.

Clayton, R. and Pontusson, J. (1998) 'Welfare-state retrenchment revisited – entitlement cuts, public sector restructuring and inegalitarian trends in advanced capitalist societies', *World Politics*, 51: 67–98.

Davidsson, J.B. (2011) 'An analytical overview of labour market reforms across the EU: making sense of the variation', Working Paper 11/1, Laboratorio Revelli.

DeGrauwe, P. (2012) *Economics of monetary union*, Oxford: Oxford University Press.

DeLong, B. and Summers, L. (2012) 'Fiscal policy in a depressed economy', *Brookings Papers on Economic Activity*, Spring: 233–74.

Eichhorst, W. and Konle-Seidl, R. (2008) *Contingent convergence: A comparative analysis of activation policies*, IZA discussion paper No.3905, Bonn: IZA.

Emmenegger, P., Häusermann, S., Palier, B. and Seeleib-Kaiser, M. (eds) (2012) *The age of dualization. The changing face of inequality in deindustrializing societies*, Oxford: Oxford University Press.

Esping-Andersen, G. (1999) *Social foundations of postindustrial economies*, Oxford: Oxford University Press.

Esping-Andersen, G., Gallie, D. and Hemerijck, A. (eds) (2002) *Why we need a new welfare state*, Oxford: Oxford University Press.

Estevez-Abe, M., Iversen, T. and Soskice, D. (2001) 'Social protection and the formation of skills: a reinterpretation of the welfare state', in P.A. Hall and D. Soskice (eds) *Varieties of capitalism: The institutional foundations of comparative advantage*, Oxford: Oxford University Press.

Hacker, J.S. (2004) 'Privatizing risk without privatizing the welfare state: the hidden politics of social policy retrenchment in the United States', *American Political Science Review*, 98: 243–60.

Hausermann, S. (2010) *The politics of welfare state reform in continental Europe*, Cambridge: Cambridge University Press.

Häusermann, S. (2012) 'The politics of old and new social policies', in G. Bonoli and D. Natali (eds) *The politics of the 'new' welfare state*, Oxford: Oxford University Press.

Hemerijck, A. (2006) 'Recalibrating Europe's semi-sovereign welfare states', WZB Discussion Paper 2006/103, Berlin.

Huber, E. and Stephens, J.D. (2015) 'Postindustrial social policy', in P. Beramendi, S. Hausermann, H. Kitschelt and H. Kriesi (eds) *The politics of advanced capitalism*, Cambridge: Cambridge University Press.

Iversen, T. and Wren, A. (1998) 'Equality, employment and budgetary restraint: the trilemma of the service economy', *World Politics*, 50: 507–46.

Jenson, J. (2012) 'A new politics of the social investment perspective: objectives, instruments, and areas of intervention in welfare regimes', in G. Bonoli and D. Natali (eds) *The politics of the new welfare state*, Oxford: Oxford University Press.

Jessoula, M., Graziano, P.R. and Madama, I. (2010) '"Selective flexicurity" in segmented labour markets: the case of Italian "mid-siders"', *Journal of Social Policy*, 39: 561–83.

Kluve, J. (2010) 'The effectiveness of European active labour market programmes', *Labour Economics*, 17(6): 904–18.

Korpi, W. and Palme, J. (2003) 'New politics and class politics in the context of austerity and globalization: welfare state regress in 18 countries 1975–1995', *American Political Science Review*, 97: 425–46.

Krugman, P. (2013) 'Europe's Keynesian problem', The Conscience of Liberal blog. Available at: http://krugman.blogs.nytimes.com/2013/05/25/europes-keynesian-problem/ (accessed 25 May 2014).

Leibfried, S. (2010) 'Social policy: left to the judges and the markets?', in H. Wallace, M.A. Pollack and A.R. Young (eds) *Policy-making in the European Union*, Oxford: Oxford University Press.

Leibfried, S. and Pierson, P. (1995) *European social policy: Between fragmentation and integration*, Washington, DC: The Brookings Institution.

Mabbett, D. and Schelkle, W. (2016) 'Searching under the lamppost: the evolution of fiscal surveillance', in J.A. Caporaso and M. Rhodes (eds) *The political and economic dynamics of the Eurozone crisis*, Oxford: Oxford University Press.

Matsaganis, M. (2018) 'Income support policies and labour market reforms under austerity in Greece', in S. Theodoropoulou (ed) *Labour market policies in the era of pervasive austerity: a European perspective*, Bristol: The Policy Press.

OECD (Organisation for Economic Co-operation and Development) (1994) *The OECD jobs strategy*, Paris: OECD.

Pierson, P. (1994) *Dismantling the welfare state?*, New York, NY: Cambridge University Press.

Pierson, P. (1996) 'The new politics of the welfare state', *World Politics*, 48: 143–79.

Pierson, P. (1998) 'Irresistible forces, immovable objects: postindustrial welfare states confront permanent austerity', *Journal of European Public Policy*, 5: 539–60.

Pierson, P. (ed) (2001) *The new politics of the welfare state*, Oxford: Oxford University Press.

Rueda, D. (2007) *Social democracy inside-out: Partisanship and labour market policy in industrialized democracies*, Cambridge: Cambridge University Press.

Starke, P. (2006) 'The politics of welfare state retrenchment: a literature review', *Social Policy and Administration*, 40: 104–20.

Streeck, W. and Thelen, K. (2005) 'Introduction: institutional change in advanced political economies', in W. Streeck and K. Thelen (eds) *Beyond continuity: Institutional change in advanced political economies*, Oxford: Oxford University Press.

Theodoropoulou, S. (2015) 'National social and labour market policy reforms in the shadow of EU bail-out conditionality: the cases of Greece and Portugal', *Comparative European Politics*, 13: 29–55.

Vis, B. and Hemerijck, A. (2014) 'The Great Recession and welfare state reform: is retrenchment really the only game left in town?', *Social Policy and Administration*, 48: 883–904.

Vlandas, T. (2013) 'The politics of temporary work deregulation in Europe: solving the French puzzle', *Politics and Society*, 41: 425–60.

Weaver, K. (1986) 'The politics of credit claiming', *Journal of Public Policy*, 6: 371–98.

Wren, A., Mate, F. and Theodoropoulou, S. (2013) 'The trilemma revisited: implications for inequality and employment creation of the ICT revolution and the expansion of service trade', in A. Wren (ed) *The political economy of service transition*, Oxford: Oxford University Press.

Wren-Lewis, S. (2013) 'The "official" cost of austerity', Mainly Macro blog. Available at: http://mainlymacro.blogspot.be/2013/10/the-official-cost-of-austerity.html (accessed 28 October 2014).

Wren-Lewis, S. (2015) 'Eurozone fiscal policy – still not getting it', Mainly Macro. Available at: https://mainlymacro.blogspot.be/ (accessed 1 March 2015).

Wren-Lewis, S. (2016) 'A general theory of austerity', BSG Working Paper BSG-WP-2016/014, May, Oxford: Blavatnik School of Government, University of Oxford.

TWO

Structural reforms in Europe: a comparative overview

Chiara Agostini and David Natali

Introduction

The present chapter provides an overview of structural reforms (SRs) – measures to improve economic growth prospects and the ability of economies to adjust to economic shocks – introduced in Europe between 1999 and 2012 and, in particular, during the Great Recession (2008–12). Such a cross-policy analysis – including social protection (eg pensions), education policy, research and development (R&D) and public sector reforms – makes it possible to shed light on the complex interaction of the labour market policies that are at the core of this volume with social policies (aimed at welfare production and redistribution) and economic policies (aimed at economic production).

While the concept of SRs is highly debated in the literature and needs some revision of its normative roots, we consider it a good descriptive tool: it helps to trace reform trends in a number of policy areas and to understand the overall functioning of a socio-economic system. The present chapter proposes a new typology of SRs for a more detailed analysis of SRs trends in Europe.

Through the analysis of reforms between 1999 and 2012, we address two key questions: 'Is there a common reform trend of a 'race to the bottom' in relation to social and employment rights?'; and 'What has been the impact of the Great Recession? Do we see overall continuity or a shift between the pre- and post-crisis?'. In the following, we analyse five country clusters – Anglo-Saxon, Nordic, Continental European, Southern European and Visegrad countries, which are consistent with the different varieties of capitalism and employment regimes – and we provide evidence of diverse reform trends over time.

The present contribution is organised as follows. The second section presents the research questions at the core of the chapter and provides a brief review of the literature on socio-economic reforms in Europe over the last decades. The third section lays out the definition of SRs and the complementarity between socio-economic policies before and since the Great Recession. The fourth section provides an overview of SRs in the European Union (EU), with a focus on reform trends and outputs. The fifth section draws some conclusions.

Socio-economic reforms in Europe: common path or different strategies?

Recent contributions on the political economy of socio-economic reforms have followed a cross-policy perspective. The contemporary literature has proposed different concepts, including employment models (Bosch et al, 2009), social models (Dølvik and Martin, 2014) and social and growth models (Palier and Boisson-Cohen, 2015).

This cross-policy perspective, which we use in the chapter too, has some analytical advantages. First, it is possible to examine the complex interplay of policy decisions and the importance of institutional complementarities. As shown by Eichorst et al (2010), institutions do not work in isolation. On the contrary, they form complex institutional arrangements. System coordination and institutional complementarities are key elements of capitalist models, and 'when present in the "right" form, mutually reinforce each other' (Hassel, 2014: 11). Complementarities are also important to assess reforms in one policy area: labour market reforms, for instance, can be assessed only when considering other policy areas that they interact with (eg education, training, etc). Second, a cross-policy perspective enables the tracing of common and coherent trends where these exist, or, in the opposite case, helps to avoid overestimations of policy coherence and stability. It makes it possible to map different socio-economic models and their performance. Third, such an analytical perspective facilitates the assessment of the convergence/divergence of different socio-economic models. In line with neo-institutionalism, rather than one model for economic growth and prosperity, many models may coexist (Hall and Soskice, 2001).

Such a framework allows us to address two research questions:

- Question 1: Is there a common reform trend of a 'race to the bottom' in relation to social and employment rights?
- Question 2: What has been the impact of the Great Recession? Do we see overall continuity or a shift between the pre- and post-crisis?

The contemporary literature has provided different and partly contradicting answers. As far as the first question is concerned, some authors have hypothesised a gradual liberalisation and retrenchment of social and labour rights in all different varieties of welfare capitalism. For Streeck (2009), globalisation and the progressive decline in the power of organised labour have weakened the more coordinated and egalitarian forms of capitalism. Evidence of this downturn is provided by the overall retrenchment of social policy and unemployment insurance, and the relaxation of employment protection legislation. Baccaro and Howell (2011) share this point of view with respect to industrial relations. The latter have experienced a long trend of decentralisation and deregulation, accompanied by institutional conversion, across different varieties of industrial relations systems. All this is consistent with the supply-side interpretation of socio-economic reforms.

Certain authors, however, stress the ongoing divergence between different varieties of socio-economic and labour market policies. This is the case of Hall and Gingerich (2009), who find different varieties of capitalism reacting through different strategies to common challenges, as well as Hemerijck (2013), who sees examples of recalibration, and not retrenchment, in the Nordic and some Continental European countries that have invested in human capital. This is also the position of Palier and Boisson-Cohen (2015) and Hassel (2014), who have proposed a complex reform trajectory involving geographical regions and time periods. Continental and Nordic countries experienced a first step – austerity measures and wage freezing – in the 1990s and early 2000s. More recently, the same countries have promoted social investment and less severe retrenchment (in line with a '*high road*' to economic growth and competitiveness). The South, on the contrary, was very timid in promoting retrenchment and wage stability in the 1990s but was then forced in the context of the crisis to make massive cuts in social protection and investment (along the '*low road*'). Eventually, Central and Eastern European (CEE) countries followed different reform paths due to their own position in the global economy and in the EU. Countries that are members of the Economic and Monetary Union (EMU) have seen more stringent budgetary policies, while those with a more marginal implication in the integration process have had more room for alternative reform paths (Schweiger, 2014).

As for the second question, some have argued that since the crisis, European countries have started reforms intended to reduce public spending, deregulate labour markets and radically alter the traits of the European social model. As stressed by Pochet and Degryse (2011: 214), none of the reforms adopted in the fields of labour law and social protection can be regarded as an improvement in social legislation. Others have identified a more diversified reform trend much more coherent with the pre-crisis reforms. For Schroeder et al (2015), while those countries less affected by the crisis (such as Germany) have not altered their social and employment models, those that have experienced a more pronounced decline have followed two different strategies. Nordic countries have followed an anti-cyclical path of increased active labour market policies, while others (eg the Netherlands) have adopted a pro-cyclical set of retrenchment and cost-containment measures. Dølvik and Martin (2014) provide a more nuanced reading of socio-economic performances across Europe. In particular, they stress the uncertain prospects for the Nordic model, with the risk of a future 'piecemeal withering and retrenchment' of social policies. In the same line, Davidsson (2011) outlines the long-term increased inequality and declined protection in the Nordic labour markets.

Structural reforms in the European Union: some conceptual clarification

In order to contextualise the labour market reforms analysed in the other chapters, we focus on SRs. SRs are a key concept in scientific and political debate. They are proposed by economists as a key component of growth strategies and are at the top of the agenda supported by international organisations[1] and the EU (Rubio, 2014). At the origin of the concept there is a typical neoliberal interpretation of the subject: SRs aim at promoting the liberalisation of product markets and the deregulation of labour markets (see Alesina et al, 2010). However, a recent strand of the literature adopts a more neutral perspective. According to this logic, restructuring is part of a broad strategy to improve a country's economic growth potential with effects on the demand side of the economy (Dølvik and Martin, 2014).

In line with Canton et al (2014: 2), we can define these SRs as measures 'to improve economic growth prospects and the ability of economies to adjust to shocks'. Even if the effective link between reforms and growth is still debated (see IMF, 2015), SRs are a useful 'umbrella' concept to look at the evolution of the European socio-economic models.

In what follows, we focus on pensions as belonging to the set of social protection, investment in human capital (education policy and innovation [R&D]) and public sector reforms to examine the strategies followed by national policymakers to improve the efficacy and efficiency of the state. While the in-depth comparative study of labour market policies is provided by Theodoropoulou in this volume, we will briefly refer to reforms of passive and active labour market policies, as well as employment protection legislation. The latter areas allow for a more encompassing analysis of reforms in Europe.

Table 2.1 proposes a typology of SRs based on two dimensions: investment and protection. Echoing Polanyi (see Bohle and Greskovits, 2012), these dimensions reflect two organising principles of contemporary welfare capitalism: economic liberalism and social and industrial protection. These two principles inspire two policy agendas that are both included in SRs: one focused on investment in productive capacities (to increase the country's competitiveness); the other on protection (against market forces).

Table 2.1 shows two polar opposites. On the one hand, we have *social standards devaluation*. This is consistent with the 'supply-side' interpretation of SRs (Dølvik and Martin, 2014). According to this approach, SRs consists of the deregulation of product markets – through the limitation of entry barriers, price control, public ownership and so on – and of labour markets – through the decentralisation of collective bargaining, stricter definition of wage setting targets and reform of unemployment protection. This recalls the 'low road' to economic competitiveness based on cost-cutting, conflictual labour relations and a narrow set of social programmes (Millberg and Houston, 2005).

On the other hand, we have *social standards improvement*. This reflects a broader 'supply-side and demand-side' interpretation. According to this, economic growth and competitiveness is achieved through high-quality social services and efficient welfare protection as an alternative to cost containment (Dølvik and Martin, 2014). This is the 'high road' to economic competitiveness based on accumulated capital, a qualified workforce, material and immaterial infrastructures, an effective tax system and public administration, cooperative labour relations, high-quality production and higher wages, and costly welfare programmes (Schmid, 2013: 3).

There are a number of possible policy mixes between these two polar opposites: policy packages involving social devaluation in some

Table 2.1: A typology of structural reform trends

		Investment	
		Decrease	Increase
Protection	Decrease	Social standards devaluation	Selective investment
	Increase	Socio-economic protectionism	Social standards improvement

Source: Agostini et al (2016)

areas and improvements in some others. The third ideal-type we propose here is *selective investment* in productive capacity. It consists of an expansion of investment in some areas (those with a direct effect on competitiveness but limited redistribution, eg, R&D and education) and, in parallel, a reduction of protection in some others (social and labour market protections). Social investment can be part of this strategy, with investments in human capital and knowledge to support labour market participation or to confront new social risks (Morel et al, 2012). A Schumpeterian workfare state approach can also be part of this type of SRs. It is based on: 'the promotion of product, process, organizational, and market innovation; the enhancement of the structural competitiveness of open economies mainly through supply-side intervention; and the subordination of social policy to the demands of labour market flexibility and structural competitiveness' (Jessop, 1993: 9). The fourth ideal-type is *socio-economic protectionism*, with an increase or stability in the protection of social standards for some categories and in some economic sectors (those related to the old industrial economy) even at the cost of lower investments. This reform path aims at improving growth through domestic demand and to safeguard social peace (Hausermann, 2012; Thelen, 2014).

Structural reform trends: a cluster-by-cluster overview

This section sheds light on the major trends in SRs in the EU. We look at five country clusters: Anglo-Saxon, Nordic, Continental, Southern and Visegrad countries.[2] In the following, we provide a brief summary of SRs. Qualitative information is combined with quantitative indicators. We look at reform trends and the evolution of public spending and social rights protections in the pre-crisis years (between 1999 and 2008) and the crisis period (between 2008 and 2012). A decline in spending on pensions, education, R&D and/or the public sector is interpreted as a sign of *social standards devaluation*. A decline in employment protection legislation is a further sign of a 'low road' to competitiveness. By contrast, an overall increase in spending, investments and standards indicates a 'high road' to competitiveness and *social standards improvement*. As far as the intermediate cases are concerned, when investments in education, R&D and active labour market policies are increased while spending on pensions and passive labour market policies are retrenched, we see a signal of *selective investment*. When the opposite is evident, we see *socio-economic protectionism* in continuity with the old industrial logic and 'passive' social policy.

Anglo-Saxon countries

Anglo-Saxon countries (Ireland and the UK) have been the European front-runners in implementing measures for containing the public budget and increasing labour market flexibility since the 1980s. Conservative governments in the UK between the 1980s and 1990s, as well as the 1981–87 Fine Gael–Labour government and the Fianna Fáil government since 1987 in Ireland, implemented austerity measures and deregulation (*social standards devaluation*).

Pensions policy was a target of retrenchment. Figure 2.1 in the Appendix demonstrates a slight increase in public pensions expenditure as a share of GDP in the two countries in the late 1990s and early 2000s (1 percentage point between 1999 and 2008). The apparent contradiction between reforms and their impact on spending needs some explanation. While, at first glance, this increase seems to suggest higher levels of protection, it is, in fact, the result of many factors. First, demographic trends have had a clear impact. Second, the economic cycle has had a huge impact. The increase in spending since the crisis seems a typical mirror image of the recession that hit many EU countries. Such a trend is also partly an effect of the anti-cyclical measures introduced in 2009/10 to buffer the social consequences of the recession. These elements tend to hide the impact of the cutbacks identified in the literature. The retrenchment of public benefits has a long-term component, which could lead to the decline of provision in the near future but is not yet visible. A second indicator – the net replacement rate (NRR) – allows us to neutralise some of the effects of demographic and gross domestic product (GDP) trends. Between 2006 and 2008, we see a decline in pension benefits in Anglo-Saxon countries (see Figure 2.2).

The end of the 20th century saw good economic performance in both the UK and Ireland. Both countries experienced a decline in unemployment, a rise in GDP and stable budgetary policy. Yet, the economic strategies of the two countries were not the same. Since 1997, the Irish path was characterised by cheap credit, tax reductions and increased internal demand. The latter were the main promoters of economic growth and accompanied longer-term policy measures consistent with public investments, increased foreign direct investment (FDI) and tax cuts. The entry into the Eurozone in 2000 'opened up a huge reserve of low interest rates and cheap credit for the Irish economy' (Regan, 2011). The 1990s and 2000s were thus characterised by increased public spending on active labour market policies, poverty prevention and education policy, while wages largely increased. Ireland was thus a typical example of *social standard improvements*.

Over the same years, the UK – under the New Labour government – saw, to some extent, the perpetuation of flexible labour market policies initiated by Thatcher, as well as an increase in public spending on some policies. Since 2000, the Blair government increased public spending on health, reaching about 9% of GDP in 2009. In particular, the 2001 reform revised the rules about health-care provision, with more autonomy for hospitals and open competition between public and private providers. The Working Family Tax Credit of 1998 was an integral part of the New Deal arrangement for activating youth and other disadvantaged groups and thus promoting employment. In parallel, public expenditure on education policy increased up to 5% of GDP, together with an overall increase in public investment (Mayhew and Wickham Jones, 2014).

Figures 2.3 to 2.6 in the Appendix allow the tracing of the evolution of different public policies addressed by SRs. First of all, we consider the public expenditure invested in education as a percentage of GDP. Between 1999 and 2008, we see an increase of public spending in the Anglo-Saxon cluster (1.6 percentage points). Such a trend is confirmed by public education expenditure as a share of total public expenditure (see Figure 2.4). This indicator is useful in reflecting the policy priorities of countries while neutralising the effect of GDP variation. In the period 1999–2008, we see an overall increase in Ireland and the UK. As for R&D, if we consider the evolution of expenditure between 1999 and 2008, the Anglo-Saxon countries proved stable. By public sector spending, we refer to the expenditure on the remuneration of government employees (wages, salaries and other related costs) (as a percentage of GDP). We see an increase in Anglo-Saxon countries (1.1 percentage points) (see Figure 2.6). We also consider the number of employees in public administration, defence and compulsory social security, where there was an upward trend during that period (Eurostat, 2016)

The post-crisis period has been characterised by some reduction of social standards in the two cases but with different magnitudes and some qualification for the UK. In the case of Ireland, *social standards devaluation* has been driven by the deep recession, the extraordinary worsening of the public budget and EU constraints. The latter has consisted of the Memorandum of Understanding (MoU). Pension reforms have been at the heart of the fiscal consolidation efforts of Irish governments over the crisis years. Measures implemented since 2009 have included cuts in pensions, changes concerning the retirement age and access conditions, and cuts in public support to pre-funded pension schemes (Agostini et al, 2016).

In the same period, the UK has followed a two-step pattern that is common to many European countries. The first response to the crisis was consistent with an anti-cyclical logic: public spending – namely, in pensions – was increased to buffer the main negative social consequences of the crisis. The second step, since 2010, has consisted in the reduction of public benefits (through a revision of indexation) and the increase of the retirement age. In the case of the UK, a key measure affected civil servants and public sector employees. Their pension benefit calculation has been brought into line with that of other dependent workers. Between 2008 and 2012, we see a clear overall increase of public pension spending. In parallel, NRRs increased in Anglo-Saxon countries (see Figure 2.2). We see the latter trend as the effect of anti-cyclical measures taken in the UK and the parallel decline in wages.

The two countries have taken measures to increase the equality of educational opportunities. In Ireland, despite severe budget constraints and cutbacks, a number of measures concerning the education system have been implemented since 2010. A strategy to improve the quality of early childhood, primary and secondary education – the National Strategy to Improve Literacy and Numeracy among Children and Young People – was launched in July 2011, with a budget of €9 million. The strategy set a number of performance targets to be reached by 2020 and foresees the implementation of a series of concrete actions over the years (Agostini et al, 2016). Between 2008 and 2011, the Anglo-Saxon cluster saw an increase in public spending as a percentage of GDP and the stability of the ratio of public expenditure on education as a percentage of total public expenditure (see Figures 2.3 and 2.4).

In the last few decades, R&D reforms have been fairly intense, although they have declined more recently. Ireland has increased public support for R&D activities through tax credits, public grants or subsidies targeted at innovative small- and medium-sized enterprises (SMEs), and by strengthening university–industry linkages and better protecting intellectual property rights. The implementation of those measures, however, took place in a context characterised by fiscal consolidation priorities. Yet, the increase of investment in the UK leads to the growth of R&D spending in the Anglo-Saxon cluster (see Figure 2.5).

Since the eruption of the crisis, we have seen an unprecedented decline in employment in parts of the public sector in Ireland. In the Irish MoU, the 'reduction of public service in terms of numbers', the implementation of the provisions concerning public servant pensions and a 10% pay reduction for new entrants were outlined. In any case, the reduction in the number of public service workers, to be completed by 2015, was quantified in the National Recovery Plan 2011–14 – presented by the Cowen government in November 2010 – at approximately 24,750 people compared with the 2008 level. The UK Coalition government also reduced public spending, in particular, through lower transfers to local government and public sector reforms, but we saw resistance to cost containment in pensions and health care (Mayhew and Wickham Jones, 2014). As for the reform trends in the public sector, between 2008 and 2012, we see a general contraction of the level of expenditure on the remuneration of employees as a share of GDP in the Anglo-Saxon countries (–0.7 percentage points) (see Figure 2.6). This trend is confirmed by the decline in the number of public employees in public administration, defence and compulsory social security (–7.6 percentage points) (own calculations based on Eurostat, 2016).

Nordic countries

Nordic countries (Denmark, Finland and Sweden) have traditionally been considered examples of a 'high road' to economic growth and competitiveness, characterised by the desire to combine sound budgetary conditions, high-quality production and innovation-driven growth, and fairly high wages and social standards. This development model was consolidated over the 1990s and 2000s, when a series of reforms in various policy areas strengthened the 'social investment orientation' of the Nordic model, though at the cost of some cuts to social benefits, which contributed to an increase in income inequality (Dølvik et al, 2014).

Yet, reforms passed in these countries since the 1990s prove that the model has changed and some *selective investment* has taken place. In particular, we refer to the constant decline in active labour market policies in Sweden, with the parallel increased role of social partners in addressing unemployment risks and inactivity traps (Jansson et al, 2016). Pensions suffered cutbacks in all the Nordic countries, with paradigmatic changes both in Sweden, through the 1998 reform, and in Denmark, with the spread of occupational pension funds since 1991. These measures are consistent with the slight increase in pension public spending as a share of GDP (0.5 percentage points) between 1999 and 2008 (see Figure 2.1) and the decline of NRRs up to 2006 and beyond (see Figure 2.2). Passive labour market support was then subject to stricter conditionality. However, investment on education and vocational education and training increased. As stressed by Dølvik et al (2014), this was the case of the Danish apprentice-based system, with the growing emphasis on lifelong learning. On top of that, the labour market did not experience any systematic deregulation, with the exception of the liberalisation of temporary jobs in Sweden and the decline in labour market regulation in Denmark.

The 2000s were characterised by signs of both change and continuity. The former was represented by the reform of the Swedish Ghent system – similar reforms were implemented in Finland and Denmark – with the parallel decline of the benefits and the regulatory and administrative role of trade unions (Jansson et al, 2016). However, these and other reforms did not entail an overall increase of inequality between insiders and outsiders while the supply of labour and skills was increased through new measures on the reconciliation of work and family life. The latter were supported by the persistent generosity of income security schemes (Dølvik et al, 2014). In the field of education and R&D, reforms passed between 1999 and 2008 led Nordic countries (with the exception of Finland) to decrease their public investment in education (by 0.4 percentage points) even if education expenditure as a percentage of total public expenditure increased (see Figure 2.4). Investments in research and innovation as a percentage of GDP increased in the period 1999–2008 but slightly declined (0.1 percentage points) between 2008 and 2012 (see Figure 2.5).

The same mixed trend is evident for the public sector. Public expenditure on employment remuneration slightly fluctuated at around 13.8% of GDP in the immediate pre-crisis period, while it increased between 2008 and 2012 (see Figure 2.6). As for the number of employees in public administration, defence and compulsory social security, during the pre-crisis period (1999–2008), we see a general expansion of public administration (Eurostat, 2016). In a comparative perspective, this upward trend was particularly evident in the case of the Nordic countries.

Since 2011, more restrictive measures (*social standards devaluation*) have been implemented, although they have sometimes been accompanied by investment-oriented initiatives (in R&D). Particularly worrisome signals are coming from two key sectors of the Finnish development model: education and R&D. The former has been heavily hit by budget cuts undertaken since 2011, although public spending on education is still above the EU average and various measures aimed at improving the efficiency and effectiveness of the system have been implemented. Similarly, although it is still the highest in the EU, gross domestic expenditure on R&D as a percentage of GDP declined in 2009 and 2010 (Agostini et al, 2016).

In the wake of the crisis, Nordic countries have proven to accelerate the path of SRs of welfare and labour market policies. On the one hand, the Danish case stands out for in-depth reforms: the tightening of social protection measures and the strength of conditionality in the aid for unmarried people are just some examples of more explicit reductions of social standards, at least for a part of the population (Dølvik et al, 2014). On the other hand, pensions reform proved a more balanced policy mix. Measures have been introduced to increase old-age protection for those more at risk of poverty: this is the case of the new 'guaranteed pension' in Finland and the more gentle revision of benefit coefficients in Sweden. A reduction of taxes on pensions has been a crucial tool in reducing the potential negative effects of the crisis and improving the level of benefits. In the pensions field, between 2008 and 2012, we see a decline in NRRs combined with an increase in public pension spending. As stressed earlier for Anglo-Saxon countries, the latter indicator is not particularly reliable due to the impact of GDP decline and the effect of some longer-term factors like population ageing.

Education policy spending slightly increased between 2008 and 2011. In the meantime, Nordic countries (eg Finland) have reformed their R&D policy in order to improve cooperation between public institutions and private business, while also rationalising the interaction between education and research bodies. In parallel, tax subsidies have increased. In the period 2008–2012, Nordic countries have slightly reduced their overall investment as a share of GDP in this area (–0.1 percentage points).

Public sector reforms have not been massive, except in Finland. By 2011, the Finnish State Productivity Programme had reduced the central public administration by 8,000 jobs, with the aim of reducing costs and improving the efficiency of the system. The reform of local administrations – when fully implemented between 2015 and 2017 – is expected to reduce of €1 billion of expenditures (Agostini et al, 2016). All in all, in the post-crisis phase, Nordic countries increased their investment in the public sector, both in terms of general expenditure on the remuneration of government employees as share of GDP and the number of employees in public administration, defence and compulsory social security.

Continental countries

Continental Europe (Austria, Belgium, France, Germany, Luxembourg and the Netherlands) has proven heterogeneous. Many of these counties present the main characteristics of coordinated market economies, with export-led growth models, high levels of wage coordination, large investments in vocational training and R&D, and continuous innovation (Hall, 2014).

As stressed by Palier and Boisson-Cohen (2015), these countries experienced far-reaching reforms between the 1980s and early 2000s. In some countries, welfare and labour market policies underwent significant restrictive changes in the years before the crisis and continued to undergo adjustments in its aftermath. The reforms ultimately led to the shrinking of the welfare state and the dualisation of the labour market. This is the case of Germany, which embraced pensions retrenchment already in the 1980s together with flexibilisation at the margins of the labour market (Carlin et al, 2014). The Riester Reform of 2001 and the Hartz Reforms between 2002 and 2004 clarify the logic of SRs in Germany: cost containment in social protection (both old-age and unemployment schemes) was combined with the launch of supplementary pension funds and atypical jobs. As stressed by Carlin et al (2014), changes in wage setting and collective bargaining in general hugely contributed to boost productivity and German firms' competitiveness. This trend was paralleled by the increased investment in R&D, up to 2.5% of GDP, and the high level of spending in education and vocational education and training (VET). The latter went through the reform of 2005, which increased the role of firms and the interplay between public and private providers. Reforms between 1990 and the 2000s are thus a typical case of SRs consistent with *selective investment*.

Later on, the German system went through the crisis with counter-cyclical measures made possible by the austerity of the previous decades. Some public spending expansion consisted of the reduction of employers' social contributions and the boost of short-time working schemes for both typical and (some) atypical categories of workers. In the wake of the crisis, a new tendency towards *social standards improvements* was launched through the adoption of the pension reform that increased total public spending and the establishment of a national minimum wage (Agostini et al, 2016).

While many Continental EU countries followed such a strategy, France has been characterised by a largely different path. The French socio-economic model has been lightly revised through the complex balance of cost containment (especially through pensions reforms) and increased revenues (higher taxation). This is a case of *socio-economic protectionism*. In the pensions field, France has been one of the few countries in Europe that has reversed cost-containment measures (introduced by the right-of-centre governments in 2007 and 2010) through the reduction of retirement age limits in the Ayrault reform of 2013. The setting up of the *Revenue de Solidarité Active* (RSA) in 2008 was an example of active social policy, with more emphasis on job seeking but limited effects on the French labour market (Le Cacheux and Ross, 2014).

The whole Continental European cluster has been characterised by the decline in social protection in the 1990s. Public spending on pensions as a share of GDP declined between 1999 and 2008 (−0.5 percentage points), as well as the level of pension benefits (NRRs) (see Figure 2.2). This trend was confirmed in the post-crisis period (except for the slight increase in total spending as a percentage of GDP) (see Figure 2.1). As for education and R&D, the opposite is true. The upward trend is clear when we focus on public spending as a percentage of GDP (see Figures 2.4 and 2.5). Eventually, the trends in the public sector confirm the reform path of the pre-crisis period: general expenditure on the remuneration of government employees declined in the Continental cluster (−0.4 percentage points − see Figure 2.6) but there was an increase in the number of public employees (Eurostat, 2016). In the post-crisis phase, we see a slight increase in the remuneration of government employees but a marked decline in the number of employees in the public administration (−5.5%).

Southern Europe

Southern European countries (Greece, Italy, Portugal and Spain) are often referred to as mixed market economies based on a low level of social spending, low employment rates, high labour market segmentation and a very fragmented production system (with a key role for SMEs and the informal sector) marked by a lack of competitiveness. Such common traits mask, in fact, very different socio-economic institutions that have led to quite different reform paths (Perez and Rhodes, 2014).

In the 1990s and early 2000s, this group of countries experienced labour market reforms consistent with the progressive dualisation of the labour force: insiders were well protected from the deregulation of labour contracts while flexibility was introduced at the margins, with an increase of atypical jobs concentrated on young generations. This trend had repercussions on social rights protections, with the progressive segmentation of social protection systems across sectors, occupational groups and genders. At the same time, the gap in social spending between southern countries and the EU average was only partly reduced. As stressed elsewhere, large-scale reforms intended to address both excessive costs and inequalities have been paralleled by persistent high-level public spending and the segmentation of pensions rights across social and occupational groups (this was particularly the case in Italy and Greece). Other countries (eg Spain) saw an increase in welfare spending and a reorientation towards active labour market policies and the protection of new social risks: expansion took place (in terms of access and funding) in paid parental leave, financial support for working mothers, means-tested unemployment benefits and education (Pavolini et al, 2015). Data on public pension spending prove that the period 1999–2008 saw an upward trend (by 0.9 percentage points) in line with the increase of pension benefits (NRRs) (see Figures 2.1 and 2.2).

Economic reforms tended to revive growth but much of the latter was related to the impact of the run-up to EMU and its first implementation. Spain, as well as Greece and Portugal, benefited from the common currency area and its extraordinary low interest rates. Italy, by contrast, had a sluggish economic trend, with persistent budgetary strains due to the enormous public debt. More than investment in R&D and education – which, in fact, did not lead to the expected increase of productivity – economic trends were shaped by favourable monetary policy and the real-estate bubble, both consistent with the increase of private debt. Between 1999 and 2008, southern countries experienced a decline in public spending on education, both in terms of the percentage of GDP (–0.1 percentage points) and as a percentage of total public expenditures (–0.4 percentage points) (see Figures 2.3 and 2.4). In the same period, Southern Europe experienced the most significant increase in public spending in R&D but the gap with the more advanced and innovative European economies was not reduced that much (see Figure 2.5).

Since the crisis, all four countries have shared the path towards *social standards devaluation*. This was extremely evident in the case of Greece and Portugal, which were under the MoU programme (already seen in the Irish case). In the wake of the 'sovereign debt crisis', the four countries started a plan of welfare cuts – especially in the pensions field – together with a general retrenchment of public spending. As stressed by Agostini et al (2016), the Italian reform pattern – as well as that of the other countries of the region seems consistent with the 'low road' to economic growth and competitiveness, a model reliant mainly on cost containment in the different policies under scrutiny. Budgetary cutbacks have been the main goal of the reforms implemented since 2009 in the domains of pensions, unemployment, education, R&D

and the public sector. All these fields have experienced retrenchment in both the long and short term. As proved by Figures 2.1 and 2.2, despite the increase of public pensions spending, the level of pension benefits started to decline. In parallel, between 2008 and 2012, we see the decline of public spending on education as a percentage of total public spending, the stability of expenditures on R&D (which, in a context of a sharp decline in GDP, means that there was not a major focus on the policy) and the evident decrease of public spending on the public sector (see Figure 2.6). The latter saw a decline of public spending on both the remuneration of public employees (−0.1 percentage points) and the number of employees in public administration (a reduction of −8.8% in the number of employees in public administration in Southern Europe). The outcomes have been extremely clear in terms of an overall reduction in social rights protections and the resurgence of poverty, unemployment and health diseases.

Visegrad countries

In the 1990s, the main challenge for the region (Czech Republic, Hungary, Poland and Slovakia) was the transformation of politico-economic institutions inherited from the socialist regimes while boosting economic growth. Reforms in that decade were thus consistent with the twofold aim of increasing the growth potential of the countries through liberalisation and protecting citizens from the negative effects of such a transformation. Visegrad countries acceded to the EU with a GDP below the Western EU average but soon started to fill the gap. Between 2003 and 2007, average GDP growth rates in Visegrad countries were between 3% and 10%, while in the same period, Western EU members saw an average GDP growth rate below 3% (Schweiger, 2014).

In the 1990s, this group of countries started labour market reforms consistent with the progressive liberalisation of labour contracts and increased flexibility. In the same years, CEE countries saw the growth of social spending to buffer the impact of economic and labour market reforms. Hungary's social welfare system, extensively using disability and early retirement schemes, was among the most generous in the region (Bohle and Greskovits, 2012).

However, by the end of the century in many countries, a new strategy of retrenchment was put in place. The reduced generosity of public pensions has taken place in parallel to the establishment of incentives for the development of supplementary private schemes: this has reflected a partial privatisation of the system. The latter trend has been particularly evident in the Visegrad countries, with the setting up of mandatory private schemes since the end of the 1990s. Between 1999 and 2008, we see different trends on pensions: an increase in public spending (2.2 percentage points – see Figure 2.1) but a decline in pension benefits (in terms of NRRs) (see Figure 2.2).

Within the public sphere, decision-making processes were redesigned to create a legal framework with authority and legitimacy, as well as to establish a more efficient and transparent public sector infrastructure. In some cases, these reforms related to the remuneration of certain segments of the public sector, such as ministries (eg in the Visegrad countries), or certain occupational groups, such as teachers. This is confirmed by quantitative indicators: total spending on the remuneration of public employees declined in the pre-crisis period (see Figure 2.6) but the number of public employees increased (Eurostat, 2016). As outlined by Bohle and Greskovits (2012), the Visegrad states tried to mitigate the impact of market shocks on their industrial legacy and, at the same time, accelerate foreign capital infusion by protective regulation and tariffs, export zones, foreign trade and investment agencies, investment support funds, tax exemption regimes, and public development banks. Figures on education policy show the stability of public spending (at about 4.4% of GDP) but its increase as a percentage of total public expenditures (see Figures 2.3 and 2.4). As for R&D, we see much stability in total public spending (see Figure 2.5).

All these trends are consistent with a good performance of the labour market. This has been deemed to be the consequence of both migration flows towards the west and domestic reforms. As stressed by Schweiger (2014), in Poland, the number of temporary jobs and the self-employed increased substantially, from 11% of all workers in 2001 to 28% in 2007.

In the context of the crisis, the path to SRs undertaken in the region reflected, to some extent, a *social standards devaluation* strategy, combined with limited investment, especially in policy sectors defined as growth-enhancing, such as education and R&D. The unemployment protection cutbacks of 2010 and the retrenchment of education policy in 2011 in the Czech Republic are proof of such a trend. Yet, cost-containment and austerity measures have not been accompanied by further waves of privatisation. A typical case is represented by pensions policy, where countries first decided to put contributions to pension funds on hold. This was followed by a more radical intervention. Hungary rolled back mandatory pension funds in 2010. In Poland from 2014, the contribution to mandatory pension funds decreased from 7.3% to 2.92% of wages. Several other countries have significantly reduced contributions (eg Slovakia). Data on spending confirm the following trends: pension benefits declined between 2008 and 2012 despite an overall increase of public spending (see Figures 2.1 and 2.2).

Visegrad countries have invested in the digital agenda, driven by strong information and communication technology (ICT) laws. Governments have invested in their enterprise environment to support innovation. Yet, these countries have been characterised by persistent shortcomings: a lack of available researchers, the low registration of patents and industrial designs, and little collaboration between universities and the private sector in research (WEF, 2014). In the post-crisis period, education policy saw a decline as a percentage of total public expenditure but total spending on R&D increased (see Figure 2.5). Eventually, the public sector saw a general increase of both spending and the number of employees (see Figure 2.6).

Summary

Summing up, as for the first question mentioned at the beginning of the chapter – 'Is there a common reform trend of a 'race to the bottom' in relation to social and employment rights?' – in the period between 1999 and 2012, we do not see any evidence of a common trend towards *social standards devaluation* or *improvement*. Instead, we see a diversified trend. Table 2.2 in the Appendix provides a summary of reform trends in pensions, education, R&D, public sector and labour market policies.

Nordic and Southern countries experienced a more evident decline in social and labour market standards. Nordic countries saw a decline in labour and pension benefits, and, in parallel, increased public investment in education, R&D and the public sector.[3] This cluster represents an interesting case of *selective investment*: improving the countries' productive capacity while reducing social and labour market protection. Southern countries experienced a decline in pensions, education and employment protection legislation, while labour market spending increased, together with investment in R&D. Up to the crisis, this cluster was an example of *socio-economic protectionism*. Since the crisis, the shift towards *social standards devaluation* seems more evident.

The other clusters show more expansionary trends. There is an upward trend in the Anglo-Saxon countries, largely determined by Ireland and its growth up to the crisis. The UK is characterised by a decline between 1999 and 2012 in labour market spending per unemployed person, as well as a decline in R&D spending as a share of

GDP. However, this is not a devaluation scenario because of increased employment protection and increased public spending on pensions, education and the public sector. In Continental Europe, we see an increase in labour market, education, R&D and public sector spending. With the exception of pensions, we see a trend towards *social standards improvement* since the crisis. Yet, we need to consider the huge internal variation, with Germany being a case of *selective investment*, while France is a case of *socio-economic protectionism*, with an increase in labour market and pensions spending, and R&D, a decline in education, and no major activation of labour market policies. Overall, improvement characterised the Visegrad countries, even if more recent trends are consistent with *social standards devaluation*.

Looking at the second question we asked at the beginning of the chapter – 'What has been the impact of the Great Recession?' – we see evidence of an explicit and general shift towards *social standards devaluation*. Between 2008 and 2012, active and passive labour market policies (LMP) expenditure per unemployed person decreased in Anglo-Saxon, Nordic and Visegrad countries, with a more mixed trend in Southern Europe and an overall increase in Continental Europe. Pensions benefits declined in all clusters except Anglo-Saxon countries, while public investments in education fell in Continental, Southern and Visegrad countries. Spending on the public sector decreased in Anglo-Saxon and Southern countries. The trend towards *social standards devaluation* seems particularly significant in Southern and Visegrad countries. In the Nordic countries, there is a risk of a shift from a *selective investment* path to *social standards devaluation* (see the decline in R&D and the mixed trend in public sector reforms). In Continental Europe, there is evidence of a more mixed trend: increased labour market spending, stable employment protection legislation and a decline in pensions and education spending. However, the variation between countries belonging to this cluster is still high.

Concluding remarks

The comparative analysis of SRs (see Table 2.2) allows us to draw some conclusions. In the whole period under scrutiny, we see a more intense decline in social standards in Southern European countries and, to some extent, in Nordic countries, while the other country clusters show a more contrasted trend. Since the crisis and up to 2012, we see evidence of a more generalised decline in social standards.

From a more analytical point of view, we propose three further remarks. First, while the period under scrutiny does not prove any major convergence, a longer-term perspective gives evidence of a more general trend of social devaluation. At the end of the 20th century, Anglo-Saxon, Nordic and Continental European countries started ambitious programmes of public spending cutbacks and the deregulation of the labour market. This partly explains their more mixed reform record since the early 2000s and in the wake of the crisis.

Second, the definition of different varieties of socio-economic policies risks overestimating the coherence of the reforms and policy trends in the different countries. Each cluster shows evident differences between countries: France and Germany in Continental Europe, Italy and Spain in Southern Europe, and UK and Ireland in the Anglo-Saxon camp all demonstrate different socio-economic institutions and trends in SRs.

Third, the typology of SRs proposed in the chapter is a first attempt to qualify socio-economic policies in the EU countries but further research is needed. The Nordic countries, for instance, have been characterised by what we have called selective investment, but the reform record mentioned earlier leaves the possibility of a shift from social investment to workfare, where social standards are compressed to make the whole economic system more competitive and innovative. Such a future possible trajectory should be further investigated through a more fine-grained analytical and conceptual toolkit.

Notes

[1] Both the Organisation for Economic Co-operation and Development (OECD, 2014) and the European Commission concentrate on long lists of policies: labour and product market policies, education, health, innovation, housing policies, the efficiency of public sectors, tax systems, unemployment benefit reform, human capital investment, and R&D.

[2] These groups of countries correspond to different labour market and welfare regimes (for a review of different definitions of socio-economic models in Europe, see Agostini et al, 2016).

[3] In 1999, Nordic countries spent more than 7% of their GDP on education. This was the highest level in the EU. Three different clusters spent above 4% of GDP: Continental countries (5.3%) and the Southern and Anglo-Saxon countries (around 4%). In 2008, the Nordic countries showed the highest level of expenditure (6.8%), followed by the Anglo-Saxon and Continental countries, both clustered at around 5.5% of their GDP. As for R&D, in 1999, Nordic countries had the highest level (2.9% of GDP) compared with 2% in Continental Europe, about 1.5% in the Anglo-Saxon

countries, 0.8% in Visegrad countries and Southern countries, 0.5% in South-Eastern countries, and 0.4% in the Baltic countries. In 2008, the big spenders remain the Nordic countries (3.3%) followed by the Continental countries (2.1%) and the Anglo-Saxon (1.5%) countries.

References

Agostini, C., Lisi, V., Natali, D. and Sabato, S. (2016) *Structural reforms in the EU countries*, Brussels: ETUI.

Alesina, A., Ardagna, S. and Galasso, V. (2010) 'The Euro and structural reforms', *Review of Economics and Institutions*, 2(1): art 2.

Baccaro, L. and Howell, C. (2011) 'A common neoliberal trajectory: the transformation of industrial relations in advanced capitalism', *Politics and Society*, 39(4): 521–63.

Bohle, D. and Greskovits, B. (2012) *Capitalist diversity on Europe's periphery*, Cornell, NY: CUP.

Bosch, G., Lehndorff, S. and Rubery, J. (eds) (2009) *European employment models in flux: A comparison of institutional change in nine European countries*, Basingstoke: Palgrave Macmillan.

Canton, E., Grilo, I., Monteagudo, J., Pierini, F. and Turrini, A. (2014) 'The role of structural reform for adjustment and growth', *Ecfin Economic Brief*, no. 34.

Carlin, W., Hassel, A., Martin, A. and Soskice, D. (2014) 'The German social model in transition', in E. Dølvik and A. Martin (eds) *European social models from crisis to crisis: Employment and inequality in the era of monetary integration*, Oxford: Oxford University Press, pp 49–104.

Davidsson, J.B. (2011) 'An analytical overview of labour market reforms across the EU: making sense of the variation', working paper, Laboratorio Revelli, 11/1.

Dølvik, E. and Martin, A. (2014) *European social models from crisis to crisis: Employment and inequality in the era of monetary integration*, Oxford: Oxford University Press.

Dølvik, E., Andersen, J.G. and Vartiainen, J. (2014) 'The Nordic social model in turbulent times. Consolidation and flexible adaptation', in E. Dølvik and A. Martin (eds) *European social models from crisis to crisis: Employment and inequality in the era of monetary integration*, Oxford: Oxford University Press, pp 246–86.

Eichorst, W., Feil, M. and Marx, P. (2010) 'Crisis, what crisis? Patterns of adaptation in European labor markets', *Applied Economics Quarterly Supplement*, 56(61): 29–64.

Eurostat (2016) Eurostat online database – Labour Force Survey series – detailed annual survey data, http://ec.europa.eu/eurostat/data/database

Hall, P. (2014) 'Varieties of capitalism and the Euro crisis', *West European Politics*, 37(6): 1223–43.

Hall, P. and Gingerich, D. (2009) 'Varieties of capitalism and institutional complementarities in the political economy', *British Journal of Political Science*, 39: 449–82.

Hall, P. and Soskice, D. (2001) *Varieties of capitalism: The institutional foundations of comparative advantage*, Oxford: Oxford University Press.

Hassel, A. (2014) 'Adjustment in the Eurozone: varieties of capitalism and the crisis of Southern Europe', *LSE Europe in Question Discussion Paper Series*, no. 76, pp 1–41.

Hausermann, S. (2012) 'The politics of old and new social policies', in G. Bonoli and D. Natali (eds) *The politics of the new welfare state*, Oxford: Oxford University Press, pp 111–32.

Hemerijck, A. (2013) *Changing welfare states*, Oxford: Oxford University Press.

IMF (International Monetary Fund) (2015) *World economic outlook*, Washington, DC: International Monetary Fund.

Jansson, O., Ottosson, J., Muhrem, M. and Magnusson, L. (2016) 'Unemployment and pensions protection in Europe: the changing role of social partners, Sweden', Ose working paper, no. 26, pp 1–60. Available at: http://www.ose.be/EN/publications/ose_paper_series_prowelfare.htm

Jessop, B. (1993) 'Towards a Schumpeterian workfare state? Preliminary remarks on post-Fordist political economy', *Studies in Political Economy*, 40: 7–39.

Le Cacheux, J. and Ross, G. (2014) 'France in the middle', in E. Dølvik and A. Martin (eds) *European social models from crisis to crisis: Employment and inequality in the era of monetary integration*, Oxford: Oxford University Press, pp 105–43.

Mayhew, K. and Wickham Jones, M. (2014) 'United Kingdom's social model: from the New Labour to the crisis and the Coalition government', in E. Dølvik and A. Martin (eds) *European social models from crisis to crisis: Employment and inequality in the era of monetary integration*, Oxford: Oxford University Press, pp 144–76.

Milberg, W. and Houston, E. (2005) 'The high road and the low road to international competitiveness: extending the neo-Schumpeterian trade model beyond technology', *International Review of Applied Economics*, 19(2): 137–62.

Morel, N., Palier, B. and Palme, J. (eds) (2012) *Towards a social investment welfare state? Ideas, policies and challenges*, Bristol: The Policy Press.

OECD (2014) *Economic policy reform 2014: Going for growth interim report*, Paris: OECD Publishing.

OECD (2015) *Pensions at a glance: OECD and G20 indicators*, Paris: OECD Publishing.

Palier, B. and Boisson-Cohen, M. (2015) 'Les trajectoires post-crise des pays de la zone euro: vers une dualisation économique et sociale de l'Europe'. Available at: http://www.congres-afsp.fr/st/st1/st1boissonpalier2.pdf

Pavolini, E., Leon, M., Guillèn, A.M. and Ascoli, U. (2015) 'From austerity to permanent strain? EU and welfare reforms in Italy and Spain', *Comparative European Politics*, 13(1): 56–76.

Perez, S. and Rhodes, M. (2014) 'The evolution and crisis of the social models in Italy and Spain', in E. Dølvik and A. Martin (eds) *European social models from crisis to crisis: Employment and inequality in the era of monetary integration*, Oxford: Oxford University Press, pp 177–213.

Pochet, P. and Degryse, C. (2011) 'The programmatic dismantling of the European social model'. Available at: http://www.intereconomics.eu/archive/year/2012/4/823/

Regan, A. (2011) 'From boom to bust: How the Irish economy became addicted to cheap money', Politico blog, published on 21 January 2011, available at www.politico.ie/archive/boom-bust-how-irish-economy-became-addicted-cheap-money. Accessed on 29/10/2017

Rubio, E. (2014) 'Promoting structural reforms in the euro area: what for and how?', working paper, no. 119, Notre Europe.

Schmid, G. (2013) 'Inclusive growth. What role for the European social model?', *OSE Working Paper Series*, 13/5, p 12.

Schroeder, W., Futh, S.K. and Jantz, B. (2015) 'Change through convergence? Reform measures of European welfare states in comparison', Friedrich Ebert Stiftung Foundation Study. Available at: http://library.fes.de/pdf-files/id/11448.pdf

Schweiger, C. (2014) *The EU and the global financial crisis, new varieties of capitalism*, Cheltenham and Northampton, MA: Edward Elgar.

Streeck, W. (2009) *Re-forming capitalism*, Oxford: Oxford University Press.

Thelen, K. (2014) *Varieties of liberalisation and the politics of social solidarity*, Cambridge: CUP.

WEF (World Economic Forum) (2014) 'The Europe 2020 competitiveness report 2014 edition'. Available at: http://reports.weforum.org/europe-2020-competitiveness-report-2014/

Appendix

Figure 2.1: Public pensions expenditure as a percentage of GDP, 1999–2012

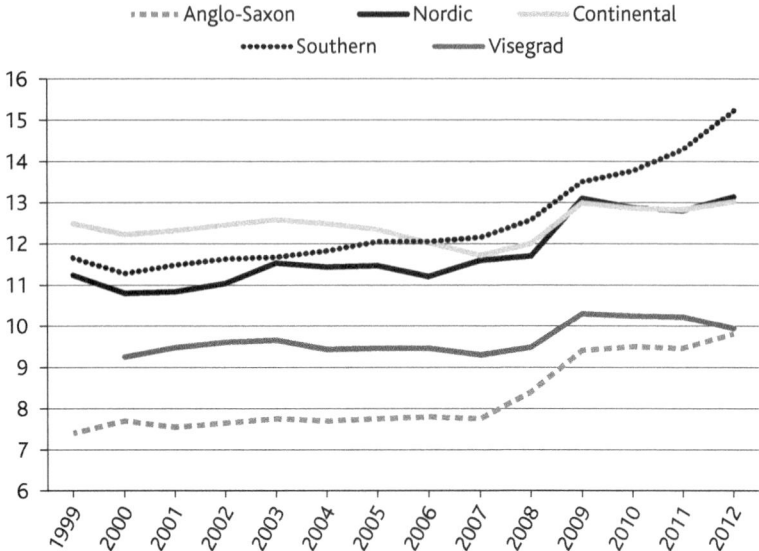

Source: Elaboration on Eurostat dataset (last updated on 12 November 2014; accessed 30 January 2015)

Figure 2.2: Net replacement rates, pensions, 2006, 2008, 2010, 2012

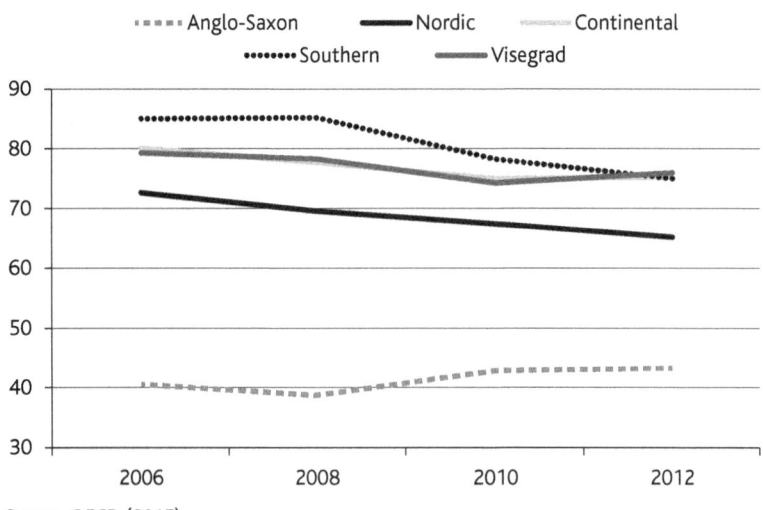

Source: OECD (2015)

Figure 2.3: Public expenditure on education as a percentage of GDP, 1999–2011

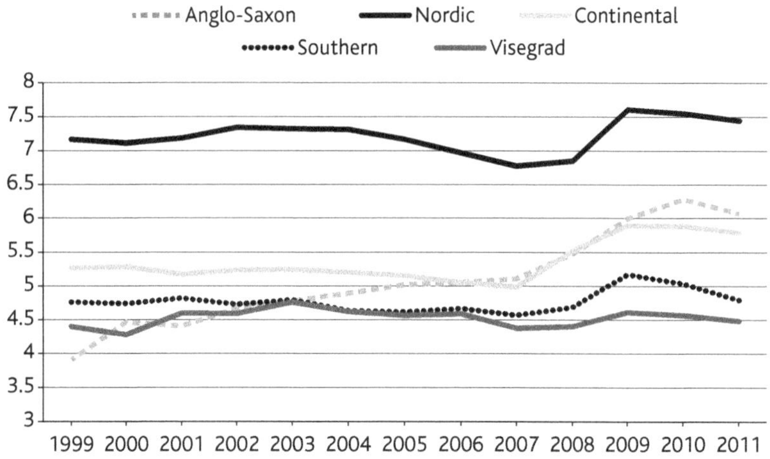

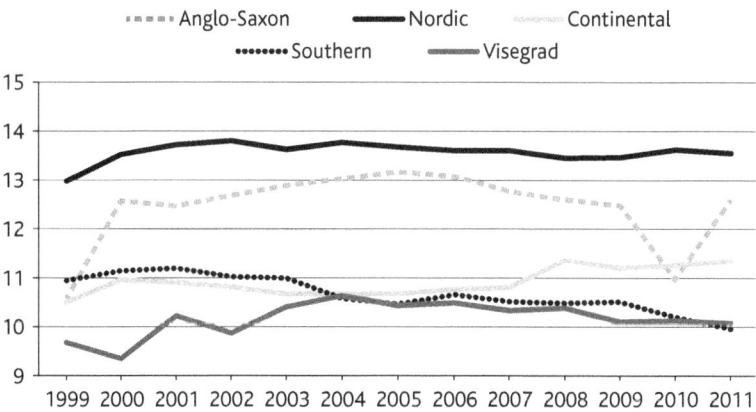

Source: Elaboration on Eurostat dataset (last updated on 28 November 2014; accessed 7 December 2014)

Figure 2.4: Public expenditure on education as a share of total public expenditure 1999–2011

Source: Elaboration on Eurostat dataset (last updated on 24 July 2014; accessed 2 February 2015).

Figure 2.5: Public expenditure on R&D and the public sector, 1999–2012

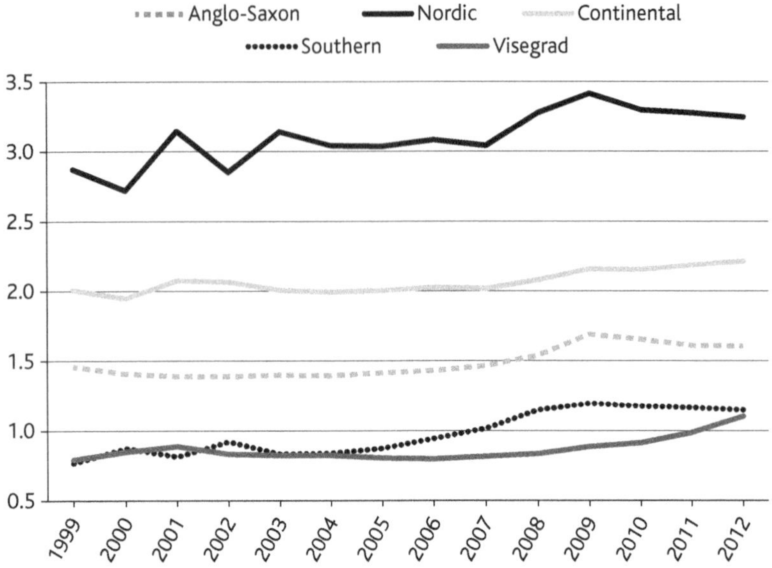

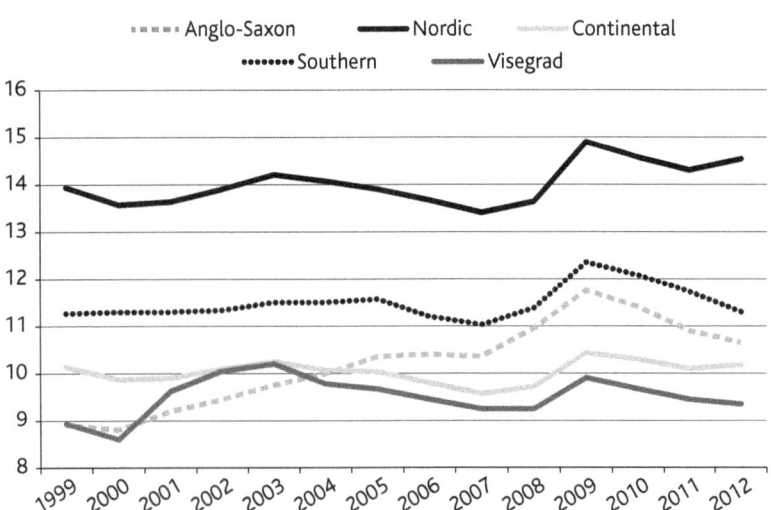

Source: Elaboration on Eurostat dataset (last updated on 28 November 2014; accessed 7 December 2014)

Figure 2.6: General government expenditure in the remuneration of employees as a share of GDP, 1999–2012

Source: Elaboration on Eurostat dataset (last updated on 18 February 2015; accessed 10 March 2015)

Structural reforms in Europe

Table 2.2: Overview of structural reforms in Europe

	Anglo-Saxon*		Nordic		Continental		Southern†		Visegrad	
	1999–2012	Pre-crisis Crisis	1999–2012	Pre-crisis Crisis	1999–2012	Pre-crisis Crisis	1999–2012	Pre-crisis Crisis	1999–2012	Pre-crisis Crisis
Labour market‡										
PLMP										
ALMP										
EPL										
Pensions§										
Education¶										
R&D										
Public sector										

■ = Increase of social standards
▨ = Stability and/or mixed trends
▨ = Decrease of social standards

Notes:

PLMP = Passive Labour Market Policies; ALMP = Active Labour Market Policies; EPL = Employment Protection Legislation; R&D = Research and Development.

* Ireland largely shapes the average level of the indicators on structural reforms: labour market spending and R&D spending are the result of a divergent trend between IE (growth) and UK (with a clear downward trend).

† The trend of education expenditures is about three Southern European countries, Greece is not covered due to a lack of information.

‡ PLMP and ALMP are expressed in terms of spending per unemployed while EPL concerns both regular and temporary contracts;

§ pensions net replacement rates; ¶ spending per total public expenditure.

Source: Eurostat, OECD and WEF

THREE

Income support policies and labour market reforms under austerity in Greece

Manos Matsaganis

Introduction

One of the most surprising features of the social situation in Greece over the past few years has been the almost complete failure of the social safety net to cope with the fallout from the recession, the most severe in the euro area. Indeed, it would be no exaggeration to say that the 'supply' of social protection in the country fell just as the 'demand' – that is, the need – for it increased dramatically.

During 2007–13, the Greek economy contracted by 26.5% in real terms. The loss in output was far greater than in other Southern European economies (Portugal: –7.6%; Spain: –7.5%; and Italy: –8.7%; or Ireland: –7.0%) over the same period. To find another example of such a harsh and drawn-out recession in the peacetime economic history of advanced economies, one would have to go back to the US Great Depression (–30% of gross domestic product [GDP] during 1929–32).

The steep rise in joblessness is no doubt the most characteristic feature of the Great Recession in Greece. Before the crisis, in May 2008, unemployment had reached its lowest level for over a decade (6.7% of the labour force). Thereafter, it started to rise again, gathering pace as the recession deepened.

The unemployment rate peaked at 28.7% in November 2013, and remained as high as 21.4% in April 2017. The decrease in employment was greater than the increase in unemployment: during 2008–13, the number of employed workers declined by 1,064,000, while the number of unemployed ones rose by 942,000. The total employment rate stood at 52.0% in 2016, having fallen to as low as 48.8% in 2013. In 2008, it had been 61.4%.

Since the Greek crisis has been protracted as well as deep, it is hardly surprising that the stock of unemployed workers out of work for over 12 months has risen so much. The long-term unemployment rate peaked at 19.5% in 2014, and was still as high as 17.0% in 2016, relative to 3.7% in 2008.

Policy responses to increased unemployment in all countries and at all times are constrained by fiscal considerations. However, in Greece during the Great Recession, these constraints have been much tighter than is usually the case as the government has operated under conditions of extreme 'austerity'. In 2010, in the aftermath of the sovereign debt crisis, the country was placed under international supervision by the European Union (EU)/European Central Bank (ECB)/International Monetary Fund (IMF) 'Troika' of lenders. The 'Greek Programme' aimed for significant primary surpluses (net of interest payments on debt), even as the economy slid into recession, while also introducing sweeping labour market 'reforms'.

On the other hand, policy responses were also conditioned by a legacy of pre-existing factors that limited their effectiveness. Some of these were 'objective', in the sense that they were related to the structure of the labour market: a high incidence of informal work, a large share of self-employment and small firm sizes. Others were rather more self-inflicted: poor administrative capacity, low sophistication in policy design and implementation, and skills mismatches.

Until the onset of the crisis, labour market institutions and norms (eg those concerning hiring and firing practices), whether formal or informal, tended to protect male breadwinners in stable jobs. Workers' rights and social protections had been expanded since the mid-1970s. In the 1980s, in response to rising unemployment, labour market regulation was tightened for permanent employees, and became more flexible for temporary ones on fixed-term contracts, thereby deepening labour market segmentation. During 1998–2000, ambitious policy reforms aimed to reduce unemployment by making standard work more flexible, and non-standard employment better protected. However, as they were poorly designed and clumsily executed, they failed to win the support of employers and labour unions, and eventually came to very little (Papadimitriou, 2005). Meanwhile, the adequacy and coverage of income support for unemployed workers remained low. On the eve of the crisis, although enforcement was weak, Greece ranked highly in terms of the strictness of employment protection legislation (EPL). This was to change dramatically under the impact of the crisis.

In this chapter, we review the changes in labour market policies under conditions of harsh austerity and mass unemployment in Greece since 2010. Three policy areas are covered: income support to the unemployed; active labour market policies (ALMPs); and EPL. The main changes are summarized in Table 3.1.

Income support

In a recession, eligibility conditions for unemployment benefits may be relaxed temporarily and benefit rates improved and their duration extended, with minimal adverse effects in terms of lower job-search intensity or higher reservation wages. This policy was actually put into effect in Germany, Italy and several other countries – including the US – and was welcomed by international organisations such as the Organisation for Economic Co-operation and Development (OECD, 2011) and the European Commission (CEC, 2013a). As a recent report by the latter explained:

> During economic downturns, eligibility conditions and replacement rates need to cater for the increased rate of job destruction and the stronger need for stabilising incomes, and the duration needs to be adapted in line with the reduced chances of finding a job.... Conversely, during recoveries, the unemployment benefit system needs to provide stronger incentives to re-enter the labour market in order to prevent cyclical unemployment from becoming structural. (CEC, 2013a: 210)

In Greece, the adjustment of unemployment benefits in response to the massive rise in joblessness was rather more equivocal. Nothing much happened in the early stages of the recession, as the Public Employment Service (OAEΔ), charged with the provision of unemployment benefits, was caught between a rise in benefit claims and a fall in contribution income (as well as bureaucratic inertia). Later on, under the provisions of the austerity programme, significant policy change with respect to unemployment benefits did take place. However, the direction of change differed greatly by instrument.

In a nutshell, contributory unemployment insurance was retrenched: the benefit rate was reduced and eligibility conditions were tightened. Means-tested unemployment assistance was expanded in terms of eligibility conditions but not in terms of benefit rates. Finally, in a further attempt to improve coverage, a new benefit for (formerly) self-employed workers was also introduced.

Unemployment insurance

The main instrument of income support to unemployed workers in Greece is contributory unemployment insurance, funded by employer and employee contributions. Unemployment insurance benefit is paid to dependent workers who are involuntarily unemployed, capable and available for work, and registered with the Public Employment Service, provided that they have accumulated an adequate contributions record.

In the case of first-time claimants, the required contributory record is: either (1) 80 days per year over the past two years, at least 125 days of which were in the past 14 months, excluding the past two months; or (2) 200 days in the past two years excluding the past two months, of which at least 80 days were in each of the past two years. Second-time claimants are required to have 125 contribution days over the past 14 months, excluding the past two months. Slightly modified conditions apply to seasonal workers (100 days over the past 12 months) and to construction workers and fishermen (100 days over the past 14 months).

Benefit duration is five to 12 months, depending on the redundant worker's contribution record. The benefit is paid at a flat rate. In 2010, the rate was €454 per month (61% of the minimum wage). Holiday and dependant allowances are also paid.

Coverage is incomplete. Four categories of workers are excluded. The first two by design: contributory conditions exclude new entrants to the labour market, while the maximum duration of support (12 months) excludes the long-term unemployed. Another two categories are excluded de facto: undeclared workers and the self-employed, the latter also including 'self-employed workers providing services to a single work provider in a continuous manner, hence acting *de facto* as employees' (OECD, 2010). As a result of all that, fewer than half of all jobless workers claimed unemployment insurance benefit. Specifically, in the first quarter of 2010, just before the 'bail-out' agreement was signed, the proportion of unemployed workers receiving unemployment insurance benefit was 45.6%.

Until recently, unemployment insurance seemed to function most efficiently as a subsidy to seasonal workers, or, rather, their employers. It was common practice for hotel managers, owners of 'cramming schools' and others to fire personnel at the end of the tourist season and the school year, respectively, only to hire them back a few months later at the start of the new season. In such cases, unemployment insurance benefit acted as a bridging device. In 2010 (yearly average), 29% of all recipients were defined as 'seasonal workers in tourism' (Matsaganis, 2011).

Eligibility conditions for unemployment benefit were actually worsened in 2011, when a ceiling was set on the total duration of separate spells of benefit receipt (400 days since 2014), over a period of four years. Furthermore, as a result of sweeping changes concerning the minimum wage, the benefit level paid under unemployment insurance was slashed in February 2012, from €454 to €360 per month.

Since unemployment insurance benefit was cut at the same rate as the minimum wage, the replacement rate of the benefit (vis-a-vis the minimum wage) was not altered much. Before the crisis, as a result of ad hoc indexation, it had fluctuated between 51% and 62%: it was 57% in the mid-1990s, 54% in the early 2000s, 58% in 2004, 51% in 2006, 59% in 2008, 61% in 2009/10, 62% in 2011, and 61% since 2012.

As a result of changes in both eligibility rules and the composition of the pool of jobless workers – more new entrants and more long-term unemployed – the number of unemployment insurance benefit recipients dwindled just as the number of unemployed workers skyrocketed. In 2010, an average of 224,000 persons received unemployment insurance benefit, out of a total of 624,000 unemployed.

In 2016, the average number of those claiming unemployment insurance benefit had fallen by almost half to 127,000, while the number of jobless workers had nearly doubled to 1,126,000. In view of that, the coverage rate fell from 35.9% in 2010 to 11.3% in 2016.

Unemployment assistance

The gaps in coverage of unemployment insurance might be less grave if compensated by a well-functioning programme of unemployment assistance, providing income support on a means-tested basis to those no longer (or not yet) eligible for unemployment insurance. However, this is not the case. Unemployment assistance benefit was only introduced in 2001, under the name 'long-term unemployment benefit'. Even so, the benefit can only be described as modest, while eligibility conditions for access are unusually restrictive.

The new benefit was initially worth €150 per month, raised to €200 per month in 2003, payable for a maximum period of 12 months. The income threshold for access to unemployment assistance benefit, at €5,000 annually plus €587 per dependent child – already rather low at the time of its introduction – was not indexed and was not adjusted until 2012. As a result of 'fiscal drag', the income test became ever-more biting and the benefit ever-more narrowly targeted: as a proportion of median income, the income threshold (for a couple with one child) fell from 35% in 2004 to 26% in 2010.

Other eligibility conditions were even more unreasonable. Access was restricted to those aged over 45. Also, only the long-term unemployed could apply. What is more, only former recipients of (contributory) unemployment insurance benefit were eligible and only if they had already drawn that benefit for the full 12 months (the maximum duration of unemployment insurance).

In view of its short duration, stringent eligibility conditions and low take-up rates, unemployment assistance failed to play the major role envisaged at the time of its introduction and drifted into irrelevance. In 2009, on the eve of the Greek crisis, unemployment assistance benefit was claimed by as few as 939 people (0.2% of all unemployed or 0.5% of the long-term unemployed).

More recently, eligibility conditions have been extended. The annual personal income threshold below which unemployment assistance may be granted was raised in 2012 (from €5,000 to €12,000), then reduced again in 2014 (to €10,000). In the same year, the age condition was relaxed to 20–66 years (relative to 45–65 years, as was the case until then).

On the other hand, the generosity of unemployment assistance was not improved. The benefit rate remained at €200 per month (unchanged in nominal terms since 2003, when it was raised from €150), for a maximum duration of 12 months. As a result of no indexation, the value of unemployment assistance benefit relative to the minimum wage drifted steadily from 38% in 2003 to 27% in 2011, while – somewhat paradoxically – it bounced back to 34% after the 2012 cut in the minimum wage.

Moreover, the unusually stringent structure of adjustments to the annual income threshold in order to account for additional family members (nothing for spouses but €587 per dependent child) remained in place. The rather peculiar requirement to have first claimed unemployment insurance benefit for the full 12 months, which de facto disenfranchised the majority of unemployment assistance applicants, was also left intact. Furthermore, an annual cash limit of €35 million extra spending (€100 million total spending) restricted the number of beneficiaries to far short of the total number of unemployed in low-income families. In 2015, the number of unemployment assistance recipients was estimated at 21,350 (1.8% of all unemployed or 2.4% of all long-term unemployed). In 2016, it fell further to 13,250.

Unemployment insurance for the self-employed

In 2013, unemployment insurance was extended to self-employed workers. The categories involved were mainly own-account workers and freelance workers in various professions. Claimants were required: (1) to have ceased their activity not earlier than 1 January 2012; (2) to have regularly paid social contributions for at least 12 months out of a total insurance period of at least three years before then; (3) to meet an income test (see later); and (4) to have settled any social security contributions owed. This last condition proved the hardest to meet: as an IMF study found (De Mets 2013), among contributors to the own-account workers' social security fund (OAEE), insuring most potential recipients of the new benefit, 664,000 (86%) were in arrears with contributions in September 2013, while as many as 388,000 (50%) owed over €5,000.

Eligibility for the new benefit was also subject to income conditions: annual personal income had to be below €10,000 and annual family income below €20,000 (averaged over two years prior to claiming). The benefit level was €360 per month (the same as for ordinary unemployment insurance benefit, but with no allowance for dependants), payable for a period of three to nine months, depending on contributory record. Applications for the new benefit started in April 2013. In 2015, the number of successful applicants was 6,740. In 2016, it stood at a mere 4,125.

Coverage rate of unemployment benefits

As discussed earlier, the policy mix of recent years has included measures that expanded coverage and others that limited access to income support for jobless workers. Stressing the former while downplaying the latter, Blanchard et al (2014: 20) claimed that, on IMF advice, the coverage of unemployment benefits in Greece 'expanded'.

As a matter of fact, the opposite was true. The net effect of the changes, taking into account improvements as well as reductions in eligibility, was a steady decline of the aggregate coverage rate of all unemployment benefits combined. In particular, the expansion of unemployment assistance for the long-term unemployed and the introduction of unemployment insurance for the self-employed, though welcome, were far too modest to compensate for the sharp reduction in the proportion of unemployed workers receiving the main instrument of income support for jobless workers, namely, unemployment insurance for wage earners. This is shown in Figure 3.1.

Figure 3.1: Coverage rate of unemployment benefits in Greece, 2010–16

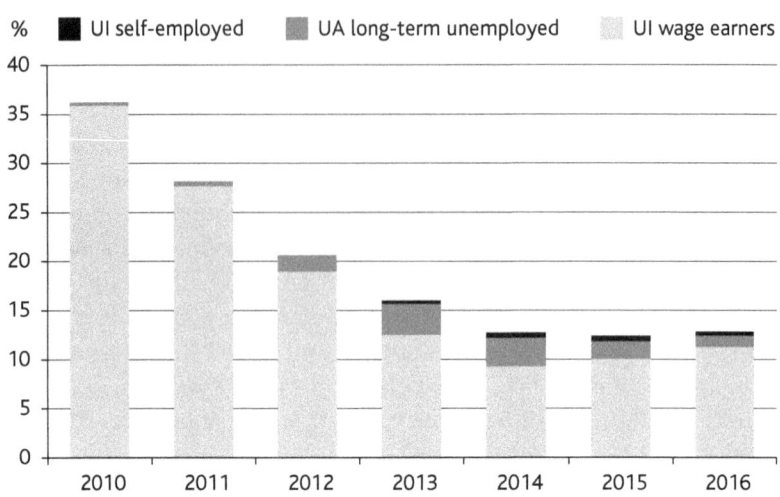

Note: UA = unemployment assistance; UI = unemployment insurance.
Source: ElStat (unemployment), Ministry of Labour (UB receipt)

Active labour market policies

'Activation' became popular among policymakers following concerns that excessive reliance on income support alone might prolong unemployment spells and hence breed dependency. The publication of *The OECD jobs study* (OECD, 1994) provided a conceptual framework that helped to strengthen the case for ALMPs to improve access to jobs, develop job-related skills and promote more efficient labour markets.

In Europe, ALMPs became an essential component of the European Employment Strategy. The latter, implemented from the mid-1990s via the Open Method of Coordination, and supported by grants from the European Social Fund (ESF), was the closest the EU has come so far to pursuing a common policy in that area (Zeitlin et al, 2005). In particular, the emphasis on 'activation' was a key pillar of the new policy paradigm of 'flexicurity', itself inspired by the labour market policies underpinning employment growth while preventing in-work poverty in Denmark and the Netherlands (Viebrock and Clasen, 2009). ALMPs usually comprise three types of programme: (1) training courses to upgrade skills; (2) job-search assistance to improve the matching process between vacancies and job-seekers; and (3) direct job creation schemes via subsidies to public and private employers.

Effectiveness of active labour market policies in Europe and beyond

As it turned out, evaluation studies comparing the effects of ALMPs on a sample of participants (the 'treatment group') relative to the labour market outcomes of non-participants (the 'control group') have failed to produce overwhelming evidence of their effectiveness. In particular, the presence of deadweight effects (arising when hirings from the treatment group would have also occurred in the absence of the programme being evaluated) and substitution or displacement effects (when jobs taken by participants would have simply been occupied by non-participants had the programme not existed) may significantly limit the net positive effect of ALMPs on employment and/or earnings.

For instance, a meta-analysis of ALMPs by Card et al (2010), examining 199 programmes drawn from 97 studies over the period 1995 to 2007, found that the number of programmes with a significantly positive outcome only marginally outnumbered those with a significantly negative outcome, even though that margin would appear to lengthen in the longer run. Another meta-analysis by Kluve (2010) of nearly 100 studies from Europe alone reached similar conclusions, adding that it is often the type of ALMPs that matters. Specifically, direct job-creation schemes in the public sector do not seem to work, while wage subsidies and job-search programmes – the latter supported by sanctions (the suspension or reduction of unemployment benefit when participants fail to look for a job actively enough or when they refuse an acceptable job offer) – seem to be more effective.

Effectiveness of active labour market policies in Greece

Uncertainties remain about the effectiveness of activation policies implemented in Greece due to the absence of an evaluation culture. The Public Employment Service has claimed that the ALMPs introduced during 2010–12 have halted the increase in unemployment by five to seven percentage points. Nevertheless, this is not based on a thorough assessment of outcomes of the programmes pursued, in terms of employment creation or retention net of displacement effects, which makes it impossible to establish attribution to ALMPs. A survey carried out by the author on behalf of the Ministry of Labour in 2009 found no evidence that a single job was created (or saved) as an effect of all the ALMP schemes put into operation during 2000–08 (at a cost of approximately €1 billion in ESF grants).

This is quite consistent with the key conclusion of a recent detailed study, which found that the main channels through which the European Employment Strategy seemed to operate in peripheral countries were financial conditionality and the domestic empowerment of policy entrepreneurs rather than policy learning, as most of the literature had previously assumed. In the particular case of Greece, employment policy was preoccupied predominantly with balancing the demands of employers for lower labour costs with those of workers for higher real wages. Policy initiatives emanating from Europe, aiming instead at bringing forward positive-sum solutions for both parties (activation, gender equality, reconciliation of work and family, flexicurity), were seen by Greek policymakers (even those with a pro-European outlook, eg, during the reign of Costas Simitis and his socialist modernisers [1996–2004]) as alien and irrelevant to domestic concerns (even when promoted by personalities that were politically akin and culturally close to their Greek counterparts, such as Portuguese Prime Minister António Gutierrez during 1995–2001) (Zartaloudis, 2014).

Nevertheless, because European initiatives were readily translated into ESF priorities and the latter came with lavish funding for AMLPs (and, what is more, in a policy area perennially starved of domestic resources), Greek policymakers, administrators and businessmen learned to behave as if ESF priorities were also their own, which was patently not the case. Passive, skin-deep adjustment and 'follow the money' became the name of the game. In such a context, the very purpose of ALMPs – to boost employment – was relegated to a secondary concern in Greece.

Successive reforms of the Public Employment Service (in 1998, 2001, 2003 and 2006) seem to have failed to engineer a change of approach (Zartaloudis, 2014; see also Papadimitriou, 2005). As for the more intense efforts of recent years to upgrade Public Employment Service (PES) capacities, with technical assistance from the European Commission's Task Force for Greece, it is too soon to tell what, if any, effect they may have had. This seems to stand in stark contrast with the experience of other EU countries, such as Belgium, where ESF-supported schemes had a significant impact on innovation even though they amounted to no more than 2% of ALMPs, compared with an estimated 40% in Greece (Verschraegen et al, 2011).

High youth unemployment

In Greece, ALMPs have been most prominently pursued over the past three decades in the context of youth unemployment, which was higher in Greece than in most other EU countries even before the crisis (Matsaganis, 2015). This was also the case for highly qualified persons in their late 20s. For instance, the unemployment rate of individuals aged 25–29 holding university degrees at bachelor, master's or doctoral level (International Standard Classification of Education (ISCED) levels 5–8) in the first quarter of 2008 stood at 2.3 times the euro area average (15.5% versus 6.8%). Six years later, it had gone up to 3.2 times as high (35.2% versus 11.0%). Plenty of other evidence confirms that the transition from education to employment has always been slower and more incomplete in Greece than in most other European countries, and has become even more so under the impact of the current crisis (Mitrakos et al, 2010; Eurofound, 2014).

Skills mismatches are a crucial factor here, caused by problems on the demand as well as the supply side. To start with, the skills mix produced by the education system at all levels seems poorly designed for the needs of a dynamic economy. Parents tend to hold manual labour in low esteem, so vocational education is eschewed by schoolchildren of average ability and above, who overwhelmingly opt for general education leading to university. As a result, vocational schools are perceived – and often are – of inferior quality, and so end up catering for low performers, typically from low-income families, often with a foreign migrant background (CEDEFOP, 2014; Ioannidou, 2014).

As for universities, those in highest demand prepare graduates for careers in the so-called liberal professions of medicine, law and engineering or architecture, and the rest for jobs in the civil service and the broader public sector. As a result, employers find that young people applying for jobs lack the skills they value. As a recent McKinsey (2014) study found, the skills missing the most include 'hard skills' such as proficiency in English and 'hands-on experience', as well as softer skills such as 'work ethic' and 'problem solving and analysis'. The same study established that small firms faced greater difficulties in recruiting suitable new hires and were less likely to work with education providers and with other employers to tackle their skills problems.

If initial vocational education is perceived to be of poor quality, so is continuing vocational education and training following entry to the labour market. Training-related ALMPs, to a large extent financed by the ESF and other EU institutions, have grown exponentially over the past few decades but seem to operate on the assumption that the absorption of available resources must be maximised at all costs. Usually, this implies that the acquisition of skills is of secondary importance. In such a context, it should not be surprising that training providers have successfully resisted occasional attempts by the Ministry of Labour to force them to follow up on former trainees in order to monitor how they fare in the labour market on the grounds that this would interfere with maximising the use of earmarked EU funding.

In 2013, mounting concern that the generation of young workers entering the labour market during the Great Recession, or in its immediate aftermath, may in fact be a lost generation led the European Commission to launch the Youth Guarantee initiative. This takes the form of a pledge by member states to ensure that young people under 25 (whether or not they are registered in the public employment services) receive either an offer of employment, continued education, an apprenticeship or training within four months of becoming unemployed or leaving formal education.

Under the Youth Guarantee plan, a total of €340 million (including €170 million from the ESF allocation in 2014–20) was earmarked for Greece in 2014/15. A recent report commissioned by the Task Force for Greece (Coquet, 2014) set out a rather detailed implementation plan, which incidentally advocated against wage subsidies in private firms and in favour of apprenticeship schemes, youth entrepreneurship programmes and direct job creation in the public sector.

In view of the failings of vocational education and training policy in Greece, discussed earlier, the Memorandum of Understanding committed the Greek government to 'closely align the Youth Guarantee Implementation Plan with the roadmap for the modernisation and expansion of vocational education and training and providing immediate relief for the hardest-hit young people' by December 2014 (CEC, 2014: 195). Needless to add, the resignation of the previous government in December 2014 and the subsequent election of a new government in January 2015 seem to have put this plan on hold.

As argued in a recent collection of essays (Dolado, 2015; Felgueroso and Jansen, 2015), the Youth Guarantee contains useful elements, drawn from the successful experience of Nordic and other EU countries, such as Germany and Austria. Nevertheless, it may prove hard to replicate this success by providing immediate relief in the labour markets of peripheral countries, where youth unemployment is high but aggregate demand remains depressed. Moreover, poor administration and fraud (as revealed by a recent spate of scandals in Spain), as well as structural problems concerning the transition from education to employment, labour market segmentation and low firm sizes, may further limit the effectiveness of the Youth Guarantee.

Public works

As discussed earlier, recent reviews of the economic literature, offering systematic meta-analyses of evaluation studies (Card et al, 2010; Kluve, 2010), do not seem to provide much support for the effectiveness of direct job-creation schemes. Nevertheless, as also discussed earlier, there is no real evidence that vocational training schemes, as implemented in Greece, have contributed to the creation or retention of jobs. On the other hand, the Public Employment Service, largely because of bureaucratic inertia and staff shortages, also seems to suffer from chronic incapacity to provide unemployed workers with valuable assistance with job search.

In view of the foregoing, public works have come to be seen as relatively more attractive almost by default. An early study, sponsored by the Labour Institute of the Greek General Confederation of Workers, argued that:

> Remediating employment policies, including workweek reductions and employment subsidies, abound but have failed to answer the call satisfactorily. Direct public-service job creation, instead, enables communities to mitigate risks and vulnerabilities that rise especially in turbulent times by actively transforming their own economic and social environment. (Antonopoulos et al, 2011, n.p.)

Eventually, that became the consensus view among policymakers. In July 2013, a public works programme was launched, aiming to create 50,000 temporary jobs using €216 million from EU structural funds. The Task Force for Greece, a European Commission agency specially created to provide technical support to the Greek government, became heavily involved in helping to design the programme (CEC, 2013b). The IMF was also supportive (IMF, 2014). In the meantime, 'public work programmes targeted at jobless households, the long-term unemployed and young people not in education, employment or training as a measure of emergency and temporary nature while labour demand remains sluggish' had been elevated to the status of 'prior action', that is, listed in the Memorandum of Understanding agreed between the Troika and the Greek government, committing the latter to a number of actions that must be taken prior to the disbursement of financial aid (CEC, 2014: 106).

The programme was targeted at the long-term unemployed in jobless households. Passing an income test was also required. The programme provided for five months of subsidised community work with a monthly wage of up to €490 for workers over 25 years of age, and up to €427 for those aged below 25. The first phase of the programme, employing 50,000 people, was completed in early 2014. The next phase, intended to cover at least another 50,000 people (CEC, 2014) – up to 90,000 according to the International Labour Office (ILO, 2014) – was still under discussion in late 2014, when an early general election was called.

The appointment of Rania Antonopoulos, the author of the Levy Institute report cited earlier, to the position of deputy minister of labour following the general election, and the (rare) political consensus discussed earlier, point to the likely rise in importance of public works programmes in Greece. The new deputy minister has announced her intention to create 550,000 jobs (rather than merely 50,000 as the current plan has it).

Employment protection legislation

Labour market reform is a broad concept, also comprising legislative changes affecting wage-setting institutions, working time regulations, labour taxation and minimum wages, as well as job protection. This section focuses on EPL alone.

Labour market segmentation

The defining feature of the Greek labour market before the crisis was its polarisation between hyper-protected insiders, under-protected 'mid-siders' and unprotected outsiders (Jessoula et al, 2010; Matsaganis, 2011). On the one hand, jobs in the public sector (and especially public utilities) provided family wages, generous social benefits, lax work practices and absolute employment protection. The partial privatisation of certain public enterprises and/or the liberalisation of the respective industries had reduced the employment protection of younger and/or newly hired workers but had not affected the hyper-protection of core workers there. On the other hand, for the overwhelming majority of Greek workers ('mid-siders'), typically employed in small firms, jobs paid less on average and came with less generous benefits and reduced employment protection. Furthermore, in certain sectors of the economy (such as the construction industry, tourism and other services), informal employment was the norm, allowing many employers to flout regulatory constraints in the form of dismissal protection, minimum wages and social insurance. As a result, workers in such sectors faced precarious working conditions with little or no access to legal safeguards or social rights.

Changes in employment protection legislation

EPL comprises: (1) regulations protecting permanent workers; and (2) rules limiting firms' recourse to temporary work. As regards permanent workers, a battery of measures significantly reduced firing costs. Key changes included the following:

- the threshold at which dismissals are considered collective was raised (for firms with 20–150 employees: from four to six dismissals per month);
- the length of notice required prior to dismissal was shortened considerably for white-collar workers and severance pay was reduced for all workers;
- the length of trial periods for newly hired workers was increased (from two to 12 months); and
- an earlier provision under which employers were required to pay part of unemployment benefit in case of dismissals arising from mergers or acquisitions was also abolished.

Concerning temporary work, various steps were taken to increase flexibility:

- the maximum duration of fixed-term contracts before they are automatically converted to indefinite-duration contracts was extended to three years (otherwise, their renewal without restriction was allowed under certain circumstances);
- the scope for temporary work was extended, as was its duration (from 18 to 36 months, or indefinitely if contracts are separated by a 23-day interval);
- several restrictions on the scope of temporary work agencies were lifted or eased;
- the requirement that temporary work agencies may provide services only for 'transitory, extraordinary, or seasonal' positions was abolished;
- the length of time before hiring via temporary work agencies is allowed following redundancies for economic reasons was reduced (from six to three months for individual redundancies and from 12 to six months for collective dismissals);

- the use of temporary work agencies in large public works contracts was permitted; and
- the list of hazardous positions closed to workers supplied by temporary work agencies was limited.

Public employment

According to recent estimates (CEC, 2014: 38), employment in the broader public sector shrank from 907,351 people in 2009 to 651,717 in 2014. What is more, in proportional terms, this reduction (28.2%) was significantly greater than for total employment (a fall of 21.7% between the first three quarters of 2009 and the same period in 2014). While this reduction was largely achieved through attrition (early retirement, the non-renewal of fixed-term contracts and the elimination of temporary positions) and a more rigorous application of the 1:5 rule (one new hiring for every five separations), the termination of permanent positions has also taken place.

The latter was mostly done via a 'mobility scheme', in which redundant workers were placed for a period of eight months on 75% of their last salary. By the time the eight-month period expired, they could be transferred to a new public sector position. If not, they exited public employment altogether. By March 2014, approximately 300 workers who had been placed in mobility with the first wave (July 2013) had left the public administration. At the same time, a total of 25,000 public employees were in mobility, of whom about 15,000 were 'expected to find a new job, after transiting through the scheme, in departments suffering from understaffing' (CEC, 2014: 39).

In fact, even the Memorandum of Understanding seemed to acknowledge that staff shortages in the public sector had gone too far:

> While the horizontal application of [the 1:5] rule has contributed to reducing the size of the civil service, it is now essential, in order for it to deliver the necessary quality of services, to hire new employees in a timely fashion, and following a rigorous, skill-based selection process. (CEC, 2014: 38)

The 2015 budget agreed by the Troika and the previous government allowed for 15,000 new hires. In January 2015, the incoming government's minister for public administration announced that approximately 3,500 civil servants would be reinstated, with an offsetting reduction of the number of new hires planned.

Assessment

As a result of the foregoing, in a very short time, the Greek labour market was deregulated. A European Commission assessment based on the Labour Market Reforms (LABREF) database concluded that 'Greece was at the top of the countries in adopting reforms that decreased the stringency of labour market regulations' (CEC, 2014: 49). While this assessment was also influenced by sweeping changes in wage setting (not reviewed here), it was not restricted to these alone: 'In the areas of job protection [EPL] and working time, Greece has also been a very active reformer even if other countries have been changing their institutions, too' (CEC, 2014: 49). As a recent ILO report also noted: 'Between 2010 and 2013, the OECD index of EPL has shown Greece to have the second highest decrease in the EU for permanent employees – after Portugal – and the highest drop for temporary employees' (ILO, 2014: 88).

It is worth noting that most of the changes discussed earlier occurred in the early phase of the Greek programme (2010–12). In later years, especially after the drastic cut to minimum wages (February 2012), labour reform ran out of steam. As the most recent IMF review drily noted: 'The authorities were unable to deliver on most labour market reform commitments, given political realities' (IMF, 2014: 19–20). Pending items included 'excessive restrictions … that raise the cost of doing business and inhibit the establishment or expansion of larger-sized firms', 'legislative change [concerning disputed collective dismissals] to establish simple and easily verifiable statutory requirements, remove the required approval of the Minister of Labour, and ensure that the employer internalizes the social cost of its actions', and action to remove maturity allowances adding up to 30% (for employees with nine or more years of experience) of the statutory minimum wage (IMF, 2014: 19–20).

Has labour market deregulation been successful in terms of higher employment? In fact, the total number of jobs continued to fall until the third quarter of 2014. At most, it can be argued that by reducing labour costs, recent changes have averted job losses (eg by enabling some firms to survive the crisis). On the other hand, there is evidence that EPL reforms had little effect on job creation, merely encouraging the transformation of more secure contracts into less secure ones. For instance, the total number of existing full-time contracts transformed into either part-time or intermittent contracts increased from 26,253 in 2010 to 84,290 in 2012 (ILO, 2014). Moreover, the joint effect of legislative reforms and the economic downturn has been a deterioration in the quality of non-standard employment, as shown by the rise in involuntary temporary and part-time work (on involuntary part-time work, see Veliziotis et al, 2015).

Evidence from the analysis of labour market flows seems to bear that out:

> The labour market reforms presented above have also increased employment polarization between standard and non-standard (e.g. temporary, part-time) forms of employment. In particular, in the most recent years, non-standard employment has increasingly represented a step towards labour market exclusion (i.e. unemployment or inactivity) rather than a temporary solution with a view to more stable employment. (ILO, 2014: 96)

Conclusion

On the whole, labour market policies (in common with all other welfare state institutions) in Greece have failed to rise to the challenge of harsh austerity and mass unemployment. A legacy of backwardness, neglect and a general lack of sophistication proved difficult, if not impossible, to overturn under the emergency conditions prevailing since 2010. Moreover, as regards the less controversial aspects of the structural reforms demanded by the country's creditors under the bail-out agreements (for instance, supporting job creation, upgrading the Public Employment Service and improving the absorption, as well as the effectiveness, of EU funding), the domestic actors' preferred approach of passively adjusting to European funding opportunities rather than genuinely puzzling for solutions left no room for a more constructive engagement. The adverse effects of the resulting handicap are there for all to see.

On the other hand, as far as the more controversial aspects of recent structural reforms are concerned, there can be little doubt that over the past six years, the Greek labour market has become more flexible for firms but considerably less secure for workers. In other words, reform has emphatically not followed the much-discussed 'flexicurity' approach (Viebrock and Clasen, 2009), officially promoted by the European Commission, which aims to reduce segmentation by combining lower job and employment protections for core workers, on the one hand, with greater income and social protections for non-standard workers, on the other. Indeed, as Heyes (2013) has shown, the implementation of austerity measures in Ireland and elsewhere undermined conditions for implementing those components of flexicurity that have appealed most to trade unions. Similarly, in Greece, far from aiming at flexicurity, reform has taken the more mundane route of deregulation across the board, with reductions in job security accompanied by a drastic cut in minimum wages, as well as in unemployment insurance benefits, at the same time as industrial relations deteriorated and collective bargaining was virtually abandoned (Matsaganis, 2013; Kornelakis and Voskeritsian, 2014; Theodoropoulou, 2015). The wisdom and political sustainability of this approach at the European level is questionable and has, in fact, been questioned for some time (Boeri and Garibaldi, 2009). Recent events in Greece and elsewhere seem to bear that out.

While political rhetoric tends to paint a dark picture ('Middle Ages for labour'), on closer inspection, a more nuanced portrait emerges. To be sure, there is little doubt that labour market reform, set against a background of mass unemployment and low unionisation, has further shifted the balance of power at workplaces against workers. Nonetheless, whether deregulation has also actually reduced segmentation is an open question.

It is true that newly hired workers in public utilities now enjoy fewer advantages. The mobility scheme has shattered the conviction of civil servants in general government that their job was for life, and changes in EPL (and in collective bargaining) have weakened the position of private sector workers. As a result, it can be argued that many insiders have now moved closer to the position formerly occupied by 'mid-siders', while most of the latter have moved closer to that occupied by outsiders. Pay cuts have been roughly just as drastic for both categories, leaving the public sector pay premium largely intact (Christopoulou and Monastiriotis, 2014; see also Ioannou, 2013).

Nevertheless, the gap between (some) hyper-protected insiders and unprotected outsiders remains as great as ever. Even under conditions of extreme austerity, workers in public utilities (a less numerous category than 'normal' civil servants) have mostly kept their privileges in terms of employment protections and social benefits. For instance, the Telecommunications Company Union 'accepted dualisation, exacerbating the insider–outsider cleavage' (Kornelakis, 2016: 403), in other words, it successfully defended the advantages of existing employees at the expense of newly hired workers. Also, neither the government nor the Troika saw fit to question the €500 million annual subsidy paid to the few thousand pensioners of the Public Power Corporation, who continued to retire under extremely favourable terms. As for precarious workers in informal or undocumented jobs, their situation can hardly be said to have improved and in many respects – pay, benefits, employment opportunities – seems certain to have deteriorated further.

Imbalances in union membership reinforce the insider–outsider gap. For many decades, and hence irrespective of the upheavals of recent years, Greek unions have been more unevenly spread between different segments of the labour market and have suffered a steeper fall in union density compared with their European counterparts. Union density is very low outside the enclaves of the civil service, banking and the public utilities (in other words, in the private firms employing the overwhelming majority of all wage earners). According to the Institutional Characteristics of Trade Unions, Wage Setting, State Intervention and Social Pacts (ICTWSS), 'Database on institutional characteristics of trade unions, wage setting, state intervention and social pacts' (Visser, 2015, n.p.), compiled by Jelle Visser and his team at the Amsterdam Institute for Advanced Labour Studies (AIAS), the union density rate in 2011 was 64.7% in the public sector, compared with 14.3% in private firms (including banking).

In view of that, the typical union member – and especially union leader – in Greece is a tenured public sector worker, member of a special social insurance scheme, predominantly male and middle-aged, and exclusively Greek. In contrast, the typical worker is younger, employed (often 'flexibly') by private firms, insured with the general social insurance scheme and in an increasingly feminised and multi-ethnic workforce.

In other words, at a time when ordinary workers need their unions more than ever, the latter appear to be growing increasingly alienated from the former. The recent resurgence of militant, highly politicised, independent labour organisations, holding official unions in contempt, seems to confirm this process of gradual alienation. As is the case everywhere else, the future of Greek unions seems to hinge on their capacity to successfully promote the aspirations of all workers for more jobs on better pay and conditions.

References

Antonopoulos, R., Papadimitriou, D.B. and Toay, T. (2011) *Direct job creation for turbulent times in Greece*, The Levy Economics Institute with the Labour Institute of the Greek General Confederation of Workers, Annandale-on-Hudson, NY: Bard College, www.levyinstitute.org/publications/direct-job-creation-for-turbulent-times-in-greece

Blanchard, O.J., Jaumotte, F. and Loungani, P. (2014) 'Labor market policies and IMF advice in advanced economies during the Great Recession', *IZA Journal of Labor Policy*, 3(2): 1–23.

Boeri, T. and Garibaldi, P. (2009) 'Beyond Eurosclerosis', *Economic Policy*, 24(59): 409–61.

Card, D., Kluve, J. and Weber, A. (2010) 'Active labour market policy evaluations: a meta-analysis', *The Economic Journal*, 120: F452–77.

CEC (Commission of the European Communities) (2013a) *Employment and social developments in Europe 2012*, Brussels: European Commission.

CEC (2013b) *Task Force for Greece: fifth activity report*, Brussels: European Commission.

CEC (2014) *The second economic adjustment programme for Greece: Fourth review*, European Economy Occasional Paper 192, Brussels: European Commission.

CEDEFOP (European Centre for the Development of Vocational Training) (2014) *Vocational education and training in Greece: Short description*, Luxembourg: Publications Office of the European Union.

Christopoulou, R., and Monastiriotis, V. (2014) *The public–private duality in wage reforms and adjustment during the Greek crisis*, Crisis Observatory Research Paper No. 9/2014, Athens: Hellenic Foundation for European and Foreign Policy (ELIAMEP).

Coquet, B. (2014) 'Youth Guarantee Implementation Plan in Greece: policy making under extremely severe economic conditions', report for the Task Force for Greece.

De Mets, P. (2013) 'Greece: reforming the collection of social security contributions', Fiscal Affairs Department, International Monetary Fund.

Dolado, J.J. (2015) 'Introduction', in J.J. Dolado (ed) *No country for young people? Youth labour market problems in Europe*, a VoxEU e-book, London: Centre for Economic Policy Research (CEPR) Press, pp 1–14.

Eurofound (2014) *Mapping youth transitions in Europe*, European Foundation for the Improvement of Living and Working Conditions, Luxembourg: Publications Office of the European Union.

Felgueroso, F. and Jansen, M. (2015) 'The Youth Guarantee: theory or reality?', in J. Dolado (ed) *No country for young people? Youth labour market problems in Europe*, a VoxEU e-book, London: Centre for Economic Policy Research (CEPR) Press, pp 129–37.

Heyes, J. (2013) 'Flexicurity in crisis: European labour market policies in a time of austerity', *European Journal of Industrial Relations*, 19(1): 71–86.

ILO (International Labour Office) (2014) *Productive jobs for Greece*, Research Department, Geneva: International Labour Office.

IMF (International Monetary Fund) (2014) *Greece: Fifth review under the extended arrangement under the extended fund facility, and request for waiver of non-observance of performance criterion and rephasing of access*, IMF Country Report, no. 14/151, Washington, DC: International Monetary Fund.

Ioannidou, A. (2014) *Die Situation der Jugendlichen auf dem griechischen Arbeitsmarkt*, Berlin: Friedrich Ebert Stiftung.

Ioannou, C. (2013) 'Greek public service employment relations: a Gordian knot in the era of sovereign default', *European Journal of Industrial Relations*, 19(4): 295–308.

Jessoula, M., Graziano, P. and Madama, I. (2010) '"Selective flexicurity" in segmented labour markets: the case of Italian "mid-siders"', *Journal of Social Policy*, 39(4): 561–83.

Kluve, J. (2010) 'The effectiveness of European active labour market programs', *Labour Economics*, 17(6): 904–18.

Kornelakis, A. (2016) 'Inclusion or dualization? The political economy of employment relations in Italian and Greek telecommunications', *British Journal of Industrial Relations*, 54(2): 385–408.

Kornelakis, A. and Voskeritsian, H. (2014) 'The transformation of employment regulation in Greece: towards a dysfunctional liberal market economy?', *Relations industrielles/Industrial Relations*, 69(2): 344–65.

Matsaganis, M. (2011) 'The welfare state and the crisis: the case of Greece', *Journal of European Social Policy*, 21(5): 501–12.

Matsaganis, M. (2013) *The Greek crisis: Social impact and policy responses*, Berlin: Friedrich-Ebert-Stiftung.

Matsaganis, M. (2015) 'Youth unemployment and the Great Recession in Greece', in J.J. Dolado (ed) *No country for young people? Youth labour market problems in Europe*, a VoxEU e-book, London: Centre for Economic Policy Research (CEPR) Press, pp 77–88.

McKinsey (2014) 'Education to employment: getting Europe's youth into work', McKinsey Center for Government.

Mitrakos, T., Tsakloglou, P. and Cholezas, I. (2010) 'Determinants of youth unemployment in Greece with an emphasis on tertiary education graduates', *Economic Bulletin*, 33: 21–62.

OECD (Organisation for Economic Co-operation and Development) (1994) *The OECD jobs study: Facts, analysis, strategies*, Paris: OECD.

OECD (2010) *Jobs for youth: Greece*, Paris: OECD.

OECD (2011) *Persistence of high unemployment: What risks? What policies?*, Economics Department Policy Notes No. 5, Paris: OECD.

Papadimitriou, D. (2005) 'The limits of engineering collective escape: the 2000 reform of the Greek labour market', *West European Politics*, 28(2): 381–401.

Theodoropoulou, S. (2015) 'National social and labour market policy reforms in the shadow of EU bail-out conditionality: the cases of Greece and Portugal', *Comparative European Politics*, 13(1): 29–55.

Veliziotis, M., Matsaganis, M. and Karakitsios, A. (2015) 'Involuntary part-time employment: perspectives from two European labour markets', ImPRovE Working Paper, 15/02, University of Antwerp.

Verschraegen, G., Vanhercke, B. and Verpoorten, R. (2011) 'The European Social Fund and domestic activation policies: Europeanization mechanisms', *Journal of European Social Policy*, 21(1): 55–72.

Viebrock, E. and Clasen, J. (2009) 'Flexicurity and welfare reform: a review', *Socioeconomic Review*, 7(2): 305–31.

Visser, J. (2015) ICTWSS Data base. Version 5.0. Amsterdam: Amsterdam Institute for Advanced Labour Studies AIAS, www.uva-aias.net/nl/data/ictwss

Zartaloudis, S. (2014) *The impact of European Employment Strategy in Greece and Portugal: Europeanization in a world of neglect*, Basingstoke: Palgrave Macmillan.

Zeitlin, J., Pochet, P. and Magnussen, L. (eds) (2005) *The Open Method of Co-ordination in action: the European employment and social inclusion strategies*, Brussels: Peter Lang.

Appendix

See Table 3.1.

Table 3.1: Changes in labour market policies in Greece from 2010 onwards

	Unemployment Benefits – Insurance	Unemployment Benefits – Assistance	Active labour market policies	Employment protection legislation Regular contracts
Eligibility	Expansion: Extension to self-employed workers subject to income testing (2013)	Retrenchment: Income threshold (€5,000 p.a. plus €587 per dependent child) not adjusted or indexed until 2012 a income threshold (for couple + 1 child) fell from 35 to 26% of the median income in 2010	Supported employment/training Expansion: Youth Guarantee plan: Apprenticeship schemes, youth entrepreneurship programmes and direct job creation in the public sector (2013)	Retrenchment: Threshold of collective dismissals was raised from 4 to 6 for firms with 20–150 employees (2010)
Level/replacement rate		Expansion: Extension of income threshold from €5,000 to €12,000 p.a. (2012) and then back to €10,000 (2014)	Expansion: Public works programme launched (€216mn for 50,000 temporary jobs) targeted at the long-term unemployed in jobless households, subject to income test; up to 5 months of community work subsidized at €490 per month for workers aged >25 years and at €427 per month for workers aged <25 years (2013)	Retrenchment: Length of required notice prior to dismissal was shortened for white-collars (2010)
	Retrenchment: Reduction of benefit from €454 to €360 per month due to cuts in the minimum wage (on the basis of which the benefit is calculated) (2012)	Expansion: Age condition extended from 45–65 years to 20–66 years (2014).		Retrenchment: Severance pay was reduced for all workers (2010)

(continued)

Income support policies and labour market reforms under austerity in Greece

Unemployment Benefits – Insurance	Unemployment Benefits – Assistance	Active labour market policies	Employment protection legislation
	Retrenchment: Annual cash limit of €35m extra spending (€100m total spending) imposed restricting the number of beneficiaries (2014)		Retrenchment: Abolition of employers' obligation to pay part of the unemployment benefit in case of dismissals arising from mergers or acquisitions (2012)
	Level/replacement rate		**Temporary contracts**
	Retrenchment: Benefit level not adjusted or indexed between 2003 and 2011à Replacement rate relative to minimum wage declined from 38 to 27% (24% in 2012 following minimum wage cuts)		Retrenchment: Probationary period of contracts increased from 2 to 12 months (2010)
Duration			Retrenchment: Maximum duration of fixed-term contracts before becoming indefinite duration contracts was extended to 3 years (2011)
Retrenchment: Establishment of ceiling on total duration of separate spells of benefit receipt over a period of 4 years (previously none) (2012)			Retrenchment: Renewal of fixed-term contracts without restriction was allowed when certain circumstances prevail (2011)
			Retrenchment: Intermittent work made easier for employers; maximum duration of the period involved was extended from 6 to 9 months (2010)

(continued)

Table 3.1: Changes in labour market policies in Greece from 2010 onwards (continued)

Unemployment Benefits – Insurance	Unemployment Benefits – Assistance	Active labour market policies	Employment protection legislation
			Retrenchment: Duration of temporary work was extended indefinitely if two contracts are separated by a 23-day interval (2011)
			Retrenchment: Restrictions on the scope of temporary work agencies (TWAs) were lifted or eased. More specifically: • Permissible duration of subcontracting of workers by TWAs extended from 18 to 36 months. • Abolition of the requirement that TWAs provide services only for 'transitory, extraordinary or seasonal positions' • Reduction of the length of time before hiring via TWAs was allowed following redundancies for economic reasons from 6 to 3 months for individual dismissals and from 12 to 6 months for collective dismissals • Permission to use TWAs in large public work contracts granted • List of hazardous positions closed to workers supplied by TWAs was limited.

FOUR

The Italian labour market policy reforms and the economic crisis: coming towards the end of Italian exceptionalism?

Patrik Vesan and Emmanuele Pavolini

Introduction

The Italian labour market has been put under very strong pressure since the onset of the financial and economic crisis. In the years since 2007, the number of job-seekers has doubled and a series of long-standing critical issues, such as youth and long-term unemployment, have dramatically worsened. The Italian government initially responded to the Great Recession by maintaining previous institutional arrangements, trying to adapt them in order to cushion the social consequences of the recession. Nevertheless, after the 2011 sovereign debt crisis, the situation changed and a new wave of reforms started.

The present chapter describes these changes and assesses the direction that they have taken by comparing policies before and after the onset of the recent economic downturn. Although it is not possible to detect a single trajectory of change in Italian labour market policies, our argument is that we can observe an overall tendency towards a peculiar version of 'welfare readjustment' (Häusermann, 2012), a pattern of reform in which governments curtail industrial-type policy instruments, such as income or job protections for insiders, while adopting new social policies. In Italy, this 'readjustment process' in the domain of labour market policies has been realised through the adoption of some provisions that favour 'outsiders' and, at the same time, the drastic retrenchment of labour rights for workers on open-ended contracts. As a result, the boundaries between 'insiders' and 'outsiders' now appear more blurred than they were before the outbreak of the Great Recession.

The chapter is divided into four sections. The second section shows the main facets of the Italian labour market since the 1990s. The third section illustrates labour market reforms before the economic crisis. The fourth section focuses on the most recent changes since 2008. The last section offers an interpretation of labour market reforms in Italy since the crisis.

Main aspects of the Italian labour market before and since the onset of the crisis

In order to provide an overview of the Italian labour market's functioning over time, Tables 4.1 to 4.6 offer some basic information on its specificities and similarities compared with the European Union 15 countries (EU15) on average. The tables take into consideration five moments in time (1995, 2000, 2007, 2014 and 2015) in order to compare the situation before and after the onset of the crisis. The year 2015 was added because in that year, the situation slowly started to improve, at least in terms of unemployment rates compared with the previous years. Moreover, apart from focusing on the greater part of the labour market (taking into consideration what has happened to those aged between 15 and 64), it is important to look at two specific profiles in a life-cycle perspective: young people (aged between 15 and 24) and the older adult population (aged between 55 and 64).

Activity rates in Italy during the whole period considered here (1995–2015) were lower than in the EU15 on average (see Table 4.1). Although the Italian rates for 15–64 year olds have been constantly around 10 percentage points lower than in the rest of Western Europe, they have increased over time (thanks mainly to the larger participation of women in the labour market). The situation among young people, however, has profoundly worsened: the gap between the EU15 and

Table 4.1: Activity rates over time, Italy and the EU15

	15 to 24 years of age		15 to 64 years of age*		50 to 64 years of age	
	EU15	Italy	EU15	Italy	EU15	Italy
1995	47.2	38.7	67.2 (56.8)	57.6 (42.4)	40.1	29.2
2000	47.5	38.1	69.0 (59.9)	59.9 (46.2)	40.7	29.0
2007	48.0	30.8	71.9 (64.6)	62.4 (50.6)	49.1	34.5
2014	44.3	27.1	73.4 (67.8)	63.9 (54.4)	58.2	48.9
2015	43.9	26.2	73.5 (68.0)	64.0 (54.1)	59.6	51.1

Note: * Female activity rates in parentheses.
Source: Eurostat (2016) online labour market database

Italy grew larger (8.5% in 1995 and 17.7% in 2015) and there was a dramatic drop in the activity rate (from 38.7% in 1995 to 26.2% in 2015). In relation to this phenomenon, it should be added that the trend started well before the current economic crisis: already in 2007, the Italian rate had fallen and the gap with the EU15 was around 17 percentage points. Moreover, the Italian female activity rate remained lower than the EU15 average, although it increased over time.

Temporary employment in Italy was very limited in the 1990s and below the Western European average (see Table 4.2). However, it reached the EU15 level by 2007. A similar pattern can be detected for older adult workers, but the situation is totally different among young workers: in 1995, around 19% of Italians aged between 15 and 24 had temporary contracts, compared with around 32% among young Western Europeans on average. In 2015, the situation had reversed: more than half of young Italians (57.1%) had temporary contracts, whereas the percentage among Western Europeans was 43.6% on average. Also in this case, the situation had already changed before the onset of the crisis: in 2007, the incidence of temporary employees in the total number of employees was practically the same in Italy and Western Europe.

Temporary employment in Italy has another characteristic in a comparative perspective: it is involuntary (see Table 4.3). In 2015, almost three quarters of temporary workers in Italy declared that they had such a contract because they could not find a permanent job (this percentage was around 61% in the EU15). Temporary work was a problem before the crisis but Italy had not deviated from the EU15 average so much as in 2015.

The unemployment rate for those 15–64 years of age in Italy has traditionally been only slightly above the EU15 average: during the first part of the last decade, it even dropped below the average, and in

Table 4.2: Temporary employees as a percentage of the total number of employees over time, Italy and EU15

	15 to 24 years		15 to 64 years		55 to 64 years	
	EU15	Italy	EU15	Italy	EU15	Italy
1995	32.3	18.7	11.5	7.2	5.0	3.8
2000	39.4	26.2	13.6	10.1	6.2	6.0
2007	42.7	42.2	14.9	13.2	6.4	6.2
2014	43.4	56.0	13.8	13.6	5.7	5.4
2015	43.6	57.1	14.0	14.1	5.8	5.7

Source: Eurostat (2016) online labour market database

Table 4.3: Main reason for temporary employment, Italy and EU15

	Could not find permanent job		Did not want a permanent job		In education or training		Probationary period		Total	
	EU15	Italy	EU15	Italy	EU15	Italy	EU15	Italy	EU15	Italy
1995	–	61.9	–	4.9	–	28.7	–	4.4	–	100.0
1999*	52.1	50.2	13.5	5.2	27.7	38.7	6.6	4.9	100.0	100.0
2007	57.8	65.0	13.1	6.9	20.8	20.8	8.5	7.4	100.0	100.0
2014	60.3	72.7	11.0	2.3	19.3	15.8	9.0	9.2	100.0	100.0
2015	61.2	73.5	11.2	2.2	18.8	14.8	8.8	9.5	100.0	100.0

Note: *Data for year 2000 missing for the EU15 and therefore 1999 was used.
Source: Eurostat (2016) online labour market database

2015, it was around two percentage points higher (see Table 4.4). Older workers in Italy have been less exposed to the risk of unemployment and generally less than in Western Europe as a whole (even in 2015). By contrast, youth unemployment has hit Italy harder than the EU15, and the recent economic crisis helped to widen the gap.

Finally, if we shift our attention from rates to absolute numbers (see Table 4.5), we can grasp the drama of what has been happening in Italy since 2007: the number of unemployed more than doubled from 1.5 to 3 million in just a few years (+104.8% between 2007 and 2015), while in Western Europe, the same figure increased by 'only' around 45%. At the same time, there was a reduction in employment of 2.0% of the employed (compared with a 0.3% rise in the EU15).

In sum, when the crisis started, the Italian labour market already presented many problematic facets, in particular, a lower female activity rate (not shown in the tables) and youth inclusion in the labour market. As will be shown in the third section, policies aimed at reforming the labour market 'at the margin' before 2008 had already created a very

Table 4.4: Unemployment rates, Italy and EU15

	15 to 24 years		15 to 64 years		55 to 64 years	
	EU15	Italy	EU15	Italy	EU15	Italy
1995	21.2	33.5	10.7	11.7	7.8	4.3
2000	16.1	31.5	8.4	10.9	6.9	4.6
2007	14.9	20.3	7.0	6.1	5.4	2.5
2014	21.9	42.7	10.7	12.9	7.5	5.5
2015	20.3	40.3	9.9	12.1	7.2	5.5

Source: Eurostat (2016) online labour market database

Table 4.5: Number of unemployed and employed and their relative variation over time, Italy and EU15

	2007	2015	Variation 2007–15
Unemployed			
EU15	13,071	19,013	+45.5%
Italy	1,481	3,033	+104.8%
Employed			
EU15	174,558	175,049	+0.3%
Italy	22,846	22,395	–2.0%

Source: Eurostat (2016) online labour market database

dualised situation (on the basis of age). The economic crisis has 'simply' amplified these facets, doubling the number of unemployed, fostering a mostly 'involuntary' use of temporary contracts and bringing the youth unemployment rate to unprecedented levels.

Changes in the traditional model: from the mid-1990s until the crisis

In the international literature, Italian labour market policy has often been considered a case of a 'sub-protective unemployment welfare regime' (Gallie and Paugam, 2000), characterised by low coverage, limited benefit generosity and a lack of investment in active labour market policies (ALMPs). This was certainly true until the mid-1990s, when Italy, along with other Mediterranean countries, consolidated a specific 'guaranteed labour market policy' model (Ferrera and Gualmini, 2004) strictly committed to the protection of the full-time and open-ended employment of male breadwinners who worked in medium and big firms. This model rested on three main pillars.

The first pillar was represented by the highly fragmented unemployment compensation system. Unlike other European countries, in Italy, this system was based on a single-tier unemployment insurance (*indennità ordinaria di disoccupazione*), and on several other benefits for specific categories of workers (in industry, agriculture or construction). The most important scheme was the *Cassa integrazione Guadagni* (CIG), which provided short-time work benefits for temporary layoffs. This scheme was supplemented by the so-called 'mobility allowance' (*indennità di mobilità*), a relatively generous unemployment benefit reserved for employees of medium-sized and large firms, but only in case of collective dismissal and usually after having exhausted special CIG schemes for industrial restructuring.

Overall, these industrial-type benefits were frequently used as a functional substitute for unemployment insurance benefits because the latter offered only very weak protection to a limited number of unemployed (Sacchi et al, 2011). However, only some categories of employees – that is, the 'insiders' belonging to the most central and unionised economic sectors – could get access to the relatively generous economic support offered by the CIG scheme and the mobility allowance. By contrast, workers in micro- and small companies or with a fixed-term contract had very limited or no protection at all against unemployment, in terms of unemployment assistance schemes or national social assistance schemes (Sacchi and Vesan, 2015).

The second pillar of the Italian model of 'guaranteed labour market policies' was represented by the strict regulation of labour relationships. Until the mid-1990s, Italy, along with the other Southern European countries, showed a high level of employment protection legislation (EPL), according to Organisation for Economic Co-operation and Development (OECD) estimates. This was true especially for workers employed in firms with more than 15 employees, who were protected by Article 18 of the Workers' Statute adopted in 1970. This article established that employers were obliged to reinstate fired workers to their former position and pay the entire amount of wages and social contributions lost since the day of dismissal if the court declared that the dismissal had been illegitimate.[1] In addition, stringent rules were also laid down to limit the use of fixed-term contracts.

Finally, the third pillar of the Italian model of 'guaranteed labour market policies' was represented by the public monopoly of job-placement services (and therefore the prohibition of private employment agencies) and by the rigid procedure that obliged employers to hire the unemployed registered on a compulsory list managed by local public employment centres. By contrast, ALMPs had a residual role and the spending on them was limited compared with that of other European countries (Bonoli, 2013).

Since the mid-1990s and until the beginning of the recent economic crisis in 2008, this labour market policy model had undergone several important changes, which followed two main trajectories (Vesan, 2016a). As in most European countries, the first trend of reforms was the sharp liberalisation of employment regulations. These reforms were typically introduced 'at the margin' because they aimed at easing the rules on temporary labour without changing the regulation on 'core workers', namely, those employed on an open-ended contract (Berton et al, 2012). From 1995 to 2012, the norms on the dismissal of core workers basically remained the same, while EPL for temporary workers drastically decreased (from 4.75 in the mid-1990s to 2 in 2003),[2] as a consequence of the liberalisation of temporary agency work and other fixed-term contracts promoted by both centre-left and centre-right governments.[3]

A second trajectory of change concerned the gradual shift, at least in normative terms, towards a more proactive orientation in relation to labour policies, with a stronger focus on active measures and the conditionality of unemployment benefits (Sacchi and Vesan, 2015). On the one hand, greater investments were made in ALMPs, which began to increase in the mid-1990s and exceeded the total expenditure on passive policies at the beginning of the 2000s.[4] However, this was not a stable trend because the gap between higher passive measures and lower ALMPs has been widening once again since the mid-2000s. On the other hand, the tightening of the unemployment benefit conditionality criteria was not implemented systematically (Jessoula and Vesan, 2011).

The first significant change was related to the organisation of public and private employment centres. In line with the decentralisation processes that affected several social policy domains in the 1990s (Kazepov, 2010), competences with regard to ALMPs and public employment services were devolved to the regions and the provinces. Moreover, the public monopoly of placement services was abolished in 1997 and the provision of job centres was gradually opened up to private agencies. This has led to the emergence of a fragmented model of governance in which public–private networks of employment services are regulated differently at regional and provincial levels.

Moreover, unlike employment regulation and ALMPs, reforms in unemployment benefits were only incremental. The generosity of unemployment insurance benefits rose from 25% for three months in 1994 to 60% for eight to 12 months in 2008 (depending on the age of recipients and geographical area). Nevertheless, their coverage continued to be limited due to the strict eligibility conditions, while no variations were made in the setting of the CIG scheme and the mobility allowance, which were used intensively in order to tackle the economic crisis at the beginning of the 1990s.

Towards a new institutional landscape: the 'long jump' of labour market policy reforms during the economic crisis

The policy responses adopted since the beginning of the recent economic crisis have profoundly altered the 'institutional landscape' of the Italian labour market. Since 2012, Italy has left the path of reforms 'at the margin', which characterised the first wave of liberalisation, for a more comprehensive strategy based on the promotion of external forms of flexibilisation, also with reference to open-ended workers. This approach has been complemented by other far-reaching policy changes, especially in the domain of unemployment benefits. In what follows, we will distinguish three phases – run-up, take-off and final push – which marked this new wave of reforms of Italian labour market policy.

Run-up: 2008–11

When the new centre-right government led by Berlusconi came to power in May 2008, Italy entered the first trimester of a long recession that lasted until the end of 2014. In order to cushion the social impact of the economic crisis, the first strategy was a massive recourse to 'emergency social shock absorbers' (*ammortizzatori sociali in deroga*) by temporarily extending the duration and coverage of CIG schemes and mobility allowances (Sacchi, 2015).[5] These measures were originally thought of as ad hoc provisions, which reflected the early interpretation of the economic crisis (and of its suitable response) in terms of 'demand shock' (Clasen et al, 2012) and were financed by a specific budget periodically allocated by the government. In other words, these emergency short-term work schemes were used as economic stabilisers aimed at mitigating the social impacts of the economic crisis and temporarily sustaining consumer demand. Therefore, no 'disruptive innovation' was adopted in this first phase. Nevertheless, the recourse to these emergency tools indirectly contributed to open up a window of opportunity for a more transformative intervention in the Italian unemployment compensation system.

A further 'run-up movement' towards a far-reaching reform of Italian labour market policy can also be observed with reference to employment regulation. After the failed attempt at reforming Article 18 of the Workers' Statute at the beginning of the 2000s, a new law adopted in 2011 opened up the possibility of derogating from the discipline of individual employment relationships (also in the domain of dismissal regulation) through collective bargaining agreements at the territorial or industrial level (so-called 'proximity agreements'). Nevertheless, this provision had a marginal impact as such derogations could only be established on a voluntary basis, while the diffusion of this kind of agreement remained rather limited.

Take-off: 2012–14

The real 'take-off' of the reform phase came in 2012 with the adoption of a sweeping reform (Law 92/2012) passed by the Monti government, which came to power at the end of 2011 after the resignation of Berlusconi and right in the middle of the sovereign debt crisis. The most important aspect of Law 92/2012 was the revision of illegitimate dismissal (Article 18 of the Workers' Statute). In order to reduce the length and uncertainty of litigation, a compulsory conciliation procedure was established, while monetary compensation was introduced as the general rule for economic dismissals deemed to be unfair. Nevertheless, thanks to a compromise promoted by the leading Italian centre-left party (the *Partito democratico* [PD]), Law 92/2012 left judges with some room to manoeuvre in determining both the fairness of the dismissal and its consequences (Sestito and Viviano, 2016).

Law 92/2012 also introduced important changes in the domain of unemployment compensation by adopting a new 'social insurance for employment' (*Assegno sociale per l'impiego* [ASPI]). The ASPI was more generous compared with the previous unemployment insurance benefit and was extended to apprentices and cooperative workers. Nevertheless, the ASPI maintained the same strict eligibility criteria fixed by the old benefit – in particular, two years of social security seniority – which seriously limited access to unemployment benefits for workers recently entering the labour market (Berton et al, 2012).[6] The main goals of this reform were to make the ASPI the most important Italian unemployment benefit scheme. As a matter of fact, a further innovation was the abolition of the mobility allowance (starting from 2017) and the attempt to reform the CIG schemes, which, however, remain largely incomplete.

Final push: from autumn 2014 onwards

After the 2013 elections, the Italian political system was stuck in a long stalemate. Such a stalemate was only partially overcome by the formation of a new government led by Enrico Letta, which lasted less than a year. In February 2014, Matteo Renzi, the newly elected leader of the PD, replaced Letta as prime minister and a new wave of far-reaching reforms came onto the government's agenda.

As far as labour market policy reforms were concerned, at the end of 2014, the Italian Parliament passed Law 183/2014, the so-called 'Jobs Act', which delegated the Renzi cabinet to adopt measures in several domains, such as employment regulation, unemployment benefits and ALMPs.

A first important change introduced by the Jobs Act concerned the new open-ended contract (*contratto a tutele crescenti*), which limited the reinstatement of open-ended workers for discriminatory dismissal and some forms of disciplinary dismissal. By contrast, economic dismissals ruled unfair by a judge can only be subject to monetary compensation, which is now strictly set by law.[7]

In addition to this new open-ended employment contract, the Renzi government introduced a further liberalisation of fixed-term contracts and eased the possibility to downgrade workers to a less-qualified level in case of organisational need. At the same time, the government stopped recourse to the so-called '*collaborazioni coordinate e continuative a progetto*' (a type of 'economic-dependent employment' relationship), with the declared aim of limiting precarious employment. Nevertheless, this provision runs the risk of having unexpected negative consequences, such as fostering the diffusion of irregular work or of job vouchers, which have skyrocketed in Italy in recent years.

Another important novelty pertains to the reform of the unemployment benefits system. With the adoption of the Jobs Act, the ASPI and the mini-ASPI were moulded into a single insurance benefit, the NASPI (Nuova Assicurazione Sociale per l'Impiego – the New Social Insurance for Employment), which has significantly lowered the eligibility threshold of unemployment insurance (in particular, the seniority insurance rule). In order to get the NASPI, the job-seeker must have paid three months of contributions in the past four years and worked for at least 30 days in the past year before the beginning of the event of unemployment. The amount of the NASPI has been set at 75% of the previous salary up to €1,195 (for 2015), and 25% for the part exceeding that amount up to a maximum ceiling (equal to €1,300), while its duration depends on contributory seniority (half the number of weekly contributions paid by the worker up to a maximum of two years).

A further important change is represented by the introduction of a social assistance allowance for the unemployed (*assegno sociale per la disoccupazione* [ASDI]), but only for poor workers (with dependent children or more than 55 years of age) who have exhausted the NASPI. This scheme is means-tested and gives access to a sum equal to two thirds of the last NASPI benefit for a duration of six months. Due to budgetary restrictions, this new scheme was initially introduced on an experimental basis, but in summer 2015, the government transformed this experimental measure into a structural one.

In 2016, this innovation was accompanied by the extension of the experiment of 'support for active inclusion' (SIA), a means-tested benefit reserved for poor people, to the whole national territory. The SIA provides social services and cash benefits of up to €400 per month for larger families that have at least one minor or disabled child or a pregnant woman.[8]

The Jobs Act also introduced an important reform of short-time working schemes (CIG) by reducing the duration of these benefits, revisiting the rules on their financing and extending their coverage. This reform represents another step towards abandoning Italian exceptionalism in labour market policies, within the framework of which, as we have seen, short-time working schemes have often been used as a functional substitute for a weak unemployment insurance system. Overall, it is fair to say that the Jobs Act laid the ground for the creation of a new multi-tiered unemployment compensation system in Italy, which now appears more similar to the system adopted by France, the UK, Spain and Portugal.

Finally, it is also possible to observe some important novelties in the domain of ALMPs. In September 2015, the government adopted a reform of the governance of the public employment system through the creation of a National Agency of Active Labour Market Policies (ANPAL). At the present, ANPAL will have two important tasks. On the one hand, it will set national guidelines for the activation of the unemployed and coordinate the new Italian network for employment services (both private and public).[9] On the other hand, ANPAL will define the main characteristics of a new policy instrument, the so-called 'outplacement allowance' (*assegno individuale di ricollocamento*), a voucher that unemployed people can use to buy outplacement services, also on the private market.

Further novelties are related to the adoption of new rights in the domains of work–family reconciliation policies in order to tackle the low Italian female employment rate (Mallone, 2016) and in the domain of school-to-work transition policies, with the aim of reducing school drop-outs and youth unemployment (Vesan, 2016b). In particular, within the framework of a comprehensive reform of the Italian education system (called 'The Good School' – '*La Buona Scuola*'), the Renzi government decided to strengthen the link between school and work, in particular, by providing additional resources for school-to-work alternation initiatives that have become compulsory in secondary schools.

In conclusion, if we consider the reforms adopted since the onset of the Great Recession, a clear strategy of employment liberalisation has been carried out by different Italian governments. This strategy has followed a threefold approach:

- Its first and main component is the abolition of the reinstatement of workers in case of illegitimate economic dismissal, in favour of simple monetary compensation.
- The second component of the strategy concerns the liberalisation of temporary contracts, accompanied by the reregulation of other forms of atypical contracts (eg for economically independent workers) in order to limit their diffusion and misuse.
- The third component concerns the deregulation of working conditions at both individual and firm levels and the promotion of collective bargaining decentralisation.

As a result, the overall strategy pursued by the Jobs Act and the previous reform since 2011 have led to the transition from a regime of *job protection* to (some sort of) *flexicurity* regime, where the possibility of a more stable employment (with related rights) has been exchanged for the possibility of easier dismissals and workforce reorganisation according to business needs. Such a liberalisation has been accompanied by a thoughtful reform of unemployment benefits that aimed at extending protection to some previously uncovered categories of workers and reversing the typical industrial logic of the former compensation system. As we will argue in the fifth section, this has been the only reform, together with some changes related to child benefits, parental leave and school-to-work transitions, which has promoted the partial post-industrial turn of Italian labour market policies. However, this reorientation process is far from being accomplished.

Interpreting the changing nature of Italian labour market policies

As illustrated in the previous sections, Italian labour market policy has traditionally shown important peculiarities compared with other continental Bismarckian welfare states: low generosity (apart from for 'insiders') and coverage of workers; the absence of a social assistance scheme for the unemployed and of a minimum income scheme; and the very strong (even for Bismarckian countries) divide between 'insiders' and 'outsiders' in terms of rights and employment protections. Reform developments until 2011 did not substantially challenge this approach. However, since the beginning of the sovereign debt crisis, there have been important changes going in different directions.

In order to study the trajectories of these reforms, we will adopt the analytical framework proposed by Häusermann (2012). Häusermann distinguishes between 'industrial social policies' and 'post-industrial social policies' (in this latter case, she also distinguishes between 'activation/social investment policies' and 'needs-based social protection policies'). When applied to labour market policies, industrial policies are based on passive income support for unemployed 'insiders' (people eligible for unemployment insurance benefits) and EPL. Post-industrial activation/social investment policies are based on ALMPs and investment in training and human capital formation, whereas 'needs-based' social protection focuses on the provision of social security to groups of the population/labour force that, in the context of industrial logic policies, would not be entitled to any protection, for example, those with atypical career paths or the long-term unemployed. As shown in Table 4.6, reforms introduced in Italy since the beginning of the recent economic crisis have followed different directions, according to the specific policy tools.

The overall trajectory of the Italian labour market policy changes can be characterised as a 'welfare readjustment' process, where it is possible to observe a predominant trajectory of retrenchment with reference to industrial-type policy tools, accompanied by some emerging elements of post-industrial recalibration.

In particular, a very strong reduction in EPL has taken place. The reforms in 2012 and 2014 focused for the first time on insiders, substantially reducing their employment protections: individual and collective dismissals in the case of workers with open-ended contracts have become easier for enterprises, while recent governments' intention has been to regulate temporary contracts more. The trajectory of reform in EPL therefore seems to be heading towards a 'liberal' model: a relatively low level of protection of open-ended contracts, potentially matched by a more limited recourse to temporary contracts by enterprises (given the fact that it should narrow down the difference between open-ended and fixed-term contracts in terms of employee protections).

Other evidence of this reform trajectory can be found with reference to passive benefits. The first policy response to the Great Recession was characterised by the expansion of some old policy instruments, in particular, short-term working schemes, beyond their traditional scope. Nevertheless, the sovereign debt crisis and the persistent recession pushed Italian governments to reform the unemployment benefit system. As we have seen in previous sections, the mobility allowance – the unemployment scheme reserved to some categories of

Table 4.6: Industrial and post-industrial labour market policy instruments since the recent economic crisis, Italy

Type of policy	Instrument	Direction of change in coverage/protection/generosity	Content of changes
Industrial social policies (income and job protection for insiders)	EPL	Retrenchment	Drastic reduction in employment protections for workers with open-ended contracts (insiders). The protection in case of illegitimate dismissals shifted from compulsory reinstatement to the previous job position (+ the payment of lost wage and social contributions) to the provision of an economic compensation. No severance payment benefits have been foreseen.
	Passive benefits I	Expansionary	Extensive use of temporary emergency unemployment benefits as first policy response to the economic crisis
	Passive benefits II (income replacement for insiders post-2015)	Retrenchment	Abolition of the mobility allowance. Several changes in CIG aimed to rationalise the use of these schemes: extension of eligibility criteria to cover previously unprotected categories of workers; equalisation of social contributions paid by employers and introduction of a 'bonus-malus' principle (contributions rise on the basis of the actual use of the benefits); stricter rules for the duration of CIG schemes; prohibition to use CIG schemes in case of plant closure.
Post-industrial social policies	Needs-based income support for the (long-term) unemployed and 'outsiders'	Expansionary	Insurance-based unemployment benefits more generous and including more outsiders (ASPI, then NASPI): a) In 2011, the replacement rate was equal to 60% of gross wage. After the introduction of the NASPI, it shifted to 75% of the average wage in the last four years up to an annual ceiling (in 2015, the ceiling was equal to €1,195) + 25% of the difference between the average wage and the ceiling. However, the benefit cannot exceed the amount of €1,300 per month. b) The duration of the unemployment insurance shifted from 180 days to a maximum of two years. More in detail, the duration of the NASPI is equal to half the number of weeks of contributions paid in the four years before the termination of employment. However, the weeks that already gave rise to the payment of the benefit are excluded from the computation of its duration. The eligibility rules have also been reviewed: – In 2011: two years' insurance seniority and 52 full weekly contributory requirements in the last two years. – In 2015: 13 weeks of contributions in the last four years preceding the termination of employment and 30 working days in the last 12 months. Introduction of new unemployment protection schemes: – A social assistance allowance for the unemployed (Asdi). – Unemployment benefit for dependent self-employed (Dis-coll). – Extension at the national level of SIA.
	Social investment/ALMPs	Retrenchment (up to 2015) Limited expansion (since 2015)	– Expenditure cuts and shift of resources from ALMPs to passive benefits. – Limited investments in work-family reconciliation policies and in school-to-work alternation initiatives. – Creation of the National Agency for Active Labour Market Policy. – Introduction of a job-assistance voucher on an experimental basis. – Tightening of conditionality rules.

workers in case of collective dismissal – was abolished, while the Italian government adopted a comprehensive reform of short-time working schemes (the Italian system of CIG) in order to limit their use and save money to finance the new unemployment benefits schemes introduced in 2015. Such new schemes – in particular, unemployment insurance (NASPI), unemployment assistance (ASDI) and, later, support for active inclusion (SIA) – have extended the level of protections guaranteed to Italian job-seekers and poor people. Therefore, from this perspective, we can observe a shift in Italian labour market policy from a system based essentially on industrial-type policy instruments to a system that has introduced some post-industrial recalibration elements (Häusermann, 2012).

Nevertheless, the overall retrenchment of old industrial policy tools, combined with the expansion of needs-based social protection policies, has not led to the complete transformation of Italian labour market policy into a system based on a post-industrial logic. As a matter of fact, investments in both activation and social investment policies have been reduced during the economic crisis (Kazepov and Ranci, forthcoming).

Expenditure on ALMPs decreased during the first phase of the economic crisis. Investments declined from €6.2 billion (35% of total expenditure on labour market policies) in 2008 to €4.9 billion (19% of total expenditure on labour market policies) in 2011 (Ministry of Labour, 2012). By contrast, recent increases in spending on activation have relied mainly on the implementation of European-funded programmes, such as the Youth Guarantee and the regional initiatives adopted within the framework of the European Social Fund. However, ALMP investment is still largely insufficient to cover the wide Italian gap with other European countries, while the main institutional novelties introduced by the Jobs Act (such as ANPAL and the outplacement allowance) still remain on paper.

As far as social investment-oriented policies are concerned, Italy lags behind in childcare (and also long-term care) service provision compared with many other Western European countries (Albertini and Pavolini, 2015; Leon, 2015), while only some partial changes have been introduced to support work–family life reconciliation. Moreover, the cuts to local government, the primary providers of social care services, due to austerity measures are having an impact on their capacity not only to expand, but even to maintain reconciliation services (Albertini and Pavolini, 2015; Leon, 2015). Eurostat EU-SILC data show that in 2005, 25% of children under three years of age attended formal childcare (in the EU15, this was 29%), while in

2013, the Italian percentage went down to 20% (whereas in the EU15, it went up to 33%).

In conclusion, recent reforms have led to the retrenchment of open-ended workers' rights and some 'old' industrial-type instruments, as well as to some improvements in needs-based social income support policies. Nevertheless, the post-industrial turn of Italian labour market policies is still in the future, while the process of welfare readjustment remains fragile.

A fragile and still incomplete path towards a new labour market policy regime

Since the outbreak of the recent economic crisis, Italian labour market policies have entered a period of intense reform. This most recent wave of reforms represents a further and more clear-cut departure from the trajectory of policy change that began in the mid-1990s. Before 2008, the intervention strategy focused on the liberalisation of employment relationships 'at the margin', accompanied by an incremental increase in the comparatively low replacement rate of unemployment benefits. After a 'honeymoon period' of employment growth (Boeri and Garibaldi, 2007), the reforms adopted before the Great Recession led to a strong increase in labour market dualisation. As we have shown, the share of fixed-term workers skyrocketed from 7.2% in 1995 to 13.3% in 2007 (Eurostat Labour Force Statistics), while 1.6 million employees were left without income support in case of dismissal because of the strict unemployment benefit eligibility criteria (Sacchi and Vesan, 2015). Moreover, such an increase in dualisation has also had negative consequences on productivity growth (Sacchi and Vesan, 2015).

The recent economic crisis exacerbated some of the main weaknesses that have always characterised the Italian labour market. At the same time, the economic crisis provided a window of opportunity to adopt some reforms that were previously rejected due to the strong veto powers of different coalitions of actors. This new opportunity was strongly influenced by supranational and international actors. The worsening of the financial situation pushed Italian governments to ask for 'indirect' help, mainly in terms of European Central Bank purchases in the secondary bond markets (Sacchi, 2015). Such help was made conditional on the adoption of fiscal austerity measures and 'structural reforms', also in the domain of labour market policies. In other words, the 2011 financial storm and the need to quickly restore credibility at the international level, on the one hand, reinforced the agenda-setting powers of the Monti and Renzi governments and, on the other hand, narrowed the choice of policy alternatives.

The new wave of reforms that have been adopted since 2012 were aimed at profoundly revising the Italian labour market policy model. Three main changes mark the departure from the previous policy path but, at the same time, show the fragility of the emerging new model. First, the Monti government introduced, and the Renzi governments completed, a historical reform of the dismissal rules of open-ended workers. This reform can be described as an 'institutional retrenchment' strategy (Green-Pedersen, 2004) because it aimed at curtailing the social rights of employees. The liberalisation of open-ended employment relationships was legitimised by the Renzi government as a means to increase the share of permanent contracts by promoting a transition from a highly segmented labour market to a labour market more flexible for all. In order to promote this change, in 2015, the government invested substantial resources in employment incentives for hiring people with the new open-ended contracts (*contratto a tutele crescenti*). The impact of these new open-ended contracts, accompanied by strong employment incentives, has been the object of several controversies at the academic and political level. Nevertheless, recent studies show some evidence of some positive outcomes, at least with reference to 2015, when the share of open-ended workers increased by 2.4% (INPS, 2016). Unfortunately, the available data for 2016 seem not to confirm such a positive trend; this is probably because the incentives attached to the new open-ended contracts have been reduced (from a maximum of about €24,000 in three years to €6,500 in two years). These strong incentives were originally aimed at promoting the diffusion of the new open-ended contracts in a context of limited economic growth. Nevertheless, this has been particularly expensive and is unsustainable in the long run. Also for this reason, the Renzi government is currently studying the proposal to cut non-wage labour costs in a permanent way. The idea is to make open-ended contracts more convenient for employers in order to promote an improvement in working conditions and productivity. In fact, the impact of this measure will depend on several factors, such as whether relief will be based on social contributions or taxes, the conditions attached to the reduction of non-wage labour costs, and the capacity of this kind of intervention to really affect employers' choices.[10]

Second, two important reforms of unemployment benefits were carried out in 2012 and 2015. The main goal was to extend the coverage of unemployment insurance – which can now be considered almost universal – and increase its generosity. At the same time, these reforms tried to increase equality in the treatment of different categories of workers and to bring back short-time working schemes (CIG) to their original function as a complementary instrument embedded in a more robust unemployment insurance system. Overall, the new trajectory of these policy changes points to the 'normalisation' of the Italian model, that is, to reducing the distance from other European countries such as France or Germany. However, this catching-up process is fragile in a number of ways.

On the one hand, the 'readjustment path' has to be completed. The new unemployment assistance scheme (ASDI) is an important measure, but its eligibility conditions are so strict that its 'selective universalism' rationale can be called into question. A similar consideration can be advanced with reference to the extension of the SIA scheme at the national level. While the introduction of this measure can be welcomed as a further step in creating a full multi-tiered compensation system in Italy, the limited amount of resources invested by the government, its strict eligibility conditions and therefore its reduced potential coverage strongly limit the innovative scope of the provision.

A final element of the fragility of the recent reforms concerns ALMPs. This domain remains largely underdeveloped, in particular, with reference to the job-assistance service. The reform adopted in 2015 introduced some important novelties by revising the governance of the employment services network. Nevertheless, the potential of any reform in this sub-area strictly depends on its implementation. The legacy of fragmented and often inefficient local bureaucracies (at least in some parts of the country), the lack of resources, and the limited coordination capabilities of the central administration represent important hindrances to a process of change that requires strong determination and guidance.

At the same time, Italy has not yet seriously engaged in the recalibration of its welfare state towards a social investment approach. As highlighted by Kazepov and Ranci (forthcoming), since 2000, Italy has had the lowest share of family/children, ALMP and tertiary education expenditure as a percentage of gross domestic product (GDP) (with the sole exception of Poland) in Europe. This is due to several reasons. The unbalanced structure of social expenditure (which privileges public spending on old-age pensions) and the overall low per capita social expenditure, combined with the huge Italian debt and the fiscal constraints imposed by the European Stability and Growth Pact, have severely hampered the development of social investment policies. At the same time, the absence of structural preconditions[11] could make the implementation of these policies in an 'immature' context such as Italy not only ineffective, but also counterproductive (Kazepov and Ranci, forthcoming).

In conclusion, in recent years, Italy has followed a trajectory of reform aimed at abandoning some aspects of its labour market policy exceptionalism. This ongoing process has involved retrenchment in the regulation of labour relations, but we can also observe improvements in the unemployment benefit system. Nevertheless, efforts at 'progressive recalibration' have remained fragile since only modest progress has been made in work–family reconciliation and school-to-work policies.

Notes

1. The main contested aspect of Article 18 was the uncertainty regarding both the contents and the timing of judges' decisions, which sometimes led to very high firing costs for employers.
2. OECD Labour Force Survey (LFS) – Strictness of EPL – temporary employment, version 1.
3. It is worth noting that in Italy, EPL for temporary workers was strongly restricted between 1990 and 2008 (Berton et al, 2012).
4. Overall, labour market expenditure remained relatively stable during these years, despite significant variations in the unemployment rate.
5. These anti-crisis measures were important because they helped to reduce the number of employees not covered by unemployment compensation from over 3 million to 1.6 million in the first years of the economic crisis (Berton et al, 2012).
6. The seniority insurance rule was repealed in order to get access to the so-called 'mini-ASPI'. However, this represented an unemployment insurance benefit with reduced requirements that could last for a maximum of six months.
7. Such compensation amounts to two months for each year of seniority, from a minimum of four months up to 24 months. In case of conciliation between the fired workers and the employer, this compensation is equal to one month for each year worked, with a ceiling of 18 months. The same amount of money is foreseen for workers at firms with fewer than 15 employees who have been illegitimately dismissed, but with a ceiling of six months.
8. Proposed legislation that is currently under the scrutiny of Parliament mandates the government to reform the Italian anti-poverty measures,

among other things, by introducing a national means-tested benefit called 'inclusion income', which will be provided only to unemployed persons aged 55 and over who meet the eligibility criteria already laid down for the SIA.

[9.] A process of constitutional reform is currently under way in Italy. If approved, it will recentralise ALMP, thereby reversing the devolution carried out at the beginning of the 2000s.

[10.] For a critical comment on this proposal, see Raitano (2016).

[11.] According to Kazepov and Ranci (forthcoming), the absence of three preconditions hampers not only the development of social investment policies in Italy, but also the possibility of these policies having positive impacts. These preconditions are: (1) a strong functional connection between the education system and labour market demand; (2) a high level of gender parity; and (3) a low risk of being trapped in low-quality jobs (especially for young people).

References

Albertini, M. and Pavolini, E. (2015) 'Care policies in Italy between a national frozen landscape and local dynamism', in U. Ascoli and E. Pavolini (eds) *The Italian welfare state in a European perspective*, Bristol: The Policy Press, pp 132–55.

Berton, F., Richiardi, M. and Sacchi, S. (2012) *The political economy of work security and flexibility*, Bristol: The Policy Press.

Boeri, T. and Garibaldi, P. (2007) 'Two tier reforms of employment protection: a honeymoon effect?', *The Economic Journal*, 521(117): 357–85.

Bonoli, G. (2013) *The origins of active social policy*, Oxford: Oxford University Press.

Clasen, J., Clegg, D. and Kvist, J. (2012) 'European labour market policies in (the) crisis', ETUI Working Paper, 12.

Eurostat (2016), Eurostat online database - Labour Force Survey series – detailed annual survey data, http://ec.europa.eu/eurostat/data/database

Ferrera, M. and Gualmini, E. (2004) *Rescued by Europe? Social and labour market reforms in Italy from Maastricht to Berlusconi*, Amsterdam: Amsterdam University Press.

Gallie, D. and Paugam, S. (2000) 'The experience of unemployment in Europe: the debate', in D. Gallie and S. Paugam (eds) *Welfare regimes and the experience of unemployment in Europe*, Oxford: Oxford University Press, pp 1–24.

Green-Pedersen, C. (2004) 'The dependent variable problem within the study of welfare state retrenchment: defining the problem and looking for solutions', *Journal of Comparative Policy Analysis: Research and Practice*, 6(1): 3–14.

Häusermann, S. (2012) 'The politics of old and new social policies. the politics of the "new" welfare state', in G. Bonoli and D. Natali (eds) *The politics of the new welfare state*, New York, NY: Oxford University Press, pp 111–32.

INPS (Italian National Institute of Social Security) (2016) *Annual report*, Rome: INPS.

Jessoula, M. and Vesan, P. (2011) 'Italy: limited adaptation of an atypical system', in J. Clasen and D. Clegg (eds) *Regulating the risk of unemployment. National adaptations to post-industrial labour markets in Europe*, Oxford: Oxford University Press, pp 142–63.

Kazepov, Y. (ed) (2010) *Rescaling social policies: Towards multilevel governance in Europe*, London: Ashgate Publishing.

Kazepov, Y. and Ranci, C. (forthcoming) 'Is every country fit for social investment? Italy as an adverse case', *Journal of European Social Policy*.

Leon, M. (ed) (2015) *Care regimes in transitional European societies*, Basingstoke: Palgrave.

Mallone, G. (2016) 'The Italian Jobs Act: new opportunity for parents?', *Percorsi di Secondo Welfare*, 21 February.

Ministry of Labour (2012) 'Spesa per le politiche occupazionali. Anno 2012', *Quaderni di studi e statistiche sul mercato del lavoro*, No. 6.

Raitano, M. (2016) 'Le molte ombre della proposta di decontribuzione strutturale', *Eticaeconomia Menabò*, April.

Sacchi, S. (2015) 'Conditionality by other means. EU involvement in Italy's structural reforms in the sovereign debt crisis', *Comparative European Politics*, advance online publication, 13 October 2014.

Sacchi, S. and Vesan, P. (2015) 'Employment policy: segmentation, deregulation and reforms in the Italian labour market', in U. Ascoli and E. Pavolini (eds) *The Italian welfare in a European perspective*, Bristol: The Policy Press, pp 71–99.

Sacchi, S., Pancaldi, F. and Arisi, C. (2011) 'The economic crisis as a trigger of convergence? Short-time work in Italy, Germany and Austria', *Social Policy and Administration*, 45(4): 465–87.

Sestito, P. and Viviano, E. (2016) 'Hiring incentives and/or firing cost reduction? Evaluating the impact of the 2015 policies on the Italian labour market', Bank of Italy Occasional Paper, 325, March.

Vesan, P. (2016a) 'Labour market policics and politics', in M. Gilbert, E. Jones and G. Pasquino (eds) *The Oxford handbook of Italian politics*, Oxford: Oxford University Press.

Vesan, P. (2016b) 'Per uno schema europeo di sostegno alle transizioni attive: prime riflessioni a partire dalle politiche per l'occupazione giovanile in Italia', *Politiche sociali/Social Policies*, 3(2): 269–86.

FIVE

French employment market policies: dualisation and destabilisation

Hélène Caune and Sotiria Theodoropoulou

Introduction

In this chapter, we ask whether the direction of labour market reforms in France has changed since 2010 by comparison with the previous two decades. In 2009, in the aftermath of the global financial crisis and the coordinated fiscal stimulus in Europe, France's general government budget deficit reached 7.2% of gross domestic product (GDP). This prompted the European Commission to propose placing France under the corrective arm of the excessive deficit procedure in order to bring this deficit below the 3% of GDP limit stipulated by the Stability and Growth Pact. A similar shift in fiscal policies, from stimulus to austerity, took place across pretty much the whole European Union (EU) during 2009–12.

France is a particularly interesting case from a comparative perspective. Characterised by a conservative-corporatist labour market regime, it stands in between member states with corporatist labour market regimes in Southern Europe (Italy, Greece), which have faced overt or covert pressures for reform in a certain direction since 2010 due to real or impending fiscal crises, and member states such as Germany, in which fiscal pressures, although present and self-inflicted due to domestic politics, have been much weaker. In this chapter, we look into broad labour market policy areas, namely, income support for the unemployed, active labour market policies and employment protection legislation before and after 2009, and ask the following questions. What form has retrenchment taken under the recent fiscal pressures and how has it been distributed across these policy domains? Has the emphasis of active labour market policy instruments changed? How have policy changes affected insiders and outsiders in the labour market?

We show that during the economic crisis and the subsequent fiscal austerity period, there were no paradigmatic changes in French labour market policies, which continued to develop along a path pursued since the early 2000s. Successive governments, both centre-right and centre-left, have implemented flexicurity à la *française*, with a focus on flexibility at the expense of security. External flexibility – firms' ability to hire and dismiss workers – has been developed for both core workers and more precarious forms of employment (temporary work). Furthermore, new measures also introduced important changes in the field of internal flexibility (working-time organisation, wages) (Eichhorst and Konle-Seidl, 2008).

The chapter is structured as follows. The second section provides some background for the policy developments that will be illustrated by discussing the characteristics of the French labour market and the effects that the crisis has had on it and on the French macroeconomy. The third section illustrates the patterns of French labour market policies and their reforms from the 1980s to 2008, and, more specifically, how the traditional conservative-corporatist French labour market policies gradually shifted towards dualisation. In the fourth section, we present the policy changes implemented since 2009 under the aegis of EU-induced fiscal austerity. The final section concludes.

Macroeconomic and labour market background

Effects of the crisis on the French macroeconomy and labour market

Although France recorded two consecutive years of zero or negative growth during 2008–09 – the first time since the Second World War – output growth recovered from 2010, while GDP remained relatively stable from 2012, with low but positive growth rates. While GDP fell sharply at the end of 2008, France also experienced 300,000 job losses during 2008–09. From 2009 to 2013, headcount employment remained stable, while the total annual hours worked, which dropped by more than employment during 2008–09, fluctuated. Employment started growing again in 2013 (see Figure 5.1).

The French economy had been rather protected from the effects of the crisis endured in other European countries, mainly due to its relatively low reliance on external trade and stable private consumption rates. However, France's budget deficit expanded during the recession to reach 7.2% of GDP in 2009, higher than the euro-area average of 6.2%. This led the European Commission to initiate an excessive deficit procedure in the context of the Stability and Growth Pact. Since 2010, successive French governments – including the new

Figure 5.1: Real GDP, employment (in 000s) and total average annual hours worked growth (2007=100), France, 2007–16

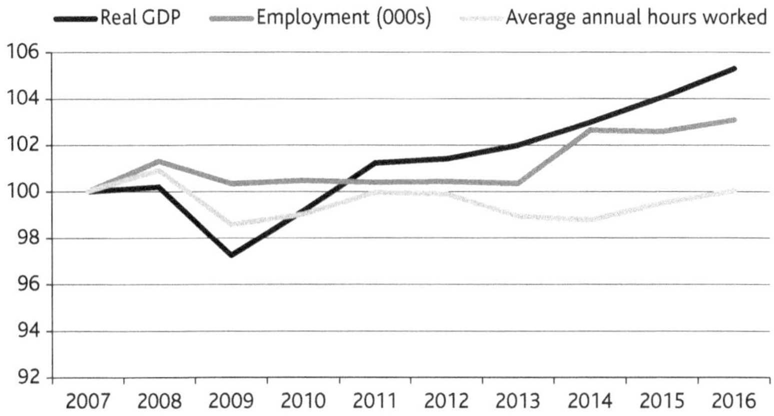

Source: Own calculations using Eurostat data (nama_10_gdp, lfsa_egan series) and Annual Macro-economic database of the European Commission (AMECO) data (NLHT series)

socialist one that was elected in 2012 – used public expenditure cuts and tax increases to reduce public deficits. Between 2010 and 2014, the cyclically adjusted budget balance (excluding interest) as a share of GDP shrank from −3.6 to −0.75 and remained around that ratio until 2016, suggesting a fiscal retrenchment effort that was pretty much in line with the average in the Eurozone. While the Commission has agreed to successive delays since then, and suspended the procedure in July 2015, it has remained very attentive to the measures planned and implemented in order to reduce the deficit. Structural reforms, especially with regards to labour market policies, are under particular European scrutiny, as will be mentioned later.

French policymakers reacted to the crisis with temporary and cyclical measures. Since 2009, to avoid a deeper recession, governments have intervened massively to save the banking system, to help the restructuring of industrial sectors facing particular difficulties, to support demand and to reduce the social costs of dismissals and increased unemployment (Freyssinet, 2011: 35). Public expenditure reduction has been partly achieved with the non-replacement of nearly 100,000 public servants between 2011 and 2013, a measure that contrasts with the exceptional expansionary fiscal measures taken during the same period.

France's economic recovery had been slow and weakened by high unemployment, especially among younger workers, who have remained an important target of policy reforms and conjectural measures (see later). Younger people have suffered the biggest employment losses from the crisis. According to calculations using Eurostat's annual labour force survey, between early 2008 and late 2009, while the average net employment loss for people aged 15–64 years of age in France was 1%, it was 9.2% for those aged 15–19, 4.9% for those aged 30–34, 2.1% for those aged 20–24 and 1.6% for those aged 25–29. By contrast, older workers, especially those above 55 years of age, registered employment gains between 2008 and 2009. Between 2010 and 2016, the overall number of those of the working-age population (15–64) in employment increased by 2.6%. By contrast, several age groups experienced employment losses. The biggest employment losses were registered by the youngest (15–24 year olds), especially 15–19 year olds, with losses of −11.4%, the younger segments of prime-aged employed people (25–29 year olds), with losses of 2.9%, but also the 35–39 year olds, the group that suffered the second-largest losses (−7.3%) after the very young. Last but not least, those with the lowest levels of educational attainment (ie those with less than primary, primary and lower-secondary education qualifications) suffered employment losses equal to 30.4% between 2010 and 2016.

The headline unemployment rate for France rose from 7.1% of the labour force (aged 15–74 according to the Eurostat definition) in 2008 to 10.1% in 2016. Although unemployment rates among the youngest have been much higher than average (a little over 30% for 15–19 year olds and a little over 20% for 20–24 year olds), the increase both in the early years of the crisis (2008–09) and after France entered the excessive deficit procedure was relatively much higher (around 33%) among elder workers (those aged 55 and above). The contrast in relative changes of employment and unemployment rates by age groups suggests that younger people, unlike older ones, responded to employment losses by exiting the labour force.

The share of part-timers in employment rose constantly between 2008 (16.8% of employed persons aged 15–64) and 2014, to peak at 18.6% of employed persons, suggesting that labour input was reduced not only through the number of people engaged in work, but also through more people among them working fewer hours. By 2016, the share of part-timers among the total employed fell slightly to 18.3%. More worryingly, involuntary part-time employment increased: the share of those working part-time because they could not find a full-time job rose sharply from 2012 onwards, from 34.2% to 44.2% of all part-time employees.

Moreover, data from the Eurostat labour force survey suggest that the share of employees in fixed-term contracts increased from 14.4%

in 2009 to 16.1% in 2016, reaching 58.6% among young people below 24 years of age. In 2010, 58% (up from 56.4% in 2008) of employees on fixed-term contracts stated that they had accepted them because they could not find a permanent job; that share rose to 61.7% in 2016. Last but not least, the share of self-employed among the total employed aged 15–64 rose substantially, from 10% in 2008 to 12% in 2016, a 20% increase.

The characteristics of the French labour market

The French labour market has been classified as a dual labour market. In the past few decades, atypical forms of employment have developed considerably and the shares of part-time work, short-time contracts and temporary agency work in total employment have increased. Whereas, in the 1970s, atypical jobs represented only 3% of all employment, their share dramatically grew to 25% by 2007. The share of temporary work in total employment rose from 10.4% in 1990 to 16.7% in 2015; the share of temporary workers employed by an employment agency grew by 130%, while normal employment rose by only 2% during the same period. Atypical jobs currently represent more than 70% of new job contracts (Palier and Thelen, 2010: 130–1). As a response to the constant rise of unemployment since the 1980s, policy responses have focused on the reduction of employers' social charges, and the financing of subsidised contracts.

The dualisation of the French labour market has been predominantly a matter of contract status. However, it is also reflected in the unemployment benefit system and the conditions of access to vocational training schemes. Short-time employment contracts tend to concern specific categories (women, the young and low-skilled workers). While these contracts have been stable since the 2000s, they have also implied more precariousness, notably, because their duration has been reduced. The share of short-time contracts in total hiring intentions increased from 48.2% in 2000 to 69.1% in 2016 (Fontaine and Malherbet, 2016).

In response to the constant rise of unemployment since the 1980s, French policymakers have focused on reducing employers' social charges and on financing subsidised contracts. Nowadays, temporary workers are still an important adjustment variable, especially in times of crisis. In the pre-crisis period of the mid-2000s, work incentives and employment assistance were developed, whereas investment in training policies remained limited (Milner, 2014: 205).

Labour market policies prior to the crisis: the gradual shift towards dualisation

Income support for the unemployed

Created in 1958, French unemployment benefit was primarily a dual system. Although it was unified in 1979, the 1984 reform divided the system into a solidarity regime (financed by the state) and an insurance regime (managed by the social partners) (Daniel, 1998; Freyssinet, 2002). The unemployment assistance scheme combined means testing and contribution conditions stricter than those required for the unemployment insurance system. From the early 1980s, the reforms introduced a differentiation between recipients according not only to age, but also to the duration of their membership of the unemployment insurance scheme. Such dualism differs from the previous unified regime in which the state participated in unemployment benefits (Daniel, 1998).

In the 1970s and 1980s, the 'social treatment of unemployment' was the main approach to unemployment (Clasen and Clegg, 2003; Castel, 2007; Clegg, 2010: 96). Labour-shedding strategies organised under the control of trade unions and employers' representatives and financed through the unemployment insurance system were progressively abandoned from the mid-1980s onwards. Since the implementation of tight economic policies in the mid-1980s, French labour market policy reforms shifted from labour-shedding strategies to social policies as an instrument of labour mobilisation (Palier, 2010).

In the early 1990s, the Allocation Unique Dégressive (AUD) generalised the degressivity of unemployment benefits. The reform decreased the level of the replacement rate[1] and reduced the duration of unemployment insurance benefits.[2] In an attempt to contain costs, the reform restricted access to unemployment insurance benefits, especially for those with shorter contribution records (Clegg, 2007: 606). From then on, unemployment insurance benefit recipients were put under even more pressure to look for jobs (Freyssinet, 2002: 6; Palier, 2012). Following the reforms of the 1990s, the coverage of unemployment insurance reached its lowest level in 1999 (42.1%). Many job seekers were left with no income and thus forced to fall back under social assurance (Clegg, 2011: 44–5).

In the 2000s, and prior to the crisis, there were again reforms of the unemployment insurance system, while the principle of degressivity was abandoned and replaced with incentives for more active job search. In contrast to the 1990s, when job seekers with short contribution records were the main losers from the reforms, the 2000s display changes in the principles underlying the unemployment system as those with a better level of protection experienced the most important losses (Clegg, 2011: 44).

Thus, to put it in a nutshell, from the 1980s to 2008, the reforms of the French unemployment benefit system were driven by cost-cutting objectives, with the emphasis on restricting eligibility conditions, strengthening the conditionality of benefits and limiting their generosity in terms of duration and replacement rates. The burden of this retrenchment fell disproportionately on the less protected and the long-term unemployed, who could be characterised as the 'outsiders'.

Activation policies before 2009: a means of flexibilisation

Between the 1980s and the late 2000s, there was an increasing focus on the activation and economic responsibilities of the jobless (Clegg, 2010: 108). From the mid-1980s, activation elements in the form of benefit conditionality were introduced into the system of income support for the unemployed in order to limit the disincentive effects of unemployment benefits and their negative effects on their recipients' integration in the labour market (Erhel, 2009). Employment assistance activation schemes (through the development of training programmes) were also developed in this period.

The 1980s and 1990s were also characterised by occupational activation, with a sharp rise of subsidised employment contracts targeted at specific groups (younger and older workers, the long-term unemployed, and social assistance recipients), which strongly favoured the development of dualisation, although such contracts were designed to ease the social and professional insertion of at-risk groups into the labour market. Job creation was particularly supported in the public and para-public sectors, illustrating the role of the state as 'employer of last resort'.

Until the end of the 1990s, activation tended to foster dualisation because participation in its schemes depended on the labour market situation of its recipients, widening the gap between social assistance claimants and unemployment insurance recipients (Clegg, 2011: 47). This dualisation trend was due mainly to the role of the social partners in managing the unemployment system. National agreements designed by employers' associations and unions thus tended to benefit their constituencies, especially the employees of large manufacturing firms and older workers (Clegg, 2011: 48).

These trends in active labour market policies were reinforced in the 2000s. In 2001, a 'back-to-work' support plan (*Plan d'aide au retour à l'emploi*) was set up so that recipients of unemployment benefits would have to sign a personalised action plan (*Plan d'action personnalisé*). The pressure to take an 'acceptable job' was also increased. In the same year, an 'employment bonus' (*Prime pour l'emploi*) was created. This new earned-income tax benefit emphasised the supply side and the 'responsibility' of job seekers (Colomb, 2012). Last but not least, in the late 2000s, the jobs that job seekers should accept after having received unemployment benefits for one year were defined (*offre raisonnable d'emploi*). This reform was an important incursion of the state into the field of the competences of the social partners, especially as trade unions were opposed to the law, which they considered would undermine recipients' rights and employment norms (Tuschizer and Eydoux, 2008).

Overall, French active labour market policies from the 1980s until the beginning of the crisis in 2008 were characterised by a mix of punitive ('demanding') instruments, reinforcing the incentives of unemployment benefit receivers for active job search, and enabling instruments, including subsidised employment and job creation schemes in the public sector. Remarkably, the eligibility conditions for participation in active labour market policies reinforced dualisation patterns in the French labour market.

Employment protection legislation before the crisis: from flexibilisation at the margins to its generalisation

Based on a conservative-corporatist logic, French employment protection legislation had been particularly protective of workers. From the second half of the 1980s onwards, flexibilisation reforms did not impose unified flexibility among all workers (Palier and Thelen, 2010: 127). Rather, core workers have relied on multiple forms of employment protection, while outsiders have faced increasing internal (working time and wage) and external flexibility (increasing the duration of probation periods). The Bismarckian–Beveridgean hybridisation of the French welfare state participated in lowering the costs of hiring workers and tended to transfer the fiscal burden to individuals, resulting in more commodification (Le Cacheux and Ross, 2015). Such measures illustrated the crucial increase in 'flexibility at the margins' (Davidsson, 2009). Mirroring activation mechanisms in the field of unemployment insurance, dualisation was also developed in the field of employment protection legislation (Davidsson, 2009), as in other Bismarckian countries, such as Germany. In the mid-2000s, the conservative government led by De Villepin firmly engaged in the flexibilisation of employment protection legislation, especially in the field of dismissal rules, thus turning the focus towards core workers. The flexibilisation trend was not abandoned, but rather renewed and reoriented, in the late 2000s.

Labour market policies since 2009: cyclical measures to support young people and flexibilisation reforms

Drift in public expenditure on labour market policies

Although public labour market policy expenditure as a share of GDP increased between 2008 and 2015 in France, looking at public expenditure per person wanting to work shows that it fell for labour market services, falling by 21% between 2010 and 2012 and rising very little (3.6%) until 2015, while it rose very little for income support measures from 2010 to 2013 and declined after that (see Figure 5.2). These developments took place against an increase in the share of the long-term unemployed in total unemployment from 40% to 46% between 2010 and 2016, whereas the long-term unemployed were 37% of the total unemployed in 2008. In other words, there has been an overall retrenchment in the form of 'drift' (compare Hacker, 2004: 246). As already mentioned, French governments did not react to the crisis by reducing public spending and this holds true as far as labour market policy is concerned as well.

Direct job creation, the second-biggest type of active labour market programme in France, was the type of active labour market programme on which expenditure rose more significantly after 2010. Spending on employment incentives also rose slightly. Public spending on training, the biggest type of programme, declined after 2012. Public spending on start-up incentives rose after 2006 but slightly declined after 2011. Turning to more qualitative details on the development of labour market policies, during the past years, changes have been focused on the guidance of the unemployed, unemployment benefits, workers' reclassification and partial unemployment.

Income support for the unemployed

The early crisis years

As a consequence of the Great Recession and the increase in long-term unemployment, 1 million jobseekers were no longer eligible for unemployment benefits by the end of 2010, 360,000 of whom

Figure 5.2: Public expenditure in different types of labour market policies as a share of GDP, France, 1998–2014

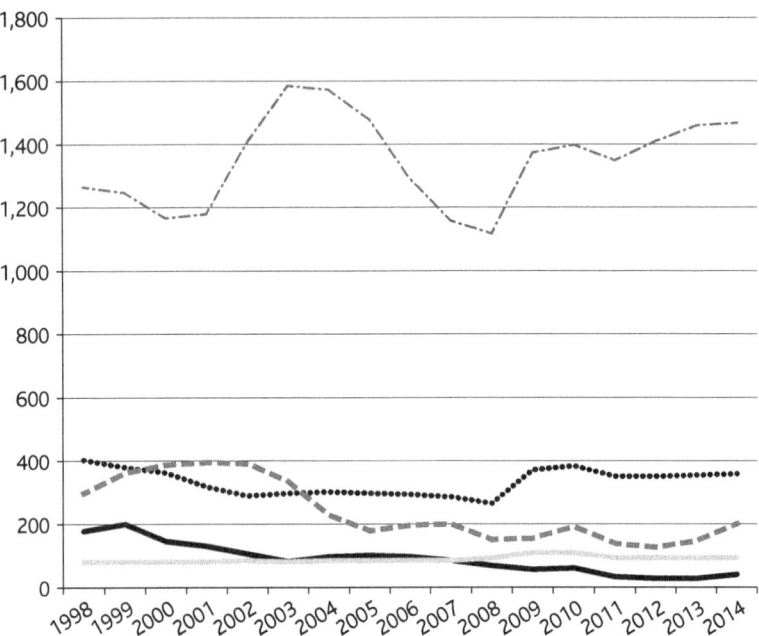

Source: European Commission (DG Empl)-Eurostat

were not even eligible for social assistance (*Revenu de solidarité active, Allocation spécifique de solidarité*). An exceptional benefit (*aide exceptionnelle pour l'emploi*) of €15.14 a day was thus established for a maximum of six months.

In February 2009, a 'social summit' introduced specific measures targeted at middle-income and better-protected workers and also set up specific measures for unemployed individuals with low contribution records. Some efforts were made to provide better coverage for more vulnerable groups (especially young people) and the long-term unemployed (Gautié, 2012: 220–1). Nonetheless, the impact of the measures was relatively low, with a total of 40,000 new recipients between April 2009 and March 2010 (Freyssinet, 2010: 87).

The unemployment benefit system was reformed in 2009. The reform was aimed at unifying job-search rules for all job seekers. The economic crisis was not the ostensible reason for the reform. The direction of policy reforms did not change in the following years. In 2009, a collective agreement among the social partners targeted the segmentation of access to unemployment benefits. Contrary to the kind of policies implemented in the 1990s, the 2009 reform of the unemployment system increased the rights of those with limited contribution periods and reduced the rights of individuals with longer contribution periods (Clegg, 2010, 2011; Freyssinet, 2010; Clasen and Clegg, 2012). As the reform benefited outsiders rather than insiders, it represents an important change.

In 2009, changes in partial activity benefit schemes (*activité partielle*) were implemented to reinforce income support for workers who saw their working hours temporarily shortened due to the recession. Such schemes existed before the crisis but they were poorly used and limited to the car and textile industries. In 2009, these schemes were extended to all sectors. These kinds of short-time working arrangements were previously referred to as 'partial unemployment'. The crisis contributed to a semantic change as they are now referred as 'partial activity'. The 2009 reform widened the coverage, increased the levels of compensation and introduced a new regime to cover long-lasting partial activity (*activité partielle de longue durée*).

Thus, changes in income support for the unemployed between 2008 and 2009 included a mixture of responses to the effects of the crisis and a continuation of previous trends of strengthening the incentives imposed on benefit recipients to search for and accept jobs, while the benefit rights of unemployed persons with limited contribution records were improved at the expense of those with longer contribution periods.

Post-2010

In 2014, a new agreement between social partners (except two unions, the Confédération Générale des Cadres (CGC) and the Confédération Général du Travail (CGT)) introduced the principle of 'rechargeable rights' (*droits rechargeables*) in the field of unemployment benefits. It allowed unemployment insurance benefit recipients to maintain entitlements that they have not used when they go back to work, and to benefit from these entitlements in the event of a subsequent period of unemployment.

The waiting period for receiving unemployment benefits (deferred compensation [*différé d'indemnisation*]) was increased for recipients with important benefits in order to deal with difficulties in financing the unemployment system. However, this measure was soon banned by the French Council of State in 2015. Policy orientations hence enhanced distributive innovative reforms (Clasen et al, 2012: 15). According to Freyssinet (2010), the extension of such programmes, which rather benefit outsiders, challenged the analysis of French employment policy reforms in terms of dualisation between insiders and outsiders.

Thus, the main change in the years since the crisis began was a tentative effort to cut costs, the burden of which fell more on insiders than outsiders. In that sense, it was aimed at reducing dualisation, even though the economic context makes this objective more difficult to achieve. At the same time, the concept of linking entitlements to career paths rather than jobs continued.

Active labour market policies: measures targeted at activating specific groups

The early crisis years

At the dawn of the crisis in 2008 (although decided beforehand), the French public employment services and the unemployment insurance system were unified in a single administration (*Pôle Emploi*), which clearly cut the management competences of the social partners (Lartigot-Hervier, 2014). The aim was not only to reduce the costs of the French public employment service, but also to make it more efficient in helping the unemployed find a job. As it integrated unemployment insurance recipients (and, among them, those who depend on activation mechanisms) and social assistance recipients (Willmann, 2009; Charpy, 2011), it ended up eliminating assistance instruments in favour of activation mechanisms. The suppression of social assistance benefits was aimed at activating their recipients while enhancing job search.

The *Revenu de Solidarité Active* (RSA) was thus introduced as a social assistance benefit that can also be obtained as a permanent in-work subsidy (Clegg, 2011). Recipients of the RSA would then be able to accumulate benefits with earned income. While this reform represented an important change of the French protection system, it must be noticed that it was also in line with diverse policies previously designed to help the unemployed to return to the labour market. It strengthened activation schemes for the people on minimum income and reconnected insertion policies with more general employment policies for job seekers (Clegg and Palier, 2007: 213). In fact, it became a third regime of benefits for the unemployed. The Great Recession crucially undermined the outcomes of the RSA. Increasing unemployment rates (from 7.7% in December 2007 to a peak of 10% in January 2010) made its implementation more difficult (Clasen et al, 2012: 14).

As noted earlier, younger and low-skilled workers suffered the biggest employment losses from the crisis. To deal with this issue, successive French governments implemented various conjectural measures on specific targeted groups. The boosting of subsidised contracts constituted a first important response to the Great Recession, but such instruments were reduced in the 2000s. For instance, it was decided that the French Public Employment Service would support long-term job seekers with a paid training programme or a subsidised contract. In spring 2009, an emergency plan was adopted and €1.3 billion was dedicated to supporting firms to hire young people on alternating training or apprenticeship contracts. Employers' associations welcomed the measure, which was aimed at strengthening the relations between training programmes and subsidised employment, but trade unions strongly rejected it on the grounds that financial incentives were directed mainly at firms.

In 2009, the plan 'Acting for young people' (*Agir pour la jeunesse*) planned to extend the RSA to fight youth poverty. However, the reform set up very strict conditions, which partly explain the low take-up (young people between 18 and 25 years of age must have worked at least two years in the past three in order to benefit from the 'youth RSA'). On the one hand, this measure was in line with the French approach to the integration of young people in the labour market, which has been a strong feature of French employment policies since the 1980s (Erhel, 2009). Nevertheless, the 'youth RSA' also constituted an important shift as the French welfare system traditionally refused social assistance to the young (Wilmann, 2009, quoted by Clegg and Palier, 2010: 221). Such a measure should also be considered in the context of important shifts in the French social assistance system.

Post-2010

In 2011, investment in apprenticeships was increased so that firms with fewer than 250 employees received almost total exemption from social charges to hire previously unemployed young people (Milner, 2014: 205). In 2012, as the Left returned to power with the election of the socialist François Hollande as President of the Republic, the government introduced two new measures dedicated to fighting youth unemployment. First, the 'future jobs' law (*contrats d'avenir*) was designed to develop job creation with the introduction of three-year employment contracts for unskilled and low-skilled young people, strongly subsidised by the state. Second, the 'cross-generation contract' (*contrat de génération*) was designed as a new kind of subsidised contract to help both the youngest and oldest employees. It was aimed at easing employment for young people, as well as at hiring older employees and maintaining them in the labour market. It was also designed to ensure the transmission of knowledge and skills.

Such measures strongly echoed previous public youth employment contracts (*emplois jeunes*) set up by the socialist government led by Lionel Jospin in 1997. However, traditionally, such measures directed towards young people do not have a strong impact on job creation to the benefit of younger workers, but they nevertheless support these groups and help to give them more chances in the labour market. Younger workers were, indeed, only able to adjust to the crisis because of the development of part-time, temporary and atypical employment contracts.

Lowering employers' social contributions was all but abandoned in this period and around 40 different types of instruments still coexisted in 2011 (Elbaum, 2011: 307–8). Social contribution exemptions and reductions of social charges are very diverse and the system became extremely complex.[3] The percentage of GDP of employers' contributions has largely increased since 2008, but if the percentage of employers' contributions in firms' added value is taken into account, it remains inferior to the 1990s.

In 2013 and 2014, employers' social contributions on fixed-term contracts were increased,[4] while employers were henceforth to be exempted from social contributions for the first three months when they hire young workers under 26 years of age (four months at firms with fewer than 50 employees). This increased the costs of using fixed-term contracts compared with regular ones. Also, some mechanisms designed to make work pay (*dispositif d'activité réduite*) were simplified.

Employment protection legislation: external and internal flexibility and the weakening of collective agreements

The early crisis years

In 2008, a multidimensional tripartite negotiation led to the adoption of an inter-professional national agreement, which was further transposed in the law on the modernisation of labour markets adopted that year. Such multidimensional negotiations have long been difficult in the French context. The failure of the 1984 tripartite negotiations was considered traumatic and impeded the development of multidimensional negotiations for several decades (Freyssinet, 2007). Although it aimed at complying with the European model of flexicurity, the law implemented 'French flexicurity' ('*flexicurité à la française*'), on balance, clearly emphasising flexibility rather than strengthening workers' security.

As far as security was concerned, the most important change was the introduction of the portability of rights (*portabilité des droits*) in case of dismissal, which made it possible for employees to preserve welfare provisions in the field of health care, as well as their training rights. Interestingly, other dispositions aimed at increasing workers' security were not introduced in the agreement, but were left out for future negotiations.

Another important change provided by this law was the introduction of dismissal by mutual consent (*rupture conventionnelle*) between employers and employees. Although the measure was supposed to increase employees' security (because they would benefit from unemployment insurance in case of dismissal and would gain partially maintained training and health insurance rights), it effectively granted employers more flexibility in dismissing employees as it allowed them to avoid long and costly legal struggles in the labour courts. A new fixed-term contract was also introduced (*contrat à objet défini*), designed to ease the hiring of white-collar workers (mostly engineers and managers) on the basis of a defined mission, which could last up to three years. Moreover, protective rules for non-permanent employment contracts were also eased and the duration of their probation periods was lengthened.

Two inter-professional agreements in 2009 and 2013 facilitated and further reinforced 'partial unemployment', that is, the voluntary shortening of working hours. The number of workers concerned increased dramatically in 2008 and 2009 (1.1% of the total employed workforce in mid-2009 compared with only 0.9% in early 2008) (Gautié, 2012: 204). Overall, in France, the adjustment to the shock of recession during 2008–09 was borne more by the reduction in working hours than by a decrease of real wages (Centre d'Analyse Strategique, 2012). Still, when compared with Germany or Italy, internal flexibility has, on average, been relatively moderate in France, though the pattern varies across sectors. Internal flexibility has been less developed in the non-farm business sector than in the manufacturing and construction sectors (Centre d'Analyse Stratégique, 2012: 9).

Changes in labour market policies from 2009 onwards were aimed at reducing dualisation in rights to activation and improving the prospects of young people through investment in apprenticeships and the introduction of new subsidised contracts. On the other hand, the subsidisation of employment was also introduced for fixed-term contracts, thus creating incentives for employers to recruit under atypical rather than permanent contracts.

Between 2009 and 2011, agreements between the social partners helped to redirect training rights from in-work individuals to those that are more distant from employment (Freyssinet, 2011). Access to training was also developed with the introduction of personal training hours accounts (*compte personnel formation*). Following the principle of rechargeable rights, it allowed workers to retain earned training-hour entitlements from one job to another. The personal training hours account is now included in the occupational personal account (*Compte Personnel Activité*, see earlier).

Post-2010

In 2013, the socialist government adopted an important reform, the Secure Employment Law. It sought to increase internal and external labour market flexibility and ease collective redundancy procedures. As in 2008 (see earlier), the 2013 law transposed a national agreement among social partners and can be considered the second part of the implementation of '*flexicurité à la française*'.

The law developed employers' flexibility with regard to redundancy but also strengthened the capacity of the administration to ensure that employers properly engaged in consultation and negotiation. More specifically, in the context of the economic crisis, employers were allowed, as long as a majority of representative unions agreed, to conclude a fixed-term collective agreement under which they undertook to maintain the level of employment in the company during a certain period of time in exchange for changes in work organisation (eg wage reductions or an increase in working time). In case of the dismissal of an employee who refuses to be subject to such an agreement, the employer would be exempted from the obligation to seek reclassification positions for the employee. Initially set up for a period of two years, such agreements to maintain employment (*accords de maintien de l'emploi*) were further extended to five years in 2016. The reinforcement of internal flexibility for permanent workers thus constituted an important trend of French employment policy responses in the context of the Great Recession.

At the same time, the 2013 law limited the use of part-time employment contracts (which cannot exceed 24 hours a week, except in case of an explicit agreement from the employees, which, in the context of the crisis, might be detrimental to them). Employers' contributions to unemployment insurance were also increased when they use short-time employment contracts. Such measures may not have a strong impact on the financing of the unemployment insurance system because short-term contracts designed to replace a worker (eg on maternity leave) – which represent an important part of short-term contracts in France – are not concerned with reducing employers' contributions. Also, the 2013 Secure Employment Law generalised compulsory additional health insurance to ensure that all employees can benefit from collective insurance. These rights were extended in 2014 and 2015. Hence, the 2013 law further developed dualisation as it also strengthened the rights of workers under permanent employment contracts, while temporary workers are the main victims of job losses in recent years.

In 2016, the reform of labour legislation raised an important public debate in France. The El Khomri law was so controversial and opposed by some trade unions mainly because of the changes proposed in employment protection legislation, rather than because of the few dispositions on workers' security whereby it strengthened the attachment of entitlements to career paths rather than employment status.[5] The law was also debated because of the decision-making process that was chosen by the government, which allowed it to avoid a vote in Parliament three times in the course of the parliamentary debate on the law. The law was one of the most debated under the mandate of François Hollande as President of the Republic and Manuel Valls as Prime Minister[6] but was fully endorsed by the EU, as illustrated in the Council recommendations of 2015 on the National Reform Programme of France.

The decentralisation of bargaining at the firm level was one of the most important changes introduced. The French authorities publicly stated their desire to meet European demands.[7] As EU institutions suggested, the law first extended the field of application of the agreements to maintain employment (*accords de maintien de l'emploi*), which were previously restricted to companies in serious economic difficulties. To assess companies' difficulties, the judge would now be able to take into account their international activities, not only their national ones.

Statutory employment protection in favour of collectively negotiated rights has been steadily reduced over the past 30 years, as well as in the most recent years (Milner, 2014: 210). The El Khomri law gave priority to collective agreements at the firm level as a new way of regulating working time, overtime pay, leave and rest. Such measures (referred to as Article 2 of the law) were at the centre of the debates and social mobilisation. While industry-wide collective agreements still represent an important level of collective bargaining in France, the law was a major change because company-wide collective bargaining could now prevail as the principle favouring (*principe de faveur*) collective negotiations was abandoned. With such a reform, the possibility for collective agreements at the company level to deviate from the law or from the sectoral level, even if it is less favourable to the worker, became the rule, whereas previously it was an exception. While the law made these dispositions for the field of working-time negotiation, it planned that the new rule could be extended to other areas of labour law.

Another important innovation in this field is a change of the rule to conclude collective agreements. The law provides that collective agreements must be made by majority agreement, that is, they must be approved by trade unions representing at least 50% of the recorded vote (the threshold was previously set up at 30%).[8] In short, companies were given greater leeway to make decisions about hiring, firing, pay and working hours according to economic conditions so that they would be less constrained by collective-bargaining procedures. The 2016 law also extended the 'normal' working week to 46 hours (as the counterpart of rather generous compensation arrangements from the 36th hour onwards).

One of the original aims of the law was to make employment legislation more flexible and to introduce a financial ceiling for unjust dismissals. However, because of the strong social movement raised against the Labour Code, this disposition only set up indicative rather than compulsory ceilings. All in all, the central objective was to reform the part of the Labour Code dedicated to working time and to dismissals, as well as to find a new articulation of collective norms. Beyond that, the law embraced various heterogeneous provisions. While it was aimed at 'simplifying' the Labour Code, in fact, it made it more complex.

Conclusion: France under austerity and the ambiguous attempt to tackle dualisation

Following the recent economic crisis, France faced renewed fiscal austerity pressures after being subjected to an excessive deficit procedure. On the other hand, the increase in unemployment increased financial pressures on the system. Thus, the pressures to cut the costs of labour market policies, already present since the 1990s, continued. At the beginning of the crisis and before France faced EU pressure on its fiscal policies, public expenditure per person wanting to work rose for all broad categories (income support and active labour market policies). However, from 2010 onwards, public spending on labour market policies showed signs of policy drift.

With regard to income support for the unemployed, retrenchment affected those who were better protected more than those with fewer rights. Nevertheless, the high unemployment rates have not made these changes more effective in reducing dualisation and maintaining the rights of workers across jobs. While enabling activation mechanisms have been developed specifically to increase job seekers' capacity to engage in training, the most important focus has been on incentive reinforcement activation mechanisms, specifically in the field of unemployment benefits, and on occupational activation mechanisms, with an important increase in subsidised contracts during the crisis.

In the field of employment protection legislation, the implementation of *flexicurité à la française* continued, with flexibility being privileged over security and with greater internal and external flexibilisation measures affecting the core of the workforce to the same, if not a greater, extent than those less well protected. Flexicurity has been at the centre of debates over employment policy reforms since the late 2000s. To develop its schemes, French policymakers have developed the securitisation of professional paths in parallel with the flexibilisation of employment protection, especially in the field of collective dismissals. In the French perspective, increasing workers' security in the context of the implementation of the European flexicurity model was envisaged mainly as improving workers' and job seekers' capacity to maintain their rights when they change jobs or become unemployed.

In recent years, particular measures have been discussed and sometimes implemented to reduce the dualisation of French labour markets. Indeed, the use of non-permanent contracts has been more regulated, even though there are plans to discuss the overtaxation of such contracts in the future, and other measures have been implemented to increase the rights of long-term unemployed and non-permanent workers. In the meantime, employment protection legislation for permanent workers has also been made more flexible as dismissal conditions have been relaxed by the most important labour law reforms since the crisis (2013 and 2016). In the pre-crisis years, the flexibilisation of employment protection legislation was the main target of reforms, and the provisions in favour of security implemented in the context of defining 'French flexicurity' appear rather marginal overall. These reforms largely developed both internal and external flexibility. In this way, the well-protected groups have lost out from the recent changes, while measures have been developed to ameliorate the situation of at-risk, especially young, workers. The various cyclical measures that have been taken since the beginning of the crisis were largely directed towards younger workers.

This chapter shows that the diverse measures implemented to reform the unemployment insurance system since the beginning of the Great Recession helped to blur the dividing line between insiders and outsiders. Several authors have shown that insiders and outsiders are not so homogeneous as a group and have underlined that (negative and positive) mobility between both groups is increasingly important (Freyssinet, 2010). J.-C. Barbier (2009: 99) refers to a crumbling of employment statuses ('émiettement *des statuts*'), leading to increasing diversity and inequality. The French labour market has, indeed, been very segmented but the distinction between the two categories is not that easy to make. Industrial workers dismissed on economic grounds are particularly at risk. Temporary workers are, of course, also at risk but they may also benefit from economic recovery (Freyssinet, 2010). Despite the measures in favour of outsiders, the 2013 Secure Employment Law and most recent employment policy measures have also helped to strengthen the segmentation of the French labour market. Distributive recalibration is nevertheless a noticeable trend of employment policy reform. Indeed, if new measures implemented since the crisis (eg 'partial unemployment') have particularly targeted core workers, around 500,000 new subsidised employment contracts (*contrats aidés*) were concluded in the public, para-public and private sectors in 2009, which represents a crucial increase of 40% in one year.

In the Great Recession, the social partners have neither negotiated measures that benefit insiders while abandoning outsiders, nor completely destroyed the faith of outsiders in the public authorities and social assistance schemes. 'Partial unemployment' typically targets insiders while outsiders and low-skilled workers have benefited from reforms of vocational training schemes. As Clasen, Clegg and Kvist (2012: 24) argue, the crisis points to a 'change in the pre-existing logic of institutional development and in the distributive orientation of protection for workers'. Indeed, priority groups have been supported by diverse measures. If increasing dualisation must hence be discussed, a clear development has been drawn towards an increasing fragmentation and segmentation of political logics and policy instruments that are sometimes contradictory. As Freyssinet (2010) argues, the stack of heterogeneous measures implemented since the Great Recession has not contributed at all to the management of professional transitions and even less to the reduction of illegitimate inequalities.

Notes

1. At a rate of around 17% every four months, and faster for those under 25 years of age.
2. To seven months for those with only six months' contributions in the past year (it was previously 15 months for people under 50 years of age and 21 months for people over 50).
3. As Elbaum shows, from 2009 and 2011, four mechanisms were created, six were suppressed and 12 were modified (2011).
4. An increase of 7% for contracts lasting less than one month, 5.5% for contracts between one and three months, and 4.5% for contracts of less than three months.
5. In the first version of the law, the occupational personal account (*Compte Personnel Activité* [CPA]) allowed for accumulating entitlements in two respects: training and hardship jobs. Only the account for citizen involvement (*compte engagement citoyen*) was finally added in this version of the CPA. It aimed at recognising the professional competences acquired with participation in volunteer activities.
6. The other politically controversial measure was the proposition regarding the deprivation of nationality in case of a conviction for terrorism, which was proposed after the Paris attacks of November 2015 but finally abandoned.
7. See, for instance, the Rapport d'information déposé par la Commission des affaires européennes portant observation sur le projet de loi visant à instituer de nouvelles libertés et de nouvelles protections pour les entreprises et les actifs (n°3600) and presented by Mr Philip Cordery. Filed in the Presidency of the National Assembly on 7th April 2016.
8. If the agreement is concluded by trade unions representing only 30% of the recorded vote, trade unions can ask for a referendum, which needs 50% of the workers' votes to come into force.

References

Barbier, J.-C. (2009) 'France', in P. de Beer and T. Schils (eds) *The labour market triangle. Employment protection, unemployment compensation and activation in Europe*, Cheltenham: Edward Elgar.

Castel, R. (2007) 'Au-delà du salariat ou en deçà de l'emploi? L'institutionnalisation du précariat', in S. Paugam (ed) *Repenser les solidarités. L'apport des sciences sociales*, Paris: Presses Universitaires de France, pp 415–33.

Centre d'Analyse Stratégique (2012) 'L'ajustement de l'emploi pendant la crise. Une comparaison internationale et sectorielle', *La Note d'Analyse*, No. 284, September.

Charpy, C. (2011) *La tête de l'emploi: Pôle emploi raconté par son patron*, Paris: Tallandier.

Clasen, J. and Clegg, D. (2003) 'Unemployment protection and labour market reform in France and Great Britain in the 1990s: solidarity versus activation?', *Journal of Social Policy*, 32(3): 361–81.

Clasen, J. and Clegg, D. (2012) 'Adapting labour market policy to a transformed employment structure: the politics of "triple integration"', in G. Bonoli and D. Natali (eds) *The politics of the new welfare state*, Oxford: Oxford University Press, pp 135–57.

Clasen, J., Clegg, D. and Kvist, J. (2012) 'European labour market policies in (the) crisis', ETUI Working Paper 2012.12.

Clegg, D. (2007) 'Continental drift: on unemployment policy change in Bismarckian welfare states', *Social Policy & Administration*, 41(6): 597–617.

Clegg, D. (2010) 'From insurance or insertion to rights and responsibilities: the shifting logics of unemployment protection in France', in A. Nevile (ed) *Rights and social policy: A comparative analysis of values and citizenship in OECD countries*, Cheltenham: Edward Elgar, pp 83–100.

Clegg, D. (2011) 'France – integration versus dualisation', in J. Clasen and D. Clegg (eds) *Regulating the risk of unemployment: National adaptations to post-industrial labour markets in Europe*, Oxford: Oxford University Press.

Clegg, D. and Palier, B. (2007) 'From labour shedding to labour mobilisation; The staggered transformation of French labour market policy', paper presented at the 2007 Annual Meeting of the American Political Science Association, Chicago, United States.

Colomb, F. (2012) *Les politiques de l'emploi (1960–2000). Sociologie d'une catégorie de politique publique*, Rennes: Presses Universitaires de Rennes.

Daniel, C. (1998) 'L'indemnisation du chômage depuis 1979 différenciation des droits, éclatement des statuts', *La revue de l'IRES*, 29: 5–28.

Davidsson, J.B. (2009) 'The politics of employment policy in Europe: two patterns of reform', paper presented at ECPR general conference, Lisbon, 14–19 April.

Eichhorst, W. and Konle-Seidl, R. (2008) 'Contingent convergence: a comparative analysis of activation policies', IZA Discussion Paper No. 3905, IZA, Bonn.

Elbaum, M. (2011) 'Le financement de la protection sociale: quelles perspectives au-delà des "solutions miracles"?', Document de travail de l'OFCE, no 2011–27.

Erhel, C. (2009) *Les politiques de l'emploi*, Paris: Presses Universitaires de France.

Fontaine, F. and Malherbet, F. (2016) *CDD Vs CDI: Les effets d'un dualisme contractuel*, Paris: Presses de Sciences Po.

Freyssinet, J. (2002) 'La réforme de l'indemnisation du chômage en France', *La Revue de l'IRES*, 38: 3–50.

Freyssinet, J. (2007) 'L'accord du 11 janvier 2008 sur la modernisation du marché du travail: un avenir incertain', *La Revue de l'IRES*, 54: 3–39.

Freyssinet, J. (2010) 'Les négociations collectives et les politiques publiques face aux "conséquences sociales" de la crise économique', *Revue de l'OFCE*, 4(115): 81–120.

Freyssinet, J. (2011) 'Négociations interprofessionnelles et crise économique', *La Revue de l'Ires*, 2(69): 33–67.

Gautié, J. (2012) 'France: protecting the insiders in the crisis and forgetting the outsiders?', in D. Vaughan-Whitehead (ed) *Work inequalities in the crisis: Evidence from Europe*, Geneva: International Labor Organization.

Hacker, J.S. (2004) 'Privatizing risk without privatizing the welfare state: the hidden politics of social policy retrenchment in the United States', *American Political Science Review*, 98(2): 243–60.

Lartigot-Hervier, L. (2014) 'Réformer en présence de veto players. Méta-réformes et syndicats dans les assurances chômage en France et en Allemagne', *Gouvernement et action publique*, 3(3): 55–78.

Le Cacheux, J. and Ross, G. (2015) 'France in the middle', in J.E. Dølvik and A. Martin (eds) *European social models from crisis to crisis. Employment and inequality in an era of monetary integration*, Oxford: Oxford University Press, pp 105–43.

Milner, S. (2014) 'The politics of unemployment policy in an age of austerity: France in comparative perspective', *French Politics*, 12: 193–217.

Palier, B. (ed) (2010) *A long goodbye to Bismarck? The politics of welfare reforms in Continental Europe*, Amsterdam: Amsterdam University Press.

Palier, B. (2012) 'Turning vice into vice: how Bismarckian welfare states have gone from unsustainability to dualisation', in G. Bonoli and D. Natali (eds) *The politics of the new welfare state*, Oxford: Oxford University Press.

Palier, B. and Thelen, K. (2010) 'Institutionalizing dualism: complementarities and change in France and Germany', *Politics & Society*, 38(1): 119–48.

Tuchszirer, C. and Eydoux, A. (2011) 'Du RMI au RSA: la difficile mise en place d'une gouvernance décentralisée des politiques d'insertion', *Revue française des affaires sociales*, 4(4): 90–113.

Willmann, C. (2009) 'L'autonomie des partenaires sociaux en débat: Pôle emploi et la convention d'assurance chômage du 19 février 2009', *Droit social*, 7/8: 830–41.

SIX

The German exception: welfare protectionism instead of retrenchment

Werner Eichhorst and Anke Hassel

Introduction

Since the turn of the millennium, the German model has been characterised by a period of major reforms, followed by a period of remarkable stability and growth in times of global economic crisis. In Germany, austerity-related reforms occurred between 2003 and 2005, when a fundamental restructuring of the welfare system was perceived as necessary to ensure international competitiveness and fiscal sustainability in a situation of high unemployment and repeated failure to stabilise and ensure economic growth. After the first change of government since reunification in 1998, the new centre-left government was criticised for failing to cope with the economic effects of reunification, globalisation and demographic change. Germany repeatedly failed to adhere to the fiscal discipline of the European Stability and Growth Pact, which was central to the workings of Economic and Monetary Union (EMU). Both internal and external pressure led to policy reforms and fundamental changes in the pension and unemployment insurance systems, as well as social assistance schemes. In addition, the German model experienced a relaxation of capital market regulation, accompanied by a reduction of corporate taxes. After these reforms concluded in the mid-2000s, Germany has not continued with any austerity strategy in economic or social policy beyond sticking to fiscal constraints and the debt brake. On the contrary, since the financial crisis hit Europe, the government has responded with policies promoting growth and expansion.

During 2008–09, most Organisation for Economic Co-operation and Development (OECD) countries were hit by the financial crash and subsequent crisis and have struggled to recover ever since. In contrast to most countries, Germany not only managed to respond quickly to the effects of the crisis with fiscal stabilisation policies, but also managed to reduce unemployment to a lower level than before the economic crisis. Germany experienced a severe drop in gross domestic product (GDP) of over 5% in 2009, but through various quick policy responses – such as short-time working and the car scrappage programme – German firms recovered quickly. Ever since, Germany experienced employment growth and the highest average economic growth rate within the Eurozone. In contrast to most neighbouring countries, neither economic institutions nor major economic reforms were seen as necessary to stabilise the national economy. The current policy orientation is rather one of moderate re-regulation of the labour market and welfare state expansion. However, Germany's strategy has posed problems for other Eurozone members as the country's rising exports go hand in hand with current account deficits in other Eurozone countries.

The academic discourse on welfare restructuring differentiates between two different, opposing forms of reform: welfare readjustment and welfare protectionism (Häusermann, 2010). Both forms combine elements of retrenchment and expansion between policy instruments that are categorised as following either an 'industrial logic' or a 'needs-based logic'. Welfare readjustment strategies are characterised by retrenchment in 'industrial logic' policy instruments, such as passive income support and employment protection legislation (EPL), as well as the expansion of 'needs-based' social policies, such as income subsidies for the working poor or, alternatively, activation mechanisms in labour market policies. In contrast, welfare protectionism entails the expansion of 'industrial logic' instruments and the retrenchment of 'needs-based logic' or activation strategies. Therefore, the strategy of the latter protects the old system at the expense of new participants in the labour market, whereas the former tries to incorporate and protect new participants and groups at the expense of the old system.

With regard to the German case, we will show that the major reforms during the early 2000s can be characterised as welfare state readjustment, whereas the recent changes entail at least some characteristics of welfare protectionism. The chapter first outlines the general setup of the reforms in the 2000s, highlighting the combination of deregulation and activation policies, before moving to the German arrangement to cope with the immediate effects of the 2008–09 crisis. The third major part of the chapter then addresses the core reform steps undertaken after 2010 in fields like the regulation of the labour market, active labour market policies, early retirement and vocational training.

Welfare reforms during the 2000s

The so-called Hartz reforms initiated in 2002 by the first 'red–green' (SPD–Greens) government and accomplished in January 2005 with the Hartz IV package marked a significant change to the German welfare state. The Hartz IV reform was introduced as the core activation policy in Germany (Eichhorst et al, 2008; Ebbinghaus and Eichhorst, 2009; Hassel and Schiller, 2010; Carlin et al, 2014). Initiated to simultaneously reduce the increasing level and cost of unemployment due to the high structural unemployment and economic inactivity rates in the new federal states and facilitate access to jobs, the Hartz reforms entailed policy measures that resembled the 'flexicurity' agendas in other countries. The reforms shifted employment risks from the employer to the employee and introduced more flexible forms of temporary or part-time employment. On the one hand, this increased the heterogeneity of employment structures, although on the other it led to an increased fragility in some segments of the labour market, especially in non-standard forms of employment, without questioning the regulatory pattern governing the core of the labour market. Hence, new forms of inequality have emerged within the labour market. The reforms seem to have only partially eased the issue of long-term unemployment or the number of beneficiaries of social assistance. The Hartz reforms led to various forms of deregulation that will be outlined here.

One of the primary goals of the Hartz reforms was to reactivate and reintegrate the short- and long-term unemployed. While maintaining contribution-related unemployment benefits for the initial phase of unemployment ('Unemployment Benefit I'), the reform merged the two means-tested schemes of unemployment assistance and social assistance into a single system ('Unemployment Benefit II'), changing the previous system of wage-related income support for those with some employment experience to a flat-rate benefit. The new structure, known as Hartz IV, proposed a single replacement scheme for those unemployed who had never paid contributions to unemployment insurance and those whose contribution-based benefits had expired. In contrast to the previous system, this scheme aimed to prevent poverty for those who had received social assistance before by slightly increasing their level of benefit and simplifying their access to employment services. At the same time, the system no longer secured the previous standard of living for the long-term unemployed as the old unemployment assistance scheme was abolished, mainly affecting people in Eastern Germany. The reform of the unemployment insurance system involved a cut in benefits for the long-term unemployed, who were moved to social assistance levels after a period of 12 to 18 months of unemployment. This had a psychological effect on those at risk of being transferred to social assistance.

In addition, the Hartz reforms included substantial activating tools to lower the number of unemployed persons. While in the past skilled workers had largely been protected from the expectation to retrain and were rather encouraged to keep their primary skills in a particular trade during spells of unemployment, the emphasis shifted to retraining and getting back to work more quickly if they were about to become long-term unemployed after one year (Hassel and Schiller, 2010). In particular, the focus was on the activation of the (long-term) unemployed through a cut in benefits for long-term recipients of unemployment assistance, mainly relevant in Eastern Germany, and an increase of activation efforts towards job searches, including in less attractive segments of the labour market.

At the structural level, employment agencies were transformed into so-called 'job centres', which are entitled to define stricter job suitability criteria and supervise the job placements of beneficiaries, as well as cutting benefits in cases of non-cooperation. Within the framework of 'rights and duties', beneficiaries sign integration agreements with the job centres, clarifying the responsibilities of each recipient to be reactivated into the job market and, ideally, into regular employment. For this goal, recipients are entitled to receive support in the form of training and additional qualifications, subsidised by the job centres. Regarding active labour market policies, the reform also entailed wage subsidies or start-ups as an alternative to regular employment, as well as reduced social security contribution packages for low-wage employment.

With regard to job creation, the reforms offered different, non-standard employment options, intended as first-access possibilities to the job market, such as marginal, part-time work ('mini-jobs'), agency work or temporary employment, alongside a simplified form of self-employment. These forms were intended to lower hiring costs, especially in service occupations, for persons with limited work experience or skill levels. This more dynamic scheme of activation was aimed at linking a lower level of dependency on state benefits to an increase in jobs in the labour market, especially in the service sector (Eichhorst et al, 2008; Ebbinghaus and Eichhorst, 2009). Activation strategies aimed at creating a more flexible labour market, with new forms of employment, while also making core changes within pre-existing segments.

One of the major changes had already occurred in a 2003 part of the Hartz package, with the regulation of the marginal part-time segment of the labour market. This change not only lifted the earnings threshold to €400 (€450 since 2013) per month from its previous level of €325, but also suspended the previous restriction of 15 hours per week. In addition, these so-called 'mini-jobs' were allowed as second jobs and were exempted from tax and social insurance contributions, the downside of which was that they did not provide social protection either. From the employers' perspective, these marginal forms of employment entailed only minimal employers' contributions as long as the wage remained below the €400 (€450) threshold. If the wage exceeded €400 (€450) or the employee had more than one of these mini-jobs, full taxation and social insurance gradually applied, which gave more incentive for employers, as well as employees, to remain under the threshold. Mini-jobs became an attractive supplement for a second job or secondary earners such as spouses, as well as students and pensioners, as they were exempt from mandatory employee contributions and income taxation. This created an incentive for employers to pay lower gross wages.

The extent to which employees entered the labour market via mini-jobs and then moved towards full-time employment is questionable. Recent research has claimed that mini-jobs are replacing former regular forms of employment in service sectors, such as hotels and restaurants/catering. Evidence shows that employers use the mini-job mechanism to reduce hourly wages and labour costs (Eichhorst et al, 2012; Hohendanner and Stegmaier, 2012). Concomitant to the introduction of marginal, part-time work was the reform simplifying social assistance for low-wage earners. Studies show that the number of employees working in marginal, part-time work has increased since 2007, amounting to approximately 30% of the beneficiaries of social assistance (Bruckmeier et al, 2013). Before the introduction of the minimum wage law in 2013, the clause excluding wages and hours could lead to lower gross wages in the marginal, part-time segment.

The Hartz reforms only marginally touched upon dismissal protection legislation and social protection for permanent and regularly insured employees. The reforms referring to dismissal protection were already introduced during the mid-1990s, narrowing the definition of fair dismissals. For workers, the maximum duration of unemployment insurance benefits was shortened from 32 months to 24 months. These changes, which contributed to an increase in the secondary segment of the market, also created fears that this flexibilisation would contribute to a deterioration of wages and employment stability as the protection for labour market insiders was hardly challenged. Despite little empirical evidence, these concerns have been readdressed since the mid-2000s and later, when the financial crisis opened up the debate on the reregulation of the German labour market.

Germany during the crisis

Germany was one of the few countries with declining unemployment and increasing employment during and after the 2008–09 global recession, as Figures 6.1 and 6.2 show. By now, it is best known for its short-time working arrangements, which contributed to the remarkable stability of manufacturing employment during the crisis, which was surprising given previous experiences.

In Germany, short-time working has been an established policy instrument for decades, so it was well known to employers, who had already used it in the past. During the crisis, specific policy action was important, in particular the extension of the maximum duration of short-time working allowance from six to 24 months and an increase in the maximum support available to employers. In contrast to the situation up to autumn 2008, employers were entitled to the full compensation of social security contributions for hours not worked, starting from the sixth month of short-time work or from

Figure 6.1: Employment rates as a percentage of the working-age population (age 15–64), various EU countries, 2000–15

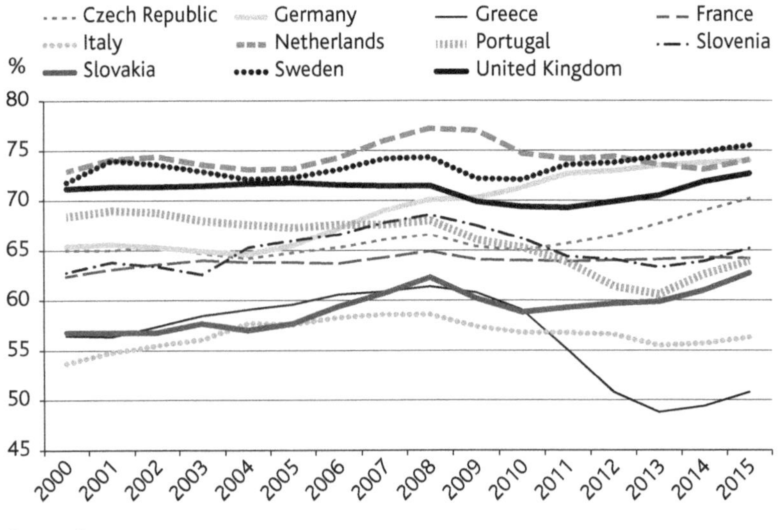

Source: Eurostat

Figure 6.2: Unemployment rates as a percentage of the labour force, various EU countries, 2000–15

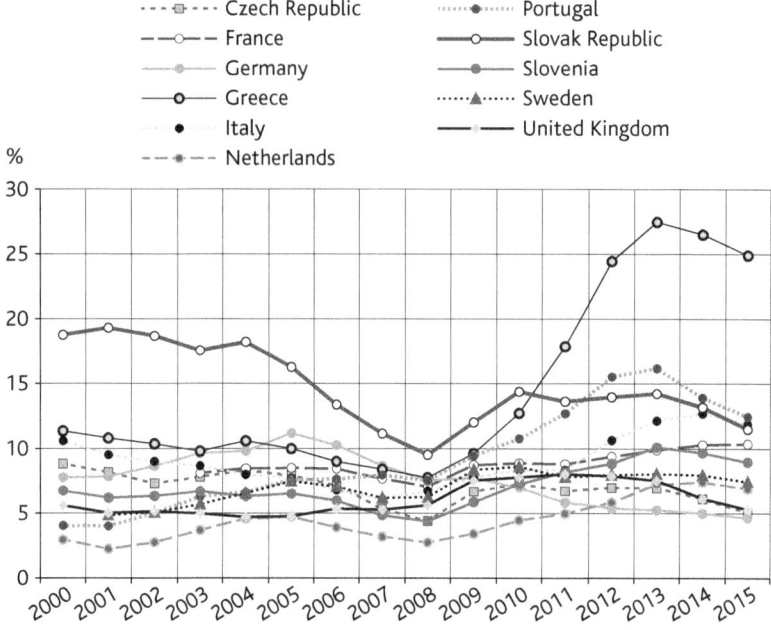

Source: OECD

the beginning if training was provided (see Figure 6.3). However, in contrast to the widely-shared view, policy reforms regarding short-time work were only one element of internal adjustment. Most of the flexible adjustment via working time reduction occurred at the company level, in particular in the case of reduced overtime work and by using surpluses on working time accounts that had grown for German exporters during the good years before the crisis. This could be done without institutional or policy changes.

Overall, many observers found the smooth development of employment figures in German manufacturing to be quite unexpected. Only a change in employers' behaviour can explain this. German manufacturing employers acted very cautiously during the 2008–09 crisis. Past experience had taught them that dismissing skilled workers during a temporary downturn can lead to severe skill shortages when demand recovers. This is particularly true in situations of adverse demographic change, which results in smaller cohorts of young workers entering the labour market. In fact, there is evidence that those sectors in which firms had experienced difficulties in recruiting

Figure 6.3: Short-time workers in Germany, 2005–16

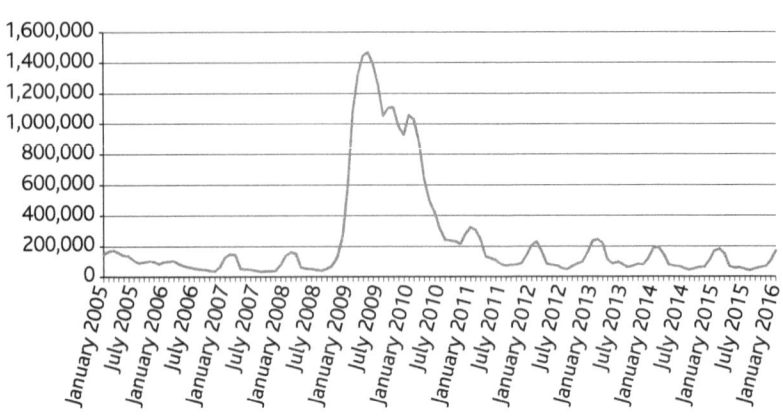

Source: Federal Employment Agency

before the crisis were the hardest hit by it and employers were therefore very reluctant to dismiss workers at short notice (Möller, 2010).

Furthermore, as routine manual tasks had been allocated to temporary agency workers, manufacturing employers could terminate a substantial part of these contracts at short notice, as well as not renewing some fixed-term jobs (Hohendanner, 2010). Hence, the secondary segment of manufacturing workers on fixed-term and agency work contracts had to bear a major part of the external adjustment during the crisis, although with the subsequent recovery employment in agency work picked up again quickly, as shown in Table 6.1. Later on, regular employment in manufacturing picked up again, but earlier than expected by many and stimulated by external demand from outside Europe.

Reducing the depth of the value chain in core businesses while focusing on the most innovative parts, more outsourcing and a longer supply chain, both national and global, can explain this, together with the increased flexibility of employment relations within both the core labour force and the marginal segment. One can argue that the 2008–09 economic crisis led to a dual pattern of adjustment in the German case, with both internal and external flexibility. The general pattern of labour market segmentation in Germany was mirrored during the response to the crisis as the marginal labour force took a major part of the burden, thus easing pressure on the core workforce, which was also protected by channels of internal adjustment (Eichhorst and Tobsch, 2013; Hassel, 2014).

Table 6.1: German labour market reforms, 2009–2017

Year/government composition	Employment protection legislation	Minimum wages	Unemployment assistance benefits	Early retirement	Vocational education and training
2009–13: Christian Democrats/ Liberals	2009 Crisis measure: Expansion of short-time work arrangements: 1) Extension of the maximum duration of short-time working allowance, 6 to 24 months 2) Increase in the maximum support available to employers – full compensation of social security contributions for non-worked hours, starting from 6th month of short time or beginning if training provided	General stability	2011: Calculation refinement of UB II/ Hartz VI minimum income support levels: 1) New link to growth in prices and wages for adults (€359+5 in 2011, €409 in 2017) 2) Special in-kind education contributions for children of Hartz VI recipients (school lunches, trips, material, etc)	General stability	General stability

(continued)

Table 6.1: German labour market reforms, 2009–2017 (continued)

Year/government composition	Employment protection legislation	Minimum wages	Unemployment assistance benefits	Early retirement	Vocational education and training
2013–2017: Christian Democrats/ Social Democrats	2017 Temporary agency work reform: 1) Equal pay for temporary agency workers after nine months (after 15 months in case of sectoral agreements), 2) Maximum contract duration of 18 months (with exceptions in case of sectoral agreements) 3) Closing loopholes for contractors with clearer definition of contract types and work council information rights	2015 statutory minimum wage of €8.50 (€8.94 in 2017) Exceptions: interns up to three months, young people below the age of 18, apprentices and the long-term unemployed (max six months after taking up a job), seasonal workers	General stability	2013: Introduction of new form of early retirement: Full pension when retiring aged 63 for those born before 1952 with at least 45 years of employment with pension insurance contributions	2014: Formation of the Alliance for Education and Training of government and social partners: 1) Aim to create additional vacancies 2) Creation of 'Assisted Training' programme to help low-achievers into apprenticeships

Welfare reforms since 2010: re-regulation rather than retrenchment policies

In contrast to virtually all other countries, Germany did not adopt severe retrenchment policies after 2010. Given the robust and improving labour market situation, with the additional revenues collected by the state, a moderate expansion of welfare benefits was implemented and the past few years have seen a partial re-regulation of the labour market. These reforms can be classified as welfare protectionism, in contrast to the welfare readjustment phase in the early 2000s. While re-regulatory policies focus mainly on non-standard forms of work and low pay, they indirectly aim to stabilise the standard employment relationship.

Re-regulation of temporary agency work

As with fixed-term employment, temporary agency work has also been progressively deregulated over the past few decades, with the most important step being taken in 2003. Since then, virtually all restrictions on agency work have been lifted, such as the maximum duration of assignments, the ban on synchronicity between employment contracts and individual assignments, or the ban on rehiring. At the same time, equal pay and equal treatment were laid down by law as a general principle governing the temporary agency work sector. However, deviations were allowed for initial periods of employment after phases of unemployment and, most importantly, by way of collective agreements. This has led to virtually full coverage of the agency sector by collective agreements, although the wages set are significantly below those of major user sectors, such as the metalworking sector (see Jahn, 2010; Baumgarten et al, 2012; Jahn and Pozzoli, 2013).

While the original intention of promoting temporary work agencies was to strengthen placement capacities for the unemployed, the labour market reforms actually implemented in Germany led to the creation of a perverse wage gap between direct employees in manufacturing and temporary agency workers performing similar tasks as wage scales differ and assignments can be made for an indeterminate period of time. This has led to competition between directly employed staff and agency workers, in particular in the low- and medium-skilled segments of manufacturing. Where trade unions and works councils were strong, they could achieve agreements with employers on a step-by-step closure of the wage gap by way of earnings supplements and a better transition from a temporary agency work contract to a direct employment relationship with the user company (Spermann, 2013). As these changes cannot be established on a general basis throughout the German labour market due to the weakness of trade unions in some sectors, the current government has announced a re-regulation of temporary agency work by legislation coming into force presumably in mid-2017. This would mean the reintroduction of a maximum assignment period of 18 months and equal pay after nine months of service with a user company, although collective agreements on specific maximum assignments and sectoral earnings supplements will continue to exist. Agency work would then be more restricted again, compared with the situation in the recent past. In addition, work that is contracted out ('*Werkverträge*') would be more strictly defined.

Introduction of the minimum wage

By the beginning of 2015, Germany had introduced a statutory minimum wage of €8.50 (gross) per hour, about 50% of the median wage, which falls in the medium range of EU member states' minimum wages (see Figure 6.4). The introduction of a general minimum wage is certainly the most important labour market reform of the current decade so far. It is remarkable that Germany now has a minimum wage that basically covers all workers that was introduced without much political struggle with the current government, as it was backed by

Figure 6.4: Minimum wage in percent of median wage of full-time workers, OECD-Europe countries and US, 2014

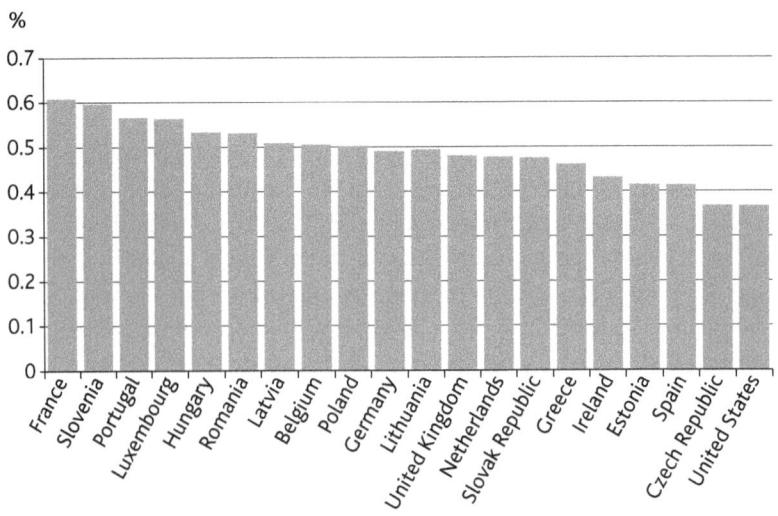

Source: OECD

all major parties and the trade unions, as well as a large share of the electorate. The introduction of a minimum wage in Germany can only be understood by taking into account its prior history of collective bargaining and low-pay sector expansion.

For many decades, trade unions in Germany were not interested in having a statutory minimum wage as collective bargaining coverage was sufficiently high to regulate wages in major parts of the labour market. This has changed over the past 20 years or so: first, with lower and declining bargaining coverage rates in Eastern Germany; and second, with the general problem in establishing wage agreements in major private service sectors (see Figure 6.5). With the move towards a more flexible (deregulated) labour market in the early 2000s, this led to a massive increase in wage dispersion and low-pay employment shares. Collective bargaining was unable to reverse this trend as bargaining structures were either non-existent or too weak in many of the crucial segments of the labour market. This led to growing public attention to low pay and a reversal of the position of major trade unions, in particular those representing service sector occupations. As a consequence, they started campaigning for a statutory minimum wage, an initiative supported by the Social Democrats. Even before the adoption of the national minimum wage, increasingly more collectively agreed minimum wages (where they could be set) were extended to cover non-organised employers and employees.

Regarding the statutory minimum wage, there are a few exemptions, in particular for interns up to three months, young people below the age of 18, apprentices and the long-term unemployed, for a maximum of six months after taking up a job. Special rules apply to seasonal

Figure 6.5: Collective bargaining coverage, as a percentage of all workers, Germany, 1998–2015

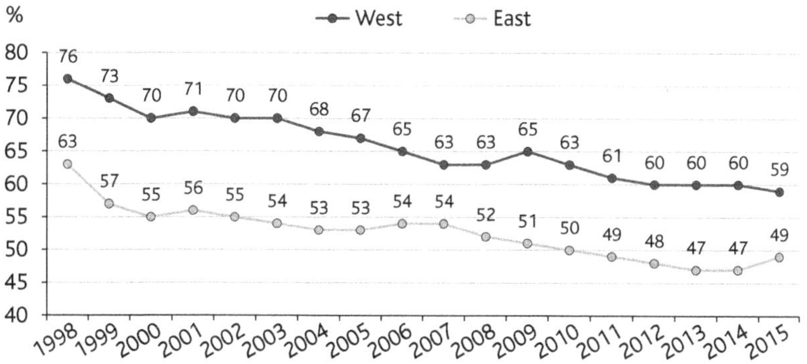

Source: Hans Boeckler Foundation Tarifarchiv

workers. Furthermore, transitory exemption clauses exist for newspaper distributors and those sectors where there are binding, collectively-agreed minimum wages below €8.50, whereby they only have to apply the statutory minimum wage by 2017. While the initial minimum wage level was set politically, and basically reflects the position of the trade unions, in the future a bipartite commission of employers' associations and trade unions will negotiate the adjustment of the minimum wage, taking into account the development of collectively-agreed wages and the situation in the labour market. Academic experts will also be consulted. This committee has recommended an increase to €8.84 in 2017.

The minimum wage has started to change the rules of the game in some segments of the German labour market. While employment and unemployment at the aggregate level do not show an impact of the minimum wage, occupations, regions and employment types dominated by low wages are more strongly affected. This holds true in particular for activities such as hairdressing, taxi driving, waiting staff, for smaller establishments, Eastern Germany and marginal, part-time work (Arni et al, 2014; Brenke, 2014). It is still too early to have gathered evidence on the dynamic and long-term effects of a minimum wage, even given the positive economic environment that made the minimum wage much less problematic to introduce than expected by some observers. However, there are hints at a mixture of employment restructuring in favour of part-time work as opposed to mini-jobs, more difficult or unrealised hirings, price increases, and a certain tendency to circumvent the minimum wage; for example, by informal unpaid overtime or a move to 'freelance' work or 'self-employment'. From a more general perspective, the minimum wage reverses some of the wage dispersion trends observed in Germany over the past 10 years or so, in particular in service occupations reliant on mini-jobs (Amlinger et al, 2016; Vom Berge et al, 2016).

Activation, income maintenance and long-term unemployment

Changes to the labour market and social policies were at the heart of the government's agenda in 2003. The Hartz I–IV reforms changed not only the institutional structure of the Federal Labour Agency and the interplay between local-level poverty relief and national unemployment insurance, but also the general policy approach towards mobilising the long-term unemployed. Although these reforms were highly contentious when they were introduced, despite some political pressure from the Left, they have not been reversed.

However, amendments have addressed many details affecting both welfare benefits and activation measures.

One of the most debated issues concerns the generosity of the minimum income support scheme in Germany, for both adults and children. The method for setting the benefit level was challenged politically and legally, resulting in a ruling by the Federal Constitutional Court in 2010. This led to a calculation refinement as laid down in formal legislation, but not to a general change in the system. There has been neither a major retrenchment nor a general increase in benefit generosity. For adults, minimum income support is determined based on the consumption patterns of low-income earners, allowing for some arbitrary adjustment. For children living in households in need, the new rules resulted in a slight increase in benefit levels. In addition to cash benefits to cover the cost of living, the German minimum income support scheme covers appropriate housing and heating, as well as specific needs and support for schoolchildren. The evolution of the level of minimum income support in Germany is related to the development of net earnings and consumer prices so that welfare benefits can keep pace with them. What has changed over time is the number of benefit recipients, under both the unemployment insurance and the minimum income support scheme, mainly due to the combined impact of the labour market reforms and a dynamic economy.

Nonetheless, some issues remain, including the relatively large group of people combining income from work with receipt of social assistance. About 1.3 million have some income from work but do not leave the benefit system. While at first glance this suggests a large number of working poor, the actual situation is not unambiguous as the majority of those 'working unemployed' work part-time, so their income from work is under no circumstances sufficient to raise them above the breadline. Here, the main issue is that some people only have very weak incentives to move from part-time work or marginal part-time work ('mini-jobs') to longer working times, in particular full-time work.

The most important reason for this is that the policy is based on an earnings-disregard clause that allows minimum income support beneficiaries to earn a limited amount before benefits are withdrawn; hence, increases in earnings would result in a progressive loss of benefits without any improvement in net income. The second concern is the lack of childcare support and other services for those taking care of children, in particular single parents, who rely on minimum income support to a very strong extent. Of course, there are also full-time workers receiving additional benefits, in particular if they have large families. However, data show that their hourly wages are not particularly low.

The second major issue is the persistent problem of unemployment. The improvement of the labour market situation in Germany since mid-2005, even during and after the 2008–09 crisis, has helped to reduce unemployment, including long-term unemployment (see Figure 6.6). However, the most disadvantaged have not benefited that much from the stronger demand for labour. This is the most difficult task: to integrate the remaining long-term unemployed into gainful employment as they lack the relevant skills and work experience, or have health problems or other obstacles to employment. This would require tailor-made services addressing the specific needs of the target group; furthermore, formally, the German legislation on active labour market policies for the long-term unemployed allows for a very flexible use of different instruments, including training, hiring incentives for employers, job-search assistance, personalised assistance and work experience programmes. Nevertheless, there seem to be significant issues with the implementation of such policies (Spermann, 2014). A reform in 2011 simplified and reduced the number of instruments, allowing for a more flexible use of the Public Employment Service in local offices, but this reform also resulted in a reduced available budget for those most dependent on support (see Figures 6.7 and 6.8), affecting in particular public employment schemes and start-up support (Law on Improving Integration Chances in the Labour Market [*Gesetz zur Verbesserung der Eingliederungschancen am Arbeitsmarkt*]). Furthermore, a new initiative to combat long-term unemployment was launched in 2014, including employer subsidies, public sector

Figure 6.6: Unemployment and long-term unemployment in Germany as a percentage of the active population, 2000–15

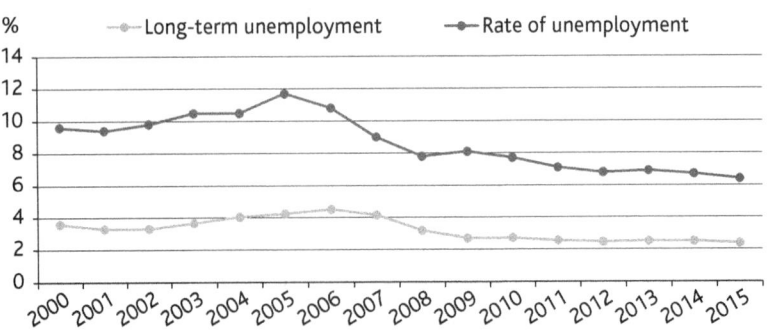

Source: Federal statistics office seasonally adjusted data

Figure 6.7: Expenditure on active labour market policies as a percentage of GDP, selected EU member states, 2000–14

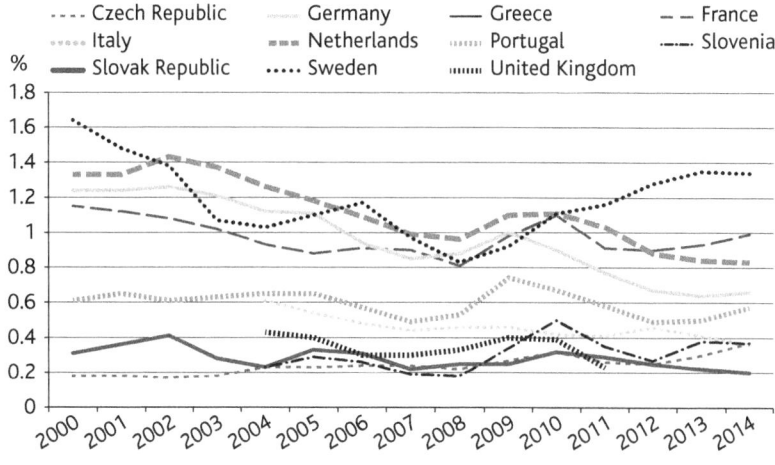

Source: OECD

Figure 6.8: Expenditure on active labour market policies as a percentage of GDP, selected EU member states

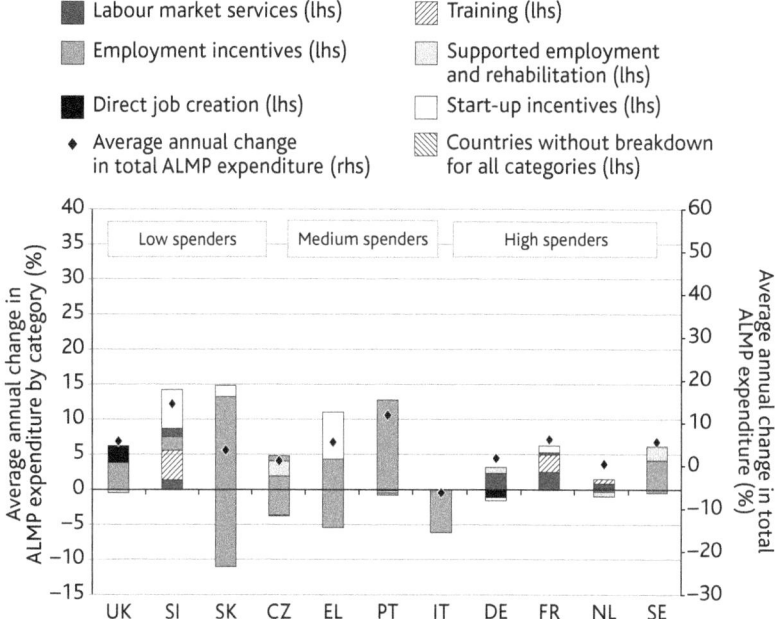

Note: UK = United Kingdom, SI = Slovenia, SK = Slovakia, CZ = Czech Republic, EL = Greece, PT = Portugal, IT = Italy, DE = Germany, FR = France, NL = Netherlands, SE = Sweden

Source: European Commission

employment opportunities and an integration pathway via part-time work and personal assistance to the long-term unemployed. However, these programmes have not been able to change the situation significantly as they are too small given the scope of the challenge.

Bringing early retirement back in

Germany adopted a long-standing path towards later retirement in the late 1990s, basically abolishing all options of a generous early exit from the labour market such as publicly subsidised old-age, part-time work ('*Altersteilzeit*') and raising the statutory retirement age step by step to 67. This policy was phased in during 2012 and it mainly affects younger and prime-aged workers. It was primarily seen as a policy to stabilise the public budget, with respect to both first pillar of pension insurance and the tax-funded general budget, as well as avoiding the premature loss of skilled labour in a rapidly ageing economy. As regards labour market performance, since the late 1990s the employment rate of older workers has increased significantly in Germany and much more strongly than in many other European countries, as Figure 6.9 shows.

As companies could not shed older workers as smoothly and cheaply as before, and given their stronger need to continue employment to a later stage in life, the increasing employment rates of older workers was mainly driven by the longer tenure of workers who would have

Figure 6.9: Employment rate of workers aged 55–64 as a percentage of the total population, selected EU member states, 2000–15

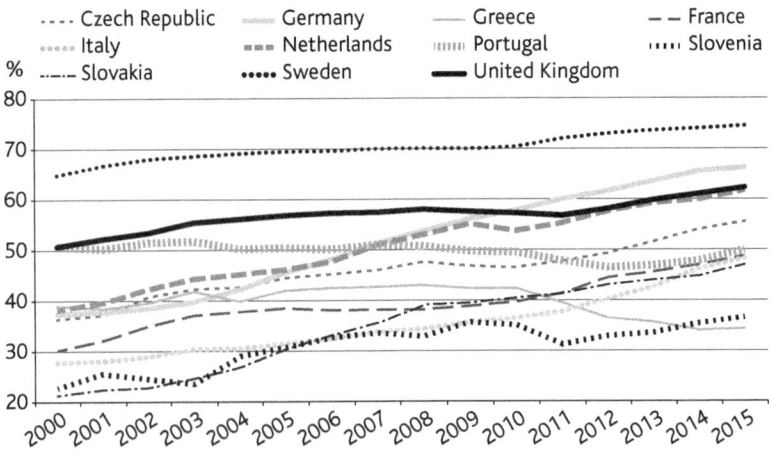

Source: Eurostat

retired earlier in the old regime. Despite some criticisms raised by trade unions and welfare associations, the general paradigm shift seemed to be largely accepted.

Against this backdrop, a quite unexpected policy change occurred. After the last general election in 2013, Germany introduced a new form of early retirement, namely the option for those born in 1952 and earlier to receive a full pension without any deduction when retiring at the age of 63, after at least 45 years of employment with pension insurance contributions. For younger people, this would be smoothly phased out again. This reform was mainly pushed for by the German trade unions in association with the Social Democrats as a policy to pave the way to an early exit for a core group of trade union members, namely skilled workers with a vocational training degree and long employment biography. This can be seen as the most explicit case of welfare protectionism, favouring labour market insiders. The Christian Democrats did not oppose this given the general popularity of early retirement policies in a situation of apparently buoyant public revenues on the one hand, as well as the need for political support for their own pet project, a pension bonus for mothers, on the other.

Retirement at 63 years of age increases the generosity of the public pension scheme. It leads to a loss in revenues from taxes and pension contributions and additional expenditure within the welfare state. Implicitly, this is a redistributive policy, from those not fulfilling the requirements of retirement at 63 to those who can benefit, namely medium-skilled workers with long employment experience and a decent wage, who are mainly active in manufacturing or the public sector. Those with a shorter or more unstable employment biography do not have access to this specific arrangement. In fact, since the legislative change, more older workers have applied for early retirement than was initially expected. In 2015, about 250,000 filed for a pension at 63. While the most generous options only apply to a certain cohort, others can get access to early pensions through extra contributions. Furthermore, policymakers are currently considering an increase in pension levels for long-term low-pay earners.

Vocational education and training

The vocational education and training (VET) system 'appears to be undergoing a period of subtle but significant change' (Thelen and Busemeyer, 2012: 89). Vocational training is still the dominant form of training after secondary education, with more than 50% taking up some form of apprenticeship. It is a highly structured approach to training, in which firms employ apprentices and train them on the job, while they also attend school for part of the time. The licensing of training and the content and examination of apprentices are organised and supervised by the local chamber of commerce. German-style vocational training has always been seen as a highly successful way of training young school leavers below the level of tertiary education. It has consistently produced low levels of youth unemployment and high levels of specialised training.

During the 1990s and 2000s, three main developments created pressure within the vocational training system (Thelen and Busemeyer, 2012: 76–8). First, the share of firms that engage in vocational training declined from 35% to 25%, which reflected the downswing of business between the mid-1990s and the mid-2000s. Second – and related to the decline of firm participation – the demand for training by school leavers could not be met. Young school leavers at the lower end of school qualifications found it increasingly difficult to find training places. As the German government is committed to providing training up to the age of 18, many of those ended up in a kind of 'transition system' (Baethge et al, 2007) of state-sponsored training. Third, the attitude of large firms towards the training needs of school leavers has changed. While in the past firms increased training capacities beyond their business needs to meet demand, this form of corporate social responsibility has significantly declined over the past decade. Firms are more reluctant to train simply to fill the gap. Outsourcing, restructuring and fierce competitive pressure have introduced a new emphasis on cost-cutting that does not allow for voluntary training.

With regard to policy change, some incremental adjustments were made. In particular, shorter training courses (two-year apprenticeships) were introduced and some of the content was removed. The government also introduced short training courses for school leavers with low skills. As school leavers increasingly either drop out of low-quality training or cannot meet the expectations of high-quality training, a school-based training regime evolved alongside the firm-based VET system. The content of apprenticeships has also become more modular and flexible. Some of these developments took place in the context of increasing Europeanisation in training standards. Even though training is not part of the core EU competencies, the European Qualifications Framework has introduced a credit system that should make VET in Germany more compatible with other countries.

While on the whole we can see institutional stability over the period under scrutiny, many training features and much content are markedly different today compared with the beginning of the period. However, given the onset of a rapid demographic change and rapidly declining numbers of school leavers, there is an expectation among policymakers and firms that the remaining schoolchildren will increasingly be pushed towards higher levels of training (Thelen and Busemeyer, 2012).

In 2014, the German vocational training system was repeatedly discussed in policy circles as well as public debates. Various observers perceive the system as being in a crisis because the number of training contracts is decreasing and the number of young people without an apprenticeship is growing. At the same time, employers complain about unsuitable applicants and unoccupied vocational training vacancies. Data on newly-concluded apprenticeship contracts show a slow but continuous decline to about 522,000 in 2015, compared with 560,000 in 2010.

The government and social partners responded by forming an Alliance for Education and Training (*Allianz für Aus- und Weiterbildung*) comprising political representatives from the national and state level, trade unions, and employers. The Alliance is the successor to the National Pact for Training and Skilled Manpower Development (*Nationaler Pakt für Ausbildung und Fachkräftenachwuchs*). It agreed on various measures to improve the situation in vocational training. One of the objectives is to create additional vocational training positions. Moreover, it introduced a programme called 'Assisted Training', which supports weaker candidates in finding an apprenticeship and finishing their training successfully.

Although the education system currently seems to be experiencing some problems, the overall diagnosis of a 'crisis' should be examined more carefully. In the past, there have been repeated phases in Germany in which the number of vocational training positions decreased. Moreover, in the vocational training and labour market, imbalances between supply and demand occur on a regular basis. Due to the regional distribution of open positions and the limited geographical mobility of potential applicants, it could be the case that young people from Eastern Germany who have not found training positions are not in a position to take up vacant apprenticeships in Southern Germany. In addition, there are significant differences in the ratio of vacant training positions and applicants between different professions. International comparisons indicate that the German vocational training system generally works well and generates very low youth unemployment. It prevents polarised structures of low-skilled school and university graduates, similar to the situation in Spain, for example. Vocational training offers a good entry into the labour market and career opportunities in professional curricula, decent working conditions and promising prospects for permanent employment, ensuring financial security and an acceptable standard of living. Hence, this path of professional qualifications is generally valued among employers and within society.

However, the vocational training system is currently shrinking and losing an increasing share to higher or academic education. Increasingly more school graduates are deciding against vocational training and for a university degree. On the one hand, this is problematic because, for example, artisanal professions face increasingly difficult challenges in finding prospective candidates, at some point endangering jobs and businesses. On the other hand, industries and large companies primarily employing university graduates welcome, and actually require, increasing levels of academic training in employees. However, since the prerequisites in many occupations for vocational training are constantly increasing, weaker candidates, for whom universities are not an option, also have difficulties in finding a vocational training position. The background to these developments is a structural change within the economy towards more complex tasks and higher qualifications.

The problems could be addressed through minor changes and a better connection between the two systems: if more combinations between training and universities were offered and universities were more available for training graduates, this would improve the attractiveness of the vocational training system. Future trainees would benefit from double degrees, further education, practical experience and improved possibilities of job and career entries. Companies would benefit by filling vacant training positions, having qualified trainees and embedding them into the companies. In addition to improving the link between vocational training and higher education, weaker candidates looking for an apprenticeship should be individually counselled and supported, even if this entails financial support from employment agencies. The strengths of young people should be determined and linked to matching vocational training positions. At the same time, it is important that working conditions in occupations with low numbers of applicants and high drop-out rates – as in hotels and catering – are improved by adjusting wages or working time. Finally, guidance and information on vocational training before and after graduating high school could be improved. Only through realistic information about the requirements at university and vocational training, and the respective professional opportunities, could wrong decisions and the resulting drop-out rates be reduced. Although existing programmes placing university drop-outs into apprenticeships are feasible, these initiatives are diversions that cost money and time and should be prevented in the first place.

However, political target setting to increase the number of vocational training positions should be evaluated critically as it might result in the artificial creation of jobs without long-term prospects. Rather, vocational training is something to be controlled by the social partners, as well as the apprentices themselves.

Although the German system of vocational training seems to be in crisis, its extent is still limited. It remains attractive for many businesses to employ apprentices as they are often motivated and productive, do not entail large costs and potentially stay in the firm in the long term. Through the proposed reforms, this interest could be strengthened. In addition, the focus of young people can increasingly be redirected towards vocational training as an education system with benefits. Presumably, this will be achieved in particular through mixed forms of vocational training and academia. In addition to a merger of these two systems, permanent shifts in the size and importance of the individual systems would eventually be acceptable as long as sufficient numbers of young people are professionally qualified as the final outcome.

Conclusion

This chapter has tried to assess the existence and extent of retrenchment policies in Germany in the aftermath of the 2008–09 recession. In contrast to the intensive phase of labour market and welfare state reforms in the context of the Hartz reform package that pointed towards 'welfare readjustment' during the early 2000s, we do not see a clear pattern of retrenchment policies in Germany. In general, the path that was adopted earlier was continued after 2005, as well as during and after the crisis. This holds for the deregulated situation of non-standard contracts such as marginal, part-time work and temporary agency work, as well as the activation policies addressing both short- and long-term unemployed people. The stability of policies can be explained by the economic conditions, which were, and remain, much more favourable than in many other EU member states. Hence, apart from some cuts in active labour market policies, we cannot see retrenchment in labour market policies. Most recently, we can identify a partial re-regulation of the labour market, most notably the introduction of a national minimum wage, a potential increase in the regulation of non-standard contracts and a reintroduction of early retirement for labour market insiders, as well as the potential expansion of active labour market policies. These policies can be classified as mainly 'welfare protectionist'. While directly addressing more disadvantaged groups of workers, the re-regulation of the low-pay sector and non-standard contracts also limits pressure on wages and working conditions for the core of the labour market.

Acknowledgements

We are grateful to the European Trade Union Institute (ETUI) for support on this piece of research and in particular to Sotiria Theodoropoulou for helpful comments on an earlier draft.

References

Amlinger, M., Bispinck, R. and Schulten, T. (2016) 'The German minimum wage: experiences and perspectives after one year', WSI Report 28e.

Arni, P., Eichhorst, W., Pestel, N., Spermann, A. and Zimmermann, K.F. (2014) 'Der gesetzliche Mindestlohn in Deutschland: Einsichten und Handlungsempfehlungen aus der Evaluationsforschung', *Schmollers Jahrbuch*, 134(2): 149–82.

Baethge, M., Solga, H. and Wieck, M. (2007) *Berufsbildung im Umbruch. Signale eines überfälligen Aufbruchs*, Berlin: Friedrich-Ebert-Stiftung.

Baumgarten, D., Kvasnicka, M., Landmann, J. and Thode, E. (2012) 'Herausforderung Zeitarbeit', Studie im Auftrag der Bertelsmann Stiftung.

Brenke, K. (2014) 'Mindestlohn. Zahl der anspruchsberechtigten Arbeitnehmer wird weit unter fünf Millionen liegen', *DIW Wochenbericht*, 5: 71–7.

Bruckmeier, K., Eggs, J., Himsel, C., Trappmann, M. and Walwei, U. (2013) 'Aufstocker im SGB II: Steinig und lang – der Weg aus dem Leistungsbezug', IAB Kurzbericht 14/2013.

Carlin, W., Hassel, A., Martin, A. and Soskice, D. (2014) 'The transformation of the German social model', in J.E. Dølvik and A. Martin (eds) *European social models from crisis to crisis: Employment and inequality in the era of monetary integration*, Oxford: Oxford University Press, pp 49–104.

Ebbinghaus, B. and Eichhorst, W. (2009) 'Germany's partial departure from passive employment policies', in P. de Beer and T. Schils (eds) *The labour market triangle – Employment protection, unemployment compensation and activation in Europe*, Cheltenham: Edward Elgar, pp 119–44.

Eichhorst, W. and Tobsch, V. (2013) 'Has atypical work become typical in Germany?', IZA Discussion Paper 7609.

Eichhorst, W., Grienberger-Zingerle, M. and Konle-Seidl, R. (2008) 'Activation policies in Germany: from status protection to basic income support', in W. Eichhorst, O. Kaufmann and R. Konle-Seidl (eds) *Bringing the jobless into work?*, Berlin: Springer (revised version published in *German Policy Studies*, 2010, 6(1): 59–100).

Eichhorst, W., Hinz, T., Marx, P., Peichl, A., Pestel, N., Siegloch, S., Thode, E. and Tobsch, V. (2012) 'Geringfügige Beschäftigung: Situation und Gestaltungsoptionen. Basierend auf einem Projekt im Auftrag der Bertelsmann Stiftung', IZA Research Report 47.

Hassel, A. (2014) 'The paradox of liberalization – understanding dualism and the recovery of the German political economy', *British Journal of Industrial Relations*, 52(1): 57–81.

Hassel, A. and Schiller, C. (2010) *Der Fall Hartz IV: Wie es zur Agenda 2010 kam und wie es weitergeht*, Frankfurt/Main: Campus Verlag.

Häusermann, S. (2010) *The politics of welfare state reform in continental Europe: Modernization in hard times*, Cambridge: Cambridge University Press.

Hohendanner, C. (2010) 'Unsichere Zeiten, unsichere Verträge? Befristete Arbeitsverträge zwischen Auf- und Abschwung', IAB Kurzbericht 14/2010.

Hohendanner, C. and Stegmaier, J. (2012) 'Geringfügige Beschäftigung in deutschen Betrieben: Umstrittene Minijobs', IAB Kurzbericht 24.

Jahn, E.J. (2010) 'Reassessing the wage penalty for temps in Germany', *Journal of Economics and Statistics*, 230: 208–33.

Jahn, E.J. and Pozzoli, D. (2013) 'The pay gap of temporary agency workers – does the temp sector experience pay off?', *Labour Economics*, 24(October): 48–57.

Möller, J. (2010) 'The German labor market response in the world recession – de-mystifying a miracle', *Zeitschrift für Arbeitsmarktforschung*, 42(4): 325–36.

Spermann, A. (2013) 'Sector Surcharges for temporary agency workers in Germany: a way out of the low-wage sector?', IZA Policy Paper 67.

Spermann, A. (2014) 'Zehn Jahre Hartz IV – Was hilft Langzeitarbeitslosen wirklich?', IZA Standpunkt 76.

Thelen, K. and Busemeyer, M.R. (2012) 'Institutional change in German vocational training: from collectivism toward segmentalism', in M.R. Busemeyer and C. Trampusch (eds) *The political economy of collective skill formation*, Oxford: Oxford University Press, pp 68–100.

Vom Berge, P., Kaimer, S., Copestake, S., Eberle, J., Klosterhuber, W., Krüger, J., Trenkle, S. and Zakrocki, V. (2016) 'Arbeitsmarktspiegel: Entwicklungen nach Einführung des Mindestlohns', IAB-Forschungsbericht 1/2016, Nürnberg.

SEVEN

The Netherlands and the crisis: from activation to 'deficiency compensation'

Marcel Hoogenboom

Introduction

In the 1980s, the Netherlands was one of the first countries in Western Europe to adapt its industrial unemployment provision system to the requirements of a new 'post-industrial age' (Clasen and Clegg, 2011a). By drastically reforming the unemployment insurance system, it was opened up to a growing number of temporary, flexible and part-time workers in the tertiary sector (Hoogenboom, 2011). In the next decade, by means of several labour law reforms, the Dutch labour market was made more flexible, resulting in rapidly growing numbers of temporary and part-time workers, as well as self-employed workers without employees (De Beer, 2011).

In the same period, the Netherlands also became one of pioneering countries in the development of 'activation policies' in the European Union (EU), that is, of active labour market policies (ALMPs), which, unlike ALMPs in earlier times, combine 'incentive reinforcement and employment assistance' (Bonoli, 2010: 450). In the late 1990s, huge investments in activation policies caused government spending on ALMPs to rise from 0.3% of gross national product (GNP) in the late 1980s to more than 0.5% in 2000. Although the proportion fell to 0.4% in the early 2000s due to falling unemployment rates and cutbacks imposed by centre-right governments on ALMP spending, the Netherlands remained one of the Organisation for Economic Co-operation and Development (OECD) countries spending most on ALMPs (OECD, 2007).

However, in the years preceding the 2008 financial and economic crisis, enthusiasm for both flexibilisation and activation had cooled in the Netherlands. Trade unions and populist political parties warned about the insecure position of the rapidly growing number of employees with precarious jobs and of involuntary self-employed workers without employees. Under electoral pressure, the centre parties also gradually withdrew their support for further flexibilisation of the Dutch labour market and cutbacks in unemployment protection.

At the same time, the results of the new activation programmes, which were basically meant to compensate for the growing flexibility of the Dutch labour market by facilitating job-to-job mobility, turned out to be disappointing. While on the eve of the financial and economic crisis in the Netherlands, the contours of a new ALMP paradigm were discussed, its implementation was thwarted by the consequences of the crisis for the government budget. During 2008–14, as a result of attempts to reduce government spending, activation programmes in both unemployment insurance and social assistance were run down. However, it will be claimed in this chapter that a new ALMP paradigm is emerging in the Netherlands, which I will dub 'deficiency compensation'. In this new paradigm, ALMPs are no longer directed at removing individual skill deficiencies by means of training and schooling programmes (as in activation), but directed at accepting and financially compensating these deficiencies. As regards unemployment provision programmes and job protection law in the Netherlands, surprisingly little was changed during the crisis. In this chapter, this absence of reforms is attributed to a 'silent uprising' on the part of the low and lower-middle classes. Through their support for two new political parties in the Dutch Parliament and a change of course by the largest trade union in the Netherlands, they prevented the main political parties from implementing new reforms after two decades of fundamental change in Dutch unemployment provision and job protection systems.

The chapter is structured as follows. The consequences of the financial and economic crisis that hit the Netherlands from the autumn of 2008 are briefly sketched in the second section. In the third section, the reform of the Dutch unemployment provision system in the period between 1980 and 2008 is analysed in order to be able to understand what happened afterwards. In the fourth section, the emergency measures in the two years of the crisis are discussed, while in the fifth section, the policy reforms in the unemployment provision and job protection systems that were implemented in reaction to the crisis are described and analysed. The final section contains the conclusion.

The consequences of the crisis and early policy reactions

As in many other Western countries, the financial crisis in the Netherlands really started with the fall of the Lehman Brothers bank in September 2008. While in the months preceding it, Dutch real gross domestic product (GDP) had been growing by about 2% annually, after that, economic contraction set in rapidly. In the last quarter of 2008 and in 2009, the Dutch economy shrank by about 4% (see Figure 7.1). One of the main causes of this downturn was the economy's heavy reliance on the financial sector, real estate and construction. With world players such as ABN-Amro Bank and ING Bank, in 2007, the balance sheet of the Dutch financial sector was about four times as large as Dutch real GDP, while homeowners owed almost €500 billion (or almost 100% of real GDP) to these banks (CPB, 2008). Therefore, the fall of Lehman Brothers set in motion a chain reaction that brought economic growth to a halt for years to come.

The fall of Lehman Brothers was almost immediately followed by acute solvency problems among some of the largest Dutch banks. In October 2008, the Dutch state rescued ABN-Amro by buying all its shares and taking full control of its activities in the Netherlands.[1] A few months later, the state rescued other banks by providing them with large capital injections. In this period, the total amount of money spent by the Dutch state to save the financial sector amounted to about €30 billion or 5% of real GDP (CPB, 2008).

A direct consequence of the crisis of the Dutch banking system was a drying up of loans for Dutch consumers and business. As for consumers, the crisis particularly prevented the banks from providing the lavish mortgages that, during the previous two decades, had inflated house prices substantially in the Netherlands. As a result, real estate and construction also went into crisis, while falling house prices led consumers to curb their spending, repay debt and try to increase their savings. When, in 2009, the financial crisis was transformed into a worldwide economic crisis, the Dutch economy went into a slowdown that, with a short upswing in 2010–11, lasted for almost five years (see Figure 7.1).

For the government budget, the financial and economic crisis had major consequences. While successive government coalitions, from both the Left and the Right, had made great efforts to reduce the government deficit after the economic crisis of the 1980s – finally resulting in a balanced budget in 2006 – in the course of only one year, this effort was nullified by the crisis, which converted a 0.2% surplus into a 5.6% deficit. Topped up by the large sums that the government spent on bailing out the banks, government debt – another preoccupation of subsequent government coalitions in the previous three decades – grew from 43% in 2007 to 57% two years later. Ultimately, it would grow to 65% in 2015.[2]

Figure 7.1: Real GDP growth and government deficit in the Netherlands, 2005–16 (% of GDP)

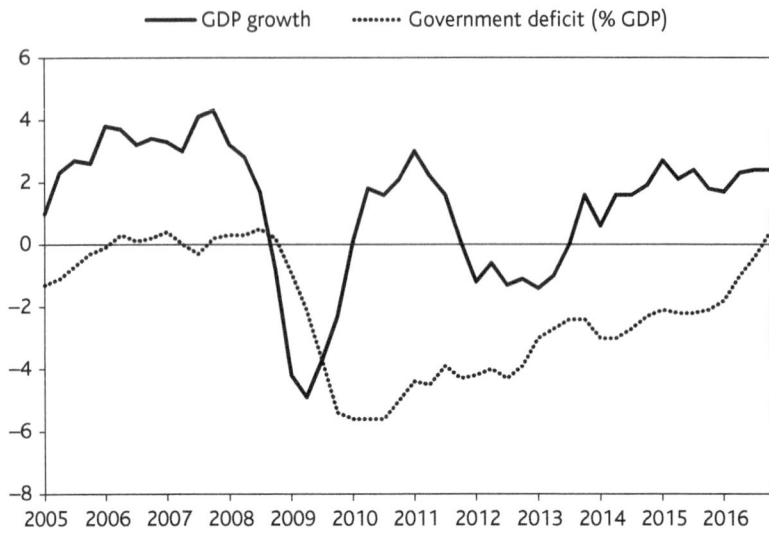

Source: www.statline.nl (accessed 26 July 2017)

However, in line with the international trend in the early days of the crisis, the first reaction of the government at the time – the Balkenende IV government, a cabinet coalition of Christian Democrats (CDA) and Social Democrats (PvdA) (for details, see Table 7.1) – was not to cut back expenditure (Den Butter, 2009). The government's main fear was that cutbacks in spending would accelerate the growth of unemployment, which was already growing substantially in the first months of the crisis (see Figure 7.2).

Table 7.1: Dutch governments, 2007–16

Government coalition*	Term	Coalition partners
Balkenende IV	February 2007–October 2010	CDA (Christian Democrats) PvdA (Social Democrats) CU (Orthodox Protestants)
Rutte I	October 2010–November 2012	VVD (Conservative Liberals) CDA (Christian Democrats) PVV (Right-wing Populist)[†]
Rutte II	November 2012–present	VVD (Conservative Liberals) PvdA (Social Democrats)

Notes:

* Named after prime minister.

[†] Formally, the PVV was not part of the government coalition (there were no PVV cabinet ministers), but it gave parliamentary support to the coalition.

Figure 7.2: Unemployment total labour force (15–65 years of age) and youth unemployment (15–35 years of age); and benefit recipients of unemployment insurance and social assistance, as a percentage of the labour force, 2004–16

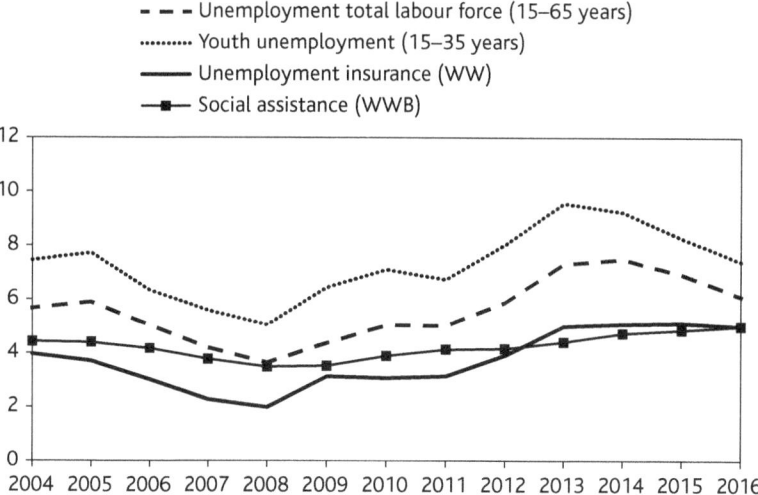

Source: Calculated on the basis of data from: www.statline.nl (accessed 26 July 2017)

Apart from the measures mentioned earlier, the government reaction to the economic crisis and its consequences was rather passive. It trusted that the first dramatic consequences of the crisis for the Dutch economy would ebb away as a result of the so-called 'automatic stabilisers'. The latter term refers to government budget doctrine, adhered to by Dutch government coalitions since the mid-1990s, which states that in order to prevent a pro-cyclical effect of government spending in times of economic downturn, *spending* on planned government policies should not be immediately cut if tax revenues dwindle as a result of the economic downturn.[3] The doctrine also states that when the economy recovers, extra government *revenues* should be cut in order to compensate for government debt built up during the economic downturn (Den Butter, 2009).

Even without the doctrine, the government had to prepare for severe budget cuts because, already in early 2009, the government deficit was in violation of the 3% Economic and Monetary Union (EMU) criterion. Therefore, in spring 2009, 20 interdepartmental working groups of civil servants were asked to come up with proposals for cutbacks that would reduce spending below the EMU criterion in the years to come. When the proposals of the working groups were published only a few months later, it became clear that in order to comply with the criterion, government spending had to be cut by about €50 billion, or 15% (Inspectie der Rijksfinanciën, 2010).

The reports of the 20 interdepartmental working groups sent shock waves through Dutch society. At once, it became clear how deep the crisis was, how brutal future cutbacks in social security and job protection would be, and how serious the ramifications would be for all citizens in the years to come. However, before the working groups had even published their advice, in February 2010, the Balkenende IV government coalition fell because of a disagreement between the CDA and the PvdA over the deployment of Dutch troops in Afghanistan. Over the next five years, two successive government coalitions (Rutte I and II) implemented many of the cutback programmes that the working groups had proposed, causing the Dutch government deficit to reach the EU threshold of 3% of real GDP in 2014.

The cutback programmes contained a wide variety of policy measures, which affected virtually all categories of Dutch citizens. Among these measures were many welfare state retrenchments, such as a gradual extension of the retirement age from 65 to 67 years, large cutbacks in long-term care budgets, a limitation of tax cuts for homeowners and the replacement of the national student scholarship system by a system of student loans (Parlement, 2012). However, unlike in many other EU countries, in the Netherlands, the cutback policies that were implemented left the unemployment provision system largely untouched. Indeed, in the period 2008–16, parts of these systems were thoroughly reformed, but they were not merely reformed in reaction to the crisis or aimed at cutting back expenditures. The reforms were already planned before the beginning of the crisis, which, at best, accelerated their implementation. The same was true of ALMPs. In the period 2008–14, ALMP policy budgets were cut severely; however, again, this was not so much in reaction to the crisis or its consequences for the state budget, but merely a continuation of pre-crisis policy trends.

Reform of the Dutch unemployment provision system and active labour market policies up to the crisis (1980s–2008)

The main reason why unemployment provision in the Netherlands was largely exempted from retrenchments was that, according to most political parties in the Dutch Parliament, the system had already been adapted to new post-industrial economic realities in the three decades before the crisis started. In the 1980s, the Netherlands was one of the first Western European countries to open up its insurance system to flexible and part-time workers, while in the 1990s, it was one of the pioneers of a new type of ALMP, 'activation policies', in social security (Clasen and Clegg, 2011a).

Reform of unemployment insurance

Since the late 1980s, the Dutch unemployment system has been composed of two main tiers.[4] At the centre of the system was the unemployment insurance scheme (*Werkloosheidswet*) known as 'WW', a compulsory insurance scheme for employees. WW was a typically Bismarckian employees' insurance scheme, financed from premiums paid by employers and employees and administered by industrial insurance agencies run by the social partners, which, in the mid-1980s, covered around 45% of the Dutch working-age population. Unemployed workers were granted – under certain conditions – benefit of 80% of their daily pay for a maximum of five years, depending on the number of years that they had been working in a certain branch of industry. After the unemployment insurance benefit period expired, unemployed persons who still had not found a new job were entitled to means-tested social assistance (*Algemene Bijstandswet* [ABW]), financed from general taxation and distributed by the municipalities, at a minimum level.[5] (See Table 7.2 for the major changes in unemployment provision, ALMP and job protection programmes in the Netherlands in the period 1987–present.)

In 1987, the unemployment system was reformed substantially. Rather than linking eligibility to the number of years that a person had been working *in a certain branch of industry*, as in the old scheme, in the new system, WW eligibility was linked to a person's *general labour history*, opening up unemployment insurance to a growing number of temporary, flexible and part-time workers in the tertiary sector. Thus, instead of requiring unemployed people to have been employed for at least 13 weeks in the previous year, in the new WW, a complex system of requirements of weeks and years was introduced to determine the maximum benefit duration for each recipient. Those unemployed who had been employed in the past year for at least 26 weeks were granted a 'loss of wages' benefit that replaced 70% of their daily pay for a period of six months. Subsequently, people who had been employed for at least three years in the past five could claim a prolongation of the benefit at the same rate for a maximum of 54 months (as from 2006: 38 months), the duration depending on their overall labour history. As a consequence of these reforms, the percentage of the active working-

Table 7.2: Major changes in unemployment provision, ALMP and job protection programmes in the Netherlands, 1987–present

Major policy measures before the crisis	
1987	Unemployment insurance (WW): benefits reduced from 80% to 70% of previous net earnings, maximum five years; eligibility linked to recipient's general labour history.
1995	Social assistance (ABW) replaced by New Social Assistance Act (nABW): obligation to apply for and accept 'suitable employment' extended to all social assistance recipients; contract between recipient, municipal social services department, and job centre on activation ('trajectory plan').
2002	Unemployment insurance (WW) administration reformed: merger of all industrial insurance agencies (run by the social partners) into one state-run administrative office (UWV).
2004	Social assistance (nABW) replaced by Work and Income Benefit Act (*Wet Werk en Bijstand* [WWB]): introduction of new funding system; municipalities obliged to outsource activation to commercial companies (obligation lifted in 2006).
2004	Unemployment insurance (WW): introduction of individual reintegration agreement between recipient, UWV and commercial and/or public activation agency.
2006	Unemployment insurance (WW): benefit level raised to 75% for the first two months of unemployment (after two months: 70%); maximum benefit duration reduced to 38 months.
Major policy measures after the start of the crisis	
2008–11	Unemployment insurance (WW): temporary activation of scheme for part-time unemployment insurance benefit (*deeltijd-WW*) for partially redundant employees, who continue to be employed by their companies but receive extra training during the hours that work is not available.
2009–11	Action Plan Youth Unemployment (*Actieplan Jeugdwerkloosheid*): regional policy programmes to prevent youth unemployment by means of a wide variety of policy measures (education, internship positions, matching job seekers and employers, etc).
2013	Social Agreement between government and social partners: • Labour contract law: ban on new and some existing flexible contract types. • Unemployment insurance: no shortening of benefit duration (as planned by government). • ALMP: participation of social partners in policy administration.
2015	Work and Security Act (*Wet Werk en Zekerheid*) implemented: reforms of unemployment insurance, job protection and labour contract law as agreed in Social Agreement (2013) implemented.
2015	Participation Act (*Participatiewet*) implemented: merger of social assistance (WWB) with benefit schemes for unemployed young people and persons with physical disabilities and/or learning difficulties and disabilities at the minimum level; introduction of 'deficiency compensation' policies which partially replace activation policies.

age population covered by the unemployment insurance scheme grew from 45% in 1980 to 70% in 2001 (Hoogenboom, 2011).

As part of the reform, formal job-seeking obligations for recipients were also toughened up considerably, both in unemployment insurance (WW) and social assistance (ABW). All benefit recipients were thus legally forced to cooperate in 'employability' assessment and improvement via education and training. Furthermore, recipients were obliged to accept 'suitable work', the definition of which was changed to include employment in other branches and, after further reforms in subsequent years, employment below one's formal qualifications and previous wage (Teulings et al, 1997; Van der Veen and Trommel, 1999).

Introduction of 'activation'

In the 1980s, some municipalities also started experimenting with new activities aimed at reintegrating 'difficult' categories of unemployed people, such as young people without qualifications and senior workers, into the labour market by means of custom-made individual education programmes, work experience places and job training. In the early 1990s, these ALMP programmes – which later came under the banner of 'activation policies' – were copied by more and more municipal social services departments (which administer social assistance) until, in the late 1990s, they were made obligatory by the national government for all social assistance benefit recipients. As from 1995, all recipients signed a so-called 'trajectory plan', a contract between the recipient, the municipal social services department and the job centre on activation. Meanwhile, the then government coalition of PvdA and Conservative Liberals (VVD) had started spending huge sums of money on subsidised labour deployment places at public institutions such as schools, municipal services departments and public transport companies. When these places were abolished by a new right-of-centre cabinet in the early 2000s, the money was transferred to the activation budgets of the municipalities and the Social Security Agency (*Uitvoeringsorgaan Werknemersverzekeringen* [UWV]) (which administers unemployment insurance [see later]). In the next few years, due to rapidly falling unemployment, overall spending could be reduced while spending per recipient remained more or less stable (see Figure 7.3).

These reforms of ALMPs were part of a first revision of social assistance in 1995, in which, again, eligibility and activation regulations were tightened up substantially and fixed national benefit norms for benefit recipients were introduced (Van Gerven, 2008). In 2004, the 'old' ABW

Figure 7.3: Spending on active labour market policies in the Netherlands: spending per recipient (€) and total spending as percentage of real GDP, 1990–2014

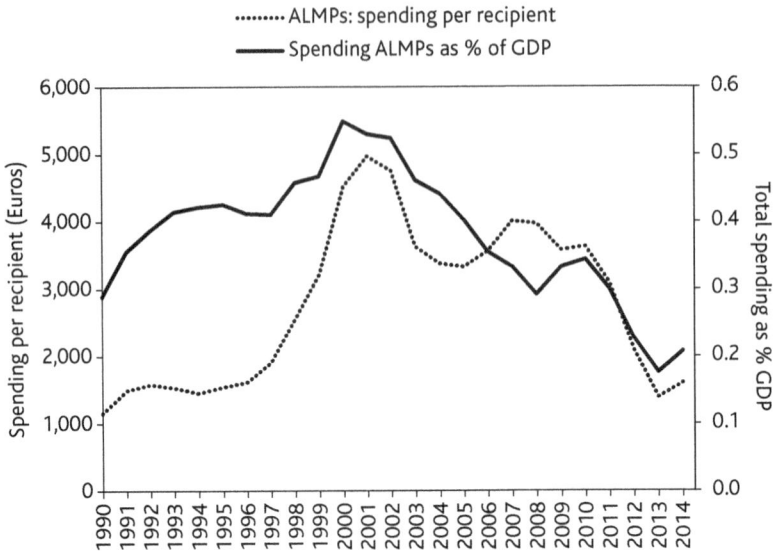

Source: Author's calculations based on the budget plans of the Ministry of Social Affairs and Employment (1990–2014)

was replaced by the Work and Income Benefit (*Wet Werk en Bijstand* [WWB]), which granted more responsibilities to the municipalities in the administration of social assistance, especially in financial terms. Each municipality now received two types of annual budget from the national government, which were fixed on the basis of statistical information: a budget for benefits and a budget for reintegration activities. To encourage municipalities to work efficiently and to reintegrate WWB recipients into the labour market early, annual surpluses on the income budget did not need to be returned to the government, while any reserves on the reintegration budget did. However, at the same time, the municipalities were relieved of their obligation to organise in-house facilities for the reintegration of social assistance beneficiaries. Instead, they were supposed to contract commercial reintegration agencies for individual reintegration trajectories, encouraging the emergence of a new 'market' for commercial reintegration activities (Van Gerven, 2008; Van Gestel et al, 2009).

Meanwhile, the administration of unemployment insurance (WW) had been revised substantially. After almost a century of social partner involvement in the administration of employees' insurance (insurance against sickness, disability and unemployment), the administration was nationalised. Thus, in 2002, the bipartite industrial insurance agencies, in which trade unions and employers' associations more or less autonomously administered employees' insurance, were abolished and replaced by a state agency, the UWV (Bannink, 2004). A few years later, the UWV was also entrusted with the assessment of social assistance beneficiaries and with the signing of activation contracts with unemployment insurance benefit recipients, which strongly resembled the contracts that were already obligatory for social assistance recipients (the so-called 'trajectory plans' [see earlier]) (Hoogenboom, 2011).

Hence, in the two decades preceding the financial and economic crisis that started in 2008, the 'old' Dutch unemployment provision system of the 1980s, which had been geared to an industrial economic structure that even then no longer existed, was transformed into a system that – at least in theory – was ready for a new post-industrial age (Clasen and Clegg, 2006, 2011b). By 2008, the system had: eligibility regulations that enabled employees to shift jobs more often and easily and to accept part-time and temporary jobs in the growing service sector; tight benefit regulations to stimulate unemployed employees to be more active in finding a new job; and a whole range of ALMPs to help them, if necessary, to acquire new skills that would make them more attractive for employers. However, a few years before the crisis started, it was claimed by a number of politicians and civil servants that two problems prevented the Dutch labour market from working as it should.

New reform plans

The *first problem* concerned the Dutch job protection system, which had largely remained unchanged since it was introduced in the 1940s. In this system, employers were only allowed to dismiss employees with a permanent or fixed-term contract after approval of the UWV (before 2002, of the bipartite industrial insurance agencies) or a cantonal judge. While it was up to the employer to choose between a procedure via the UWV or via a cantonal judge, in practice, the latter procedure was much shorter, but in most cases of unjustified dismissal, also implied the payment by the employer of a 'golden handshake', worth one month's salary for every year that the employee had worked for the employer (Dekker, 2010). This 'dual' system of job protection was deemed by the right-wing and centre parties in the Dutch Parliament and the employers' associations to be 'outdated', too slow (the UWV procedure) or too expensive (the cantonal judge procedure), and an obstacle to the further flexibilisation of the Dutch labour market. However, the left-wing parties in Parliament and the trade unions opposed any reform of the job protection system, claiming that after the reforms in social security in the previous decades, it would mean a further worsening of the position of employees.

The *second problem* that was deemed to prevent the Dutch labour market from working properly was the inability of the new activation policies to reintegrate the long-term unemployed into the labour market. Research had repeatedly shown that there was a 'granite file' of about 300,000 unemployed persons, composed of a wide variety of categories, who had been unable to find a job even in the prosperous years between 1997 and 2001 and had not benefitted from the new activation policies that were introduced in the same period. While, since the 1980s, many special projects for these categories had been unsuccessful, in 2006, a government committee – the De Vries Committee – came up with a new idea (Commissie de Vries, 2009).

This idea was based on experiences with new forms of activation for people with physical disabilities, as well as people with learning disabilities or difficulties. Until the late 1990s, as in many other Western European countries, in the Netherlands, these persons were employed by special public companies (*sociale werkvoorziening* [WSW]), where they did simple work under supervision for a minimum wage. As of the late 1990s, as part of the new activation policies, these WSW companies had started experimenting with the deployment of their personnel at public agencies and commercial companies under the supervision of social workers. The success of these experiments inspired the De Vries Committee to advise the same approach for the 'granite file' in social assistance. To benefit from the acquired experience and knowledge of the WSW companies, in its report, the committee proposed a merger of the special scheme for persons with physical disabilities and persons with learning disabilities or difficulties (WSW), a special government benefit scheme for young partially disabled persons (*Wajong*), and the social assistance act (WWB) into a new Work in Accordance with Ability Act (*Wet Werk naar Vermogen* [WWnV]).

In the years preceding the financial and economic crisis, the Committee's plan was embraced by virtually all the main political parties in the Dutch Parliament. For the centre and right-wing political parties, the plan was considered an instrument to terminate long-term benefit reliance and to cut benefit costs. For the left-wing parties, the plan was seen as an instrument to finally guarantee the long-term unemployed tailor-made activation, while, at the same time, employers would be encouraged (or forced) to employ long-term unemployed persons.

Emergency measures and reform plans (2008–10)

When, in September 2008, the financial and economic crisis hit the Netherlands, unemployment was at a historic low. With the general unemployment rate at 3.8% and youth unemployment (15–35 years) at barely 5% (see Figure 7.2), it seemed that for the first time since the early 1970s, the Netherlands had achieved a situation of almost full employment, neglecting the 300,000 or so people in the 'granite file' of social assistance. When, in spring 2009, the full extent of the crisis had become clear, the first policy reactions of the Balkenende IV government (2007–10), a coalition of the PvdA and CDA, were directed at preventing unemployment from rising rapidly.

Emergency measures

First, with the traumatic memories of the mid-1980s in mind, when youth unemployment had risen to almost 20%,[6] the government launched the 'Action Plan Youth Unemployment' (*Actieplan Jeugdwerkloosheid*) (2009–11). The Youth Plan was funded by the national government and supervised by the Ministries of Social Affairs, Education, Youth and Family, and Internal Affairs, in close collaboration with the municipalities (which administer social assistance), the UWV (which administers unemployment insurance) and various national educational organisations. It encompassed a wide variety of policy measures aimed at preventing young people from becoming unemployed by providing them with extra opportunities for education, preparing them for the labour market, organising extra internship positions at employers and matching job seekers and employers. Although supervised by national organisations, the plan was implemented at the regional level by the municipalities, the social partners, benefit agencies and schooling organisations, which had a free hand to transpose national objectives to specific local circumstances and to seek cooperation with other regional and local organisations to implement the plan (Research voor Beleid, 2011). Although the Youth Plan was never evaluated quantitatively due to its complexity and large regional differences, the commercial company that evaluated the plan concluded that in view of the relatively limited growth of youth unemployment in the Netherlands in the first years of the crisis, it seemed to have worked. In addition, the company concluded, the

Youth Plan 'has resulted in new useful labour market structures for information exchange, service provision for young people and regional cooperation, while various stakeholders have redirected their policies towards facilitating labour market transitions' (Research voor Beleid, 2011: 13).

Second, early in 2009, the national government activated an almost forgotten clause in the Unemployment Insurance Act (WW), which permitted the granting of 'part-time unemployment benefits' (*Deeltijd-WW*) by the UWV. These benefits were meant for partially redundant employees, who continued to be employed by their companies but received extra training during the hours that work was not available. Employees were eligible for the benefit if during the benefit period, they worked less than 80% of their contract, received training approved by the relevant trade union(s) and kept their jobs until the end of a period equivalent to at least one third of the benefit period after the benefit had terminated, with a minimum of three months. Employers could request part-time benefits for their employees for a period of at least 13 weeks, which could be prolonged by 13 weeks at most four times, depending on the percentage of personnel receiving benefit.[7]

In 2009, 55,000 employees were granted part-time unemployment benefit (€173 million); one year later, the figure had dropped to 21,000; and in June 2011, one month before the policy measure was terminated, fewer than 1,000 employees were still receiving benefit.[8] At its height in 2009, however, approximately 5% of all Dutch companies were using the part-time WW option, especially in construction (9%), the metal industry and real estate (both 25%), the sectors that were immediately hit by the crisis (Chkalova, 2010; Claessen and Nieuweboer, 2012).

According to a commercial research bureau that evaluated the policy measure after it had been terminated in July 2011, its results were disappointing. It could not be concluded that the measure had improved the economic position of the companies that had participated in the project or that it had prevented employers from laying off employees, although the explanation could be that more vulnerable companies had mainly participated in the project (De Groot et al, 2012).

Further reform plans

While the Youth Plan and the part-time unemployment benefit measure meant extra government spending on unemployment provision, in the meantime, the Balkenende government was considering far-reaching cuts in government spending in order to comply with the EMU's 3% government budget criterion. In spring 2009, two of the 20 interdepartmental working groups of civil servants that advised the government on this matter (see earlier) came up with proposals that, if implemented, would turn the unemployment provision system *and* the job protection system upside down. To achieve the 20% spending reduction on unemployment insurance that the working groups had set as their target, they proposed to shorten the maximum benefit duration of unemployment insurance (WW) considerably, to merge all schemes at the minimum level with severe cuts in activation programmes and to thoroughly reform the job protection system.

In the working groups' plans, the current maximum benefit duration of unemployment insurance (WW) of 38 months, in which unemployed employees received a benefit of 70% of their previous wage, was to be shortened to 12 months, after which the unemployed would enjoy a non-means-tested benefit at the minimum level. In addition, the working groups proposed to severely cut government spending on the reintegration activities of the UWV for unemployment insurance benefit recipients. At the same time, the working groups embraced the plan of the De Vries Committee to merge social assistance (WWB) with the benefit schemes for young disabled persons (*Wajong*) and persons with physical disabilities and learning difficulties or disabilities (WSW). However, while the De Vries Committee had proposed a more or less budget-neutral merger, according to the working groups, this merger should yield a cost reduction of about 20% by, among other things, substantially reducing the ALMP budgets of the municipalities.

To encourage benefit recipients to find a new job more quickly and to facilitate employers to dismiss employees more easily, the working groups advised the abolition of the legal procedure that allowed employers to dismiss employees only after approval by the UWV (which administers the unemployment insurance WW) or by a cantonal judge. Under a new Act, employers would be allowed to lay off any employee with notice of two months, while the 'golden handshake' would be retrenched from one month's salary for every year that the employee had worked for the employer to a quarter of a month's salary per year, with a maximum of six months' salaries (Inspectie der Rijksfinanciën, 2009a, 2009b).[9]

In the short run, the reports of the two working groups were very influential. In the 2010 parliamentary election campaign, many of the proposals that the working groups had formulated concerning unemployment provision and job protection systems were copied by the main political parties directly into their election programmes. Over the following five years, however, hardly any of the working groups' proposals made it into law. What happened?

The politics of reform (2010–present)

How can the virtual absence of reforms in unemployment provision in the Netherlands during the crisis be explained? It could be claimed that the main cause was a silent uprising of low- and lower-middle-income groups. These groups resisted any further reforms of what Häusermann (2011) has called 'industrial social policy instruments', that is, reforms in social insurance, job and income protection.

This silent uprising of the low- and lower-middle-income groups in the Netherlands was by no means a new phenomenon. Its roots lay in the 1990s, when two successive cabinet coalitions of social-democratic PvdA, conservative-liberal VVD and the Progressive Liberals (D66) – the 'Purple cabinet coalitions' (1994–2002) – had drastically reformed the Dutch social security, labour market and political economy. While these political parties had been sworn enemies up till then, in the 1990s, the breakthrough of the 'Third Way' ideology in the social-democratic PvdA had created a common ground between them and the conservative-liberal VVD. This common ground encompassed a drastic liberalisation and flexibilisation of the Dutch economy and labour market, with the professed aim of stimulating economic growth and job creation, which, in turn, was supposed to boost the tax revenues and social premiums necessary to sustain the Dutch welfare state. A vital part of this political programme was a partial dismantling of corporatist socio-economic structures in the Netherlands – the so-called 'Polder model' (Visser and Hemerijck, 1997) – and a reduction of the administrative power of the social partners in the area of social security. While in mainstream economic terms, the Purple coalition cabinet was very successful, with a 3–4% annual real GDP growth and a reduction of unemployment from 8% to 3% in the late 1990s, it generated its own opposition.

This opposition to the Purple cabinet's socio-economic policies was strongest among the low- and lower-middle-income groups, who experienced growing insecurity as a result of the flexibilisation of the labour market and felt that their interests were insufficiently represented in the political arena as a result of the partial dismantling of the Polder model. From the late 1990s, the uprising of the low- and lower-middle-income groups against flexibilisation and deregulation manifested itself via three channels.

First, when the social-democratic PvdA embraced and implemented Third Way socio-economic policies in the mid-1990s, more and more of its voters switched allegiance to the new Socialist Party (SP), which adheres to an orthodox socialist ideology of state intervention and is very active at the local and regional level in all sorts of social projects. Between 1994 and 2006, its share of the electorate grew from 1% to 17% in parliamentary elections (Parlement, 2015). Although the SP has never been part of a government coalition, in the 2000s, its presence on the left wing of the social-democratic PvdA forced the latter to gradually abandon its Third Way policy preferences.

Second, in 2001–02, with a political agenda that, besides anti-Islamic rhetoric, included a reversal of many of the Purple cabinet's reforms, Pim Fortuyn succeeded in mobilising voters among the low- and lower-middle-income groups, who had voted up till then for the PvdA or not at all. Fortuyn, who was assassinated 10 days before the 2002 parliamentary elections, posthumously got 17% of the vote in the elections. The PVV, the political party of Fortuyn's ideological successor, Geert Wilders, copied Fortuyn's anti-Islamic rhetoric, but initially adhered to a right-wing socio-economic agenda. In 2009, however, the party suddenly changed tack and in its new political programme, opposed further retrenchment of the welfare state and flexibilisation of the Dutch labour market. In the 2010 parliamentary election, this then uncommon combination of right- and left-wing political views won Wilders's party 15% of the vote (Parlement, 2015).

Third, the partial dismantling of the Polder model in the late 1990s and early 2000s caused a crisis in the Dutch labour movement, especially in the largest trade union (FNV), which represents about two thirds of trade union membership (15% of Dutch citizens over 18 years of age) in the Netherlands.[10] While, from the mid-1990s, the FNV was less and less consulted by the government on socio-economic issues, until the mid-2000s, it nevertheless continued a moderate and cooperative approach, which had characterised the Dutch labour movement since the establishment of corporatist socio-economic structures in the Netherlands in the 1930s (Van Bottenburg, 1995; Hoogenboom, 2004). Internally, however, this moderate approach and the unwillingness of the union leadership to employ more activist strategies met with more and more opposition, especially from the growing number of SP members, who had obtained leading positions within the sectoral branches of the FNV since the late 1990s. When, in 2009, the FNV leadership agreed to a government plan to increase the retirement age from 65 to 67 years, it was toppled and replaced by new leaders who sought a democratisation of the trade union and more activist strategies.

Radical reform plans blocked

After 2010, the three developments described earlier reached their peak and, combined, put a brake on any plans to further reform unemployment provision and the job protection system substantially. The first government coalition to experience this new reality was the Rutte I government, composed of the Christian-democratic CDA and the conservative-liberal VVD, which took office after the 2010 parliamentary elections. Since the two political parties did not command an absolute majority in both houses of Parliament, they had to seek support from a third party, the PVV.[11] As already mentioned, on socio-economic issues, the PVV claims to defend the interests of 'hard-working people', who had been hit hard by welfare state reforms during the past two decades. Therefore, Wilders's party opposed any new welfare state reforms in its negotiations with the VVD and CDA on support for the new government.[12] As a result, the Rutte I government did not enact any major reform in job protection or unemployment provision, with one exception. While its predecessor, the Balkenende IV government, had kept the ALMP budgets more or less stable in absolute terms (see Figure 7.3),[13] the Rutte I government parties and the PVV decided to confine activation in social assistance (WWB) to 'vulnerable groups' and to more than half the number of activation projects in unemployment provision (WW) (Parlement, 2010a, 2010b; for the 2012 budget, see Staten Generaal, 2011–12). In practice, this meant that the total spending on ALMPs was cut by about a third during 2010–12 (see Figure 7.3). In its coalition agreement, the Rutte I government also proposed to follow the advice of the De Vries Committee and to merge social assistance with benefit schemes for unemployed young people, people with physical disabilities and people with learning difficulties or learning disabilities at the minimum level (see earlier). In spring 2012, however, barely one-and-a-half years after its installation, the Rutte I government fell because the three parties could not reach agreement on new cuts in the government budget that were deemed necessary to comply with EMU rules.

After the fall of the Rutte I government and new elections, a new government coalition was formed in autumn 2012 – the Rutte II government – composed of the conservative-liberal VVD and the social-democratic PvdA. Initially, it seemed that the new government was going to enact far-reaching reforms in both unemployment provision and job protection. As to unemployment provision, the Rutte II government also sought a merger of various benefit schemes at the minimum level, with extra cuts in ALMP budgets, while it proposed a drastic reduction of the benefit duration of unemployment insurance. If accepted by Parliament, as of 2014, unemployment insurance (WW) benefit recipients would receive only a wage-related benefit for a maximum of one year (formerly 38 months), after which they could apply for an extra non-means-tested benefit at the minimum level for one year. Employment protection law was also to be revised. The route via the cantonal judge (see earlier) was to be abolished and the 'golden handshake' in case of unjustified dismissal was to be limited to half a month's salary per working year, up to a maximum of €75,000. In addition, the employer would have to pay for a special 'participation budget', which could be used to finance reintegration activities (Parlement, 2012).

However, the social-democratic PvdA, in particular, was eager to find support for the government's reform plans among the trade unions, especially the FNV and its grass-roots support, which is partially allied to the SP (see earlier). Therefore, in spring 2013, the government started negotiations with the social partners, which resulted in the signing of a national Social Agreement a few months later. While, after years of disagreement between the social partners and successive government coalitions, the signing of the agreement in itself was unexpected, its content was even more of a surprise. In exchange for the support of the social partners for its retrenchment policies in other domains, the government accepted a far-reaching revision of its plans on unemployment provision. Furthermore, with regard to labour contract law and the administration of unemployment insurance and ALMPs, the Social Agreement signified a clean break with government policies of the previous two decades.

Moderate change: labour contract law

In the 1990s and early 2000s, successive government coalitions had tried to make the Dutch labour market more flexible by legalising new sorts of temporary and flexible types of labour contract, resulting in rapidly growing numbers of temporary and part-time workers and self-employed workers without employees (De Beer, 2011). In the late 1990s, this development was regulated – and, at the same time, new controversial contract types legalised – by the introduction of the 'Flex Act', which, among other things, stated that an employer should offer an employee a permanent labour contract after three successive temporary contracts with less than three months between the contracts. While the new Act gave some types of flexible workers more security in the 2000s, it did not stop the growth of the number of precarious jobs, to the dismay of the trade unions.

In the Social Agreement signed by the government and social partners in 2013, it was agreed that further flexibilisation of the Dutch labour market was undesirable and that part of existing labour contract law should be revised. The government and social partners agreed to revise the Flex Act in such a way that employers would have to offer an employee a permanent labour contract after two years of employment or three temporary labour contracts with less than six (instead of three) months between them. Furthermore, some types of flexible labour contracts would be disallowed, like the so-called 'zero-hours contracts' in health care, which allowed health-care employers to unilaterally decide how many hours an employee should work in a certain period (SZW, 2013).

Moderate change: (administration of) unemployment insurance and active labour market policies

In addition to labour contract reform, the government also accepted a change of its original plans concerning unemployment insurance (WW). The government and the social partners agreed that the duration of the wage-related benefit would shortened not be to a maximum of one year, as the Rutte II government had planned, but to two years. In addition, the social partners would be allowed to agree on an extra benefit year in their branch collective agreements, which would under normal circumstances be declared legally binding for all employees in the branch by the minister of social affairs. Interestingly, this extra benefit year would be administered not by the state agency UWV, but by the social partners themselves. Moreover, it was also agreed that the nationalisation of the administration of employee insurance – which had been in the hands of the social partners between 1901 and 2002 – would be gradually reversed. As from 2020, the social partners will again become responsible for the administration of *all* employee insurance against unemployment, sickness and disability.

A similar reversal of past reforms was agreed concerning the administration of ALMPs. While the social partners had been gradually stripped of all responsibilities for ALMPs in the late 1990s and early 2000s, in the Social Agreement of 2013, the government accepted that, together with the municipalities and the state agency UWV, the social partners would participate in 35 future regional 'Work Companies'. These Work Companies will be entrusted with the placement of clients of a new benefit scheme, which will result from the merger of social assistance (WWB) with benefit schemes for unemployed young people, people with physical disabilities and people with learning disabilities or learning difficulties at the minimum level (see earlier) in the so-called 'Participation Act', which is largely modelled after the De Vries Committee plan (see earlier). Under the Act, the Work Companies will negotiate with employers over the employment of individual benefit recipients, supervised by a work coach paid by the Work Companies. If the earning capacity of the recipient is estimated by the Work Company and the employer at a certain percentage below the minimum wage level, the Work Company will compensate for that percentage by paying the employer a temporary wage subsidy. To make the Participation Act work, in the Social Agreement, the employers' associations promised that in the period 2014–26, the employers will create at least 125,000 jobs for Participation Act recipients in their companies, 100,000 in the private sector and 25,000 in the public sector.

In the two years following the Social Agreement, most of the policy reforms that the government and the social partners agreed on have been made into law. In the first half of 2014, both chambers of Parliament accepted the Work and Security Act, in which the reforms of unemployment insurance, job protection and labour contract law were clustered (Staatsblad van het Koninkrijk der Nederlanden, 2014a). In the same period, Parliament approved the Participation Act, which deals with the merger of social assistance (WWB) and benefit schemes for unemployed young people, people with physical disabilities and people with learning difficulties or learning disabilities at the minimum level (Staatsblad van het Koninkrijk der Nederlanden, 2014b).

Conclusion

In this chapter, the consequences of the financial and economic crisis for the economy and the welfare state in the Netherlands have been described and analysed, paying particular attention to unemployment benefit provision, ALMPs and job protection. From the analysis, two conclusions can be drawn.

The first conclusion is that the consequences of the far-reaching retrenchment programmes of successive Dutch governments since 2008 aimed at reducing the government budget have been limited for the unemployment system. Despite far-reaching plans to retrench unemployment insurance substantially, the system has largely survived the crisis. Indeed, in the crisis period, social assistance was reformed thoroughly, but these reforms were already planned before the crisis. Only the severe cuts in the ALMP budgets for unemployment insurance and social assistance can be linked to the crisis. In this chapter, it has been claimed that the virtual absence of reforms in the unemployment provision and job protection systems in the Netherlands during the crisis can be explained by a silent uprising of the low- and lower-middle-income groups. These groups resisted any further reforms in what Häusermann (2011) has called 'industrial social policy instruments', that is, reforms in social insurance, job and income protection. Their resistance manifested itself via two new political parties – the PVV on the Right and the SP on the Left of the political spectrum – and the main trade union, the FNV. In the period 2010–15, the growing influence of the three organisations put a brake on any plans to further reform the unemployment provision and job protection systems substantially. In 2010–12, Wilders's PVV prevented the minority Rutte I government from proposing such reforms by making its support for the government coalition dependent on rejection of any such plans. Since 2012, the social-democratic PvdA in the Rutte II government has been very reluctant to propose new reforms out of fear of losing the support of the trade unions and losing voters to the SP.

The second conclusion of the analysis in this chapter is that, in the crisis, reforms of ALMPs virtually meant the end of activation in the Netherlands. However, again, this development was only partially linked to the crisis itself. While the Netherlands had been one of the pioneering countries in the development of activation policies in the 1990s, already in the mid-2000s, some politicians and experts reached the conclusion that activation – a combination of 'incentive reinforcement and employment assistance' (Bonoli, 2010: 450) – was ineffective and too expensive (Hoogenboom, 2011). Just before the crisis, a government committee came up with an alternative for activation in social assistance: instead of offering benefit recipients all sorts of education and job-search assistance, they should be employed as soon as possible, if necessary, with the aid of job coaches and wage subsidies. During the crisis, this proposal was implemented, but with severe cuts in activation budgets, which the government committee had intended to be used for job coaching. Consequently, between 2008 and 2014, the average sum spent on activation per social assistance benefit recipient fell by almost 70% (see Figure 7.4). During the crisis, the budget for the activation of unemployment insurance

Figure 7.4: Activation budgets of social assistance and unemployment insurance: average spending per recipient (€), 2007–15

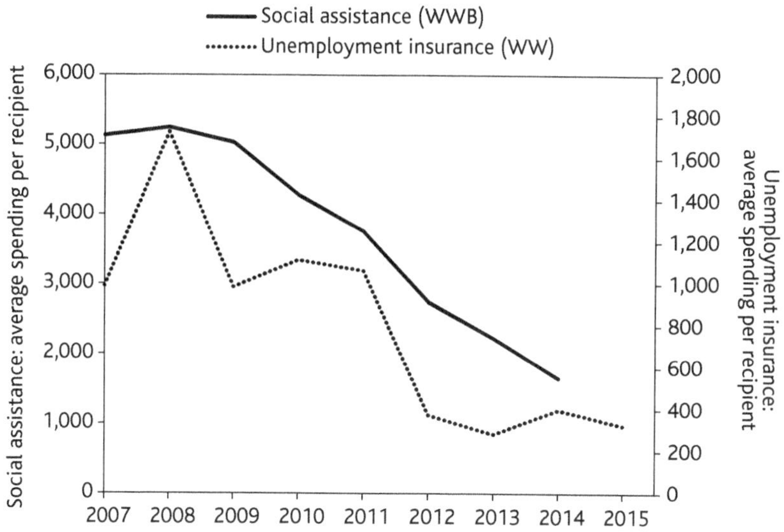

Source: Author's calculations based on the budget plans of the Ministry of Social Affairs and Employment

benefit recipients was even more severely cut, by more than 75%. In 2010, it was even decided that after 2012, no WW benefit recipient would be offered an individual activation trajectory anymore.

However, while the drastic cuts in the social assistance and unemployment insurance activation budgets seem to signify the end of an ALMP paradigm that has been dominant in the Netherlands for almost two decades, the contours of a new ALMP paradigm are emerging. In this new paradigm – which could be dubbed 'deficiency compensation' – ALMPs are directed no longer at solving individual skill deficiencies by means of training and education programmes (as in activation), but at accepting and financially compensating these deficiencies. This shift is most clearly visible in social assistance, where long-term benefit recipients are treated on a par with persons with physical disabilities and persons with learning difficulties or disabilities. In the 1990s and 2000s, large sums were spent by government agencies on programmes that should help social assistance clients to acquire the skills that are needed in a 'post-industrial economy'. Now, their lack of these skills is accepted, as is the notion that these persons will probably never be able to completely earn their own living. However, what is not accepted is the notion that these persons will never *work* again. 'In their own interest' and in the interest of society, they are forced to work, while their lack of skills is compensated by paying wage subsidies to employers who are willing to employ these persons. With this new approach, the Netherlands seems to be once again, as it was in the 1990s with activation policies, a pioneer in the development of a new ALMP paradigm.

Notes

1. In 2007, ABN-Amro had been bought by a consortium of three European banks (Royal Bank of Scotland, Fortis and Banco Santander) and subsequently split up. In October 2008, the Dutch state bought all Fortis activities in the Netherlands (which, in 2007, had acquired all ABN-Amro activities in Belgium and the Netherlands) and merged them into a new ABN holding (see Smit, 2008).
2. Data from: www.statline.nl (accessed 6 November 2016).
3. This was called the 'Zalm Doctrine' after the minister of finance who introduced it in the 1990s.
4. Until 1987, there was a third tier. After the benefits period expired, unemployment insurance (*Werkloosheidswet* [WW]) recipients and most other unemployed who were ineligible for the WW for lack of a substantial labour history could claim unemployment assistance (*Wet Werkloosheidsvoorziening* [WWV]). The WWV, which was administered by the municipalities, guaranteed a non-means-tested benefit of 75% of their daily pay for a period of up to two years, financed out of general taxes (Hoogenboom, 2011).
5. Within social assistance there was a special scheme for unemployed workers (*Rijksgroepsregeling Werkloze Werknemers* [RWW]), with separate administrative procedures and a benefit that was slightly more generous than the social assistance benefit for non-workers (for details, see Hoogenboom, 2011).
6. Data from: www.statline.nl (accessed 24 February 2015).
7. If an employer requested a benefit for less than 30% of the personnel, the maximum benefit duration was 65 weeks. This period was 52 weeks in the case of 30–60% and 39 weeks in the case of more than 60% of the personnel (Chkalova, 2010).
8. First two figures from UWV (2011: 11); last figure from Staten Generaal (2010–11: 4).
9. In its report, Working Group 10 (unemployment insurance and job protection) presented a number of variants; the variant presented in the

text is the working group's 'basic variant' (10.B) and its basic proposal for the job protection system.

10. Data from: www.statline.nl (accessed 10 March 2015).

11. The VVD, CDA and PVV commanded a majority in the (most important) Second Chamber of Parliament, but not in the Senate. To achieve a majority in the Senate, the three parties signed an agreement with the Orthodox Protestants (SGP).

12. For the PVV's ideas, see: www.pvv.nl

13. In its budget plans for 2010–12, the Balkenende IV government proposed to cut almost €400 million of activation in social assistance (WWB) and €100 million in unemployment insurance (WW) (combined, the proposed cuts would come down to about 10% of total spending on ALMP); in real terms (not per benefit recipient), it had raised the total ALMP budget by about 20% (on the proposed cuts, see Staten Generaal, 2009–10; on real spending, see Figure 7.3).

References

Bannink, D. (2004) *The reform of Dutch disability insurance*, Enschede: University of Twente.

Bonoli, G. (2010) 'The political economy of active labor-market policy', *Politics & Society*, 38: 435–57.

Centraal Planbureau (CPB) (2008) 'De kredietcrisis en de Nederlandse economie'. Available at: www.cpb.nl/publicatie/de-kredietcrisis-en-de-nederlandse-economie-acht-frequently-asked-questions (accessed 24 February 2015).

Chkalova, K. (2010) 'Deeltijd-WW in beeld'. Available at: www.cbs.nl/NR/rdonlyres/696D113D-38F4-488B-BB09-54FABF1FB906/0/2010k3v4p15art.pdf (accessed 24 February 2015).

Claessen, J. and Nieuweboer, J. (2012) 'Bedrijfsopleidingen 2010'. Available at: www.cbs.nl/NR/rdonlyres/E6551CA1-9A95-4243-AAE4-3586FB5A2496/0/2012k3v4p52art.pdf (accessed 24 February 2015).

Clasen, J. and Clegg, D. (2006) 'Beyond activation: reforming European employment protection systems in post-industrial labour markets', *European Societies*, 8(4): 527–53.

Clasen, J. and Clegg, D. (eds) (2011a) *Regulating the risk of unemployment: National adaptations to post-industrial labour markets in Europe*, Oxford: Oxford University Press.

Clasen, J. and Clegg, D. (2011b) 'Unemployment protection and labour market change in Europe: towards "triple integration"?', in J. Clasen and D. Clegg (eds) *Regulating the risk of unemployment*, Oxford: Oxford University Press, pp 1–12.

Commissie de Vries (2009) 'Werken naar vermogen: Advies van de commissie fundamentele herbezinning Wsw', Available at: https://zoek.officielebekendmakingen.nl/kst-29817-40-b1.pdf (accessed 27 February 2015).

De Beer, P. (ed) (2011) *Flexibilisering: De balans opgemaakt*, Amsterdam: De Burght.

De Groot, N., Friperson, R., Weda, J. and De Jong, P. (2012) *Werkt werktijdverkorting? Evaluatie bijzondere werktijdverkorting en deeltijd-WW*, The Hague: APE.

Dekker, F. (2010) 'Ontslagrecht in het Koninkrijk der Nederlanden (1)', *Arbeidsrechtelijke Annotaties*, 9(2): 1–24.

Den Butter, F. (2009) 'Bezuinigingsdrift als antwoord op bankiersgekte: Het crisisbeleid van het kabinet Balkenende IV', *Tijdschrift voor Openbare Financiën*, 41(5): 244–65.

Häusermann, S. (2011) 'Post-industrial social policy reforms in continental Europe: what role for social partners?', contribution prepared for presentation at the 18th Conference of Europeanists, Barcelona, Spain, 20–22 June.

Hoogenboom, M. (2004) *Standenstrijd en zekerheid: Een geschiedenis van oude orde en sociale zorg in Nederland*, Amsterdam: Boom.

Hoogenboom, M. (2011) 'The Netherlands: two tiers for all', in J. Clasen and D. Clegg (eds) *Regulating the risk of unemployment*, Oxford: Oxford University Press, pp 75–99.

Inspectie der Rijksfinanciën (2009a) 'Rapport brede heroverwegingen. 9. Op afstand van de arbeidsmarkt'. Available at: www.rijksoverheid.nl/onderwerpen/evaluaties-van-beleid/documenten-en-publicaties/rapporten/2010/04/01/9-op-afstand-van-de-arbeidsmarkt.html (accessed 27 February 2015).

Inspectie der Rijksfinanciën (2009b) 'Rapport brede heroverwegingen. 10. Werkloosheid'. Available at: www.rijksoverheid.nl/onderwerpen/evaluaties-van-beleid/documenten-en-publicaties/rapporten/2010/04/01/10-werkloosheid.html (accessed 27 February 2015).

Inspectie der Rijksfinanciën (2010) 'Brede heroverwegingen 10. Werkloosheid'. Available at: https://zoek.officielebekendmakingen.nl/blg-59842.pdf (accessed 29 November 2017).

OECD (Organisation for Economic Co-operation and Development) (2007) 'Activating the unemployed: what countries do', p 233. Available at: www.oecd.org/els/emp/40777063.pdf (accessed 28 February 2015).
Parlement (2010a) 'Vrijheid en verantwoordelijkheid. Concept Regeerakkoord VVD-CDA'. Available at: www.parlement.com/9291000/d/pdfs/regeer2010.pdf (accessed 1 March 2015).
Parlement (2010b) 'Concept Gedoogakkoord VVD-PVV-CDA'. Available at: www.parlement.com/9291000/d/pdfs/gedoog2010.pdf (accessed 1 March 2015).
Parlement (2012) 'Bruggen slaan: Regeerakkoord VVD – PvdA'. Available at: www.parlement.com/9291000/d/regeerakkoord2012.pdf (accessed 1 March 2015).
Parlement (2015) 'Verkiezingen Tweede Kamer 1918–2012'. Available at: www.parlement.com/id/vh8lnhrpmxux/verkiezingen_tweede_kamer_1918_2012 (accessed 17 March 2015).
Research voor Beleid (2011) *Samen in actie: Evaluatie Actieplan Jeugdwerkloosheid*, Eindrapport, Den Haag: Research voor Beleid.
Smit, J. (2008) *De prooi: Blinde trots breekt ABN Amro*, Amsterdam: Prometheus.
Staatsblad van het Koninkrijk der Nederlanden (2014a) 'Wet van 14 juni 2014 tot wijziging van verschillende wetten in verband met de hervorming van het ontslagrecht, wijziging van de rechtspositie van flexwerkers en wijziging van verschillende wetten in verband met het aanpassen van de Werkloosheidswet, het verruimen van de openstelling van de Wet inkomensvoorziening oudere werklozen en de beperking van de toegang tot de Wet inkomensvoorziening oudere en gedeeltelijk arbeidsongeschikte werkloze werknemers (Wet werk en zekerheid)', No. 216.
Staatsblad van het Koninkrijk der Nederlanden (2014b) 'Wet van 2 juli 2014 tot wijziging van de Wet werk en bijstand, de Wet sociale werkvoorziening, de Wet werk en arbeidsondersteuning jonggehandicapten en enige andere wetten gericht op bevordering deelname aan de arbeidsmarkt voor mensen met arbeidsvermogen en harmonisatie van deze regelingen (Invoeringswet Participatiewet)', No. 270.
Staten Generaal (2009–10), *Handelingen der Staten Generaal*, II, 2009–2010, 32123 XV, No. 2.
Staten Generaal (2010–11) *Handelingen der Staten Generaal*, II, 2010–2011, II, 32710 XV, No. 7.
Staten Generaal (2011–12) *Handelingen der Staten Generaal*, II, 2011–2012, 33000 XV, No. 2.

SZW (Ministerie van Sociale Zaken en Werkgelegenheid) (2013) 'Kamerbrief resultaten sociaal overleg', 11 April, No. 2013-0000045997. Available at: https://www.rijksoverheid.nl/documenten/kamerstukken/2013/04/11/kamerbrief-resultaten-sociaal-overleg (accessed 10 March 2015).

Teulings, C., Van der Veen, R. and Trommel, W. (1997) *Dilemma's van sociale zekerheid. Een analyse van 10 jaar herziening van het stelsel van sociale zekerheid*, Amsterdam: VUGA.

UWV (*Uitvoeringsorgaan Werknemersverzekeringen*) (2011) *Jaarverslag 2010*, Amsterdam: UWV.

Van Bottenburg, M. (1995) *'Aan den arbeid': In de wandelgangen van de Stichting van de Arbeid 1945–1995*, Amsterdam: Bert Bakker.

Van der Veen, R. and Trommel, W. (1999) 'Managed liberalization of the Dutch welfare state: a review and analysis of the reform of the Dutch social security system, 1985–1998', *Governance*, 12(3): 289–310.

Van Gerven, M. (2008) *The broad tracks of path dependent benefit reform: A longitudinal study of social benefit reforms in three European countries, 1980–2006*, Amsterdam: AIAS.

Van Gestel, N., De Beer, P. and Van der Meer, M. (2009) *Het hervormingsmoeras van de verzorgingsstaat: Veranderingen in de organisatie van de sociale zekerheid*, Amsterdam: Amsterdam University Press.

Visser, J. and Hemerijck, A. (1997) *A Dutch miracle: Job growth, welfare reform and corporatism in the Netherlands*, Amsterdam: Amsterdam University Press.

EIGHT

Dualising the Swedish model: insiders and outsiders and labour market policy reform in Sweden: an overview

Johan Bo Davidsson

Introduction

What was widely regarded as the 'Swedish model' of labour market policy no longer exists. However, it is not the fault of fiscal austerity imposed by the European Union (EU). Rather, it is the product of a long series of reforms that began with another economic crisis: the Swedish financial crisis of the early 1990s. The recurring budget deficits and the growing debt that it produced forced cutbacks in the welfare system, and the unyielding and high levels of unemployment opened the door to labour market reform. These reforms put Swedish labour market policy on a new trajectory more in line with international trends, in particular, with efforts to spur job growth in the low-skill segment of the labour market.

For many decades, it seemed that the Swedish model was immune to change. Welfare scholars saw in Sweden a paragon of an equal society based on a generous welfare state that had withstood the pressures of globalisation. While it is true that some welfare institutions are still intact, that is no longer the case in labour market policy.

This chapter traces labour market reforms in Sweden over the past two decades or so and attempts to answer the questions posed by the present volume: what areas of labour market policy have been retrenched, in what way and who bears the burden of reform?[1] The pattern suggested here is one in which labour market outsiders have borne the brunt of reforms. This can be seen in the manner in which labour market flexibility was introduced, in the fact that many of the unemployed now stand outside the social insurance system, in the declining value of social assistance benefits and, perhaps most strikingly, in the radical cuts to spending on active labour market policy. Taken together, and at odds with the literature (eg Iversen, 2009; Palier and Thelen, 2010; Pontusson, 2011), these reforms have put Sweden on a path towards labour market 'dualisation' (Davidsson and Naczyk, 2009; Emmenegger et al, 2012).

Politically, a range of forces have been in play. The Social Democrats, hamstrung by the tight economic conditions and high unemployment that followed the crisis of the early 1990s, conceded budget cuts, but also actively pursued labour market reform. Unions accepted the liberalisation of temporary employment, but were on the sidelines with regard to reforms of income protection and active labour market policy. The Conservatives actively promoted a new direction for labour market policy; the 2006 election was won on a platform of tax cuts financed by radical cuts to unemployment and sickness benefits, moving Sweden closer to the liberal welfare states.

The development of Swedish labour market policy also echoes broader trends in economic reform. The turn towards activation and the promotion of job growth in the low-productivity service sector form the backdrop against which labour market reforms were conceived and designed.

The chapter is structured as follows. In the second section, I describe the development of labour market reform in Sweden from the 1990s onwards under a number of categories: job protection legislation, income protection and active labour market policy. In the third section, I briefly discuss the EU fiscal crisis in 2008 and its (non-)impact on labour market policy in Sweden. A final section concludes.

Labour market policy reform from the 1990s and onwards

Background

The Swedish model refers, on the one hand, to the universal welfare state and, on the other, to the broader economic model associated with the two trade union economists Gösta Rehn and Rudolf Meidner (Erixon, 2008; Anxo and Niklasson, 2006). The peak of the Swedish model, in relation to both definitions, was reached somewhere in the 1970s or 1980s, with the large expansion of the public sector and social insurance, active labour market policy, and centralised wage bargaining. I will use the term 'Swedish model' to refer to the wage policy and active labour market policy of the Rehn–Meidner model and the income protection provided by the universal welfare state.

Although parts of this Swedish model have had a lasting influence abroad – most importantly, the focus on activating those out of work – it was built on a different set of policy complementarities from those favoured by international organisations today. The fundamental idea was to achieve both equality and growth by seeking to put as high a share of the workforce as possible in high-productivity jobs. This was supposed to be achieved, on the one hand, by using the wage bargaining system to make low-productivity jobs unprofitable and, on the other, by investing in active labour market policy to raise skill levels among the unemployed. Income protection, part of the universal welfare state, was regarded as a complement to flexible labour markets: transition to jobs in new sectors or moving to another part of the country would be more easily accepted if economic security was guaranteed.

The Swedish model was formed in the context of full employment. Current models, however, have emerged out of an economy afflicted by high and persistent levels of unemployment. In Sweden, the economic crisis of the early 1990s formed the background to the reforms. The sharply rising budget deficits and public debt were addressed with cutbacks in the welfare system and the high levels of unemployment opened the door for new ideas to get a foothold. The earlier social-democratic strategy of using the public sector to expand low-skill employment was, in the context of economic crisis, no longer an option (Iversen and Wren, 1998; Wren et al, 2013). Instead, policymakers looked to solutions that moved in the direction of promoting low-skill work in the private service sector.

In this context, job growth has become more important than structural transformation towards high-productivity jobs, and job growth has been understood to occur primarily in the low-productivity segments of the economy. This requires social policy that works in tandem with wage flexibility. While active labour market policy is still strongly promoted, its main function is activation, not upskilling. Therefore, the policy complementarities now advocated often combine labour market flexibility, activation and cuts in income protection (see, eg, Bassanini and Duval, 2006).

This development coincides with new patterns of welfare reform in Europe. While job protection and income protection have often been retained for labour market insiders, outsiders have been more affected by demands for increasing flexibility. In the welfare state literature, this type of reform has been labelled 'dualisation' (Davidsson and Naczyk, 2009; Emmenegger et al, 2012) and describes developments primarily in continental Europe. I will show that Sweden has also followed this reform trajectory.

Job protection in legislation and collective agreements

In most European countries, job protection was introduced or expanded during the 1970s (Emmenegger, 2014). This was also the case in Sweden. However, in Sweden, it represented perhaps a clearer break with earlier policies and the Rehn–Meidner model. The Swedish model of industrial relations was previously built on the principle of delegating labour market reforms to unions and employers, and was dependent on the good relationship that had been formed with the Saltsjöbaden Agreement in 1938 (Nycander, 2008). During this period, reforms in the area of job protection were arrived at through collective bargaining, rather than through legislation.

This model worked well but was incapable of solving the issue of job protection. The unions had been calling for stricter regulations on hiring and firing in the central collective agreement between the employers and the unions since the mid-1960s (Hamskär and Gustafsson, 2010). However, they were met by resistance from the employers. The unions then decided to break with the collective bargaining model and pushed the government to legislate on the issue.

From the point of view of the Social Democrat government, the introduction of job protection legislation was a response to a review that had highlighted the negative consequences of the Rehn–Meidner model's focus on labour market flexibility for older workers. The committee appointed in 1969 to study the introduction of job protection legislation was instructed to take into consideration the effect of the fast-paced structural transformation of the economy on older workers. It concluded that older workers could be secure only if dismissal protection was introduced (SOU, 1973: 3). The work of the committee resulted in two pieces of legislation: the 1971 law that was directed only at older workers; and the 1974 law that increased job protection for all workers. The latter included a 'last in, first out' principle in dismissal procedures, which made it very difficult to lay off older workers.

The 1974 legislation has been continually debated since its introduction. The employers' organisation and political parties on the Right have regularly called for its removal. At the same time, unions have worked hard to defend it. To be able to do so under increasing pressure for reform, they have accepted an increase in the use of fixed-term contracts, which has, in turn, led to two-tier labour market reforms (Davidsson, 2011; Davidsson and Emmenegger, 2012, 2013).

In Europe, as in Sweden, most countries have followed a pattern of two-tier labour market reform (see Figure 8.1). That is to say,

Figure 8.1: Employment protection legislation – regular and temporary contracts, Sweden, 1985–2013

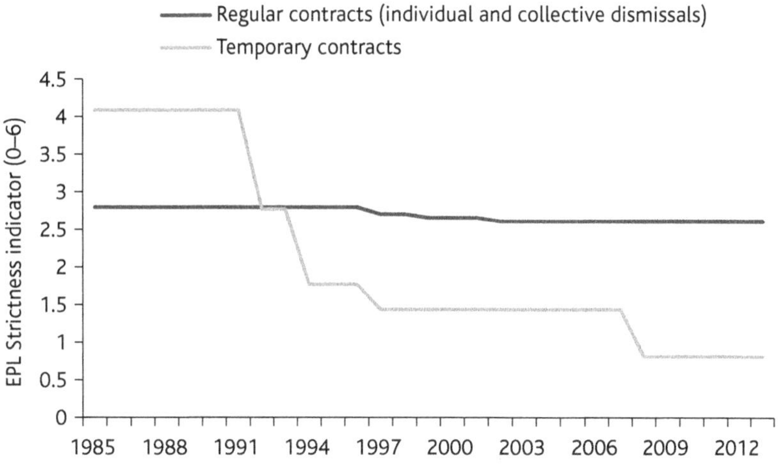

Source: OECD EPL database

the regulation of permanent contracts has remained more or less unchanged whereas the use of fixed-term contracts has been substantially deregulated. Moreover, the start of a trend of deregulation has frequently coincided with an increase in unemployment. Thus, in Continental Europe, the first reforms were introduced in the mid-1980s. In Sweden, where unemployment started to rise later, they were delayed until the 1990s. It is consequently this earlier job crisis that has been the instigator of labour market reforms in Sweden rather than the present EU fiscal crisis.

The background to the reforms was the financial and economic crisis that hit Sweden in the early 1990s. From very low unemployment levels – between 1% and 3.5% from the 1960s to the end of the 1980s – the figures rapidly increased to 11% in 1993 and have remained at a higher level since the crisis, between 6% and 8%. In response to these persistently high levels of unemployment, a number of reforms were introduced to make the labour market more flexible. It should be noted that the push for flexibility was not an immediate response to the crisis, but rather gained momentum as unemployment refused to drop in the years after. This opened the way for new thinking about labour market policy and more openness towards business demands.

Before the crisis, as late as 1990, the Social Democrat government had appointed a committee to review the existing job protection legislation. The directive that set out the task of the committee reflected demands that came from unions, including a reinforcement of the Codetermination Act and increased protection for temporary and part-time work (Dir. 1991:76). However, before the work of the committee resulted in any new legislation, there was a shift in power. After the election of 1991, a Conservative coalition came to office and issued a new directive for the committee based largely on the employers' demands for deregulation of employment protection legislation (Dir. 1991:18). The work of the committee resulted in far-reaching proposals, including the right of the employer to determine which workers to retain during collective dismissals for economic reasons (SOU, 1993: 32). The Bill that the government finally presented to Parliament included more moderate changes. The 'last in, first out' principle was retained, but the employer won the right to exempt two employees from the formal procedures.[2] Furthermore, the maximum duration for temporary employment, and the trial period of employment, was extended from six to 12 months (Prop. 1993/94:67).

Both the employers' organisation and the Conservative Party had wanted to go further, but the more moderate proposal was a result of two factors. First, the Minister of Labour, Börje Hörnlund, represented the Centre Party, which was more moderate at the time with regard to labour market policy and primarily sought changes that would benefit its constituency of small firms, hence the exemption of two employees. Second, there was a fear of union reaction if they attacked the 'last in, first out' principle (Davidsson, 2011).

The reactions from the unions and the Social Democratic Party were strongly critical. However, it was not long before the continually rising levels of unemployment forced the Social Democratic Party to reconsider its position. In a first step, in 1995, the government appointed a commission that aimed at supporting unions and employers in their negotiations on a new agreement on labour market reform. If no headway was made, legislation was presented as an alternative (Davidsson, 2011).

During the negotiations, the positions of the respective social partners were far apart and neither showed much will to compromise. The main employers' organisation (SAF) wanted a more complete liberalisation of job protection legislation. They sought primarily to get rid of the 'last in, first out' principle and/or to extend trial periods for employment. The largest union federation (LO) was strongly critical of any changes to the 'last in, first out' principle and wanted the right for workers to take a leave of absence to try out a new job and increased protection for workers on part-time contracts (Davidsson, 2011).

The combination of an aggressive employers' side and the unions' categorical refusal of any changes in the employment protection for regular workers explains the failure of the negotiations. The key point of discord was the 'last in, first out' principle (Nycander, 2008). As a result, the commission was dissolved during the spring of 1996. Even though the unions and employers were negotiating under the shadow of legislation, little headway was made.

When the failure of both the negotiations and the attempts at mediation became apparent, the Minister of Employment, Ulrica Messing, announced that the government would instead turn to legislation. At the same time, she opened up the possibility of making changes to the 'last in, first out' principle. The announcement created strong tensions within both the LO and the Social Democratic Party. The result was union acceptance of the deregulation of temporary contracts with the protection for permanent contracts upheld. The Bill introduced to parliament (Prop. 1996/97:16) increased the maximum duration of temporary employment to 12 months (limited to five employees per company) and 18 months for first-time hires. Additionally, the new law made it possible for collective agreements concluded at the local level to derogate from legislation. Earlier, such derogation was possible only with the consent of the social partners at the national level.

A decade later, the Conservatives returned to power and declared early on, to the disappointment of the employers' organisation, that they had no intention of introducing any changes to the job protection legislation concerning regular workers – in other words, the 'last in, first out' principle – during the first four years in office; this was a promise made in the election campaign. They did, however, increase the maximum duration of temporary employment to 24 months and removed the requirement for the employer to justify the need for temporary labour (Prop. 2006/07:111).

I have argued elsewhere (Davidsson, 2011; Davidsson and Emmenegger, 2012, 2013) that unions have been key actors in understanding the reform trajectory. Overall, there has been a strong push for deregulation, but unions have resisted any change to the protection of permanent work. They have done so because the protection of permanent work is linked to specific institutional power resources that are important for unions. In the Swedish case, such power resources are to be found in the 'last in, first out' principle. The principle is applied in relation to collective dismissals, where the last person to be employed should be first in consideration for dismissal. However, unions have the right to negotiate exceptions to this principle with the employers' side, a right that increases their power in negotiations. They can, for example, ask for redundancy packages for laid-off workers as compensation. Retaining such regulations that give them power over the long term has been key for unions. Under pressure to reform, they have therefore agreed to deregulate other parts of job protection legislation, most importantly, the regulation of temporary work. This choice has important consequences as those with the weakest position on the labour market face higher risk of job loss in a recession and may be trapped in temporary employment.

While job protection legislation has been important in the Swedish case since the 1970s, we should also highlight the importance of wage bargaining and collective agreements for job protection; note, for example, that some rules regarding fixed-term contracts are laid down in collective agreements, as mentioned earlier. I will briefly sketch three major developments during the period: collective bargaining has been decentralised; union membership is still high, but declining; and collective agreements still have strong coverage.

First, wage bargaining was already decentralised to the sectoral level in the mid-1980s (see, eg, Pontusson and Swenson, 1996). Second, union density has decreased significantly since the early 1990s. Union density in 1990 was 81% of the workforce; by 2013, it had declined to 70% (Kjellberg, 2009, 2014). The major drop in density rates took place in 2007 when the fees for voluntary unemployment insurance, which is administered by the unions, were drastically increased (see later).[3] This particularly affected those with high unemployment risks, who are disproportionately blue-collar workers. While, in 1990, blue-collar workers had a higher union density rate than white-collar workers – 82.2% and 80.5%, respectively (Kjellberg, 2009) – by 2013, the rate for blue-collar workers had dropped below that of white-collar workers, to 66% and 73%, respectively (Kjellberg, 2014). If we look at the sector facing the highest unemployment risks, the private service sector, union density there had declined to 54% by 2013, with hotels and restaurants showing the lowest rates, at 30% (Kjellberg, 2014). Third, the coverage of collective agreements is very high in Sweden and has not declined significantly, despite the drop in union density. This can be explained by the stable density rates of employers' organisations, which have remained at the mid-80% level since the early 1990s. The coverage of collective agreements declined from 94% in 1995 to 89% in 2013. Since everyone in the public sector is covered, the decline has occurred primarily in the private sector, where the corresponding figures are 90% in 1995 and 84% in 2013 (Kjellberg, 2014). Two issues need to be highlighted, however. First, the coverage of collective agreements is lower in sectors of the economy that are growing, such as the private service sector. Second, companies can now join employers' organisations without also joining collective agreements through so-called 'service agreements' (Karlsson and Lindberg, 2010).

In summary, Sweden has moved towards a reform trajectory in the area of job protection legislation where insiders have been privileged and outsiders have had to bear the brunt of reforms. The regulation of permanent workers has been more or less retained while the regulation of temporary workers has been substantially liberalised. We can also see that the reforms have been a side effect of the economic crisis in the early 1990s. When unemployment consistently reached high figures, the pressure to reform increased. When unions were forced to choose what protections to defend, they chose the employment protection for insiders because it was linked to unions' institutional power resources. The reforms in collective bargaining have been more limited, even though job protection can be less strong in sectors without collective agreements and/or weak unions, which are primarily to be found in private services.

Income protection

Unemployment benefits

Three tendencies, in particular, stand out for labour market reforms in the area of unemployment benefits. First, the level of the replacement rate has declined gradually but significantly since the economic crisis of the early 1990s. In turn, this has led to a rise in private supplementary unemployment benefits provided by unions in cooperation with insurance companies. Second, coverage has decreased, especially among the young, due to, on the one hand, stricter qualification requirements and, on the other, the increase in individual fees and the differentiation of fees according to unemployment risk.[4] Third, stricter sanctions have been imposed as part of activation reforms. Taken together, unemployment benefits have also developed such that insiders have enjoyed continued protection (albeit via private insurance) and outsiders face increasing difficulties in gaining access to insurance.

The reason for the decline in replacement rates can be found in the de-indexation from wage increases of the unemployment insurance ceiling, which took place during the crisis years of the early 1990s. The formal replacement rate was only reduced from 90% to 80%, but the de-indexation had much more corrosive effects. From Figure 8.2, we can see that the net replacement rate began a sharp trajectory of

Figure 8.2: Net replacement rates in the unemployment insurance, Sweden and the EU15

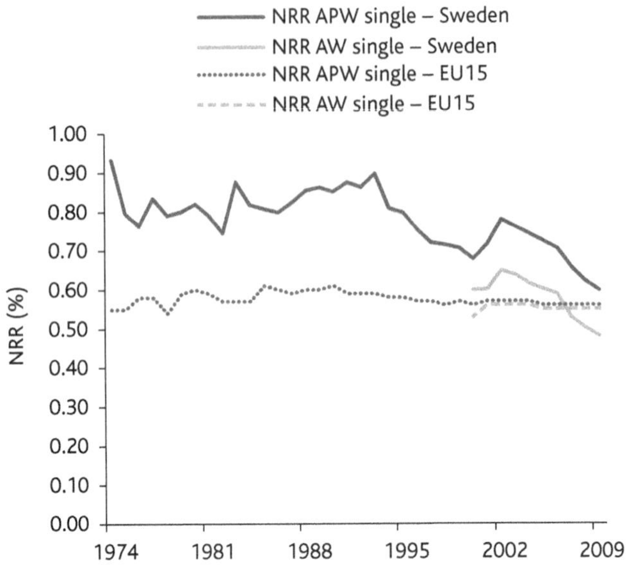

```
                — NRR APW single – Sweden
                  NRR AW single – Sweden
                ······ NRR APW single – EU15
                ----- NRR AW single – EU15
```

Notes: NRR = Net Replacement Rate; APW = Average Production Worker; AW = Average Worker.
Source: Van Vliet and Caminada (2012) 'Unemployment replacement rates dataset'

decline from 1993, shortly after de-indexation was introduced. The ceiling was raised in absolute terms on several occasions, under Social Democratic governments, but the long-term trend of decline in the replacement rate is evident. In recent years, the net replacement rate for an average worker has been below 60% for the 'average production worker', using the old Organisation for Economic Co-operation and Development (OECD) measure, and below 50% using the more recent OECD 'average worker' measure. With regard to net replacement rates, Sweden now performs worse than the EU15 average. Interestingly, continental countries such as France and Germany have kept ceilings high, whereas Sweden is moving in the direction of the flat-rate systems of the Anglo-Saxon world. Whether or not Sweden should be moving in that direction is a highly contested issue in contemporary Swedish political debate.

The Social Democratic governments that followed the Conservative government of the early 1990s did not re-index the ceiling in the insurance, but they did raise it on several occasions. At the end of the 1990s, when the economy had recovered, the issue was taken up in an internal memorandum, but the idea of re-indexing the ceiling was discarded for fiscal reasons (Davidsson, 2011). Instead, the Social

Democratic government increased the level of the ceiling in absolute terms on a number of occasions. The ceiling was raised in 1997, 2001 and 2002. This was the result of very clear policy priorities. The strategy of the Social Democratic Party throughout the post-war years has been to seek the support of the middle classes by providing high-quality services and social insurance that would crowd out private alternatives. They have always had the ambition of maintaining high ceilings, and did raise the ceiling in absolute terms again in the spring budget of 2015. The Conservative government of 2006, in contrast, cut the ceiling in absolute terms. At the time, the minister of labour responded to criticism, voiced most forcefully by unions, by saying that public insurance should serve only as basic security and that it was up to individual workers to top up with private insurance.

The downward trend in net replacement rates also comes through if we look at spending patterns. In Figure 8.3, we can see that the level of spending on unemployment insurance has decreased significantly (see total passive measures). While spending levels followed the rate of unemployment in previous years, it has begun to diverge from it since the mid-2000s. Part of the drop in spending is the lower net replacement rates, discussed here, but the decrease can also be explained partly by the lower levels of insurance coverage that were a result of increased and differentiated fees according to unemployment risks (see later).

In response to the declining quality of public unemployment insurance, private supplementary insurance run by unions in cooperation with insurance companies has emerged (Davidsson, 2014).

Figure 8.3: Spending on passive and active measures, and unemployment (standard scores), Sweden, 1985–2013

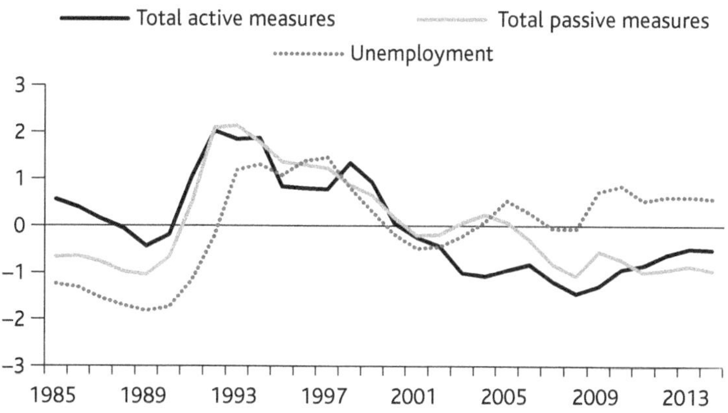

Source: Own calculations from OECD data

The private insurance raises the ceiling and reinstates an 80% net replacement rate. The rise of private insurance began in white-collar unions in the early 2000s and spread to the blue-collar unions after the public insurance ceiling was cut in 2006. Today, almost half of the workforce is covered by private supplementary insurance. However, those unions whose members have high unemployment risks have not been able to provide private supplementary insurance. Some, like the unions for retail workers or the unions for hotel and restaurant workers, decided against setting up private insurance in the first place as costs would have been too high. Others, like the unions for construction or industry workers, tried to set up insurance in 2006 but had to withdraw it in face of mounting costs.

Given the decrease in replacement rates in public insurance, it is easy to come to the conclusion that it was primarily insiders who were hit by the unemployment benefit reforms of the 1990s and 2000s, but that does not take into account that it is still relatively easy for insiders to top up with private insurance. Rather, the long-term effect has been detrimental for outsiders. Workers with high unemployment risks will have difficulties accessing the private supplementary system and the support of insiders for the public system is likely to decrease the more they become dependent on private insurance (cf Korpi and Palme, 1998).

Outsiders have also been hit by other reforms in public unemployment insurance. Two developments have led to a dramatic drop in coverage rates. First, the introduction of differentiated fees according to unemployment risk by the Conservative government in 2006 made outsiders leave (voluntary) unemployment insurance as fees rose dramatically for some workers. Second, since the 1990s, qualification requirements have become stricter, making it harder for workers on insecure contracts to qualify for unemployment benefits.

Differentiated fees in voluntary public unemployment insurance, based on the unemployment risk of the sector in which you work, were introduced in 2007. This reform meant that public unemployment insurance was, in fact, reshaped to mimic the functioning of private insurance. The effect was straightforward. In sectors with high unemployment, such as industry, construction, retail, hotels and restaurants, the fees increased radically. As a result, many abandoned the insurance. The drop in membership in the voluntary unemployment insurance was significant, from 84.4% in 2005 to 69.6% in 2014 (Kjellberg, 2014). In 2006, 80% of those who had registered as unemployed had access to unemployment benefits. In 2011, it had decreased to 40% (SO, 2012).[5] Another study finds a similar trend: up until 2006, the coverage rate was above 70%, but by 2013, the coverage rate had decreased to 41% (Arbetsförmedlingen, 2014). The strong decline in coverage is comparable to what happened in Germany when the Hartz reforms precipitated a decline in the first-tier unemployment benefit – the income-replacing benefit – from above 60% of those registered unemployed in 2005 to below 30% in 2010 (Dingeldey, 2011).

An additional explanation for the fall in coverage, although a less powerful one, is the reforms by both Left and Right governments that have made qualification requirements stricter in unemployment insurance. In 1993, the qualification period was extended from three to four months, in 1995, to five months, and in 1997, to six months. Under current rules, an unemployed person must have worked for six months to be eligible and have been a member of the insurance for 12 months. In addition, since 1996, first-time qualification for the insurance can no longer be achieved through participation in active labour market programmes. Requalification via active labour market programmes has also been impossible since 2001.

Activation in unemployment insurance

The third major change that has taken place in relation to unemployment insurance, besides lower net replacement rates and declining coverage rates, is stricter regulations on suitable employment; in other words, what type of job offers an unemployed person has to accept and stricter sanctions in the case of refusal of job offers. The major reform in this area was introduced by a Social Democratic government in 2001 (Prop. 1999/2000:139). Sanctions were ramped up with the introduction of a 'three-strikes-and-you're-out' system. The first refusal to accept a job offer resulted in a 25% reduction in the benefit (for 40 days), the second refusal in a 50% reduction (for 40 days) and the third in a loss of entitlement. The Conservative government further tightened regulations on suitable employment in 2007 (Prop. 2006/07:89). Previously, it had been possible to limit the job search during the first hundred days according to profession and geographical area, but from 2007, this was no longer possible.[6]

The development towards stronger conditionality in unemployment insurance in Sweden conforms to a more general trend whereby sanctions have become stricter in most countries. Knotz (2016) compares the development of conditionality in selected OECD countries for the period 1980 to 2012, and from his data, we can see that conditionality has increased significantly in Sweden in terms of both suitable employment and sanctions. Indeed, Sweden shows one of the largest changes towards stricter conditionality, together with countries such as Austria, Finland, Germany, Ireland and the UK.

Minimum income benefits

In Sweden, if one does not qualify for social insurance, one may apply for means-tested social benefits. During the 1970s, there were a number of proposals to remove the income test, transforming social assistance into a flat-rate insurance benefit. However, no reforms were carried out that eased eligibility conditions in this regard. An earlier problem had been that benefit levels were set at the local level and varied between municipalities. In 1982, new legislation was introduced that set a national norm concerning benefit levels and how they should be calculated. The norm was constructed to increase with changing price levels. In 1998, this was partly reversed as some of the components that make up the national norm were again to be determined at the local level (Bergmark, 2016).

Overall, social assistance benefits differ from social insurance in that they are not directly related to income. This has meant that their generosity relative to income developments has decreased over time. Bergmark (2016) compared the development of the national norm to the development of disposable income. He found that while disposable income nearly doubled in the period 1985–2014, social assistance benefits remained more or less stagnant. This was due to the choice of indexing. First, price levels increased much more slowly than wage levels. Second, the price index used is only for the basic goods and services that make up the different components in the national norm. Nelson (2013) measures generosity as the benefit share of median disposable income and finds a similar pattern, with a strong decrease in the Nordic countries between 1990 and 2008.

If we look at spending patterns, we can see, first, that they follow the unemployment level to a large degree (see Figure 8.4). Most social assistance recipients also state that the reason they claim benefits is unemployment (Bergmark, 2016). Second, it is difficult to tell from these figures the extent to which the drop in the social insurance coverage rate has affected the number of social assistance recipients. There is an increase after 2006, but that could also be due to the rise in unemployment. It should be noted, however, that the figures before 2012 include social assistance given to recently arrived immigrants whereas the figures from 2012 do not. Third, in relation to the generosity of benefits, it is, of course, telling that we do not

Figure 8.4: Social assistance, spending and household recipient rates, Sweden 1990–2015

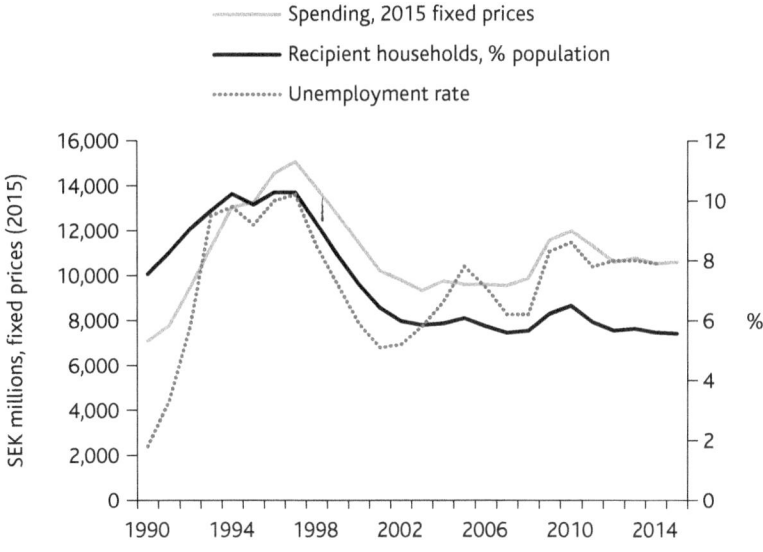

Source: Socialstyrelsen, OECD

see an increase in spending while the economy has been growing and disposable incomes have increased.

To summarise reforms in income protection, while the drop in the net replacement rate could be said to have primarily affected insiders, they could soon take advantage of the emergence of private insurance to top up public unemployment insurance. Outsiders were barred from this because private unemployment insurance was too expensive for groups with a high unemployment risk. The introduction of differentiated fees in unemployment insurance by the Conservative coalition in 2007 hit outsiders more directly and resulted in lower coverage because the policy mimicked the functioning of private insurance, where costs are based on unemployment risk. The result is an unemployment benefit that covers only about 40% of those who are registered as unemployed. For those who are unable to access the social insurance system, the fall in terms of income protection in social assistance has increased as benefit levels have decreased relative to disposable income. We have also seen the introduction of stricter definitions of suitable jobs and stricter sanctions in unemployment insurance.

Active labour market policy

At the same time as activation has been made stricter, spending on active labour market programmes (ALMPs) has been radically cut. Sweden has a long history with regard to ALMPs. As discussed earlier, they were one of the fundamental elements of the Rehn–Meidner model, which governed Swedish labour market policy from the 1950s. ALMPs are also emblematic of the Nordic welfare model, where Denmark has been the most recent case to attract praise internationally for its investment in ALMPs. Few have recognised, however, the rapid decrease in spending in this area in Sweden.[7]

The idea behind the Rehn–Meidner model in the 1950s and 1960s was to support the transformation of Sweden into a high-productivity economy. A key part of this model was a set of policies to upskill workers so that they could fill the increasing demand for jobs in the industry sector. To do this successfully, substantial investments were needed in ALMPs.

From early on, Sweden spent significant amounts on this type of training programme. ALMP expenditure increased from the 1950s on and reached 2% of GDP by the 1970s (Swenson, 2002: 274, cited in Bonoli, 2013: 73). By the 1980s, for which we have available data, Sweden spent more than twice as much as the EU average, measured as a percentage of GDP. Such figures are even more impressive when we recall that Sweden had very low levels of unemployment at the time, below 3%. This was much lower than the unemployment levels in most comparable countries. Figure 8.5 shows that Sweden was also exceptional in a Nordic context.

However, the economic crisis in the 1990s set Sweden on a different path, marked by lower spending on ALMPs. In the first years of the crisis, we can see a sharp increase in spending as unemployment nearly tripled. However, the spending per unemployed person was already decreasing then (Bengtsson, 2014). Thereafter, there is a long downward trend in levels of spending.[8] This cannot be explained by falling unemployment levels as they rose again in the early 2000s after having first declined when the economy picked up following the crisis. By the mid-2000s, we can see that Sweden converges in spending patterns in relation to both the EU15 and the Nordic countries. In recent years, we can again see a smaller increase. The increasing difference with the EU15 disappears, however, if we exclude the euro crisis countries.

This is a striking development. Even more dramatic are the sharper cuts we observe in the training element of labour market programmes,

Figure 8.5: Labour-market programmes, spending on active measures, Sweden, EU15 and Nordic countries, 1985–2015

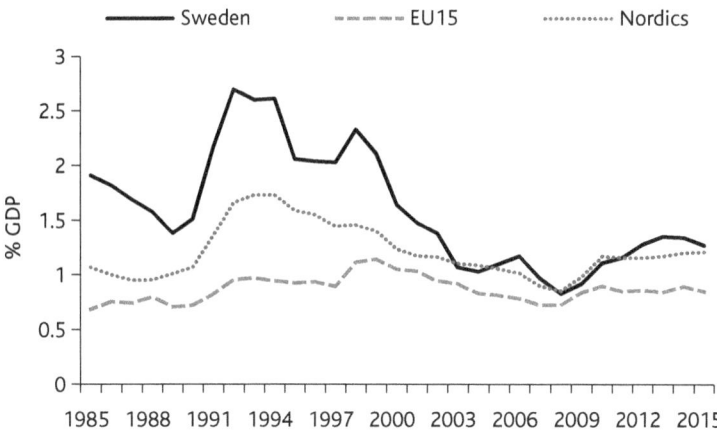

Source: OECD. Nordic figures excluding Iceland

which we can see in Figure 8.6. Training, which was key to the Swedish model and generally seen as the most high-quality policy instrument within ALMPs, has undergone cuts pushing spending levels below the EU15 and Nordic average. There was a spike in the training component in the late 1990s and early 2000s with the introduction of youth guarantees, but they were soon abandoned. Today, Sweden has gone from spending three times the EU15 average in the mid-1980s,

Figure 8.6: Labour market programmes, spending on training, Sweden, EU15 and Nordic countries, 1985–2015

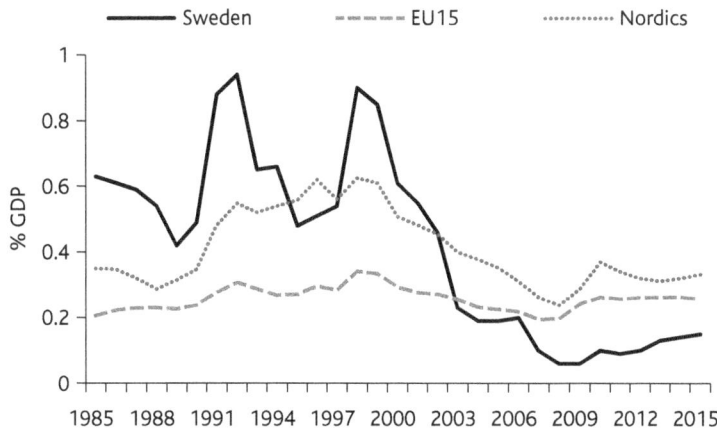

Source: OECD. Nordic figures excluding Iceland

and twice the average of the Nordic countries, to spending – as just mentioned – below both the EU15 and Nordic average.

If we look at the different components that make up the active measure in the OECD statistic on labour market programmes, we can see that while there has been a sharp decline in training, during the same period, there has been an increase in the use of employment incentives (see Figure 8.7). The trend indicates that there has been a move away from supply-side measures that seek to increase the skill levels of the unemployed and thereby increase matching efficiency on the labour market. Instead, demand measures that seek to limit costs to the employer have increased. This is true not only for Sweden, but also more broadly (Bonoli, 2013: 32). This shift in policy is a good fit with new ideas based on theories of skill-biased technological change and job polarisation, which holds that low-skill and high-skill jobs are increasing, combined with a decrease in the demand for jobs in the mid-range skill level (Autor et al, 2003, 2006; Goos and Manning, 2007; Autor, 2010; Acemoglu and Autor, 2012; Autor and Dorn, 2013; for a critique, see Mishel et al, 2013). Hence, instead of upskilling workers, policy aims to compensate the cost of labour in the low-productivity sectors. More in particular for Sweden, we can also see an increase in the number of those with low skills among the unemployed as a result of increasing drop-out rates in secondary

Figure 8.7: Type of active labour market programme spending, Sweden, 1985–2015

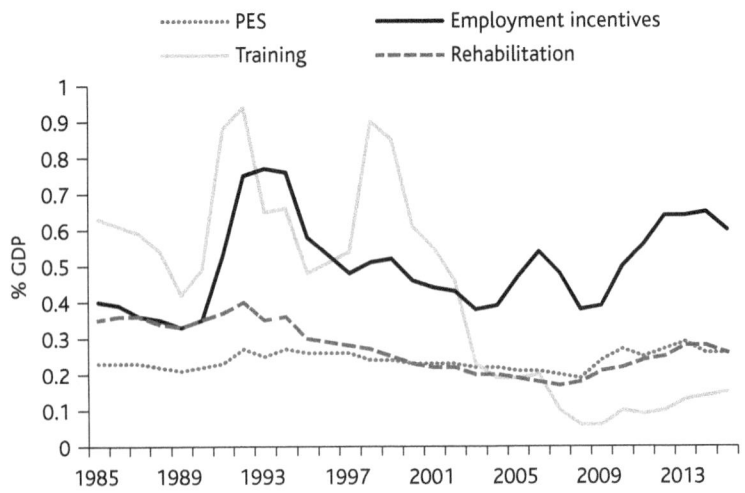

Note: PES = Public Employment Services and Administration
Source: OECD

schools and increased levels of immigration (Arbetsförmedlingen, 2016). This could provide further incentives to policymakers to move to employment subsidies if they view it as a cheaper alternative to training programmes in the context of an increasing share of the unemployed with low skill levels.

In summary, active labour market policy, which was once a defining part of the Swedish model, has been significantly retrenched. Sweden can no longer be said to be a country with strong investment in the unemployed or those in need of reskilling in order to prepare them for changes on the labour market. This is particularly harmful to outsiders, who hold a weaker position within the labour market. They are more likely to be unemployed in the first place and have the most need for upskilling.

Comparative analysis of labour market policies

Looking back on labour market reform in Sweden, the major development we can observe is a slow adjustment to the main international trend in labour market policy, which aims to create policy complementarities for a labour market increasingly geared towards the creation of low-skill jobs. Job security has been reduced through a liberalisation of temporary employment. Lower levels of income protection for labour market outsiders increase the supply of low-wage labour. With regard to activation and active labour market policy, there has been a turn towards stronger conditionality in terms of employment suitability and sanctions, and a shift in spending patterns from a strong focus on training to higher spending on employment incentives. Spending on active measures has decreased on the whole.

In terms of common typologies of labour market policy, these reforms could be said to amount to a new direction with a 'punitive' rather than an 'enabling' character (cf Eichorst and Konle-Seidl, 2008). The shift in spending patterns from training to employment incentives is also noteworthy. Training aims to upgrade skills in order for workers to secure employment in high-productivity sectors, whereas employment incentives subsidise low-skill jobs in high-wage economies. Thus, there seems to be a development under way in which labour market policy becomes more 'punitive' to fit with job creation in the low-skill sectors. This should be considered in conjunction with the sharp increase in the share of young cohorts pursuing university degrees. Taken together, labour market policy, as it is developing in Sweden, may risk reinforcing polarisation. Table 8.1 lists the major reforms discussed in the chapter.

Table 8.1: Major labour market policy reforms in Sweden, 1990–2016

		Income protection			Job protection
1991	(R)	De-indexation of the benefit ceiling			
1993	(R)	Qualification period extended from four to five months. Requalification to a new period of 300 days though ALMPs removed.	1993	(R)	Maximum allowed duration for fixed-term contracts increased from six to 12 months. Temporary agency work is legalised.
1993	(R)	Replacement rate lowered from 90% to 80%, ceiling lowered (SEK598 to SEK564).	1993	(R)	Two exceptions to 'last in, first out'.
1994	(L)	Repeal of the increase in the qualification period.	1994	(L)	Repeal of both the increased maximum duration and the two exceptions.
1995	(L)	Qualification period is extended to five months.			
1996	(L)	First-time qualification can only be done through ordinary work, that is, not from ALMPs			
1996	(L)	Replacement rate is lowered to 75%.			
1997	(L)	Replacement rate is raised from 75% to 80%. Ceiling is raised to SEK580.	1997	(L)	Maximum duration of fixed-term contracts increased to 12 months (18 for first-time hires). Derogation made possible through collective bargaining.
1997	(L)	Qualification period extended to six months.			
2001	(L)	Ceiling is raised: SEK680 first 20 weeks, then SEK580.	2001	(L)	Two exceptions to 'last in, first out'*
2001	(L)	Stricter acceptance requirements. No requalification to passive benefits.			
2002	(L)	Ceiling is raised. SEK730 first 20 weeks, then SEK680.			
2007	(R)	Differentiated fees in the unemployment insurance.	2007	(R)	Maximum duration 24 months. No restrictions on use.
2007	(R)	Stricter qualification requirements.			
2007	(R)	Ceiling lowered to SEK680. Degressive benefits: 80%, 70%, 65%.			
2013	(R)	Repeal of differentiated fees in the unemployment insurance.			
2015	(L)	Ceiling raised to SEK910.			
			2016	(L)	Restrictions on the cumulation of temporary contracts.

Notes: R = right-wing government; L = left-wing government. * The Social Democrats were in minority government in 2001, but the reform was voted through in Parliament by the right-wing parties and the Green Party.

Recent developments: labour market policy and economic crisis

The main theme of this edited volume is whether the pattern of change of labour market policies has changed during the period of fiscal austerity imposed by the EU's fiscal rules. My argument in the case of Sweden is that EU fiscal austerity had very little to do with the major labour market reforms that we have seen. Rather, it was the first economic crisis in the early 1990s, and the fiscal austerity and ideational change that followed it, which triggered a change away from what we previously have come to associate with the Swedish model and the Swedish welfare state in the area of labour market policy.

The explanation for the limited effects of EU fiscal austerity on the Swedish welfare state is straightforward. First, budget deficits were smaller in Sweden compared with most European countries. In 2009, the Swedish budget deficit as a percentage of GDP was 0.7% while the EU average was 6.7%, and the budget deficits have remained below 2% from 2009 up until today. This should be compared with the budget deficits during the economic crisis in the early 1990s, which were above 7% for the years 1992–95. Second, there was a comparatively small rise in unemployment as a result of the crisis. If we compare the years previous to the crisis, the unemployment rate only went up by about 1%, from around 7% to around 8%. While this, of course, increases costs, it is not comparable to the economic crisis in the early 1990s, when there was an increase from below 3% average unemployment to over 10% unemployment.

Almost all of the major reforms discussed earlier were already introduced before the 2008 economic crisis. The Social Democratic governments, faced with budget constraints and high levels of unemployment, responded by retrenching the unemployment benefit system and ALMPs. In order to spur job growth, they also deregulated job security protection for temporary employment and introduced activation measures. The subsequent Conservative governments continued with similar reforms, but also went further, as with the introduction of differentiated fees in the unemployment insurance.

Chung and Thewissen (2011) have argued that Sweden followed a path-dependent trend during the 2008 economic crisis, which they claim follows the tradition of its universal welfare state. This underestimates the quite radical reforms that were put in place after the economic crisis of the early 1990s, as described earlier. The measures that were introduced after 2008 were marginal. They primarily included extra finances for ALMPs and cost reductions of the individual fees for unemployment insurance, as well as the abolition of the work requirement for joining unemployment funds (however, qualification for benefits still depended on 12 months' membership in the fund and six months' work within the past 12-month period). No short-term work schemes were introduced in Sweden, as they were in many of the other continental countries. Rather, unions agreed to temporary layoffs, reductions of working time or wage cuts to save jobs without support from the government.

Conclusion

The overall conclusion is twofold. First, EU-driven fiscal austerity has not had any important effect on the development of labour market policy in Sweden. Rather, it was the financial and economic crisis of the early 1990s that triggered a move away from the Swedish model. The sharp rise in unemployment and large and increasing government deficits led to a cost crisis in which governments from both sides of the partisan divide reduced investments in labour market policy, deregulated job protection legislation and strengthened conditionality measures in the benefit systems.

Second, the burden of retrenchment fell hardest on labour market outsiders. When job protection legislation was reformed, insiders were protected by the unions and deregulation was introduced only with regard to temporary work. While the drop in the net replacement rate could be argued to have primarily affected insiders, they could soon take advantage of the emergence of private insurance to top up the public unemployment insurance. Outsiders were barred from accessing private unemployment insurance because it was too expensive for groups with high unemployment risks. The introduction of differentiated fees according to unemployment risk in public unemployment insurance resulted in a sharp drop in coverage rates. Outsiders, who, by definition, have higher unemployment risks, were hit hardest. The reduction in spending in ALMPs was also, of course, detrimental for outsiders, as was stricter conditionality and sanctions in the unemployment benefit. All in all, in the area of labour market policy, Sweden has moved away from a universal model and approached the dualised model that has been more common in continental countries with clearer divisions between insiders and outsiders in relation to the labour market and the welfare system.

Notes

1. For an earlier overview of Swedish labour market policy, see also Sjöberg (2011).

2. While the right of the employer to decide on two employees to be exempted from the 'last in, first out' principle may seem a small number, it was an important reform for small business.

3. The drop in membership in voluntary unemployment insurance was larger than the decrease in union membership, from 84.4% in 2005 to 69.6% in 2014 (Kjellberg, 2014).

4. Sweden has voluntary unemployment insurance and although much of the cost of the insurance is subsidised by the state, opting in to the insurance requires the payment of monthly individual fees.

5. The differentiated fees were abandoned in 2013.

6. In 1998, activation measures were also introduced in social assistance schemes.

7. For two exceptions, see Lindvall (2011) and Bengtsson (2014).

8. See also Palme and Cronert (2015), who show a slightly decreasing trend between 2001 and 2012 when using a measure of expenditure per programme participant. They also show a spike in 2005 and 2006. The Social Democratic government expanded ALMPs in those years, but the reforms were revoked by the Conservative coalition after they gained power in 2006.

References

Acemoglu, D. and Autor, D. (2012) 'What does human capital do? A review of Goldin and Katz's *The race between education and technology*', *Journal of Economic Literature*, 50(2): 426–63.

Anxo, D. and Niklasson, H. (2006) 'The Swedish model in turbulent times: decline or renaissance?', *International Labour Review*, 145(4): 339–71.

Arbetsförmedlingen (2014) 'Arbetsmarknadsrapport', Stockholm, Sweden.

Arbetsförmedlnigen (2016) 'Arbetsmarknadsrapport', Stockholm, Sweden.

Autor, D. (2010) *The polarization of job opportunities in the U.S. labor market, implications for employment and earnings*, Washington, DC: Center for American Progress and Brookings Institution, The Hamilton Project.

Autor, D. and Dorn, D. (2013) 'The growth of low-skill service jobs and the polarization of the U.S. labor market', *American Economic Review*, 103(5): 1553–97.

Autor, D., Levy, F. and Murnane, R.J. (2003) 'The skill content of recent technological change: an empirical exploration', *Quarterly Journal of Economics*, 116(4): 1279–333.

Autor, D., Katz, L.F. and Kearney, M.S. (2006) 'The polarization of the U.S. labor market', NBER Working Paper, 11986.

Bassanini, A. and Duval, R. (2006) 'Employment patterns in OECD countries: Reassessing the role of policies and institutions', Social, Employment and Migration Working Papers No. 35. Paris: OECD.

Bengtsson, M. (2014) 'Toward standby-ability: Swedish and Danish activation policies in flux', *International Journal of Social Welfare*, 23: 54–70.

Bergmark, Å. (2016) *Ekonomiskt bistånd: försörjningsvillkor och marginalisering – ett hinder för jämlik hälsa?*, Stockholm: Socialstyrelsen.

Bonoli, G. (2013) *The origins of active social policy: Labour market and childcare policies in a comparative perspective*, Oxford: Oxford University Press.

Chung, H. and Thewissen, S. (2011) 'Falling back on old habits? A comparison of the social and unemployment crisis reactive policy strategies in Germany, the UK and Sweden', *Social Policy & Administration*, 45(4): 354–70.

Davidsson, J.B. (2011) 'Unions in hard times: Labour market politics in Western Europe', PhD thesis, European University Institute, Florence.

Davidsson, J.B. (2014) 'The limits of solidarity: unions, redistribution and the rise of private unemployment insurance in Sweden', presentation at the Max Planck Institut für Gesellschaftsforschung, Cologne, 24–25 July.

Davidsson, J.B. and Emmenegger, P. (2012) 'Insider–outsider dynamics and the reform of job security legislation', in G. Bonoli and D. Natali (eds) *The politics of the new welfare state*, Oxford: Oxford University Press.

Davidsson, J.B. and Emmenegger, P. (2013) 'Defending the organisation, not the members: unions and the reform of job protection legislation in Western Europe', *European Journal of Political Research*, 52: 339–63.

Davidsson, J.B. and Naczyk, M. (2009) 'The ins and outs of dualization: a literature review', REC-WP 02/09.

Dingeldey, I. (2011) 'Germany: moving towards integration whilst maintaining segmentation', in J. Clasen and D. Clegg (eds) *Regulating the risk of unemployment: National adaptations to post-industrial labour markets in Europe*, Oxford: Oxford University Press.

Eichorst, W. and Konle-Seidl, R. (2008) 'Contingent convergence: a comparative analysis of activation policy', IZA Discussion Paper, No. 3095.

Emmenegger, P. (2014) *The power to dismiss: Trade unions and the regulation of job security in Western Europe*, Oxford: Oxford University Press.

Emmenegger, P., Häusermann, S., Palier, B. and Seeleib-Kaiser, M. (2012) *The age of dualization: The changing face of inequality in deindustrializing societies*, Oxford: Oxford University Press.

Erixon, L. (2008) 'The Rehn–Meidner model in Sweden: its rise, challenges and survival', Working Paper, Department of Economics, Stockholm University.

Goos, M. and Manning, A. (2007) 'Lousy and lovely jobs: the rising polarization of work in Britain', *Review of Economics and Statistics*, 89(1): 118–33.

Hamskär, I. and Gustafsson, S. (2010) 'Framtidens arbetsrätt bör byggas på fakta', *Lag & avtal*, 27 August.

Iversen, T. (2009) 'Dualism and political coalitions: inclusionary versus exclusionary reforms in an age of rising inequality', paper presented at the Annual Meeting of the American Political Science Association, Toronto, Canada.

Iversen, T. and Wren, A. (1998) 'Equality, employment, and budgetary restraint: the trilemma of the service economy', *World Politics*, 50(4): 507–46.

Karlsson, N. and Lindberg, H. (2010) *Kollektivavtalen och framtidens arbetsmarknad*, Stockholm: Ratio.

Kjellberg, A. (2009) 'Det fackliga medlemsraset i Sverige under 2007 och 2008', *Arbetsmarknad & Arbetsliv*, 15(2): 11–28.

Kjellberg, A. (2014) 'Kollektivavtalens täckningsgrad samt organisationsgraden hos arbetsgivarförbund och fackförbund', Studies in Social Policy, Industrial Relations, Working Life and Mobility, Research Report 2013: 1.

Knotz, C. (2016) 'How tight are the screws? Conditions and sanctions for the unemployed in OECD countries, 1980–2012', Working Paper, Lund University.

Korpi, W. and Palme, J. (1998) 'The paradox of redistribution and strategies of equality: welfare state institutions, inequality, and poverty in the Western Countries', *American Sociological Review*, 63(5): 661–87.

Lindvall, J. (2011) 'Vad hände med den aktiva arbetsmarknadspolitiken?', *Ekonomisk Debatt*, 39(3): 38–45.

Mishel, L., Shierholz, H. and Schmitt, J. (2013) 'Don't blame the robots: assessing the job polarization explanation of growing wage inequality', Economic Policy Institute Working Paper, 19 November.

Nelson, K. (2013) 'Social assistance and EU poverty thresholds 1990–2008. Are European welfare systems providing just and fair protection against low income?', *European Sociological Review*, 29(2): 386–401.

Nycander, S. (2008) *Makten över arbetsmarknaden*, Stockholm: SNS Förlag.

Palier, B. and Thelen, K. (2010) 'Institutionalizing dualism: complementarities and change in France and Germany', *Politics & Society*, 38(1): 119–48.

Palme, J. and Cronert, A. (2015) 'Trends in the Swedish social investment welfare state: "the enlightened path" or "the Third Way" for "the Lions"?', IMPROVE, Discussion Paper no. 15/12.

Pontusson, J. (2011) 'Once again a model: Nordic social democracy in a globalized world', in J.E. Cronin, G.W. Ross and J. Shoch (eds) *What's left of the Left: Democrats and social democrats in challenging times*, Durham, NC: Duke University Press.

Pontusson, J. and Swenson, P. (1996) 'Labor markets, production strategies, and wage bargaining institutions: the Swedish employer offensive in comparative perspective', *Comparative Political Studies*, 29(2): 223–50.

Sjöberg, O. (2011) 'Sweden: ambivalent adjustment', J. Clasen and D. Clegg (eds) *Regulating the risk of unemployment. National adaptations to post-industrial labour markets in Europe*, Oxford: Oxford University Press.

SO (Arbetslöshetskassornas Samorganisation) (2012) 'Lägesbeskrivning av arbetslöshetsförsäkringen våren 2012', Rapport från arbetslöshetskassornas samorganisation.

Swenson, P.A. (2002) *Capitalists against markets: The making of labor markets and welfare states in the United States and Sweden*, Oxford: Oxford University Press.

Van Vliet, O. and Caminada, K. (2012) 'Unemployment replacement rates dataset'. Available at: www.law.leidenuniv.nl/org/fisceco/economie/hervormingsz/datasetreplacementrates.html (accessed 28 April 2016).

Wren, A., Fodor, M. and Theodoropoulou, S. (2013) 'The trilemma revisited: institutions, inequality, and employment creation in an era of ICT-intensive service expansion', in A. Wren (ed) *The political economy of the service transition*, Oxford: Oxford University Press.

Government documents

Dir. 1991:18. Översyn av den arbetsrättsliga lagstiftningen.
Dir. 1991:76. Utredning av den arbetsrättsliga lagstiftningen.
Prop. 1993/94:67. Om ändringar i lagen om anställningsskydd och i lagen om medbestämmande i arbetslivet.
Prop. 1996/97:16. En arbetsrätt för ökad tillväxt.
Prop. 1999/2000:139. En rättvisare och tydligare arbetslöshetsförsäkring.
Prop. 2006/07:89. Ytterligare reformer inom arbetsmarknadspolitiken m.m.
Prop. 2006/07:111. Bättre möjligheter till tidsbegränsad anställning, m.m.
SOU 1973:7. Trygghet i anställningen. Anställningsskydd och viss anställningsfrämjande åtgärder. Betänkande avgivet av utredningen rörande ökad anställningstrygghet och vidgad behörighet för arbetsdomstolen.
SOU 1993:32. Ny anställningsskyddslag.

NINE

No longer 'fit for purpose'? Consolidation and catch-up in Irish labour market policy

Fiona Dukelow

Introduction

The recent economic crisis hit Ireland hard. Its economic contraction generated sharp increases in unemployment and underemployment. Policy efforts to respond to the unemployment challenge were heavily impacted by both the lack of resources at a time of fiscal crisis and the overriding aim of fiscal consolidation. Moreover, changes to labour market policies have been guided by the idea, promoted by both domestic and international policy actors, that Ireland's policy regime prior to the crisis was no longer 'fit for purpose', being overly focused on a passive benefit system and a similarly passive approach to activation. Judged against Ireland's typically conservative and slow pace of reform, a period of deep austerity between late 2008 and 2014 instigated rapid and potentially transformative labour market policy (LMP) changes. By 2016, the government framed a new policy phase, 'activation in a time of recovery and growth' (Government of Ireland, 2016: 4); however, several issues remain problematic in terms of both the changes instigated and the legacies of the crisis.

In this chapter, three core changes related to consolidation and catch-up are identified. First, retrenchment is clearly evident across the social protection system in payments to those of working age. Moreover, retrenchment is occurring in a system in which the social insurance principle is already weak. Social assistance features strongly and several categories of means-tested payments add complexity. There is no distinction between social insurance and social assistance schemes in terms of benefit rates and a flat-rate system operates. In contrast to many other Organisation for Economic Co-operation and Development (OECD) countries, the labour market is less dualistic, with little difference in the termination costs of permanent and of temporary staff (OECD, 2014a). Changes made over the crisis period have therefore further eroded the security attached to social protection in the context of cuts and curtailments of all working-age programmes.

Second, in terms of activation, existing programmes that focused heavily on direct job creation have been somewhat curtailed and new, more market-oriented, programmes have been introduced. The simultaneous pursuit of cost containment has been borne by participants via diminished benefits and tighter eligibility requirements. Compulsion has also been strengthened, though distinctions remain in terms of which groups are activated and how. Third, and finally, major institutional redesign is leading to the greater integration of the benefit system with employment services and this redesign also involves greater use of marketisation and privatisation as policy instruments. Taking these three sets of changes together and setting them against Ireland's weak employment protection legislation regime, there is a fear that changes designed to make the social protection and activation system 'fit for purpose' are contributing to labour market precarity, which is a growing concern post-crisis. Before mapping the key changes and issues across benefit schemes, employment protection legislation, activation programmes and training, the chapter begins by establishing some core contextual points.

Setting the context: the economic crisis and its consequences for labour market policy

Ireland's economic transformation in the 1990s earned it the moniker 'Celtic Tiger'. However, by the early 2000s, the conditions for overheating took hold in what was now a very open, liberalised and financialised economy. The global credit crunch had severe implications for Ireland's banking system, which was saved from collapse by a near-blanket bank guarantee (Dukelow, 2015a). The boom-to-bust economy and the cost of saving Ireland's banking system led to a sharp deterioration in the public finances, a sovereign debt crisis and a three-year programme of financial assistance from the European Union (EU)/International Monetary Fund (IMF)/European Central Bank (ECB) 'Troika' from 2010 to 2013. Austerity policies pursued since late 2008 were reinforced by the conditions imposed by the Troika and a series of austerity budgets were implemented from 2008 to 2014. In total, these budgets achieved a consolidation of approximately 19% of gross domestic product (GDP), which was matched by a prolonged period of poor economic performance, including a double-dip recession. Figure 9.1 profiles trends in debt, deficits and economic growth since 2007.

Figure 9.1: Government deficit, government debt and GDP growth rate*, Ireland, 2007–16

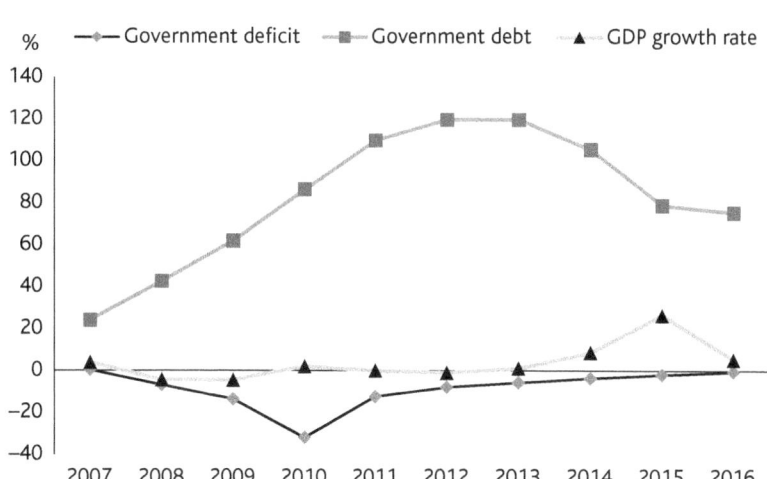

Note: *Government deficit and government debt measured as a percentage of GDP, GDP growth rate measured as a percentage of change in real GDP.
Source: Eurostat economy and finance database

The post-crisis period continues to demonstrate the volatility and weaknesses of Ireland's liberalised economic growth model. In particular, the anomalous growth rate for 2015 (26.3%) can be attributed to the activity of a small number of multinational companies onshoring intangible assets, taking advantage of Ireland's competitive tax regime in this regard in the context of international efforts to reduce tax planning and avoidance (IMF, 2016). The European Commission ruling on Irish tax concessions to Apple (European Commission, 2016) reinforces questions about Ireland's dependency on a low-tax foreign direct investment (FDI) model.

The crisis also had severe implications for employment. A large part of the economic boom was driven by a construction bubble and the bursting of this bubble had enormous fallout for those employed in the construction sector. Furthermore, across all occupations, those at lower skill levels were at much more risk of losing their jobs (NESC, 2011). Figure 9.2 profiles the unemployment and long-term unemployment rate over the long term since 1990. At the beginning of the period, both were at very high levels in the aftermath of a 1980s' economic crisis, both subsequently fell to very low levels before rising after 2008, and are now clearly falling again. However, the fall in unemployment masks other trends exacerbated by the crisis, which remain core problems. These include the fact that Ireland has a very high proportion of 'low

Figure 9.2: Unemployment and long-term unemployment rate, Ireland, 1990–2016

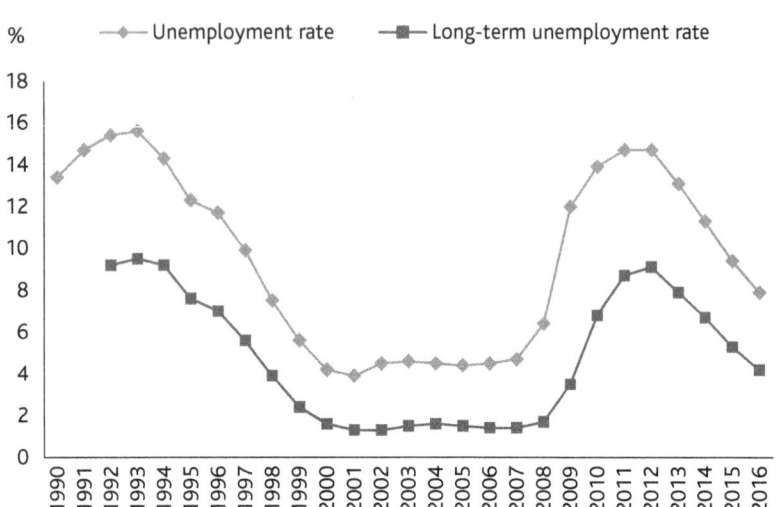

Source: Eurostat Labour Market database

work intensity households' (19.2% in 2015; the second highest in the EU28). A high proportion of young people are also not in employment, education or training (13% in 2016; the tenth highest in the EU28). Emigration potentially prevented some of these problems being even more severe. Numbers emigrating tripled between 2008 and 2012 and peaked at 89,000 people in 2013. Young people and third-level graduates were disproportionately represented, and research by Glynn et al (2015) suggests that a significant number emigrated because of dissatisfaction with the precarity of their existing job conditions and future prospects. Thus, on emigrating, 47% surveyed left full-time employment and a further 13% left part-time employment.

As for activation of the unemployed, since the early 1990s, relatively minor changes were made to measures first introduced during the 1980s. The social protection system offered some payments to support a move to work or education, which were subject to minor recalibrations over time. Training was the function of a separate agency, Foras Áiseanna Saothar/Training and Employment Authority (FÁS). This agency was also responsible for the majority of direct work schemes and for activation processes under the National Employment Action Plan introduced in 1998.

Ireland's activation institutions therefore differed from the system prevailing in the majority of OECD countries, which developed more integrated systems. Ireland's expenditure on labour market policies as a percentage of GDP was also relatively low compared with Nordic and Western European countries. The composition of LMP expenditure focused heavily on training and direct job creation, or, in terms of Bonoli's (2011) four dimensions of activation, occupation and human capital investment. This was a legacy of Irish activation policy's roots in the context of mass long-term unemployment in the 1980s.

Following this, Irish policy developments did not fully reflect the 'activation turn' from the mid-1990s, which saw policies strengthening work incentives and labour market reintegration. A number of factors erased any reform ambitions, including difficulties in streamlining what had become complex and fragmented institutional arrangements and the fact that labour shortages became one of the more pressing problems during the economic boom (Murphy, 2012a). In addition, within the social protection system, the numbers in receipt of unemployment payments declined and numbers in other payment categories increased. From 2000 to 2010, a 48% rise was recorded in three contingency-based payments: the One-Parent Family Payment, Disability Allowance and Illness Benefit (DSP, 2012a). Imervoll and Scarpetta (2012) note a similar trend in social protection payments in other countries and a subsequent effort to activate these groups. However, in Ireland, such groups were dealt with in an 'old social policy' (Häusermann, 2012) manner: the predominant focus was on income transfers while preserving category distinctions, and work was encouraged by positive incentives such as increasing earnings disregards attached to social protection payments. By the mid-2000s, as the state had more revenue and was subject to pressure from anti-poverty advocates who were bolstered by the momentum provided by the Open Method of Co-ordination (Murphy, 2012a), policy attention shifted to a greater anti-poverty focus, with payment increases across all payment types. Replacement rates improved from what had prevailed in the 1990s, which put Ireland in a comparatively higher position internationally than heretofore (NESC, 2011). This was especially the case for replacement rates for the long-term unemployed as the payment system does not taper payments by length of unemployment.

The crisis transformed this policy environment. The fiscal crisis and the rise in unemployment both exerted major pressure. Moreover, the crisis amplified existing criticisms of the activation system for its inert approach and poor employment outcomes (Grubb et al, 2009; McGuiness et al, 2013; Martin, 2015), while attention on social protection rapidly turned to seeing the system as 'overly generous and poorly policed' (NESC, 2011: 2) and a contributor to the fiscal crisis.

While such views of the social protection system were challenged, another effect of the crisis has been to narrow the range of actors influencing policy and to amplify the emphasis on fiscal discipline. The influence of trade unions and advocacy groups weakened, particularly as social partnership collapsed in 2009. New groups established to advise on labour market policies, such as the Labour Market Council set up in 2013, reflected a more centralised and top-down approach, with relatively greater input from business actors. In addition, the influence of the Troika on domestic policymaking intensified the pressure to reform the system. The Memorandum of Understanding contained a range of structural reforms, which became more specific and more urgent over the course of the agreement as domestic institutions and existing policies were opened up to greater scrutiny and long-term unemployment became a growing problem (Dukelow, 2015b). Subsequent to exiting the financial assistance programme, country-specific recommendations under the European Semester process have continued to focus on the structural reform of the social protection system and have problematised Ireland's comparatively high rate of jobless households, urging the expansion and acceleration of activation policies in this regard (Council of the European Union, 2016).

Mapping key changes in labour market policy

Benefit schemes for the unemployed

Two core trends may be identified with regard to benefit schemes for the unemployed. First, payment rates were retrenched in the general pattern of cutting all working-age payments during the crisis. Second, beyond this 'headline' retrenchment, entitlement erosion can be identified in a number of ways as regards Jobseeker's Benefit, the principal benefit to the unemployed and underemployed, as well as Illness Benefit and Invalidity Pension, the other main benefits for which workers are insured.

In 2008, the number of recipients of Jobseeker's Benefit stood at 121,763; this peaked in 2009 at 160,122, and by 2015, had fallen to 37,845 (DSP, 2016). As can be seen in Table 9.1, this benefit has seen reductions in the payment rate and payment bands, a tightening of its qualifying conditions, and a reduction in duration. The rate cuts to Jobseeker's Benefit were rationalised by the need for fiscal consolidation, but also by the idea that they would act as an activation incentive in their own right by encouraging people to 'stay close to

Table 9.1: Summary of changes to benefit schemes for the unemployed, Ireland

	2009	2016	Year of change/other comment
Jobseekers Benefit			
Payment rate	€204.30	€188	Rates cut 4% in 2010 and in 2011; child rate increased in 2010 to reduce impact of Child Benefit cuts
Qualified adult	€135.60	€124.80	
Qualified child	€26.00	€29.80	
Qualifying conditions	At least 52 contributions	At least 104 contributions and 13 in last complete contribution year prior to claim	2009
Qualification with part-time work	Unemployed for 3 days out of 6, not including Sunday	Unemployed for 3 days out of 5, including Sunday.	Number of days changed 2012, Sunday counted 2013.
Duration	Until October 2008: 15 months (>260 contributions) 12 months (<260 contributions)	9 months (>260 contributions) 6 months (<260 contributions)	Duration reduced twice: 2008 and 2013.
Earnings bands	<€80 (€91.80) €80–124 (€132.00) €124–149 (€166.10) €150+ (€204.30)	<€150 (€84.50) €150–219.99 (€121.40) €220–300 (€147.30) €300+ (€188)	2009
Half-rate entitlement	Some claimants of other payments entitled to half Illness Benefit rate	No longer applies	2012
Illness Benefit			
Payment rate	As for Jobseeker's Benefit	As for Jobseeker's Benefit	
Qualifying conditions	At least 52 contributions	At least 104 contributions	2009
	3 days' wait before qualifying	6 days' wait before qualifying	2014
Duration	Indefinite	2 years (260+ contributions) 1 year (104–259 contributions)	2009
Earnings bands	As for Jobseeker's Benefit	As for Jobseeker's Benefit	

the labour market' (Lenihan, 2009). As of 2016, these rate cuts and other changes have remained in place. Jobseeker's Benefit recipients are also subject to a more intensive activation process than previously and a tougher sanctions regime (both of which are discussed later).

The erosion of entitlements for part-time workers is particularly significant given the increase in casual and part-time working over the crisis. At the start of 2008, 21,596 of these workers were on the Live Register[1] and this number peaked at 89,790 in February 2013. By the end of 2016, the number had fallen somewhat to 59,908 (Central Statistics Office (CSO) Live Register database). The percentage of those working in involuntary part-time work as a percentage of total part-time work increased from 13.6% in 2008 to a peak of 43.1% in 2013 and remained high at 31.5% in 2016 (Eurostat Labour Market database). Changes to Jobseeker's Benefit for part-time workers, as outlined in Table 9.1, added further disentitlements to Ireland's 'days worked' as opposed to 'hours worked' system. Under the latter system, which is the more common model across Europe, individuals whose part-time work is spread across a number of days are more likely to retain entitlement to an unemployment payment (Joint Oireachtas Committee on Jobs, Social Protection and Education, 2012) and, in this regard, the 'days worked' system is justified by the Department of Social Protection (DSP) in cost-containment terms (O'Sullivan et al, 2015).

The reforms to the ways in which part-time work can be combined with a Jobseeker's Benefit payment are also intended as an incentivisation measure, this time to encourage the take-up of full-time work (Government of Ireland, 2012). However, given the substantial increase in involuntary part-time work, the incentivisation effect of these changes is questionable. To the contrary, such reforms have been found to add to the precarity of low-paid part-time workers, for whom it has made it more difficult to combine work and welfare (Loftus, 2012; Murphy and Loftus, 2015).

The two main benefits besides Jobseeker's Benefit in terms of recipient numbers are Illness Benefit and Invalidity Pension. Illness Benefit is paid to workers who become ill and are unable to work; Invalidity Pension is paid to those permanently incapable of work before transferring to a state pension. As evident in Table 9.1, the rules relating to Illness Benefit, in particular, duration, have been altered substantially, and claimant numbers declined by 23% between 2008 and 2014. More broadly, Grubb et al (2009: 106) mention Ireland's 'weak gate-keeping arrangements' for disability payments and suggest that, in some cases, claimants may be miscategorised as disabled people rather than as long-term unemployed, and that people who potentially have at least some work capacity are not being activated. Invalidity Pension claimant numbers have remained largely stable, but the rise in the number of appeals in relation to these payments during the crisis is suggestive of more stringent eligibility tests. Social welfare appeals rose quite significantly across the system during the crisis, although a particularly high increase in the rate of appeals against Invalidity Pension decisions is evident; these grew from 526 in 2008 to 4,765 in 2012 before declining to 1,857 in 2015 (Social Welfare Appeals Office, 2016). Of those appeals decided in 2015, 53.5% were allowed, which is the highest rate decided in favour of the appellant across all payment categories.

The introduction of a new benefit in 2012, Partial Incapacity Benefit, represented a modest turn to activation for individuals in receipt of Illness Benefit or Invalidity Pension. Previously, recipients could receive an 'exemption' to work part-time. Now, those who wish to work part-time may transfer to Partial Incapacity Benefit, the rate of which is decided based on the extent of incapacity determined by a medical examination. As such, Partial Incapacity Benefit may represent a more supportive route to activation for people with disabilities as opposed to the reforms occurring in relation to the One-Parent Family Payment (discussed later).

In sum, therefore, the overriding trend with respect to benefits for the unemployed has been retrenchment. However, after several years of cuts and what are essentially negative reinforcements, there are modest signs of a turn to what might be considered flexicurity. Specifically, the introduction of a Back to Work Family Dividend in 2015 is an example of a more positive activation reinforcement by way of an in-work benefit. The payment, which is the equivalent of the Qualified Child Allowance, is paid on a weekly basis for the first year of employment and reduced to half that amount in the second year.

Minimum income schemes/needs-based social protection for the unemployed

Once entitlement to Jobseeker's Benefit is exhausted or one is ineligible, unemployed people may apply for a means-tested Jobseeker's Allowance payment. Over the course of the crisis, the number of people claiming Jobseeker's Allowance increased substantially, from 113,603 claimants at the end of 2008 to 295,077 by the end of 2013, before falling back somewhat to 246,536 at the end of 2015 (DSP, 2016). Following the same logic of fiscal consolidation and incentivisation that applied to changes to Jobseeker's Benefit, Jobseeker's Allowance has also been subject to a number of cuts and curtailments, with younger claimants targeted in particular (see Table 9.2). Changes to One-Parent Family Payment are also particularly significant. In a 'risk re-categorisation' move (Clasen and Clegg, 2011), lone parents' social protection status has switched from lone parenthood to jobseeker at an earlier stage. Although reforms to the age-related work obligation were mooted almost a decade earlier (DSFA, 2006), the changes bring Ireland somewhat closer in line with age limits used in other OECD countries (see Finn and Gloster, 2010). As evident in Table 9.2, qualifying conditions and earnings disregards have been substantially tightened. In the past, One-Parent Family Payment recipients were encouraged to participate in part-time work with more generous income disregards than those pertaining to Jobseeker's Allowance, which were justified by the lack of affordable childcare provision (Grubb et al, 2009). As a result of changes to One-Parent Family Payment, the proportion of recipients working in 2014 was 36% in comparison to 60% in 2012, when age limit reforms began (EAPN Ireland, 2015), while the deprivation rate for one-parent households rose from 48.5% to 58.7% over the same period (CSO SILC [Survey of Income and Living Conditions]). Once entitlement to One-Parent Family Payment ends, recipients transfer to Jobseeker's Allowance and are thus subject to the activation processes that come with being classified as available for work. Alternatively, lone parents may apply for a new payment, known as Jobseeker's Transitional payment. Introduced to moderate the transition to Jobseeker's Allowance, it exempts lone parents from the condition of being available for work until their youngest child reaches 14. In other respects, Jobseeker's Transitional payment mirrors Jobseeker's Allowance, except that it facilitates more flexible part-time working arrangements by not stipulating that the parent must be unemployed for four days out of seven, and by allowing an earnings disregard of €90 per week – which are minor concessions in a policy move that has been described as 'careless activation' (Murphy, 2012b), especially in the context of continued poor childcare access and affordability (European Commission, 2015).

Employment protection legislation

Ireland entered the crisis with the least restrictive employment protection system in the EU, apart from that of the UK, as measured by OECD indicators of strictness. Over the period 2008 to 2013, Ireland's scores on the OECD index increased marginally, mainly

Table 9.2: Summary of changes to Jobseeker's Allowance and One-Parent Family Payment, Ireland

	2009	2016	Year of change/other comment
Jobseeker's Allowance			
Payment rate	€204.30	€188	Rates cut 4% in 2010 and in 2011; child rate increased in 2010 to reduce impact of Child Benefit cuts
Qualified adult	€135.60	€124.80	
Qualified child	€26.00	€29.80	
Payment rates for young people			
18–24	As above (until April 2009)	€100	April 2009: Jobseeker's Allowance for under 20s reduced to €100 – gradual extension of age-related cuts to 2014.
25		€144	
Qualification with part-time work	Unemployed for 3 days out of 6	Unemployed for 4 days out of 7	2013
Earnings disregard	€20 per day for 3 days	€20 per day for 3 days	No change
One-Parent Family Payment			
Payment rate	As for Jobseeker's Allowance	As for Jobseeker's Allowance	As for Jobseeker's Allowance
Qualifying conditions	Payable until youngest child reaches 18, or 22 if in full-time education	Payable until youngest child reaches 7	Gradual reduction in qualifying age from 2012 to 2015.
Earnings disregards	First €146.50 weekly gross earnings + half remainder up to €425.	First €90 weekly gross earnings + half remainder up to €425.	Gradual reduction from 2012 to 2014

due to changes in the regulation of temporary employment,[2] but only after the government unsuccessfully attempted to achieve an exemption to the effect that temporary agency workers would have a six-month wait before gaining equal treatment (*Irish Times*, 2011). As employment protection legislation was already very liberalised, greater change is evident in related areas, such as wages and wage bargaining, as internal devaluation was pursued to restore the economy to what was considered its 'super-competitive' position in the very early 2000s (Pina, 2011). The social partnership in place since 1987 collapsed in 2009 and subsequent changes to wage bargaining in certain low-paid sectors, as Whitson (2014: 420) observes, mark a shift 'towards greater reliance on minimal individual rights, market forces and a reinforcement of managerial prerogative'.

On the other hand, a Low-Pay Commission was set up in 2014 to provide for regular review of the adequacy of the national minimum wage rate and related issues. After the Commission's first report on the national minimum wage, an increase from €8.65 to €9.15 per hour was implemented in January 2016. While it means that low pay has been put on the policy agenda, it remains to be seen how effective the activities of the Commission will be in addressing its high incidence. At 25.1% of workers in 2014, Ireland had the highest incidence of low-paid work in the OECD and this rate has been rising steadily since 2004, when it stood at 17.6% (OECD, 2016). Focus on the national minimum wage means that the response to the deterioration of labour market conditions remains within the 'floor of rights' paradigm and can be considered a matter of 'tinkering around the edges' of this model (Doherty, 2016: 28).

Similar uncertainty and caution may be observed with the establishment of a Workplace Relations Commission in October 2015 following the enactment of the Workplace Relations Act 2015. The Commission is the result of plans to streamline a complex raft of existing employer law and related institutions, and is intended to make it easier for both employees and employers to deal with employment, equality and industrial relations disputes. However, the reform has also been driven by a cost-cutting agenda. For example, the National Employment Rights Authority (NERA), responsible for labour law compliance and now subsumed under the Workplace Relations Commission, had its staff numbers reduced by 23.7% between 2008 and 2015 (NERA, no date). This emphasis on cost-cutting, combined with the stress on wage competitiveness, led to fears that the new Commission will bring about a downgrading of compliance and enforcement mechanisms for employment protection, with which Ireland already has a poor track record (Murphy and Loftus, 2015).

Activation

The policy guiding transformation of the activation system is *Pathways to work*, whose development was required under the Troika reforms. Four iterations of the policy document have been published, taking account of changing conditions (Government of Ireland, 2012, 2013, 2015, 2016), but all emphasising greater engagement with the unemployed, greater targeting of activation programmes, incentivisation and institutional reform. *Pathways to work 2016–2020* (Government of Ireland, 2016) is significant, in particular, for what might tentatively be characterised as 'risk re-categorisation' (Clasen and Clegg, 2011) in its plans to extend activation to people with disabilities, part-time workers, carers ceasing their caring role and qualified adult dependants of Jobseeker payments. Framed as activation in a time of economic recovery, this is 'to help ensure a supply of labour at competitive rates and to minimise welfare dependency' (Government of Ireland, 2016: 14). The current government also plans to publish a dedicated *Pathways to work for jobless households*, among which are high numbers of lone parents and people with disabilities (O'Rorke, 2016).

As already mentioned, Irish activation expenditure has, in the past, been heavily oriented towards direct job creation and training. Reforms since the crisis have focused on curbing the occupation elements of the system and strengthening incentive reinforcement. These reforms potentially encompass both sides of the well-established binary of positive and negative incentivisation (Bonoli, 2013) but with, to date, manifestly greater emphasis on the negative in the ways in which existing schemes are being curtailed and new ones designed. Other changes to activation-related payments have seen a trend of widened access but curtailed benefits and a push towards entrepreneurship/self-employment. In both these types of change, the Irish system might be said to be catching up with what Lødemel and Moreira (2014) labelled first-wave activation reforms, taking place in the 1990s and 2000s. However, new institutional developments, in particular, the establishment of an integrated activation and social protection service (Intreo), reflect what Lødemel and Moreira identify as second-wave reform, relating, in particular, to how activation systems are governed. We shall look at these three areas of change in turn.

The crisis has seen an effort to curtail the main occupational scheme, Community Employment. Community Employment was introduced in 1994 at a time when unemployment was still very high. Its primary function is to provide direct employment with a training element in the social/non-market economy to the long-term unemployed in order to enhance participants' employability and provide local services. Community Employment was, and still is, the largest active labour market programme, although it has been subject to much criticism for its poor employment outcomes. However, in contrast to a more expansionary approach to Community Employment in the past, when up to 40,000 individuals were participants, the crisis-related rise in places has been relatively restrained. Community Employment recruitment has also changed; participants must now be recruited via individuals referred by the DSP, reflecting a more 'directed' recruitment approach (DSP, 2012b). The scheme is also being streamlined to favour a shorter one-year placement, with a target of 75% of Community Employment places set for this option, as opposed to a three-year placement option (DSP, 2015). As evident in Table 9.3, significant cuts have been made to Community Employment benefits.

Despite criticism of Community Employment, two new direct occupational programmes have been introduced during the crisis, although of a 'leaner', more stringent, design: Tús in 2011 and Gateway in 2013. Both offer non-market work placements to the long-term unemployed and both provide a top-up of €22.50 to one's existing social welfare payment in return for 19.5 hours work a week. Recruitment to these schemes illustrates the growing compulsive nature of Ireland's activation regime and a blurring of activation and workfare. In the case of Tús, as described by the DSP (2012a: 20):

> participants are randomly selected from the Live Register and sanctions apply to those who do not avail of offer of placement. While the scheme aims to contribute to the work readiness of the long-term unemployed, it also contributes to the management of the Live Register in highlighting those who are unemployed but may not be actively seeking work.

Gateway operates in a similar manner, although poor take-up led to altered criteria, with the result that eligible participants can now also voluntarily apply (Rogers, 2014), an option that was also extended to Tús in 2015.

In addition to direct work schemes, JobBridge, in operation between 2011 and 2017, is a new departure, emblematic of the policy aspiration of reorienting Ireland's activation system towards labour market reintegration. It was organised around host organisations, principally private companies but also public sector bodies and voluntary and community organisations, providing internships. Participants received an internship allowance comprising their existing social welfare payment plus €52.50 for between 30 and 40 hours of work a week. JobBridge compared less favourably with Community Employment, Tús and Gateway on social protection and employment protection grounds. An employer PRSI (Pay Related Social Insurance) contribution applies in the case of Community Employment, Tús and Gateway but not JobBridge. Also, JobBridge participants were not legally defined as employees. Many protections relating to internships, as categorised by the EC (European Commission) (Murphy, 2015), either do not exist or are unclear in the Irish context. JobBridge generated a swathe of controversy for the quality of work experience it provided, the lack of support for interns and the inadequacy of the top-up payment in meeting costs associated with participation (Doorley, 2015). Its potential for deadweight and job displacement, and the fear that it may become a route to more precarious employment post-crisis, while subsidising employer labour costs and potentially driving down wages, were also raised (Murphy, 2015; Joint Committee on Jobs, Enterprise and Innovation, 2015). Whilst JobBridge is now closed, the current intention appears to be to retain the model by developing a targeted scheme more appropriate to post-crisis labour market conditions; a move that also appears to be in line with an OECD (2014b) recommendation that JobBridge be targeted at more disadvantaged groups.

The DSP also provides payments designed to encourage a return to work or to education, open to the unemployed, lone parents, carers and people with disabilities. In these cases, curtailments to existing payments in terms of benefits and duration are evident, alongside a widening of access and a preference for enterprise-related activation, as documented in Table 9.3. Enterprise has also been encouraged by the introduction of a new payment in 2009: the Short-Term Enterprise Allowance. Immediate access is granted on becoming unemployed if one qualifies for Jobseeker's Benefit and it is paid at the same rate as that for a maximum of nine months. However, little is known about the long-term success or otherwise of participants on enterprise schemes (DSP, 2012b). In the case of the Back to Education Allowance, however, a recent evaluation found that it was performing poorly in terms of labour market outcomes (Kelly et al, 2015). Consequently, the widening of access to this programme early in the crisis has been curtailed and there has been a substantial drop in the number of recipients (see Tables 9.3 and 9.4).

Table 9.3: Summary of changes to existing activation programmes and payments, Ireland

Programme/payment	2009	2016	Year of change/other comment
Community Employment			
Payment rate	Retention of portion of existing social welfare payment plus Community Employment allowance (€208 in 2011)	Existing social welfare payment plus €22.50	2012; previously lone parents and people with disabilities allowed to retain most/all of existing payment.
Qualified child increase	Increase allowed for both payments	Single increase allowed	2012
Grants for training and materials	€1,500 per participant	€500 per participant	2012 (though later eased somewhat after review of financial viability of schemes following cuts) (DSP, 2012c)
Back to Work Allowance			
Payment rate etc	Retention of social welfare payment and secondary benefits on tapered basis for 3 years	Closed	2009
Back to Work Enterprise Allowance			
Payment rate	€204.30	€188	4% cut in 2010 and in 2011
Qualifying condition	Unemployed for 2 years	Unemployed for 1 year or in receipt of another social welfare payment	2009
Duration	Retention of social welfare payment and secondary benefits on tapered basis for 4 years	Retention of social welfare payment and secondary benefits on tapered basis for 2 years	2009

(continued)

Table 9.3: Summary of changes to existing activation programmes and payments, Ireland (continued)

Programme/payment	2009	2016	Year of change/other comment
Back to Education Allowance			
Payment rate	As for Back to Work Enterprise Allowance	As for Back to Work Enterprise Allowance	
Qualifying conditions	Between 6 and 12 months unemployment	Between 3 and 6 months unemployment	2009
	No prior DSP approval required	Approval must be attained from DSP	2014
	Jobseeker's Benefit recipients receive Back to Education Allowance for full course of study	Once entitlement to Jobseeker's Benefit ends Back to Education Allowance eligibility depends on qualification for an alternative (means-tested) payment	2015
	Part-time earnings disregarded	Part-time earnings assessed as per primary payment rules	2016/17
Student support grant	Eligible to apply	Eligibility to apply removed	2010
Annual cost of education allowance	€500	Abolished	2013

Table 9.4: Participant numbers, activation payments and programmes, Ireland, 2008–15

	2008	2009	2010	2011	2012	2013	2014	2015
Payment/programmes in operation prior to 2009								
Back to Work Allowance	3,558	2,012	851	182	18	11	2	0
Back to Work Enterprise Allowance	4,604	4,591	7,958	10,751	10,810	10,098	11,166	11,881
Back to Education Allowance	7,886	15,877	21,147	24,666	24,910	24,175	22,714	18,345
Part-time job incentive*	184	173	161	180	215	290	373	421
Job initiative*	1,464	1,407	1,310	1,211	1,149	1,051	1,031	958
Community Employment	22,896	25,512	23,193	22,589	22,445	22,575	23,249	22,813
Rural social scheme*	2,597	2,595	2,591	2,537	2,591	2,537	2,576	2,532
Total end of year participation	**43,184**	**52,167**	**57,211**	**62,116**	**62,261**	**62,105**	**61,111**	**56,950**
Payment/programmes introduced since 2009								
Short-Term Enterprise Allowance	–	1,152	1,364	1,285	1,052	559	458	396
Work placement programme graduate*	–	71	575	455	142	15	Nav	Nav
Work placement programme open*	–	85	260	87	29	81	Nav	Nav
Tús	–	–	–	2,077	4,530	6,999	7,877	7,939
JobBridge	–	–	–	2,993	5,160	6,058	6,047	4,683
Gateway	–	–	–	–	–	5	1,685	2,350
Total end of year participation	**–**	**1,308**	**2,199**	**6,897**	**10,980**	**13,717**	**16,067**	**15,368**
Total participants pre- and post-2009	**43,184**	**53,475**	**59,410**	**69,013**	**73,241**	**75,822**	**77,178**	**72,318**

Note: *These programmes have not been discussed due either to their relatively small numbers or their minor activation element.

Sources: DSP, FÁS and Pobal Annual Reports, and Eurostat Labour Market Policy database

As for numbers of participants across activation programmes and payments, Table 9.4 shows an overall rise in participation in existing schemes until 2014, with increases in Back to Work Enterprise Allowance and Back to Education Allowance participation being responsible for the bulk of this trend. New schemes were generally on a growth path until 2015, with a fall in participants in JobBridge responsible for the recent decline in overall numbers. However, between all the changes that have taken place, occupational schemes, albeit now leaner in design compared with pre-crisis times, still dominate.

Moving to the third area of change, the role of the DSP with regard to activation has been substantially transformed. A key word in policy discourse is the 'passive' nature of Ireland's approach to activation (Government of Ireland, 2012: 10; 2013: 14). This focus on the passivity of the system was echoed in other appraisals, including by the OECD (Grubb et al, 2009), whose evaluation Martin (2015: 9) likened to finding 'the emperor who had no clothes' for its poor implementation of activation policy. Grubb et al (2009: 55) drew attention to the fact that the National Employment Action Plan interview was the only 'quasi-compulsory' element of the activation process. Moreover, this was apparently a 'lax' process, with McGuinness et al (2013: 13) finding that unemployed people who were invited for an interview were 15% less likely to move off the Live Register to employment within 12 months. Poor coordination between agencies was also highlighted, as was the lack of resources to fully implement activation provisions. In the crisis context, such issues have led to major institutional reorganisation by transferring employment services from FÁS to the DSP and integrating them with benefit provision in a new service provision model called Intreo.

Under Intreo, instead of a time-based intervention system, as is the case with the National Employment Action Plan process, on becoming unemployed, individuals are assessed and assigned a Probability of Exit score, which is used to determine the appropriate level of service intervention via caseworkers. Lack of resources partly drove a decision to outsource such services for the long-term unemployed. Thus, in 2015, a new service called JobPath was introduced for this group and the service is being extended to part-time and casual workers, who also count as long-term unemployed on the Live Register in 2016/17. The model adopted emphasises a work-first approach through a payment-by-results basis for placement in the labour market and is relatively lacking in service-user empowerment (Wiggan, 2015). Outsourcing to private providers is another major departure, and with substantial involvement of UK companies in the contracts awarded, it is reflective of broader trends in marketised and internationalised activation services (Van Berkel and Borghi, 2007). The marketisation of existing activation services contracted to community providers, namely, Local Employment Services and Jobs Clubs, which were established in the early 1990s when public resources were also scarce, is also being considered by extending the payment-by-results model to these services (Government of Ireland, 2016). A tailored activation process for disadvantaged young people as part of Ireland's youth guarantee is also being developed, called First Steps, which, it is intended, will involve compulsory internships. Participants are selected by the DSP and participation is effectively mandatory.

The new approach to activation closely follows the OECD's 'mutual obligations model', in which a record of mutual commitment is signed by a caseworker and the unemployed person. Obligations outlined in the record are backed up by the introduction of new sanctions and their greater use, reflecting a greater disciplinary dimension in how unemployed people are activated. The Social Welfare Miscellaneous Provisions Act 2010 introduced penalty rates to payments to the unemployed for refusal or failure to participate in approved training and other programmes. The Act provided for a cut (currently €44) for up to three weeks to the full rate of payment, with corresponding cuts to lower payment rates. In the Social Welfare Act 2013, the circumstances that would attract a penalty rate of payment were widened to include refusal or failure to attend activation meetings. If refusal or failure to attend continued under the penalty rate, the Act provided for a disqualification from the payment for up to nine weeks. Since their introduction, the number of penalty rates applied to those in receipt of Jobseeker payments has increased from a total of 359 in 2011 to 10,867 in 2016 (Dáil Debates, 2017). Such trends have met with approval from the OECD. It notes that sanction rates are becoming comparable to OECD norms, though it problematises the fact that decisions are made at caseworkers' discretion, and in characteristic new public management mode, it recommends the adoption of more objective criteria for sanction decisions (OECD, 2015).

Training

Besides direct job creation, the other main area to which Ireland has devoted a high proportion of its activation expenditure is training, and Ireland's further education and training system has been described as 'a massive sector full of diversity' (Department of Education and Skills,

2012: 12). Since the crisis, three core changes have been occurring, which are dealt with in turn in this section: major institutional reconfiguration; an expansion of training programmes and new modes of provision; and cutbacks in participant access and benefits.

Early in the crisis, many serious governance and funding issues came to light in how FÁS managed its affairs, which paved the way for a fundamental reconfiguration of services announced in March 2010. This was further spurred by a Troika stipulation that Ireland review its further education and training provision for its activation and labour market relevance (McGauran, 2013). Consequently, FÁS responsibility for activation services and programmes was transferred to the DSP, as discussed earlier, and its training activities were transferred to the Department of Education and Skills. These are now managed under a new further education and training authority called Solas, established in 2013. Also coming under Solas's remit, Vocational Education Committees providing further education to the unemployed were reorganised and streamlined into a smaller number of Educational Training Boards (33 to 16) with which FÁS training services were merged at the local level from 2014. This is a major change in the governance of services, particularly in the case of the transfer of FÁS employment services to the DSP, which had been mooted as early as the beginning of the 1990s (Murphy, 2012a). The merger of training and further education provision under one body is also significant as an attempt to coordinate a long-standing twin-track approach to these activities.

In response to escalating unemployment, a decision was made to target training efforts at four priority groups: younger people; those who lost jobs in sectors unlikely to recover to boom levels; those unemployed for more than one year; and those with low levels of skills and education (NESC, 2011). As an indication of how training expenditure increased but was stretched over a greater number of participants, expenditure on training increased by 40%, from €474.8 million in 2008 to €665.4 million in 2013, while the number of participants (stock figure) on training courses rose even more, rising 63%, from 34,457 people in 2008 to 56,137 people in 2013 (Eurostat Labour Market database). In order to cater for an increase in training needs, the duration of FÁS/Solas course offerings to the unemployed was shortened in many cases. For example, the largest course offering targeted at unemployed people, Specific Skills Training, was restructured to include the provision of shorter discreet modules, turning typical 30-week programmes into 10-week courses. The provision of online, blended, part-time and evening courses also increased. While these changes raised the numbers of people trained, concerns were also raised about the quality of training provided and the likelihood of progression and employment outcomes (NESC, 2011; Murphy, 2015).

Outside of existing training programmes, under the government's *Action plan for jobs*, a number of specific funding programmes were announced in an effort to stimulate the provision of more market-oriented courses, which are open to tender by private, public and not-for-profit providers. An example of this new approach is Momentum, a programme launched at the end of 2012 under the Labour Market Education and Training Fund and targeted at the long-term unemployed. Initially, 6,500 places were offered, for which participants are identified by the DSP. Operating on a payment-by-results model, payment to course providers is partly based on the length of time participants remain in work. Under Solas's strategic plan (Solas, 2014: 33), it is anticipated that this funding model and outsourcing of training to private providers will become more widespread in the sector. In line with changes to activation programmes under DSP responsibility, Momentum also represents a leaner approach to training. Participants receive either a Jobseeker's Allowance or Back to Education Allowance, but no travel or subsistence allowances are paid, which remains the case with other Solas training programmes. By the end of 2014, 5,894 participants had begun the programme, 3,538 had finished and 24% of finishers found full-time employment (Exodea Consulting, 2014).

A number of changes have also been made to training allowances and access to existing FÁS/Solas programmes. Training allowances have been reduced in line with reductions to working-age social protection payments, with attendant complex and fragmented differences related to age and the type of welfare payment that the trainee is entitled to. Participants who are long-term unemployed received a further weekly 'training bonus' of €31.80 per week. By 2014, this was abolished for new participants. More fundamentally in terms of access, only participants with an underlying entitlement to Jobseekers Allowance or Jobseeker's Benefit have been paid training allowances since 2010. This affects previously entitled social welfare recipients such as those in receipt of One-Parent Family Payment and disability payments and others who are not on the Live Register (Joint Oireachtas Committee on Education and Social Protection, 2014).

Concluding remarks

As documented in this chapter, major change has been taking place in almost all areas of Ireland's LMP. The crisis has instigated significant efforts to reorient elements of the existing system. The notion of the shift from 'passive' to 'active' refers not only to a shift in focus from social protection to activation, but also to an internal shift in activation policy from an emphasis on occupation to labour market integration and a mutual obligations model of employment services. While the shift in emphasis from occupation to labour market integration is, in reality, still limited, at the same time, existing activation programmes have been retrenched and newer programmes are typically characterised by a shorter duration and lesser benefits. A tougher incentivisation regime, with greater emphasis on negative incentives for the unemployed, particularly the long-term unemployed, youth unemployed and lone parents, is also evident. New institutional and governance arrangements are also significant, involving the belated integration of social protection and activation services, as well as shifts towards more marketisation and privatisation of services.

The changes occurring in Ireland's LMP regime have yet to settle. In particular, the implications of the ways in which institutions have been reconfigured and how the shift from 'passive' to 'active' services will unfold in the longer term have yet be discerned as new agencies and practices are in their infancy, and as attention potentially extends from those officially classified as unemployed to other risk categories in the social protection system. As the pressures of fiscal consolidation seem to abate, greater scope may arise for more positive forms of incentivisation, with minor signs of this emerging in the 2015 Budget, along with some moderation of the more stringent reforms of One-Parent Family Payment. However, the bigger question that remains open is activation into what or to what purpose the system is being reformed. Ireland's employment protection regime remains weak, the incidence of low-paid employment is high and involuntary part-time employment remains high. In this context, the question arises as to whether changes may not so much be giving way to flexicurity as contributing to sustained labour market precarity, elements of which grew during the crisis and about which there appears to be a degree of acceptance as part of a continuing strategy of cost containment and economic competitiveness.

Notes

1. The Live Register is a register of the unemployed, compiled monthly by the DSP. It comprises individuals claiming unemployed benefits, including those also working part-time or casually.

2. Under the Protection of Employment (Temporary Agency Work) Act 2012, which gives effect to the EU Directive on Temporary Agency Work (Directive 2008/104/EC), temporary agency workers are granted equal treatment with temporary workers who were directly hired.

References

Bonoli, G. (2011) 'Active labour market policy in a changing economic context', in J. Clasen and D. Clegg (eds) *Regulating the risk of unemployment*, Oxford: Oxford UP, pp 318–32.

Bonoli, G. (2013) *The origins of active social policy*, Oxford: Oxford UP.

Clasen, J. and Clegg, D. (eds) (2011) *Regulating the risk of unemployment*, Oxford: Oxford UP.

Council of the European Union (2016) 'Recommendation for a COUNCIL RECOMMENDATION on the 2016 national reform programme of Ireland and delivering a Council opinion on the 2016 stability programme of Ireland'. Available at: https://ec.europa.eu/info/publications/2016-european-semester-country-specific recommendations-commission-recommendations_en

Dáil Debates (2017) 'Written Answers Nos. 313-335, Labour activation measures', *Dáil Éireann Debate*, 951(3). Available at: http://oireachtasdebates.oireachtas.ie/debates%20authoring/DebatesWebPack.nsf/takes/dail2017052300068?opendocument&highlight=10%2C867#WRP00100

Department of Education and Skills (2012) *An action plan for Solas*, Dublin: Department of Education and Skills.

Doherty, M. (2016) 'New morning? Irish labour law post-austerity', Maynooth University, Department of Law. Available at: http://papers.ssrn.com/sol3/papers.cfm?abstract_id=2827256

Doorley, J. (2015) *JobBridge: Stepping stone or dead end?*, Dublin: National Youth Council of Ireland.

DSFA (Department of Social and Family Affairs) (2006) *Government discussion paper: Proposals for supporting lone parents*, Dublin: DSFA.

DSP (Department of Social Protection) (2012a) *A review of Department of Social Protection employment support schemes*, Dublin: DSP.

DSP (2012b) *High level issues paper emanating from review of Department of Social Protection employment support schemes*, Dublin: DSP.

DSP (2012c) *Community employment financial review of schemes*, Dublin: DSP.
DSP (2015) *Community employment procedures manual*, Dublin: DSP.
DSP (2016) 'Statistical information on social welfare services 2015: Section A summary and financial'. Available at: www.welfare.ie/en/Pages/Annual-SWS-Statistical-Information-Report-2015.aspx
Dukelow, F. (2015a) 'State to the rescue: the bank guarantee and Ireland's financialised neo-liberal growth model', in R. Meade and F. Dukelow (eds) *Defining events: Power, resistance and identity in twenty-first-century Ireland*, Manchester: Manchester UP, pp 143–60.
Dukelow, F. (2015b) '"Pushing against an open door": reinforcing the neo-liberal policy paradigm in Ireland and the impact of EU intrusion', *Comparative European Politics*, 13(1): 93–111.
EAPN Ireland (European Anti-Poverty Network Ireland) (2015) 'Position paper on positive activation'. Available at: http://www.eapn.ie/eapn/position-paper-on-positive-activation-2
European Commission (2015) *Macroeconomic imbalances: Country report Ireland*, Brussels: European Commission.
European Commission (2016) 'State aid: Ireland gave illegal tax benefits to Apple worth up to €13 billion', European Commission Press release, 30 August. Available at: http://europa.eu/rapid/press-release_IP-16-2923_en.htm
Exodea Consulting (2014) *Programme evaluation: Momentum programme for projects under the labour market education and training fund*, Dublin: Solas.
Finn, D. and Gloster, R. (2010) *Lone parent obligations: A review of recent evidence on the work-related requirements within the benefit systems of different countries*, London: Department for Work and Pensions.
Glynn, I., with Kelly, T. and Mac Éinrí, P. (2015) *The re-emergence of emigration from Ireland: New trends in an old story*, Washington, DC: Migration Policy Institute.
Government of Ireland (2012) *Pathways to work: Government statement on labour market activation*, Dublin: Government of Ireland.
Government of Ireland (2013) *Pathways to work 2013*, Dublin: Government of Ireland.
Government of Ireland (2015) *Pathways to work 2015*, Dublin: Government of Ireland.
Government of Ireland (2016) *Pathways to work 2016–2020*, Dublin: Government of Ireland.
Grubb, D., Singh, S. and Tergeist, P. (2009) 'Activation policies in Ireland', OECD Social, Employment and Migration Working Papers, No. 75.

Häusermann, S. (2012) 'The politics of old and new social policies', in G. Bonoli and D. Natali (eds) *The politics of the new welfare state*, Oxford: Oxford UP, pp 111–32.

IMF (International Monetary Fund) (2016) 'Ireland staff report for the 2016 Article IV Consultation and fifth post programme monitoring discussions'. Available at: http://www.imf.org/external/pubs/ft/scr/2016/cr16256.pdf

Immervoll, H. and Scarpetta, L. (2012) 'Activation and employment support policies in OECD countries. An overview of current approaches', *IZA Journal of Labour Policy*, 1(9): 1–20.

Irish Times (2011) 'Exemption sought on agency pay', *Irish Times*, 2 September.

Joint Oireachtas Committee on Jobs, Enterprise and Innovation (2015) *Report on low pay, decent work and a living wage, November 2015*, Dublin: Houses of the Oireachtas.

Joint Oireachtas Committee on Jobs, Education and Social Protection (2012) *A review of the status of casual workers in Ireland*, Dublin: Houses of the Oireachtas.

Joint Oireachtas Committee on Social Protection and Education (2014) 'Eligibility for employment activation measures: Discussion', 12 June. Available at: http://oireachtasdebates.oireachtas.ie/Debates%20Authoring/DebatesWebPack.nsf/committeetakes/EDJ2014061200001?opendocument

Kelly, E., McGuinness, S. and Walsh, J. (2015) *An evaluation of the Back to Education Allowance*, Dublin: ESRI.

Lenihan, B. (2009) 'Financial statement of the Minister for Finance Mr. Brian Lenihan, T.D.', 9 December. Available at: http://www.budget.gov.ie

Lødemel, I. and Moreira, A. (2014) *Activation or workfare? Governance and the neo-liberal convergence*, Oxford: Oxford UP.

Loftus, C. (2012) *Decent work? The impact of the recession on low paid workers*, Dublin: Mandate Trade Union.

Martin, J.P. (2015) 'Activation and active labour market policies in OECD countries: stylised facts and evidence on their effectiveness', *IZA Journal of Labour Policy*, 4(4): 1–29.

McGauran, A.M. (2013) *Activation*, NESC Secretariat Papers, Paper No.8, Dublin: NESC.

McGuinness, S., O'Connell, P.J. and Kelly, E. (2013) *Carrots, no stick, no driver: The employment impact of job search assistance in a regime with minimal monitoring and sanctions*, Dublin: UCD Geary Institute.

Murphy, M.P. (2012a) 'The politics of Irish labour activation 1980 to 2010', *Administration*, 60(2): 27–49.

Murphy, M.P. (2012b) *Careless to careful activation: Making activation work for women*, Dublin: National Women's Council of Ireland.

Murphy, M.P. (2015) *JobBridge: Time to start again?*, Dublin: Impact Trade Union.

Murphy, M.P. and Loftus, C. (2015) 'A precarious future: an Irish example of flex-insecurity', in S. Ó'Riain, F. Behling, R. Ciccia and E. Flaherty (eds) *The changing worlds and workplaces of capitalism*, Basingstoke: Palgrave, pp 98–117.

NERA (National Employment Rights Authority) (no date) 'Review 1st January to 30th September 2015'. Available at: www.workplacerelations.ie/en/Publications_Forms/NERA-Review-2015.pdf

NESC (National Economic and Social Council) (2011) *Supports and services for unemployed jobseekers: Challenges and opportunities in a time of recession*, Dublin: NESC.

OECD (Organisation for Economic Co-operation and Development) (2014a) 'How does Ireland compare? OECD employment outlook 2014'. Available at: http://webcache.googleusercontent.com/search?q=cache:96L3MQBncOQJ:www.oecd.org/ireland/EMO-IRL-EN.pdf+&cd=1&hl=en&ct=clnk&gl=uk

OECD (2014b) *Ireland's action plan for jobs: A preliminary review*, Paris: OECD.

OECD (2015) *Economic surveys Ireland September 2015 overview*, Paris: OECD.

OECD (2016) *Employment outlook*, Paris: OECD.

O'Rorke, G. (2016) *Characteristics and implications of the level of household joblessness in Ireland*, Staff Paper, Dublin: Department of Public Expenditure and Reform.

O'Sullivan, M., Turner, T., McMahon, J., Ryan, L., Lavelle, J., Murphy, C., O'Brien, M. and Gunnigle, P. (2015) *A study on the prevalence of zero hours contracts among Irish employers and their impact on employees*, Limerick: Kemmy Business School, University of Limerick.

Pina, Á. (2011) 'Structural reforms to reduce unemployment and restore competitiveness in Ireland', OECD Economics Department Working Papers, No. 910.

Rogers, S. (2014) 'Poor uptake prompts Gateway reform', *Irish Examiner*, 16 June.

Social Welfare Appeals Office (2016) *Annual report 2015*, Dublin: Social Welfare Appeals Office.

Solas (2014) *Further education and training strategy 2014–2019*, Dublin: Solas.

Van Berkel, R. and Borghi, V. (2007) 'New modes of governance in activation policies', *International Journal of Sociology and Social Policy*, 27(7/8): 277–86.

Whitson, C. (2014) 'The reform of joint labour committees – the re-commodification of labour?', *Industrial Relations Journal*, 45(5): 409–23.

Wiggan, J. (2015) 'What variety of employment service quasi-market? Ireland's JobPath as a private power market', in Z. Irving, M. Fenger and J. Husdon (eds) *Social policy review 27*, Bristol: The Policy Press, pp 151–70.

TEN

Retrenchment, conditionality and flexibility – UK labour market policies in the era of austerity

Elke Heins and Hayley Bennett

Introduction

The UK is a typical example of both a liberal market economy (Hall and Soskice, 2001) and liberal welfare state regime (Esping-Andersen, 1990). From the outset, it is important to stress that the UK does not fit a framework that distinguishes between an 'industrial logic' and a 'post-industrial logic' when it comes to labour market policies and public unemployment benefits as the industrial logic was never relevant here to begin with and the crisis did not change this. It is also important to bear in mind that – even before the vote to leave the European Union (EU) – the EU's influence on social policy in the UK was relatively limited and that 'soft' unbinding policy recommendations had little impact.

This is not to say, however, that no change in labour market policies has taken place since the crisis. The following analysis will first examine the impact of the crisis on Britain and then map the changes and continuities in the areas of unemployment benefits, employment protection legislation, active labour market policies (ALMPs), training and human capital formation, and needs-based social protection for the unemployed. The year 2010 represents a key turning point in two respects: it was the year in which the full onset of the crisis was felt in Britain, and also the year when the government changed to a Conservative-dominated coalition with the Liberal Democrats (in 2015, replaced by a Conservative majority government), resulting in a number of significant welfare and labour market reforms.

We argue that since the crisis, the pattern of labour market and unemployment policies has changed towards even more flexibility and less income protection despite growing problems of precariousness. Many of the existing programmes that aimed at human capital formation have either been redefined as a work test or turned into an opportunity for employers to undercut existing employment protection legislation and the minimum wage. With the exception of a brief 'Keynesian' moment in which the focus was on fiscal stimulus and one temporary direct labour market programme was introduced, the emphasis has been on 'deficit reduction'. Rather than seeing the crisis as a turning point, a policy path taken since the 1980s was continued. Any 'old industrial logic' of income and job protection – which was never particularly relevant in the British experience in any case – has been further undermined over the decades, while any tentative efforts towards social investment-type policies in line with a post-industrial logic have been cut back.

The UK crisis context

In the UK, the crisis was, first and foremost, financial in character as British banks have been deeply entangled in the international financing system that was negatively affected by the US sub-prime mortgage crisis. Due to the importance of the financial sector and the construction industry, as well as the strong reliance on credit-fuelled domestic demand – or 'privatised Keynesianism' as Crouch (2011) put it – the British economy was hit severely after the country's housing bubble burst (Farnsworth, 2011; Barnes and Wren, 2012). Fears of a bank run and collapses of major mortgage lenders first emerged in autumn 2007 and were prevented only by major banking bail-out packages. Within a year, the financial crisis therefore led to an economic crisis, as expressed in rising unemployment (see Figure 10.1) and decreasing gross domestic product (GDP) rates (see Figure 10.2).

Figure 10.1 shows an increase in unemployment from under 6% in 2008 to around 8% in 2010/11. While the general trend runs in parallel with European-wide unemployment figures, the overall level was lower in the UK, and in contrast to the EU28 figures, the UK was one of the few countries in which unemployment rates have declined since 2011. By the end of 2015, it dropped to close to 5% (ONS, 2015b).

However, what looks like a positive labour market development is based on a strong increase in self-employment. In 2014, 4.6 million people (15% of those in work) were self-employed in their main job, a record number in the past four decades. Across the EU, the UK has had the third-largest percentage rise in self-employment since 2009 (ONS, 2014a). Importantly, the average income from self-employment has fallen by 22%, even more than employee incomes, since 2008/09. Self-employed workers are thus at risk of being less well-paid, but also

Figure 10.1: Unemployment rates, EU28 and UK, 2007–16

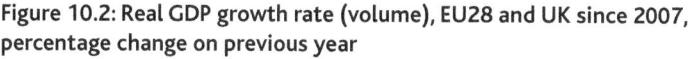

Source: Eurostat

Figure 10.2: Real GDP growth rate (volume), EU28 and UK since 2007, percentage change on previous year

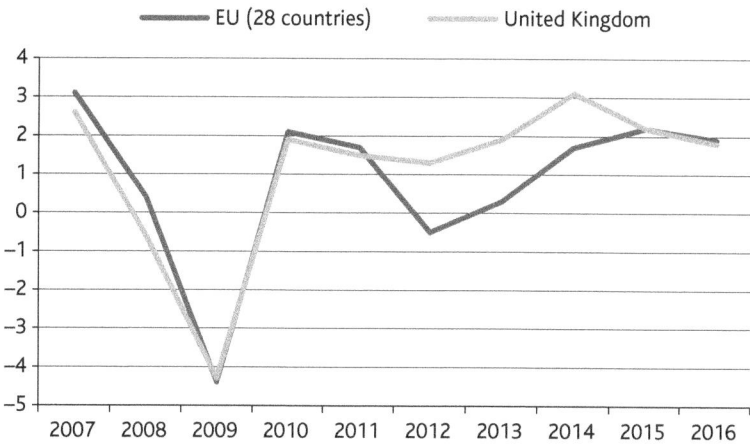

Source: Eurostat

less secure and unable to obtain social security coverage for illness or maternity.

After a huge contraction of the economy in 2008/09 – the economy shrank by 6% between the first quarter of 2008 and the second quarter of 2009 – the UK returned to a growth pattern quite rapidly thereafter (see Figure 10.2). By the end of 2014, GDP levels were estimated to have been about 3% higher than at the beginning of 2008 (ONS, 2014b).

The immediate response to the crisis by the Labour government led by Prime Minister Gordon Brown represented a short 'Keynesianist' revival (Clegg, 2010; Farnsworth, 2011). The *Pre-Budget report* of November 2008 included a number of short-term stimulus packages (HM Treasury, 2008), which added to the public debt that had already increased significantly due to the rescue measures for several UK banks (see Figure 10.3). Importantly, with the exception of the Future Jobs Fund (FJF) (see later), the stimulus measures were not aimed at keeping up employment directly, but consisted of fiscal measures such as a lowering of the value added tax (VAT) rate and other tax rate changes.

As the following analysis of different labour market policy instruments will show, this 'Keynesianist' moment was very short-lived. After the general election in May 2010, a Coalition government was formed between the Conservatives and Liberal Democrats that put so-called 'austerity' in economic and social policy firmly on the agenda.

Figure 10.3: UK gross government debt as percentage of GDP since 2007

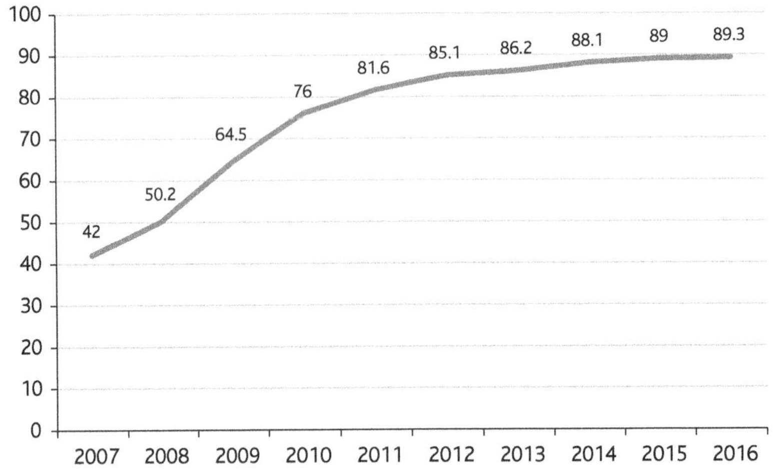

Source: Eurostat

Unemployment benefits: Jobseeker's Allowance

Labour market policies based on an industrial logic – that is, serving an income-replacement function for labour market 'insiders' – had been eroded long before the onset of the crisis. In fact, it could be argued that unemployment benefits were never really 'insider-oriented' as they always primarily fulfilled a poverty-alleviation rather than an income-replacement function due to the low level of benefits. Although

Beveridge had originally envisaged that the post-war British welfare state should be based on a reciprocal principle, the link between National Insurance contributions and benefits had been weakened over time. Apart from a period in the 1960s and 1970s when earnings-related supplements were available, unemployment benefit levels have been flat-rate and contribution-based benefits converged with needs-based assistance (Clasen, 2005).

Already decades before the crisis, the focus of unemployment benefits shifted towards targeted and means-tested welfare and tighter controls (Sinfield, 2013). When we compare the expenditure on contribution-based benefits with those on means-tested benefits, we see how irrelevant the former is (see Figure 10.4). In 1996/97, they made up 10% of total social security spending, but only 5% in 2014/15 (Hills, 2015: 26). The decline in contribution-based benefits over time is partly a result of the changed character of unemployment (from relatively short durations, on average, to more long-term unemployment) but also of the tightening of contributory and other requirements (Clasen, 2009).

Tellingly, unemployment benefits were renamed Jobseeker's Allowance (JSA) in 1996 to emphasise the function of seeking new employment rather than offering income support for those who have lost their work, and subsequent governments have not done anything to alter this (Slater, 2012: 956). JSA is separated into two

Figure 10.4: Jobseeker's Allowance expenditure, UK, 2001–17

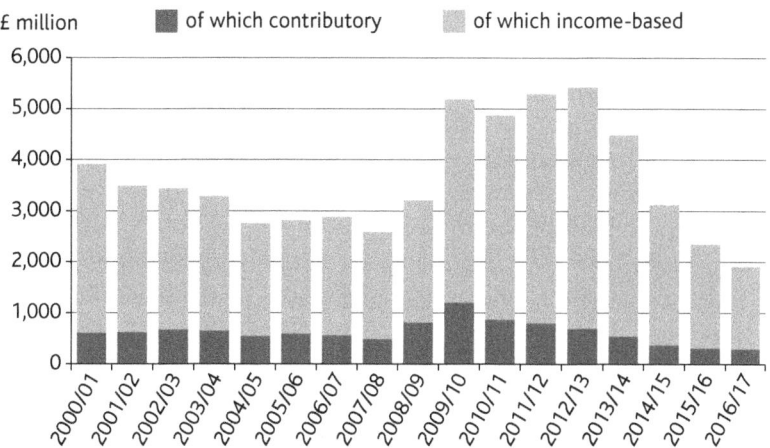

Notes: Data for year 2016/17 is a forecast; all other years show actual expenditure. Figures are adjusted to 2016/2017 prices. Figures for Great Britain only (excludes Northern Ireland).
Source: DWP expenditure and caseloads data, and 2016 Autumn Statement

components, a contribution-based and an income-based part, but paid at the same basic level. The distinction between contribution-based and means-tested benefits is thus mainly an administrative matter and has little relevance in public perception. Contribution-based JSA can be claimed for a maximum of six months by those who meet the eligibility requirements of having worked for a minimum of 26 weeks in the two years before claiming benefits and having paid sufficient National Insurance contributions. The flat-rate benefit in 2016/17 was £73.10 per week, with a lower rate for the under-25s (£57.90).

Although the rates have been increased over the years, the general trend regarding this type of labour market policy is slow retrenchment in the form of 'policy drift', which had already started under previous governments before the crisis. While benefits received by disabled people and pensioners (which are protected by a triple lock that makes sure pensions will increase by whatever is highest – inflation, wages or 2.5%) increased from 2013 to 2015 in line with consumer-price inflation (2.7%), benefits and tax credits for working-age people were increased by only 1%. This typically lower-than-inflation increase is part of the government's professed aim to 'ensure the overall affordability of the welfare system' (HM Treasury, 2012: para 1.155). Despite the lack of strong automatic stabilisers that maintain demand during economic downturns in the UK welfare system, there was no attempt to increase income support for the unemployed in response to the crisis (Clegg, 2010). Working-age benefits unrelated to having children already fell under the Labour government, despite the effects of the economic crisis (Hills, 2015: 23). However, it is important to recognise the existence of 'functional equivalents'. Higher-income and short-term unemployed can often rely on private unemployment insurance in the form of mortgage protection plans (Clasen, 2007), as well as non-statutory redundancy payments (Clasen, 2009). Thus, if we want to speak of an insider/outsider problem, then this refers not to the effects of public benefits, as in other European countries, but to wider inequalities in the types of employment: executives and other high-income employees often receive very generous 'golden handshakes', while other types of employees receive little or no redundancy pay at all.

Employment protection legislation

Overall, the UK is characterised by a very flexible labour market, with the most lax employment protection among Organisation for Economic Co-operation and Development (OECD) countries before and after the crisis (Venn, 2009). Importantly, employment protection legislation in the UK was used not to support collective bargaining, but to reduce its relevance, as it was seen as a hindrance to 'flexibility' (Clasen, 2009: 82). After the crisis, minor improvements in protecting employee rights introduced under the Employment Act 2002 were reversed again and the OECD employment protection legislation index for regular workers decreased in 2013 to the pre-2000 value of 1.03 (OECD, 2013).

Since 2010, the Conservative-led Coalition/Conservative government have removed or reduced 1,900 substantive regulations to support employers by removing 'bureaucratic burdens' (UK Government, 2013). The government presented employment protection legislation reform as a necessary response to the global crisis and to maintain Britain's competitiveness. Consequently, many employment protection legislation reforms affect workers' rights. For example, one major reform to employment tribunal legislation means that employees now have to wait longer and participate in mediation before approaching a tribunal, employers are no longer required to provide supporting evidence for the applicant's case, and it is now more difficult for employees to access Legal Aid to support a case (TUC, 2014). In addition, since 2013, employees have had to pay an upfront fee of up to £1,200, which considerably raises the stakes for low-income workers (Phillips, 2013). Redressing cases before an employment tribunal has thus become financially risky for employees.

The government claims that the changes to employment tribunals will save businesses £40 million per year (UK Government, 2013). The number of cases brought to tribunals has decreased, and as a result of the changes, it is suspected that many employers may find it easier to break employment laws without being held accountable through the tribunal system (TUC, 2012; The Law Society of Scotland, 2014). For example, cases have come to light in which redundant workers were rehired by the same company to do the same job for less pay or on less secure contracts (Malik, 2014; Meikle, 2014). There are also claims that regular employees are being replaced by people put on unpaid mandatory work placements by the benefit agency (HOC, 2012).

Many of the recent changes to employment protection legislation also reduce the security and rights of temporary employees. Many employment rights – such as the right not to be unfairly dismissed or the right to redundancy pay – rely on the legal definition of 'employee'. Since 2010, there has been an increase in employment contracts using the term 'worker' rather than 'employee'. In general, workers are entitled to the same rights as employees: protection from unlawful deductions, the national minimum wage, holiday pay and working time regulations regarding rest breaks, the 48-hour week and its opt-out clause. They are also entitled to statutory maternity, paternity and adoption pay. 'Workers', however, do not automatically have the right to maternity, paternity or adoption leave, or the right to request flexible working or time off for emergencies. They also do not have the automatic right to protection from unfair dismissal, a minimum notice period to terminate their employment or statutory redundancy pay. Furthermore, the government has increased the qualifying period of continuous employment for unfair dismissal claims to two years (Pullan, 2013).

On the whole, much employment has become more flexible and less protected since the crisis. There has been a significant increase not only in low-paid self-employment, but also in the number of contracts with no stated working hours. These so-called 'zero-hour contracts' are a prime example of the increase in flexible labour arrangements as they require individuals to be ready for work but with no certainty about how many hours of work (and thus income) there will be from week to week. In 2008, there were approximately 143,000 zero-hour workers in the UK (CIPD, 2013); by the end of 2014, there were nearly 700,000 (2.3% of all people in employment) (ONS, 2015a).

Zero-hour workers are extremely vulnerable to poverty or exploitation by employers as they can – like all workers – be refused benefits for voluntarily leaving a job. It is therefore difficult for zero-hour workers to leave employment when the hours are reduced. Despite these tensions, in the six months leading up to April 2013, 27% of Jobcentre Plus advertised vacancies had no guaranteed income (HOC Scottish Affairs Committee, 2014: 42). Not only do these entail a precarious position with regard to employment legislation, but these staff earned an average of £9 an hour, compared with £15 an hour for other employees (Pennycook et al, 2013). About 25% of workers on zero-hour contracts are full-time students, but 70% are in permanent jobs. A total of 26% stated that they would like to work longer hours (Pullan, 2013; Brinkley, 2013).

The government's recent employment protection legislation reforms are part of a much larger policy reform process that seeks to increase the flexibility of workers, reduce employment protection and legislation, and consequently, for many people, affect the relationship between employment and welfare provision. Even without substantial formal changes to employment protection legislation and despite a very low protection starting point, retrenchment has taken place as employment is now even less protected than before the crisis and more and more people are being moved into very precarious jobs.

Active labour market policies

The Labour government initiated large-scale activation reforms after 1997, introducing a suite of 'New Deal' welfare-to-work programmes and, in 2000, creating Jobcentre Plus to act as a 'one-stop shop', coordinating activities between benefit claims and activation and support programmes. These welfare-to-work programmes also reached out to a range of working-age groups outside the labour market and were often administered as part of a new 'quasi-market' system (Finn, 2011; Griggs et al, 2014).

While some of the New Deal programmes incorporated training, wage subsidy and job creation options, on the whole, this was a work-first, supply-side approach to move individuals into the labour market as quickly as possible. Such programmes were introduced during times of better labour market performance and provided support for individuals struggling to enter the labour market. The early welfare-to-work programmes were also voluntary for most out-of-work groups, although participation became increasingly mandatory for the young unemployed and for some long-term unemployed (Finn, 2011). For particularly deprived areas, the government also introduced place-based programmes involving more support options than the national schemes. For example, the Employment Zone (EZ) initiatives were aimed at the long-term unemployed in unemployment 'hot spots'. For people not finding work through the New Deal programmes, the government introduced the 'Step Up' programme, in which participants were mandated onto 12-month national minimum wage employment placements (Finn, 2003; McGuinness and Dar, 2014).

Most of the New Deal and local programmes were merged into the 'Flexible New Deal' in 2008. This welfare-to-work programme became mandatory for more categories of claimants and contracted providers and Jobcentre Plus (to an extent) complemented mainstream provision with special support programmes. However, on the whole, the government did not amend ALMP programmes in response to the crisis; instead, reforms were in line with strategies devised pre-crisis (Slater, 2012; McKnight, 2015).

Even under the Labour government, expenditure on ALMPs had increased only modestly (Clasen, 2009). The Conservative–Liberal Democrat Coalition government then abolished most place-based funds, cancelled existing activation programmes and increased the 'marketisation' of activation programmes by making them even more target-based than they were before. The biggest change has been the introduction of the 'Work Programme' in 2010 to replace the 'Flexible New Deal'. Participation is now mandatory for most groups of claimants, including long-term health benefit claimants and lone parents, who had previously been seen as having 'legitimate' reasons for being out of work.

While the previous Labour government planned a similar large-scale welfare-to-work programme reform ('Flexible New Deal' phase 2), the Coalition's changes have since led to a number of changes to the services offered to job seekers. First, the Work Programme is delivered predominately by private-sector organisations and contracts follow a 'black-box' approach whereby providers design and include whatever services and training they consider suitable for job seekers (Bennett, 2017; Mirza-Davies, 2014). The government therefore no longer outlines specific training and human investment requirements and most Work Programme providers do not offer accredited training for job seekers. Second, the amalgamation of programmes has led to a decoupling of locally provided, publicly funded training provision from the mainstream welfare-to-work activity that some job seekers previously accessed to supplement mainstream welfare-to-work support (Bennett and Clegg, 2013). Finally, alongside the Work Programme, the government introduced new conditionality measures and toughened the sanctioning regime. In this way, the Work Programme not only lacks funding for and political interest in social investment initiatives, but is also embedded within a more punitive system.

The government has introduced a swathe of programmes that require job seekers to undertake particular tasks and Jobcentre Plus may sanction those who do not comply. On top of a renewed Jobseeker's Agreement, which sets out what a claimant has agreed to do to find work, some individuals may be mandated to take part in the new 'Help to Work' scheme, which entails either visiting the job centre daily or taking up 'community work placements' comprising work-related activity for the benefit of the community for up to 30 weeks (CAB, 2015; McKnight, 2015). There is also a separate 'Work Experience Programme' that is voluntary to join but becomes compulsory once the claimant has accepted a place offer. The Mandatory Work Activity Scheme, introduced in 2010 and delivered by private organisations, provides (unpaid) work or work-related activity for up to 30 hours a week over a four-week period. Overall, these new measures seek to 'correct' job-seeking behaviour and, in some cases, adopt a 'work for your benefit' approach (McGuinness and Dar, 2014). A final notable change is that the Jobcentre Plus portfolio of services for job seekers has been reduced as part of the general cuts across the public service. Due to recent reforms to benefit administration, such as an increase in conditionality, Jobcentre Plus has become a benefit administrator only, emphasising its controlling rather than supportive function.

Overall, we see an increased turn towards mandatory 'workfare' in the provision of national activation programmes. Supplementary 'enabling' social-investment-type policies delivered through Jobcentre Plus are being cut back or left out of contract requirements in order to reduce costs. This is particularly the case in England, as we will highlight in the next section.

Training and human capital formation

Leaving training mainly to employers, the UK has never had a strong public tradition in this policy area. In the early 1980s, a range of programmes – including job-creation schemes – were introduced to address rising unemployment, but after a short expansionary phase, these were scaled back again in the late 1980s and the focus shifted from training for the adult unemployed to providing work incentives and subsidising work experience for the long-term unemployed (Clasen, 2009).

As outlined earlier, most UK activation and employment programmes implemented since the economic crises are 'work-first' and mandatory in nature. An exception to this was the 'Young Person's Guarantee' (YPG). The YPG was introduced in the 2009 Budget and involved the creation of temporary, full-time (25 hours per week) jobs undertaking work of 'social benefit'. All young people (aged 18–24) unemployed for 12 months or longer would be guaranteed a job, the opportunity of work experience or work-focused training. The YPG was formally introduced in January 2010 and operated until March 2011 (Harari, 2011).

A notable part of the YPG was the FJF, a £1 billion fund to provide up to 150,000 guaranteed jobs. As an explicit crisis measure, the FJF was a temporary job-creation scheme designed in response to concerns about the long-term effects of rising youth unemployment. The Labour government thus acknowledged that, for some people, unemployment was a demand-side issue requiring job-creation policy responses. The Department for Work and Pensions (DWP) therefore provided funding to subsidise temporary paid jobs lasting six months for young people and those living in disadvantaged areas.

Long-term unemployed young people were also offered a number of other options: sectoral routes, which involved training in specific sectors (those with growing employment) with employer support; participation on a Community Task Force (which involved work experience placements); work-focused training; assistance with self-employment; or provision through the New Deal for Young People in specific areas (DWP, 2012). However, within the context of a growing punitive discourse from the Conservative Party in opposition, the Labour government later announced that all those in the 18–24 age bracket unemployed for over 10 months were *required* to participate in one of the options offered under the YPG (Harari, 2011). In the event of failure to do so, participation in a Community Task Force became mandatory, with the possibility of benefit sanctions (DWP, 2012). In 2010, the new government extended the fund by one year to provide an additional 200,000 jobs at an extra cost of £300 million, but then abolished it, citing high costs. By the close of the programme in 2011, 105,220 temporary employment positions were filled (Fishwick et al, 2011), 85% of which were in the 18–24 age group (DWP, 2012).

Excluding the FJF, the government did not introduce notable training and human development initiatives. On the contrary, driven by the austerity agenda, funding and resources for this policy area have since been reduced. For example, large-scale reductions to public service spending included a 20% reduction in the further education budget for adults during the spending review period of 2014–15 (HM Treasury, 2010). However, mapping changes in this policy area is not straightforward. The governance structure of adult learning and training programmes is complex and involves a range of central government departments, devolved administrations, government agencies and ad hoc initiatives. This is a historical arrangement and has changed little since 2010. Support for the unemployed, including training and skills as part of the work-first activation agenda, is the remit of the DWP in England, Scotland and Wales and the responsibility of the Department for Social Development (benefits) and the Department for Employment and Learning (training and skills) in Northern Ireland, whereas training, education and skills policies are arranged independently from the provision of ALMPs for the unemployed. Efforts by the previous Labour government to link adult training services provided through the Skills Funding Agency and local colleges under the remit of the Department for Business, Innovation & Skills (BIS) with the activities of Jobcentre Plus under the remit of the DWP have not been followed through by the Coalition government (Goerne and Clegg, 2013).

The fragmented picture is further complicated as training provision and lifelong learning are devolved in Scotland, Wales and Northern Ireland. There is no room to cover all the initiatives and programmes before and after the crisis throughout the UK, so we focus here only on England.

Since 2010, there has been a large increase in programmes that involve mandating benefit recipients and young people into 'work experience' positions or schemes that involve working for an employer. However, most do not pay the statutory minimum wage and participants are not legally classed as 'employees'. For young people, this includes the new 'Sector Based Work Academies', the 'Young People's Work Experience Programme' and a new 'Traineeships' scheme. The government have portrayed these three initiatives as 'skills development and human investment' schemes, despite the limited certified training provision and low (if any) pay scales. The Coalition government did not share the previous policy ambitions regarding social investment through state-funded skills and training. Instead, the new strategy highlighted the 'shared responsibility' for skills, with employers and learners being asked to contribute to the costs (Foster et al, 2011). Specific loans are offered to fund learning and training administered through private banks that must be paid back by learners once they achieve a specific wage level (Mirza-Davies, 2014: 5). Supplementary training programmes previously offered by Jobcentre Plus have been replaced by mandatory work activities outlined in the previous section and 'flexible' funding at the discretion of local Jobcentre Plus offices (CAB, 2015).

Human capital building is now taking place primarily through apprenticeships. Well before the crisis, in 2000, the Labour government revived the traditional apprenticeship scheme under which apprentices could access part-time education and training, were employed by a particular firm, and received a small weekly wage. The 'Modern Apprenticeship' scheme targeted all young people and offered employers financial assistance if they took on apprentices. In addition, a pre-apprenticeship scheme, Entry to Employment, was introduced for individuals with low educational attainment who might not normally be able to access an apprenticeship place. In 2005/06 alone, the government spent £920 million on apprenticeships and £181 million on the Entry to Employment programme. However, these figures are comparatively low in comparison with other labour market tools. Apprenticeship starts represented just 1% of the working-age population between 2005 and 2010, rising to 2% during 2010–12/13 and reverting to 1% in 2013/14.

Despite the lower number of apprenticeship starts in 2013/14 and 2014/15 compared with previous years, apprenticeships continue to play a central role post-2010. There are nearly three times as many apprenticeship starts in 2014/15 than 10 years earlier. However, through a number of reforms, the human investment and skills training aspect of apprenticeships has been diluted. Programme-led apprenticeships, delivered mainly by further education colleges, have been discontinued (Hodgson and Spours, 2011) and, in their place, employers are encouraged to take responsibility for the design of apprenticeships. Post-2010, the majority of people starting apprenticeships work in the low-paid service sector rather than the traditional manufacturing sector (Mirza-Davies, 2015: 1), raising questions about the long-term outcomes of recent apprenticeships. There has also been a threefold increase in the number of apprenticeship starts by people aged 25 and over between 2009/10 and 2013/14 (Mirza-Davies, 2015: 5), nursing suspicions that these are not serving the aim of human capital building, but simply constitute a cheap hiring option for employers.

Available figures on apprenticeships do, indeed, give reasons for concern. Data from 2010/11 show that 'workplace skills training for adults has fallen by 275,400 places, suggesting that employers have simply shifted their workers onto apprenticeships to continue getting government funding' (Lanning, 2012). There is also significant variance regarding the quality and pay of apprenticeship places, for example, 56% of engineering apprentices receive off-the-job training compared with only 24% of retail apprentices, and apprentices in construction are earning 32% more than their counterparts in other sectors (DfE and BIS, 2013: 17). The lack of definition and variable training and pay rates can be used by employers to circumvent the statutory minimum wage requirements as the minimum hourly rate for apprentices is lower than for regular jobs. Alongside the reforms to the apprenticeship schemes, the government also introduced a separate 'Traineeship' programme as a supposed pre-step to the apprenticeship scheme. While it provides funding and support to employers, trainees are exempt from receiving the already low apprentice minimum wage. In practice, therefore, apprenticeships are often exploited by employers as a way to undermine the minimum wage, while focusing less on human capital formation. As a consequence of the retrenchment of these types of policies in England and their continuation under devolved governments, we find increasing regional differences, including the centrality of social investment ideas.

Needs-based social protection for the unemployed

While we will focus on means-tested unemployment benefits in this section, it is important to bear in mind that the non-contributory support system for the unemployed in the UK is complex and consists of a vast array of further means-tested benefits and allowances. Means-tested JSA amounts to the same flat-rate payments as contributory JSA, with an additional rate for couples. It can be claimed by anyone of working age and out of work who was employed over the past two years but was exempt from paying National Insurance contributions due to low wages, as well as by those who have exhausted their six months of contribution-based JSA or who have not worked over the past two years. A limit is set for private savings and a partner must work less than 24 hours per week on average. Claimants themselves must not work more than 16 hours per week on average.

This income-based JSA is linked to activation. The New Deals since the late 1990s have expanded the definition of a 'working-age adult' to include previous 'outsiders', such as lone parents, the disabled or people from difficult backgrounds, each with different expectations regarding their activation efforts (Griggs et al, 2014). This emphasis on 'work as the best route out of poverty' is closely linked to a 'make work pay agenda', which offers wage subsidies in the form of child and working tax credits as an incentive to work, instead of benefit increases, in order to tackle so-called 'welfare dependency' (Wiggan, 2012; Deeming and Smyth, 2015).

The consensus on the issue of 'welfare dependency', as well as the focus on supply-side labour market policies, emerged in the 1990s (Clasen, 2005), but the discursive problematisation was increased by the Conservative-led government. As already mentioned, since 2010, benefit increases have been below inflation. In addition, a weekly benefit cap has been introduced that prescribes a maximum amount that can be received when claiming a number of combined benefit, allowances and tax credit types. This cap is set at £384.62 per week for couples (with or without children) and single parents and at £257.69 per week for single persons. Furthermore, the eligibility criteria for receiving income-based JSA were tightened and the plan is to replace it with the so-called 'Universal Credit' that is gradually being rolled out across Great Britain. The term 'universal' refers to the fact that it combines various different low-income household benefits; it is still means-tested and subject to sanctions.

Under the Welfare Reform Act 2012, claimants can now find their benefits suspended for up to three years if conditions are not met.

Even single parents or lead carers in a couple with a child aged one to four have to partake in 'worked-focused interviews' to keep in touch with the labour market.

Over 15 million sanctions have been issued against recipients of JSA since 2000, half of which have been in the six years since 2010. A total of 45% (over 6 million) have been implemented (see Figure 10.5). June 2010 to July 2014 was the peak period for JSA sanctions, with an average of 136,500 referred and over 640,000 sanctions applied each month during this period. More recently, sanction levels have dropped, mainly due to other agencies better supporting appeals and making job seekers more aware of their rights and claimant commitments.

The reforms also entail that less recognition is afforded to special needs, with the exception of the severely disabled. Regarding disabled claimants, so-called work capability assessments have become stricter and many were denied access to better benefits for health-related claims (Employment Support Allowance [ESA]). Disabled ESA claimants are now exposed to increased conditionality and sanctioning (see Figure 10.6). Despite a recent fall in total referrals and an improvement in appeals processes, since the introduction of the new regime in 2012, on average, over 1,900 sanctions were applied each month to people in receipt of ESA.

Discussion

Overall, it is difficult to classify the UK in terms of its labour market pattern according to the framework suggested in this book given that so much is mingled together under needs-based assistance, activation and social investment – particularly because activation can have two sides, the incentivising 'carrot' and the punitive' stick'. Morel et al (2012) distinguish between different 'worlds' and Bonoli (2009) between different 'varieties' of social investment regimes, while Deeming and Smyth (2015) differentiate between the Nordic 'heavy' (where 'old' social spending on protection is coupled with 'new' social spending on prevention through human capital building; see Kvist, 2015) and the liberal 'light' social investment strategies (which combines a focus on productive human capital investment with low social protection). Already before the crisis, the UK's social investment strategy clearly corresponded to a liberal light model.

This does not mean that there have been no changes. A key characteristic of the UK welfare provision since the 1990s is a work-first orientation as unemployment benefits and ALMPs have become more closely linked than previously (Clasen, 2009). There is a clear

UK labour market policies in the era of austerity

Figure 10.5: Jobseeker's Allowance sanctioning trends, UK, April 2000–October 2016

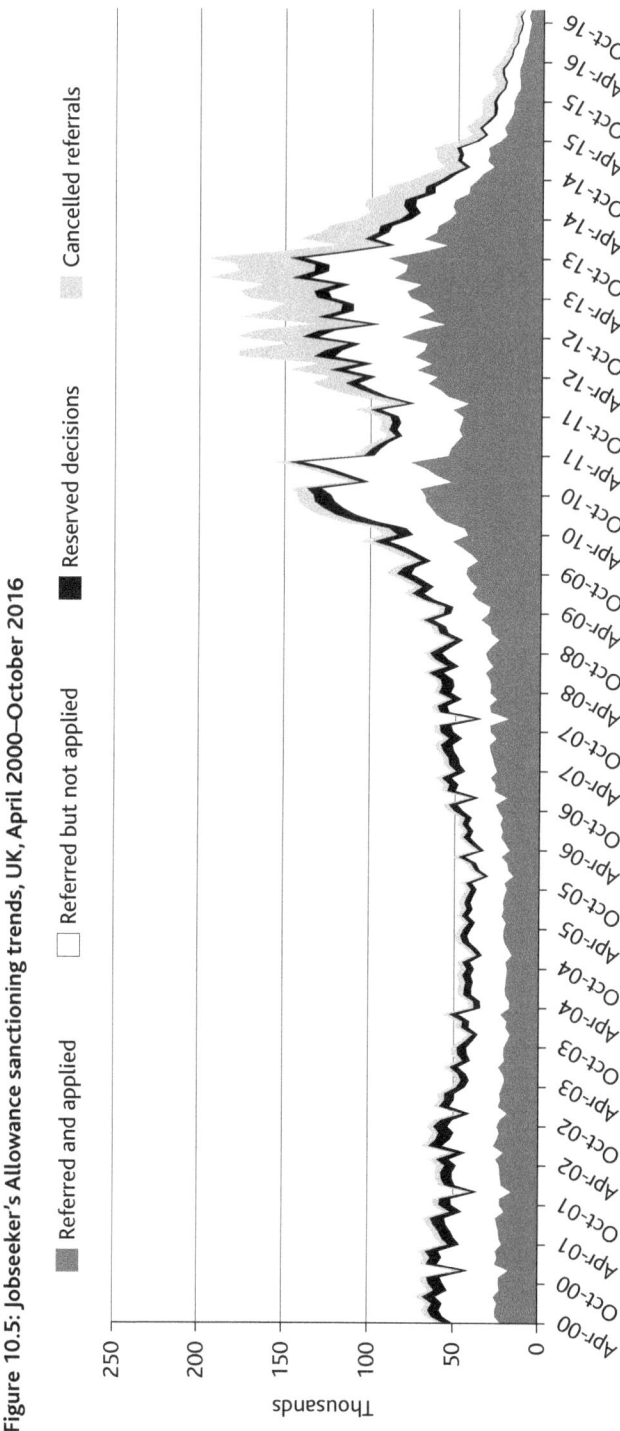

Source: DWP data, April 2000–December 2016

Figure 10.6: Employment Support Allowance sanctioning trends, Great Britain, January 2008–July 2016

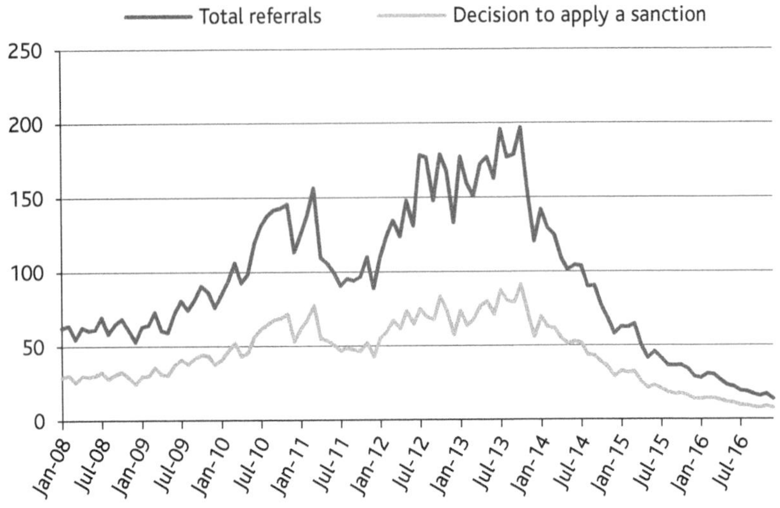

Source: DWP data (January 2008–December 2016); all figures are for Great Britain (excludes Northern Ireland)

tendency for the aim of employment growth to be promoted at the expense of, rather than as a complement to, the aim of social protection (Deeming and Smyth, 2015). The principle of conditionality, stipulating that entitlement to welfare benefits should be dependent on satisfying certain compulsory conditions, has been creeping steadily into employment policy in Britain since the Thatcher era (Peck, 2001). A main aim was not only to reduce unemployment, but also to tackle the wider problem of 'worklessness' (Wiggan, 2012) and to widen the categories of people to be 'activated'. Over time, this activation had less to do with enabling social investment and took on an increasingly punitive character.

Under the Labour governments until 2010, we could still discern ALMPs and human capital investment that represented a 'social investment type' (Bonoli, 2009) as new training programmes and strategies were devised to promote employability and to increase the job-readiness of unemployed workers (Lindsay et al, 2007; Paz-Fuchs, 2008). However, the residualisation of public welfare benefits and a trend towards a rather punitive workfare state that attempts to enforce work for all had already then begun (Deeming, 2014). This can be illustrated with two DWP-commissioned reviews of UK welfare-to-work policies. The so-called Freud report was published under the title 'Reducing dependency, increasing opportunity: options for the future of welfare to work' (Freud, 2007). At the beginning of the recession, another review of conditionality in the welfare system recommended a new regime of 'personalized conditionality', with the objective of moving as many working-age benefit recipients as possible into work in order to 'avoid long-term benefit receipt and protect the taxpayer' (Gregg, 2008: 10). Social attitude surveys correspondingly indicate a longer-term hardening of attitudes towards redistribution and welfare (Park et al, 2012).

Despite the weakness of automatic stabilisers in the liberal British welfare state and the clear structural character of unemployment during the global crisis, this route of welfare to work, which mainly blames the workless individual for not trying hard enough or not having the 'right attitude' to find work, was continued. The retrenchment of income protection for various working-age benefit claimants has even accelerated through not protecting the real value of unemployment benefits, the introduction of a benefit cap and increased conditionality. Under the Work Programme, even mandatory unpaid labour can now be stipulated as a condition for continued benefit receipt for the long-term unemployed. At the same time, the ALMP reforms and the reduction and amalgamation of Jobcentre Plus-managed training and employment support means that human capital development initiatives have been drastically reduced. There is now even less 'carrot' and even more 'stick'. The term 'social investment' is not even used in England anymore, although it is important to recognise differences in Scotland, Wales and Northern Ireland because training is a devolved responsibility.

Furthermore, an increase in the low-income self-employed and zero-hour workers point to an increasing flexibilisation and precarisation of large parts of the labour market. Various developments in the use of nominally 'human capital-forming' initiatives such as apprenticeships signify a large-scale replacement of at least somewhat secure jobs falling under standard minimum wage regulation by jobs that even undermine the already low standards of the British labour market regime. Although the UK has implemented a national minimum wage, many of the described labour market programmes actually undermine the minimum wage. For example, participants of workfare programmes only receive the regular benefit payment, but they have to work for it.

While the UK's headline employment figures may not demonstrate that the crisis created a large labour market problem, when combined with changes to employment protection legislation, the rise of precarious work and the lack of welfare support for such workers, it is clear that deep-seated labour market transitions are taking place.

Instead of the crisis being an instigator of path reversal towards strengthening either protection or social investment, the dominant logic of a low security welfare state has been maintained and the groups being affected by the harsh realities of living in a liberal welfare state have increased. Rather than speaking of 'insiders and outsiders' in relation to the public benefit system, it would be more apt to conclude that UK working-age adults are increasingly all becoming unprotected outsiders as both existing welfare rights and support to find decent employment are cut back. If we want to use the insider/outsider terminology, then this is best applied in relation to the corporate sphere, in which some individuals, depending on their skills, sector or company, are able to negotiate 'golden handshakes' and other attractive redundancy packages. Table 10.1 gives an overview of the policy areas that have experienced retrenchment or expansion and assesses whether the nature of activation policies has shifted towards enabling or more punitive forms.

Labour market policies that are typically classified as protecting incomes and jobs have never followed a replacement principle in the UK social security system, but merely fulfil a poverty-alleviation function. The low benefit levels were further reduced through non-indexation to wages or prices while employment protection was further deregulated. Furthermore, we see a clear increase in conditionality (complemented by harsher sanctions) and a reduction in social investment (in England). Needs-based social protection has always been the main policy focus due to the means-tested and low-benefit approach of the British welfare state. However, we also see retrenchment here as there is a renewed discourse on 'deservingness' that implies delegitimising unconditional public support for parents with young children and some disabled and chronically ill people, with work being the preferred route over welfare.

Conclusion

The financial pressures and increased risk of unemployment created by EU austerity have led to even less protection and increased retrenchment of labour market and unemployment policies in Britain. While the crisis in the UK is mainly a banking and private debt crisis, the main focus of the UK government has been on deficit reduction and this has led to widespread public sector and budget cuts, including for labour market programmes and support for job seekers, as well as an increase in sanctions and new conditionality for a wider range of working-age adults.

Table 10.1: Social and labour market policy instruments pre-crisis and post-crisis, UK

	Unemployment benefits	ALMPs	Needs-based social protection policies	Employment protection legislation	Training and apprenticeships
Policy aim	Income replacement	Activation/social investment	Income support for the (long-term) unemployed	Job protection	Human capital building and skills formation
Relevance before crisis	Low	Some investment	Dominant principle in comparison with others	Low	Low
Development since crisis	Retrenchment. Reduction in eligibility, introduction of 'benefit cap', uprating limited to 1%, benefit freeze at 2015/16 values	Retrenchment and increased conditionality, expansion of workfare programmes including 'community work placements' and 'Work Experience Programme'	Retrenchment through increased conditionality and increase in benefit sanctioning	Retrenched. Reform to tribunal process and legal aid support (leading to reduction in cases), increase in zero-hour contracts, and less protected self-employed workers	Retrenched (but regional differences). Reduction in training programmes, diluting of definition of apprenticeship, lower pay rates for apprentices

While a recalibration of policies from an industrial logic to a post-industrial logic is typically connected to some 'modernising compromises' (Bonoli, 2003) and trade-offs between policies, the non-existence of 'insider' benefits makes any package deals difficult, if not impossible. The fact that there is no strong advocacy for social investment or protection due to the weakness of trade unions adds to this problem. There is also no substitute for the residual protection provided through statutory employment protection legislation or JSA in the form of collective agreements.

It is difficult to disentangle the effects of the crisis from the effects of a changing government ideology, beginning with the Thatcher governments from 1979 onwards. The Labour governments after 1997 introduced some measures that acted as carrots rather than sticks but they also tightened the benefits regime for several types of 'workless' working-age adults. However, while there was then at least some attempt to create 'equality of opportunity' and to support job seekers with training and employment experience, under the Conservative-led Coalition from 2010 and then the Conservative government from 2015, labour market policies have become overly punitive, with discourses attacking a 'something for nothing' or 'welfare dependency' culture. The government has used the crisis as an opportunity to argue that 'there is no alternative' to deficit reduction and cutting back the welfare state. Instead of seeing enabling active labour market and human capital formation policies as a social investment, these are regarded as a cost factor and now mainly serve the functions of a work test. Employment protection legislation, wider social protection measures and minimum wages have been eroded or undermined for the sake of 'employer-friendliness' and supply-side economic policies.

References

Barnes, L. and Wren, A. (2012) 'The liberal model in (the) crisis: continuity and change in Great Britain and Ireland', in N. Bermeo and J. Pontusson (eds) *Coping with crisis. Government reactions to the Great Recession*, New York, NY: Russel Sage Foundation, pp 287–324.

Bennett, H. (2017) 'Re-examining British welfare-to-work contracting using a transaction cost perspective', *Journal of Social Policy*, 46(1): 129–48.

Bennett, H. and Clegg, D. (2013) 'The local arena for combating poverty', research report, COPE, Glasgow, UK.

Bonoli, G. (2003) 'Social policy through labour markets: understanding national differences in the provision of economic security to wage earners', *Comparative Political Studies*, 36(9): 1007–30.

Bonoli, G. (2009) 'Varieties of social investment in labour market policy', in N. Morel, B. Palier and J. Palme (eds) *What future for social investment?*, Stockholm: Institute for Futures Studies, pp 55–66.

Brinkley, I. (2013) *Flexibility or insecurity? Exploring the rise in zero hours contracts*, London: The Work Foundation. Available at: https://csgconsult.com/wp-content/uploads/2014/03/339_flexibility-or-insecurity-final.pdf

CAB (Citizens Advice Bureau) (2015) 'Government employment schemes'. Available at: http://www.adviceguide.org.uk/scotland/work_s/work_self_employed_or_looking_for_work_s/government_employment_schemes.htm#h_compulsory_schemes

CIPD (Chartered Institute of Personnel and Development) (2013) 'Zero-hours contracts. Myth and reality. Research report November 2013'. Available at: http://www.cipd.co.uk/binaries/zero-hours-contracts_2013-myth-reality.pdf

Clasen, J. (2005) *Reforming European welfare states: Germany and the United Kingdom compared*, Oxford: Oxford University Press.

Clasen, J. (2007) 'Distribution of responsibility for social security and labour market policy. Country report: United Kingdom', Amsterdam Institute for Advanced Labour Studies working paper 07-50, Amsterdam.

Clasen, J. (2009) 'The United Kingdom', in P. de Beer and T. Shils (eds) *The labour market triangle. Employment protection, unemployment compensation and activation in Europe*, Cheltenham: Edward Elgar, pp 70–95.

Clegg, D. (2010) 'Labour market policy and the crisis: Britain in comparative perspective', *Journal of Poverty and Social Justice* 18(1): 5–17.

Crouch, C. (2011) *The strange non-death of neoliberalism*, Cambridge: Polity Press.

Deeming, C. (2014) 'Foundations of the workfare state – reflections on the political transformation of the welfare state in Britain', *Social Policy & Administration*, 49(7): 862–86.

Deeming, C. and Smyth, P. (2015) 'Social investment after neo-liberalism: policy paradigms and political platforms', *Journal of Social Policy*, 44(2): 297–318.

DfE (Department for Education) and BIS (Department for Business, Innovation & Skills) (2013) *Rigour and responsiveness in skills*, April, London: BIS.

DWP (Department for Work and Pensions) (2012) 'Impacts and Costs and Benefits of the Future Jobs Fund, November 2012'. Available at: https://www.gov.uk/government/uploads/system/uploads/attachment_data/file/223120/impacts_costs_benefits_fjf.pdf (accessed August 2016)

Esping-Andersen, G. (1990) *The three worlds of welfare capitalism*, Princeton, NJ: Princeton University Press.

Farnsworth, K. (2011) 'From economic crisis to a new age of austerity: the UK', in K. Farnsworth and Z. Irving (eds) *Social policy in challenging times: Economic crisis and welfare systems*, Bristol: The Policy Press.

Finn, D. (2003) 'The "employment-first" welfare state: lessons from the New Deal for Young People', *Social Policy & Administration*, 37(7): 709–24.

Finn, D. (2011) 'Welfare to work after the recession: from the New Deals to the Work Programme', in C. Holden, M. Kilkey and G. Ramia (eds) *Social policy review 23. Analysis and debate in social policy, 2011*, Bristol: The Policy Press, pp 127–45.

Fishwick, T., Lane, P. and Gardiner, L. (2011) *Future Jobs Fund: An independent national evaluation. July 2011*, London: CESI.

Foster, S., Casebourne, J., Roberts, E. and Lake, L. (2011) *Integrated employment and skills: Maximising the contribution for sustainable employment*, London: CESI. Available at: https://www2.learningandwork.org.uk/publications/integrated-employment-and-skills-maximising-contribution-sustainable-employment (accessed October 2017)

Freud, D. (2007) *Reducing dependency, increasing opportunity: Options for the future of welfare to work. An independent report to the Department for Work and Pensions*, Leeds: Corporate Document Services.

Goerne, A. and Clegg, D. (2013) *National report: UK*. Combating Poverty in Europe (COPE) project report, Edinburgh: University of Edinburgh.

Gregg, P. (2008) *Realising potential: A vision for personalised conditionality and support. An independent report to the Department for Work and Pensions*, Norwich: The Stationery Office.

Griggs, J., Hammond, A. and Walker, R. (2014) 'Activation for all. Welfare reform in the United Kingdom, 1995–2009', in I. Lødemel and A. Moreira (eds) *Activation or workfare? Governance and the neo-liberal convergence*, Oxford: Oxford University Press, pp 73–100.

Hall, P.A. and Soskice, D. (eds) (2001) *Varieties of capitalism. The institutional foundations of comparative advantage*, Oxford: Oxford University Press.

Harari, D. (2011) 'Future jobs fund', House of Commons Briefing paper SN05352. Available at: http://researchbriefings.parliament.uk/ResearchBriefing/Summary/SN05352

Hills, J. (2015) *Good times, bad times: The welfare myth of them and us*, Bristol: The Policy Press.

HM Treasury (2008) *Pre-Budget report 2008: Facing global challenges, supporting people through difficult times*, Cm 7484, Norwich: The Stationery Office.

HM Treasury (2010) *Spending review 2010*, Cm 7942, Norwich: The Stationery Office.

HM Treasury (2012) *Autumn Statement 2012*, Cm 8480, Norwich: The Stationery Office.

HOC (House of Commons) (2012) 'The introduction of the Work Programme. House of Commons oral evidence taken before the Public Accounts Committee', uncorrected transcript of oral evidence, 8 February.

HOC Scottish Affairs Committee (2014) *Zero hours contracts in Scotland: Interim Report* (HC 654). London: The Stationery Office. Available at: https://www.publications.parliament.uk/pa/cm201314/cmselect/cmscotaf/654/654.pdf

Hodgson, A. and Spours, K. (2011) 'National education systems: the wider context', in: A. Hodgson, K. Spours and M. Waring (eds) *Post-compulsory education and lifelong learning across the United Kingdom: policy, organisation and governance*, London: IOE Press, pp 1–15.

Kvist, J. (2015) 'A framework for social investment strategies: integrating generational, life course and gender perspectives in the EU social investment strategy', *Comparative European Politics*, 13(1): 131–49.

Lanning, T. (2012) 'The real story behind the rise in apprenticeships under the Coalition', *The Guardian*, 11 October.

Lindsay, C., McQuaid, R. and Dutton, M. (2007) 'New approaches to employability in the UK: combining "human capital development" and "work first" strategies?', *Journal of Social Policy*, 36(4): 539–60.

Malik, S. (2014) 'DWP orders man to work without pay for company that let him go', *The Guardian*, 3 November.

McGuinness, F. and Dar, A. (2014) 'Work Programme', House of Commons Library standard note, SN/EP/6430.

McKnight A (2015) 'The Coalition's record on Employment: Policy, Spending and Outcomes 2010–2015', CASE Working Paper 15. London: LSE.

Meikle, J. (2014) 'Nearly 4,000 NHS staff laid off then rehired over three and a half years', *The Guardian*, 17 March.

Mirza-Davies, J. (2014) 'Constituency casework: training', House of Commons Library, 30 July. Available at: http://www.parliament.uk/business/publications/research/briefing-papers/SN05444/constituency-casework-training

Mirza-Davies, J. (2015) 'Apprenticeship statistics', House of Commons Library, 13 February. Available at: http://www.parliament.uk/business/publications/research/briefing-papers/SN06113/apprenticeship-statistics

Morel, N., Palier, B. and Palme, J. (2012) 'Social investment: a paradigm in search of a new economic model and political mobilisation', in N. Morel, B. Palier and J. Palme (eds) *Towards a social investment welfare state? Ideas, policies and challenges*, Bristol: The Policy Press, pp 353–76.

OECD (Organisation for Economic Co-operation and Development) (2013) *Employment outlook 2013. Protecting jobs, enhancing flexibility: A new look at employment protection legislation*, Paris: OECD.

ONS (Office for National Statistics) (2014a) 'Self-employed workers in the UK'. Available at: http://www.ons.gov.uk/ons/dcp171776_374941.pdf

ONS (2014b) 'Statistical bulletin: gross domestic product preliminary estimate, Q3 2014'. Available at: http://www.ons.gov.uk/ons/rel/gva/gross-domestic-product--preliminary-estimate/q3-2014/stb-gdp-preliminary-estimate--q3-2014.html

ONS (2015a) 'Contracts with no guaranteed hours, zero hour contracts, 2014'. Available at: http://www.ons.gov.uk/ons/rel/lmac/contracts-with-no-guaranteed-hours/zero-hour-contracts--2014/index.html

ONS (2015b) 'Labour market statistics, January 2015'. Available at: http://www.ons.gov.uk/ons/rel/lms/labour-market-statistics/january-2015/index.html

Park, A., Clery, E., Curtice, J., Phillips, M. and Utting, D. (eds) (2012) *British social attitudes: The 29th report*, London: NatCen Social Research.

Paz-Fuchs, A. (2008) *Welfare to work: Conditional rights in social policy*, Oxford: Oxford University Press.

Peck, J. (2001) *Workfare states*, London: Guilford Press.

Pennycook, M., Cory, G. and Alakeson, V. (2013) *A matter of time. The rise of zero-hour contracts*, London: The Resolution Foundation.

Phillips, L. (2013) 'Legal aid is being ruled out of court', *The Guardian*, 23 March.

Pullan, L. (2013) 'Back to basics: zero-hours contracts November 2013', *Pay and Benefits Magazine*, 28 October.

Sinfield, A. (2013) '"What unemployment means" three decades and two recessions later', in G. Ramia, K. Farnsworth and Z. Irving (eds) *Social policy review 25. Analysis and debate in social policy, 2013*, Bristol: The Policy Press, pp 207–25.

Slater, T. (2012) 'The myth of broken Britain', *Antipode*, 46(4): 948–69.

The Law Society of Scotland (2014) 'Employment tribunal fees report July 2014'. Available at: https://www.lawscot.org.uk/media/334389/employment-tribunal-fees-report.pdf

TUC (2012) 'Priced out: the impact of employment tribunal fees on access to justice'. Available at: http://www.tuc.org.uk/sites/default/files/tucfiles/pricedoutmojfeesconsultation.pdf

TUC (2014) 'At what price justice? The impact of employment tribunal fees', July. Available at: http://www.tuc.org.uk/sites/default/files/TUC_Report_At_what_price_justice.pdf

UK Government (2013) 'Government unveils Deregulation Bill'. Available at: https://www.gov.uk/government/news/government-unveils-deregulation-bill

Venn, D. (2009) *Legislation, collective bargaining and enforcement: Updating the OECD employment protection*, Paris: OECD.

Wiggan, J. (2012) 'Telling stories of 21st century welfare: the UK Coalition government and the neo-liberal discourse of worklessness and dependency', *Critical Social Policy*, 32(3): 383–405.

ELEVEN

Czechia: political experimentation or incremental reforms?

Tomáš Sirovátka

Introduction

In this chapter, we shall assess the dynamics of labour market policies and regulations during 2008–14 in Czechia. A primary focus will be developments in the unemployment benefit scheme (income replacement for insiders), active labour market policies (ALMPs) (including labour market training) and employment protection legislation. Second, we shall analyse needs-based income support (minimum income protection) and activation policies related to the minimum income scheme (MIS). Three issues will be paramount. The first concerns substantive and governance-related policy changes: whether these changes have brought expansion or retrenchment in expenditure and coverage (of benefit recipients or participants of the programmes). The second concerns whether there has been a shift in the character of the policy instruments that promote activation: whether these instruments have been rather enabling/restitutive or punitive/repressive in nature. The third concerns whether and how divisions are emerging concerning the policies between groups facing the risk of unemployment. Besides an assessment of labour market policy trends during the crisis and afterwards, the politics underlying the reforms will be discussed.

The key methodological approach is institutional policy analysis, combined with the secondary analysis of data from international and national sources. Historical institutionalism accentuates the role of institutional legacies in policies: policies and institutions are considered to be path-dependent on the institutional set-up. Institutional path dependency explains to a great extent the varieties of policy dynamics in different countries or the persistence of given features of welfare and labour market regimes over time, despite the common challenges that countries face. Studies also show that institutional path dependency is shaped by institutional traditions. Saxonberg et al (2013) explain, for example, how policy path dependency has been strong in Czechia in the area of childcare policies, even during the transition to a market democracy during the 1990s and 2000s, due to the cultural and institutional legacies of the past, in contrast to a new area, such as labour market policy, which has been subject to experimentation.

Path dependency, however, is not an obstacle to policy change. Incremental forms of institutional change can take place through '*bricolage*' or 'layering'. Accumulation of the incremental changes may, at times, lead to path-breaking change when the policy path comes to a *critical juncture* (Palier, 2005; Streeck and Thelen, 2005). Critical junctures may also emerge from exogenous shocks, such as a transformation of the political and economic systems in Central and Eastern Europe after communism or the economic crisis. Some authors expect exogenous shocks to come from other institutional changes, such as overall change in policy governance, when power relations are being drastically reshuffled. For example, such shocks emerge from the implementation of more comprehensive governance changes such as marketisation, decentralisation/recentralisation and so on. New institutionalism emphasises the role of agents such as political actors and their manoeuvring: explanation of the direction of change comes from the coalitions of actors interested in change (Hall, 2009). Another explanation of how policy may change is provided by discursive institutionalism (Schmidt, 2008). New policies often emerge due to new ideas that penetrate public and policy discourses and lay the ground for policy change.

From this perspective, the key assumption of this chapter is that labour market and activation policies since the 1990s are a new policy area in the post-communist Czechia, in contrast to, say, pensions, family policies or health care. For this reason, these policies are not path-dependent, but susceptible to experimentation and frequent policy changes, depending on political and discursive factors. In Czechia, during the crisis and post-crisis period, the reforms in this policy area were made quickly, and often left unfinished. For this reason, it is not easy to recognise the future direction of these unfinished reforms.

The chapter is organised as follows. In the second section, economic developments during the crisis are sketched. In the third section, the dynamics of labour market policies is assessed: the unemployment benefit scheme, ALMPs and employment protection legislation. In the fourth section, the dynamics of the MIS are in focus: the reforms of MIS during the crisis and post-crisis period, as well as activation policies. In the fifth section, the question of insiders and outsiders is discussed and also the politics underlying the reforms. In the concluding section, key findings are summarised and discussed.

Economic development during the crisis and related European Union regulations

In Czechia, the crisis brought about a fall in gross domestic product (GDP) of almost 5% in 2009, temporary recovery in 2010 and 2011, and slight recession again in 2012 and 2013, followed by economic recovery in 2014. In consequence, the unemployment rate (Labour Force Survey) increased from 4.4% in 2008 to 7.3% in 2010 and remained at 7% until 2013 but decreased to 6.1% in 2014 (see Table 11.1). At the same time, the government deficit in 2009 increased to 5.5%. In reaction to this development, the excessive deficit procedure for Czechia was opened in December 2009 by the Council of the European Union (2009), which called for an average annual fiscal effort of at least 1% of GDP over 2010–2013. In particular, the Council invited the Czech authorities 'to implement reforms with a view to raising potential GDP growth and reforms conducive to enhancing the quality of public finances, in particular reforms improving the efficiency and effectiveness of public spending' (Council of the European Union, 2009: 14). In addition, the Council asked the Czech authorities to continue with the necessary pension and health-care reforms.

In the following years, the government deficit went down to 4.4% (2010), 2.7% (2011) and 3.9% (2012), and in 2013, to 1.2%, thanks to a restrictive fiscal policy followed consistently by the government during 2010–2013, based on cuts in public expenditure, although the

Table 11.1: Selected macroeconomic indicators, Czechia (annual averages in %)

	2008	2009	2010	2011	2012	2013	2014
Real GDP growth	2.7	–4.8	2.3	2.0	–0.8	–0.5	2.7
Number of the employed (main job) (growth)	1.6	–1.4	–1.0	–0.3	0.4	1.0	0.8
Unemployment rate	4.4	6.7	7.3	6.7	7.0	7.0	6.1
Long-term unemployment rate	2.2	2.0	3.0	2.7	3.0	3.0	2.7
Share of registered unemployed persons in population 15–65	4.1	6.1	7.0	6.7	6.8	7.7	7.7
Real wages growth	1.4	2.3	0.7	0.6	–0.8	–1.5	2.5
Inflation rate	6.3	1.0	1.5	1.9	3.3	1.4	0.4
Government deficit (% of GDP)	–2.1	–5.5	–4.4	–2.7	–3.9	–1.2	–1.9
Gross public debt (as % of GDP)	28.7	34.1	38.2	39.8	44.5	44.9	42.2

Source: Czech Statistical Office, available at: http://www.czso.cz/, European Commission AMECO database for gross public debt figures

recommended reforms of the pension and health-care systems did not take place, apart from the implementation of co-payments in health care in 2009.

The gross public debt/GDP ratio increased between 2008 and 2013 from 28.7% to 44.9%. Czechia's general government deficit declined to 1.3% of GDP in 2013, in line with the Council's recommendation. In 2014, the Commission projected the general government gross debt to fall to 44.4% of GDP in 2014 and to increase to 45.8% of GDP in 2015, remaining below the Economic and Monetary Union's (EMU's) reference value of 60% of GDP, as a result of which the Council concluded that the Czech Republic's deficit had been corrected and terminated the excessive deficit procedure in 2014 (Council of the European Union, 2014).

Despite the aforementioned negative trends in GDP growth and labour market performance, the country's economic decline was moderate, except in 2009, and unemployment has remained among the lowest in the European Union (EU). The government deficit was also rather low compared with other EU countries and the response to the excessive deficit procedure was relatively fast and effective, although its approach was clearly restrictive. Since 2014, the economic recovery has been apparent.

Labour market policies

Unemployment protection

The unemployment benefit scheme in Czechia as it emerged during the 1990s represents a combination of the liberal and the employment-centred unemployment regime, as distinguished by Gallie and Paugam (2000): at the end of the 1990s, benefits were provided for a period of six months, the replacement rate was 50% of the previous wage for the first three months and 40% for the rest (60% when in vocational training), with a ceiling of 2.5 times the living minimum (2.8 when in vocational training). The Employment Act 2004, adopted on accession to the EU, entailed some improvements in standards, from which mainly insiders benefited: the lower level of the benefit was increased to 45% of the replacement rate in order to meet the European Social Charter standard; the period covered by unemployment benefits was prolonged to nine months for people above 50 years of age and 12 months for people above 55 years; and the ceiling of the benefit was set at the level of 0.58 times more than the average wage (0.65 times more when in vocational training).

On the other hand, increased conditionality and administrative pressures followed, aimed at restricting access to unemployment benefits based on job-search criteria. Job-search incentives have been increased, mainly by implementing a stricter definition of 'suitable job' that also describes as 'suitable' jobs that last for longer than three months and amount to 80% of full-time working. In the case of long-term unemployed persons, the job may last for an even shorter period, provided it corresponds to no less than 50% of full-time employment. It was not necessary to take into account qualifications, abilities, accommodation and accessibility by transport (only health status had to be considered). Refusal to participate in a temporary job (including subsidised jobs such as public work programmes), refusal to undergo a medical examination organised by the employment office or non-compliance with individual action plan commitments might result in sanctions (loss of benefit entitlements for a period of six months instead of three).

In 2008, the new centre-right government increased the pressure on the unemployed, shortly before the crisis hit.[1] After five months of unemployment, employment offices were obliged to elaborate an individual action plan with the unemployed. Failure to fulfil the obligations of this individual agreement (or rejection of it or the vocational training programme) entailed removal from the register and also reduced entitlements to social assistance benefits (at most, the subsistence minimum).[2] The focus on activation also implied some shortening of the period covered by unemployment benefits. From January 2009, the period covered by unemployment benefits was shortened from six to five months (and from nine [12] to eight [11] months in the case of the unemployed over 50 [55] years of age). On the other hand, the replacement rate during the two first months was increased from 50% to 65%, left at 50% for the next two months and reduced to 45% for the remaining month(s). At the same time, the period spent in education was no longer recognised as a substitute for a work record for the purpose of unemployment insurance entitlements. During 2009 when the crisis was fully being felt in the country and unemployment hit even the regular workforce, a decision was adopted by Parliament to increase temporary replacement rates in the two first months to 80% but it was not implemented because the government resigned in that year and new elections were expected.

The centre-right coalition re-elected in 2010 adopted further measures in 2011 aimed at increasing the pressure on the unemployed. People who terminated their labour contract without 'serious reasons'[3] received only a 45% replacement rate after the first month, and people who received severance pay did not get benefits during the period covered by it. On the other hand, the positive incentive for the unemployed of toleration of earnings up to half of the minimum wage in part-time temporary jobs as a supplement to unemployment benefit was abolished. The changes in the unemployment benefit scheme are summarised in Table 11.6 in the appendix.

In consequence of all these measures, access to unemployment benefits was restricted; while 39.3% of the unemployed were entitled to such benefits at the end of 2008, by 2011, it was only 26.1%, in 2013, it was only 21.2% and in 2014, it was only 21.4% (author's calculations from data from the web portal of the Ministry of Labour and Social Affairs [MLSA]).

The overall trend was to improve the position of insiders slightly and mainly to punish outsiders. As we can see from Table 11.2, replacement rates improved during 2008–14. On the other hand, eligibility for unemployment benefits was restricted.

As Table 11.2 shows, in 2014, the replacement rates of unemployment benefits in Czechia are similar to or slightly below the EU average in the case of low-wage earners but above the EU average for average wage earners.

Active labour market policies

With EU accession in 2004, new opportunities opened up for ALMPs through the European Social Fund (ESF). During 2006 and 2007, ESF projects made it possible to increase the relative number

Table 11.2: Net replacement rates for unemployment benefits for two levels of wages, different household compositions and the initial phase of unemployment (no top-up benefits included)

	67% of average wage						100% of average wage					
	Without children			2 children			Without children			2 children		
Persons	1	2	2	1	2	2	1	2	2	1	2	2
		1 EA	2 EA		1 EA	2 EA		1 EA	2 EA		1 EA	2 EA
2008	50	50	79	66	63	84	50	50	74	62	58	78
2010	65	65	87	75	74	92	65	65	83	71	69	88
2012	65	65	87	67	67	88	65	65	83	70	66	89
2014	65	65	87	67	67	88	65	65	84	70	64	89
2014 EU	68	69	84	73	74	86	58	59	76	67	65	79

Notes: EA = economically active (working). Top-up benefits may be social assistance or housing benefits. Family benefits are included.
Source: OECD (2016a)

of ALMP participants from 19% (2005) to nearly 32% (2006) and then 39% (2007) of the unemployed. At the same time, some shifts in the governance of ALMPs emerged. With the ESF programmes, the volume of outsourcing increased, with some ESF projects fully outsourced. Second, within the projects implemented by employment offices, most measures – such as individual diagnostics, counselling, labour market training and motivation programmes – have been outsourced to private agencies, non-governmental organisations (NGOs) or public education. Project-like management of ALMPs prevailed due to ESF funding and strengthened the already high level of decentralisation.[4]

The centre-right government that came to power in 2007 changed the approach to ALMPs: first, emphasis on active measures declined; and, second, the marketisation of employment services and policies was forced forward. Traditionally, Czechia has been a laggard in ALMPs but the gap with most EU countries widened further after 2008. The proportion of participants fell to about one quarter of the unemployed in 2008, and with the crisis, the number of ALMP participants increased only slightly in absolute terms, while the number of unemployed went up by about half. The trend of ALMP retrenchment culminated in 2012, while in 2013, the new caretaker government changed it. However, no dramatic improvements took place because the government was bound by the restrictive government budget adopted for 2013, and the position of the new centre-left government elected in 2014 was similar.[5] However, the number of ALMP participants increased back to the level of 2010 (see Table 11.3). The changes in ALMPs and the Public Employment Service (PES) are summarised in Table 11.6 in the appendix.

The governance reform of 2010–11 was another important step taken by the government, adopted with a cost-containment objective. Recentralisation involved the stronger subordination of local employment offices to the PES, accompanied by shifting legal competences from the local (77 local offices) to the regional level (14 regional offices). At the same time, during 2011, the number of PES employees was reduced from 8,136 to 6,237 (Úřad práce, 2014). In 2011, the minimum income scheme and social assistance administration were merged with the employment offices, shifting from the municipalities. However, only 1,953 of the original 3,642 staff working on the minimum income scheme and the social assistance agenda at municipal social departments were employed at employment offices after the merger. The understaffing of this scheme has been heavily criticised by the ombudsman (Ombudsman/Veřejný ochránce

Table 11.3: Active labour market policy during 2010–14: participants and expenditure (Public Employment Service register data)

	2008	2009	2010	2011	2012	2013	2014
Unemployed (end of year)	352,250	539,136	561,551	508,451	545,311	596,833	541,914
ALMP participants:							
Public works	16,246	19,794	22,882	21,322	12,833	21,839	22,967
Job creation in private sector	12,756	20,208	25,882	13,410	11,380	21,716	33,091
Sheltered workshops – creation	974	1,231	1,640	1,405	817	768	1,132
Sheltered workshops – maintenance	9,349	10,315	10,076	14,620	1,514	92	6,105
Work rehabilitation	134	76	120	72	55	133	–
Local projects	43	204	459	643	522	3,301	3,944
Vocational training (of which ESF)	36,451	39,831	65,453	45,521	25,199	41,438	46,454
ESF projects – not specified	16,584	10,596					
Other:							
job experience							5,944
and other measures							1,882
Total ALMP participants	92,537	102,255	126,512	96,993	52,320	89,287	123,587
as % of the unemployed	26.3	19.0	22.5	19.1	9.6	15.0	22.8
ALMP expenditure (thousand CZK)	6,131,729	4,953,467	6,171,493	3,815,886	2,595,049	4,285,714	6,426,900
out of which ESF	2,678,240	2,736,558	4,175,475	2,156,359	1,502,859	3,232,952	5,755,200
out of which ESF in %	43.7	55.2	67.6	56.5	68.0	75.4	89.5

Source: MLSA web portal, statistics on unemployment and ALMP, various years, http://portal.mpsv.cz/sz/stat

práv, 2012). At the same time, the institution of 'shared job mediation' – that is, the outsourcing of mediation and counselling to private agencies – was implemented in legislation in 2011. However, it did not work because the financial rewards offered to the private agencies were set too low.

In 2013, when it was apparent that the employment offices could barely perform their tasks effectively, the government decided to increase the staff of the employment offices by 250 permanent and 150 temporary employees, both in employment policy and the minimum income scheme and social assistance agenda (MLSA [MPSV], 2013a). With the new temporary 'caretaker government' established in July 2013, a more substantial decision was made to accept 700 new employees who would be clearly pro-client-oriented: 319 positions in 2013 and the rest in 2014 (MLSA [MPSV], 2013b). Despite these measures, the estimated understaffing (Úřad práce, 2014) was still about 20% at the beginning of 2014, compared with the situation in 2011 preceding the reform. The government also announced several measures in March 2013 (Employment Plan; see MLSA [MPSV], 2013c), the most important being employment opportunities (in the form of 12 months' work experience) for young people,[6] help for companies threatened by the crisis by supporting short-time working combined with vocational training,[7] and, lastly, more support for job creation measures for disadvantaged groups, in both the public and the private sector.

Czechia adopted a key strategic document in 2014: 'Employment Policy Strategy until 2020'. The Strategy asserted that the share of ALMP participants would be increased, as would the employment rates of people on the margins of the labour market, and, finally, the mismatch between the skills of the unemployed and the requirements of employers would also be reduced. Substantial ALMP expenditure would be necessary, as well as a strengthening of the personal and technical capacities of the institutions involved. In addition, the government adopted a so-called 'Activating Package' in May 2014, which goes into more detail in defining the specific measures. These may be clustered under two headings: increasing the effectiveness of PES by making it client- and employer-oriented; and increasing the range and scope of ALMP measures, for example, by introducing new instruments, such as lowering social insurance payments, supporting the social economy, age management and supporting flexible forms of working. As a first step, investment stimuli were boosted to regions with unemployment rates 25% higher than average and to government-approved industrial zones. Next, the principles of a social economy were supported, as well as work experience placements for students and school leavers, and labour market discrimination and all forms of illegal work were abolished.

As Clasen et al (2012: 9) suggest, in Czechia, the crisis was understood as a *demand shock* characterised by *fiscal constraints*, not as a *structural challenge*. Hence, the key labour market measure was the prevention of a recessionary spiral by protecting insiders' jobs with the help of ESF funds. At the same time, the government chose to try to reduce the public deficit, among other things, by imposing restrictions on unemployment benefit schemes and cutting spending on ALMPs. The outsiders (marginal workforce) were not a focus of the policies implemented. Greater emphasis on ALMPs and disadvantaged groups is apparent since 2013, but substantial progress has not yet been made.

Employment protection legislation

Protection of the labour force was strong before 1989 under the communist regime, which declared itself a 'working-class regime'. Subsequently, some liberalisation of labour law took place. Czechia became obliged to transpose EU labour law into national legislation when it signed the Association Agreement with the EU. Important implementing laws were Act No. 118/2000 Coll. on the protection of employees in the case of the employer's insolvency, and the amendment of the Labour Code (Act No. 155/2000 Coll.), which adopted 28 EU directives ('harmonisation amendment'), including the directives on rights to information and consultation, protection against collective redundancies, maximum length of working time, parental leave, part-time work, the posting of workers, and health and safety at work. The second EU amendment of the national Labour Code (Act No. 46/2004 Coll. of March 2004) included directives on equal treatment and anti-discrimination.

The centre-right coalition government that emerged from the 2006 elections was committed to revising the Labour Code by adopting more flexible arrangements. This plan was criticised and opposed by the trade unions, as well as by the political opposition. Finally, the government succeeded only in 2011 in pushing through the revision of the Labour Code, aimed at flexibilising the labour market, but these revisions did not bring substantial change. Traditionally, in Czechia, the protection of the regular workforce in the case of individual dismissals is stronger than in Organisation for Economic Co-operation and Development (OECD) countries on average. On the other hand, protection against collective dismissals is below average. The protection of the regular workforce is considerably better than in the case of employees on temporary contracts, but the gap is slowly closing (see Table 11.4).

On the other hand, the low level of law enforcement in Czechia has already been recognised (Falkner et al, 2008). For example, there are no labour courts, so employees have to complain in the civil courts, which work slowly due to case overload, with proceedings taking years not months. Thus, protection is less effective than what is laid down in the law.

However, the protection of temporary workers improved, especially regarding temporary agency workers (typically foreign labour). In order to prevent the acceleration of the problems with dismissed agency workers during the crisis, the government amended the Employment Act in January 2011, obliging work agencies to be insured for bankruptcy.[8] Since 2012, however, work agencies cannot employ foreigners – they have to be hired by companies directly. More security has been provided for occasional workers, such as written contracts (since 2011), and the maximum number of temporary contracts was set at two in 2012. On the other hand, a number of flexibilisation measures have also been implemented, such as the prolongation of the maximum duration of temporary contracts to nine years in 2011, an increase in the maximum limit on specific task contracts from 150 to 300 hours in 2012 and differentiation of the rules for temporary contracts with regard to specific professions and reasons (such as seasonal work, agency work, building industry) in 2013. Lastly, since 2012, the amount of severance pay has been based on the duration of the work contract. The changes in employment protection legislation are summarised in Table 11.6 in the appendix.

Table 11.4: Employment protection legislation index in the Czech Republic (OECD methodology)

	Collective and individual dismissals/ regular contracts	Individual dismissals/ regular contracts	Collective dismissals/ additional arrangements	Temporary workers
2008	2.75	3.00	2.13	1.88
2010	2.75	3.00	2.13	2.00
2012	2.66	2.88	2.13	2.13
2013	2.66	2.88	2.13	2.13
2013 OECD average	2.29	2.04	2.29	2.08

Source: OECD (2016b)

Minimum income protection and activation of long-term unemployed and social assistance recipients

Minimum income protection (social assistance) scheme

In Czechia, the Living Minimum Act[9] and the closely related Act on Social Need[10] introduced a new Minimum Income Protection/Social Assistance (MIP/SA) scheme in November 1991 that was mainly concerned with protective objectives during the first market transition period. The scheme was designed under national legislation as a basic social safety net that provided a guarantee of minimum income.

The MIP/SA scheme designed at the beginning of the 1990s was relatively generous: it provided an approximate 55% replacement of the net average wage for a single person, 99% for a couple and 181% for a family of four. No financial incentives such as disregards on earnings or back-to-work bonuses were provided to social assistance recipients.[11]

The administration of the MIP/SA scheme was not favourable for activation either. The first obstacle was an institutional split between the MIP/SA administration and the employment services administration (the administration merged in 2012; see earlier). Municipalities required only formal proof from MIP/SA benefits recipients that they were registered as job seekers at the employment office.

The reform of MIP/SA in 2006 was aimed at providing adequate minimum guarantees, while increasing incentives in order to activate welfare recipients (MLSA [MPSV], 2005; Vládní návrh, 2005). The most important of these changes was the restricted access to MIP/SA benefits for young people: according to the new legislation, adult children and parents sharing accommodation were considered to be a household when testing the means of subsistence for the purpose of the main benefit, the living allowance. In practice, this measure excluded most unemployed young people from benefit entitlements. At the same time, positive work incentives in the form of disregards on earnings were implemented: since 2007, only 70% of income from work and 80% of income from sickness and unemployment benefits have been taken into account when testing for the means of subsistence.

The reform of MIP/SA was also aimed at differentiating between 'deserving' recipients (and providing them with full rights to the MIP/SA scheme, ie, the living minimum) and 'undeserving' or inactive recipients (excluded from or provided at most with restricted MIP/SA scheme rights, ie, the subsistence minimum).[12]

In the June 2006 elections, the Social Democrat-led government lost its majority and, after difficult negotiations, the centre-right coalition government of Civic Democrats, Christian Democrats and Greens emerged with a slight majority in Parliament. Within the comprehensive package of 'social reform' Acts of August 2007, the new Parliament accepted one important change in the MIP/SA scheme: the automatic indexation to the inflation rate of the living and subsistence minimums was cancelled; it has been at the sole discretion of the government since 2007. At the same time, in-kind benefits, or benefits addressed to the so-called 'substitute recipient', were made possible in cases of misconduct (eg when not paying for housing costs such as rent or energy) instead of cash. However, although the revaluation of the living/subsistence minimum took place only in 2008 when value added tax (VAT) was increased, the replacement rates did not drop during the crisis period and have remained slightly above the EU average (see Table 11.5).

Another question is that due to the increases in VAT and housing costs (rent deregulation was completed during 2008–10), real purchasing power fell more significantly for people on low incomes.[13]

Activation of minimum income recipients and the long-term unemployed

Since the centre-right government returned to power in 2007, it has been committed to cuts in public expenditure, with a series of

Table 11.5: Net replacement rates for the total of social benefits for the long-term unemployed (60th month of unemployment), for two levels of wages and for different household composition

	67% of average wage						100% of average wage					
	Without children			2 children			Without children			2 children		
Persons	1	2	2	1	2	2	1	2	2	1	2	2
		1 EA	2 EA		1 EA	2 EA		1 EA	2 EA		1 EA	2 EA
2008	42	66	56	67	77	61	30	47	47	53	57	52
2009	45	64	56	65	75	62	32	46	47	51	55	52
2010	48	64	56	64	74	61	36	46	47	51	57	52
2011	49	63	57	64	74	62	36	45	47	50	57	52
2012	49	65	57	65	76	62	37	47	47	51	59	52
2012 EU	48	57	54	62	69	62	35	42	44	48	53	51
2014	49	64	57	65	75	62	37	47	47	51	58	52
2014 EU	47	53	54	61	68	60	33	41	44	47	54	50

Note: EA = economically active (working).
Source: OECD (2016a)

measures aimed at restricting access to social assistance benefits either by tighter conditionality and or by pushing the recipients – mostly the long-term unemployed – back into the labour market. Entitlements to MIP/SA benefits were cut again in September 2008, in effect as of January 2009. After six months, MIP/SA benefit recipients were automatically entitled to only a subsistence minimum instead of a living minimum.[14] Only in cases in which they participated in public works for a total of 20–30 hours per month were they entitled to a living minimum plus a supplement in the amount of 30% of the difference between a subsistence and a living minimum. If they worked more than 30 hours, they received a bonus on top of the subsistence minimum in the amount of half the difference between the living minimum and the subsistence minimum.[15] In August 2009, about 24,000 of the 123,000 claimants for the living allowance were evaluated to be entitled only to the lower benefit corresponding to the subsistence minimum.

The new institution of public service (a workfare condition of entitlement to a living minimum) was criticised by the ombudsman because some of the unemployed objectively could not work (due to disability or other individual problems). Furthermore, the municipalities did not offer sufficient opportunities to MIP/SA recipients to participate in the programmes for public service jobs: in 2009, only 10% of the municipalities organised these activities (MLSA [MPSV], 2010).

Due to the crisis and the government policy response, the public budget deficit increased from 2.1% to 5.5% in 2009 and 4.4% in 2010. At the same time, the number of unemployed increased by nearly 50% compared with 2008, to about 560,000 in 2010 (MLSA [MPSV], 2011; see also Table 11.3). The number of MIP/SA-recipient households nearly doubled, rising from 65,000 households in 2008 to 73,000 in 2009, 91,000 in 2010, 103,000 in 2011, 116,000 in 2012, 150,000 in 2013 and 161,000 in 2014 (average annual figures; see MLSA [MPSV], 2015).

The new activation measures adopted in 2011[16] represented a continuation of the repressive activation reforms, with great emphasis on the workfare principle. Positive incentives in the form of bonuses to the living minimum or the subsistence minimum in case of participation in public service were cancelled. Instead, all unemployed (regardless of whether they are MIP/SA recipients or unemployment benefit recipients) were obliged after two months of unemployment to participate in public service for up to 20 hours per week (which, in fact, corresponds to a part-time job). Refusal could result in exclusion from all entitlements to unemployment or social assistance benefits. Since the beginning of 2012, nearly 61,000 (mostly long-term) unemployed have participated in the public service scheme (MLSA [MPSV], 2012).

The other measure was increased control over the use of MIP/SA by recipients by introducing more in-kind benefits: in 2009, *electronic payment* was implemented in cases where recipients were suspected of misusing benefits; and from 2012, *social cards* have been implemented, aimed mainly at this category of MIP/SA benefit recipients.[17] The changes in MIP/SA and related activation measures are summarised in Table 11.6 in the appendix.

The direction of the activation reforms may be understood as a significant shift towards repressive sanctions, ending in an *explicit workfare* form. This effort culminated during the crisis (2009–12) when workfare requirements were extended to the broader category of the unemployed and positive incentives in the public service scheme were cancelled.

Politics of the reforms in labour market-related policies

Deeper divisions in the labour market

While the newly created unemployment benefits scheme and MIP/SA scheme tended to converge during the 1990s, the reforms implemented in 2004 started to differentiate them, mainly with regard to generosity. Increased conditionality was a common feature of the two schemes (Sirovátka and Hora, 2012). This trend was led by the distinction between 'deserving' and 'undeserving' unemployed or benefit recipients, which was based practically on the distinction between the regular workforce (only short-time unemployed), on the one hand, and the marginal workforce (typically the young unemployed and long-term unemployed), on the other, underpinned by a political logic aimed at redirecting resources towards the most powerful and 'legitimate' groups of the electorate (Sirovátka and Hora, 2012).

With the crisis, the trend continued: the replacement rates of unemployment benefits were increased for the short-term unemployed. On the other hand, access to unemployment benefits was restricted to a narrower group of insiders by excluding those who were fired due to misconduct and the level of benefit was reduced for those who quit their job voluntarily; the length of the benefit period was also cut. From 2012, it was made possible to demand that the unemployed participate in public service programmes in order to retain their entitlement to unemployment benefits, except for the short-term unemployed (two months).

In the MIP/SA scheme, more sanctions towards outsiders were used: entitlements were cut in 2009 by implementing the subsistence minimum and a duty of public service in order to preserve entitlement. Since 2012, positive incentives (bonuses on top of the living minimum) for those participating in public service have been abolished.

Clearly, labour market divisions between insiders and outsiders sharpened due to the crisis. At the same time, insiders – according to the legislative definition – have become a narrower group than before. This trend contrasts with the increasing numbers of regular workers who lost their jobs during the crisis.

Factors behind the divisions

The policy of fiscal consolidation and cuts in public expenditure that influenced the reforms in labour market policy, as we have seen earlier, was initiated even before the crisis by the centre-right government that emerged from the 2006 elections. The impact of the crisis was an additional factor pushing the reforms in the same direction as they were intended, irrespective of the crisis.

Thus, the reforms of 2007–12 were influenced mainly by political factors: above all, their logic was dictated by fiscal consolidation aims. In this context, welfare dependency became a key argument used by the right-wing government to legitimise welfare state reforms aimed at cutting public spending (Programové, 2007, 2010). These reforms included the implementation of fees in health care, cutting family benefits, reforming pensions by weakening the public pillar, cutting social insurance payments and implementing a flat tax on incomes.

Most importantly, there was a political push to achieve 'savings' in social expenditures, with the professed aim of achieving a lower public deficit. This motive was successfully repeated by right-wing parties in the June 2010 election campaign, although the cumulative public deficit in Czechia (at most 40% in 2010 and 2011) was among the lowest in Europe (compared with the EU average of 83%).[18]

The labour market policy reforms fitted very well into the political project outlined by centre-right governments from 2007 to 2010, whose objective was to roll back the welfare state. Above all, the labour market policy reforms helped to legitimise the other far-reaching welfare state reforms. Labour market policy reforms were easier to ratify than reforms in other fields because they represent a relative new policy field that has emerged since 1989 and path dependency did not play a prominent role (see Saxonberg et al, 2013).

The preparation and implementation of the reforms was fast due to strong political will and enforcement, which led to many substantial shortcomings. Similarly, the procedure for their approval was opaque and unusual. For example, the negotiations of the new governance reform (Act No. 73/2011 Coll.) of the employment office (public administration services) from its initial 'merit proposal' up to its submission to Parliament took only three months, while the new Employment Act No. 435/2004 Coll. took a whole year to negotiate (Kotrusová and Výborná, 2014). The majority of the social partners complained of the non-standard legislative process, which was also the reason for the rejection of this Act by the president (Parlament České republiky, Poslanecká sněmovna, 2011). In spite of this, the Parliament, when a government coalition held the majority, quickly overruled the rejection by the president. During 2012 and 2013, it became apparent that several measures implemented as activation reforms suffered from serious weaknesses. These failures were strongly criticised and most of the reforms had to be abandoned.

The most important one was the decision to dismantle the workfare principle imposed on the unemployed under the unemployment benefit scheme. Specifically, in November 2012, the Constitutional Court discontinued the institution of public service as a compulsory activity for those unemployed for more than two months, enforced through a punitive sanction (suspension of entitlement to unemployment benefits) in the case of a refusal to perform public service activities.[19] Similarly, the 'social cards' project was cancelled by the government itself (see earlier).

When assessing the factors behind the labour market reforms and other related policies, the institutionalist perspective helps us to recognise the reasons for the divergence between the policies aimed at insiders and outsiders, as well as the reasons for the rapid introduction of radical activation reforms, ending in explicit workfare measures mainly affecting outsiders. These key factors may be summarised as follows: first, a lack of path dependency (legacies) from the past; second, the crisis being used as a critical juncture to confer more legitimacy on the reforms dictated by cost-containment aims; and, finally, a discursive change contextualised by the crisis that sought to blame the unemployed, especially outsiders (long-term unemployed and benefit claimants). Such discursive and labour market policy changes were deliberately framed in order to legitimise the far-reaching welfare state reforms.

Conclusion

Our analysis has shown that in Czechia, during the crisis and post-crisis period, labour market and related reforms have been rapid, incomplete and associated with political developments. The main thrust of reforms encompassed cuts in public expenditure, limited access to benefits and other measures, and increased conditionality and activation.

In the unemployment benefit scheme, the trend was to improve the position of insiders slightly and to punish and 'flexibilise' outsiders. In particular, eligibility for unemployment benefits was restricted, while their level was increased in the first two months. In ALMPs, Czechia was always far behind most EU countries: during the crisis, the proportion of the unemployed in such measures fell and the gap between Czechia and the other EU countries widened. On the other hand, the protection of existing jobs was a clear preference. Protection of the regular workforce in the case of individual dismissals remains stronger than the OECD average and protection of temporary workers was only slightly improved in order to alleviate the government's fiscal obligations due to fired (foreign) agency workers. On the other hand, the level of protection against collective dismissals is below the OECD average.

The reform of the MIP/SA scheme was also aimed at differentiating between deserving recipients (and providing them with full entitlements) and undeserving/inactive recipients (provided at most with only restricted rights). The direction of the activation measures in this scheme was a significant shift towards repressive sanctions, ending in an *explicit workfare* form.

When assessing the factors behind the reforms in labour market policies, the institutionalist perspective helps us to recognise the reasons for the divergence between policies aimed at insiders and at outsiders. These may be summarised as follows: a lack of path dependency (legacies) from the past; crisis as a critical juncture used to confer more legitimacy on cost-containment measures; and, finally, a discursive shift aimed at blaming the unemployed, 'outsiders' in particular. This discursive change and consequent labour market policy change were intended to legitimise the far-reaching welfare state reforms; labour market policy reforms thus helped to push through the political project outlined by centre-right governments from 2007 to 2010, whose objective was to roll back the welfare state. This project, however, emerged due to political factors, irrespective of the crisis. A partial change of approach occurred from 2013 with the caretaker government and again in 2014 with the centre-left government. The policy changes, however, have been incremental.

Acknowledgement

This study was written with the support of the Czech Grant Agency (Grant 21263S: 'Welfare Attitudes in Post-Crisis Europe').

Notes

1. In Czechia, the first signs of the crisis in terms of economic slowdown were apparent only in the last quarter of 2008; the labour market was hit only in 2009 (see Table 11.1).
2. Act No 382/2008 Coll.
3. Like health-care reasons, caring obligations or dismissals due to organisational changes.
4. Since the early 1990s in the Czech Republic, there was a two-level public services administration system: the centre (Ministry of Labour and Social Affairs [MLSA]) and 77 local/district employment offices as legal subjects of their own.
5. Organisation for Economic Co-operation and Development (OECD) data indicate expenditure on ALMPs in 2008 of 0.22% of GDP, 0.27% in 2009, 0.32% in 2010, 0.27% in 2011, 0.25% in 2012, 0.30% in 2013 and 0.37% in 2014, of which 0.10–0.12% of GDP is expenditure on the administration of the Public Employment Service (PES). The share of participants in ALMPs represents something like 1% of the labour force; in 2010, it was 1.23%, and in 2014, it increased to 1.56% (OECD, 2016a).
6. To a great extent implemented as traineeships in firms financed through the ESF's Operational Programme under the Youth Guarantee.
7. A similar measure was implemented during 2009–10 as a buffer against collective dismissals financed from EU funds under the de minimis rule, which covered about 3% of the labour force.
8. The government was pushed in 2009 to launch a new programme of support for immigrants in order to enable them to return home (to provide them an airline ticket plus a lump sum of €500, later €300), although returning to their home country was often not possible because of debts they still hoped to somehow repay.
9. *Zákon o životním minimu* (Act No. 463/1991 Coll. on Living Minimum).
10. *Zákon ČNR o sociální potřebnosti* (Act No. 482/1991 Coll. on Social Need).
11. On the other hand, the Employment Act 1991 (and its amendment in 1992) established a general condition in the form of a strict definition of a suitable job (see earlier).

12. In the latter case, typically those who did not actively seek a job, did not register at the employment office or refused a suitable job, or did not fulfill the obligations of the individual action contract. The other reason might be that they did not use their property to increase their income.

13. In 2009, VAT was unified at 19%; previously, a lower level of 5% had been in place for food, books, medicine, construction works and some services.

14. This was later changed and disabled people are exempt.

15. Act No. 382/2008 Coll.

16. Act No. 354 of 6 November 2011.

17. This measure was later cancelled by the government itself because it was poorly prepared and had an evident negative impact on the recipients.

18. Data from the European Commission.

19. The proposal to the court was submitted by MPs of the opposition Social Democratic Party.

References

Clasen, J., Clegg, D. and Kvist, J. (2012) *European labour market policies in (the) crisis*, Working Paper No. 12, Brussels: ETUI.

Council of the European Union (2009) 'Council Recommendation to the Czech Republic with a view to bringing an end to the situation of an excessive government deficit', Brussels, 30 November, 15755/09 (OR. en).

Council of the European Union (2014) 'Council closes excessive deficit procedures for Belgium, Czech Republic, Denmark, Netherlands, Austria and Slovakia', Luxembourg, 20 June, 11089/14 (OR. en), PRESSE 349.

Falkner, G., Treib, O. and Holzleithner, E. (2008) *Compliance in the enlarged European Union: Living rights or dead letters?*, Aldershot: Ashgate.

Gallie, D. and Paugam, S. (2000) 'The experience of unemployment in Europe: the debate', in D. Gallie and S. Paugam (eds) *Welfare regimes and the experience of unemployment in Europe*, Oxford: Oxford University Press.

Hall, P. (2009) 'Historical institutionalism in rationalist and sociological perspective', in J. Mahoney and C. Thelen (eds) *Explaining institutional change. Ambiguity, agency, and power*, Cambridge: Cambridge University Press, pp 204–24.

Kotrusová, M. and Výborná, K. (2014) 'Zhodnocení institucionální reformy veřejných služeb zaměstnanosti v roce 2011 v České republice', *Fórum sociální politiky*, 9(6): 10–17.

MLSA (MPSV) (Ministry of Labour and Social Affairs [Ministerstvo práce a sociálních věcí]) (2005) 'Důvodová zpráva k návrhu zákona o hmotné nouzi'. Available at: http://socialnirevue.cz/media/docs/navrh-zakona-o-hmotne-nouzi-05-2005.doc (accessed 15 December 2009).

MLSA (MPSV) (2010) 'Veřejnou službu zavedlo v loňském roce 10 procent obcí', Tisková zpráva, press release, 3 June. Available at: http://www.mpsv.cz/cs/32 (accessed 20 July 2012).

MLSA (MPSV) (2011) *Analýza vývoje zaměstnanosti a nezaměstnanosti v roce 2010*, Praha: Ministerstvo práce a sociálních věcí. Available at: http://portal.mpsv.cz/sz/politikazamest/trh_prace/rok2010/Anal2010.pdf

MLSA (MPSV) (2012) 'Ve veřejné službě pracovalo 97 procent dlouhodobě nezaměstnaných', Tisková zpráva/press release, 27 December. Available at: http://www.mpsv.cz/cs/14026 (accessed 10 April 2013).

MLSA (MPSV) (2013a) 'Mullerová: Úřady práce dostanou významnou posilu: dalších 144 zaměstnanců', Tisková zpráva/press release, 29 May. Available at: http://www.mpsv.cz/files/clanky/15381/TZ_290513a2.pdf

MLSA (MPSV) (2013b) '*Úřad práce půjde do terénu a víc pomůže nezaměstnaným – díky novým zaměstnancům*', Tisková zpráva/Press release, 13 August. Available at: http://www.mpsv.cz/files/clanky/15925/TZ_130813b2.pdf

MLSA (MPSV) (2013c) 'Plán pro zaměstnanost má 7 bodů za 7 miliard', Tisková zpráva/Press release, 15 March. Available at: http://www.mpsv.cz/files/clanky/14864/TZ_150313.pdf

MLSA (MPSV) (2015) *Statistická ročenka z oblasti práce a sociálních věcí 2014*, Praha: Ministerstvo práce a sociálních věcí.

OECD (Organisation for Economic Co-operation and Development) (2016a) 'Benefits and wages, tax benefit model'. Available at: http://www.oecd.org/els/benefits-and-wages.htm

OECD (2016b) 'OECD employment database'. Available at: http://www.oecd.org/employment/emp/oecdindicatorsofemploymentprotection.htm

Ombudsman/Veřejný ochránce práv (2012) 'Příloha k Informaci o činnosti veřejného ochránce práv za první čtvrtletí roku 2012. Sociální reforma – poznatky z praxe veřejného ochránce práv'. Available at: http://www.ochrance.cz/zpravy-o-cinnosti/zpravy-pro-poslaneckou-snemovnu/ (accessed 10 April 2012).

Palier, B. (2005) 'Ambiguous agreement, cumulative change: French social policy in the 1990s', in W. Streeck and K. Thelen (eds) *Beyond continuity: Institutional change in advanced political economies*, Oxford: Oxford University Press, pp 127–44.

Parlament České republiky, Poslanecká sněmovna (2011) 'Stanovisko prezidenta republiky 2011, 131/7'.

Programové (2007) 'Programové prohlášení vlády Mirka Topolánka, 25. Leden'. Available at: http://www.vlada.cz/cz/clenove-vlady/historie-minulych-vlad/prehled-vlad-cr/1993-2007-cr/mirek-topolanek-2/prehled-ministru-24440/ (accessed 10 April 2012).

Programové (2010) 'Programové prohlášení Vlády České republiky 4. Srpna'. Available at: http://www.vlada.cz/cz/media-centrum/aktualne/programove-prohlaseni-vlady-74853/ (accessed 10 April 2012).

Saxonberg, S., Sirovátka, T. and Janoušková, M. (2013) 'When do policies become path dependent? The Czech example', *Journal of European Social Policy*, 23(4): 437–50.

Schmidt, V.A. (2008) 'Discursive institutionalism: the explanatory power of ideas and discourse', *Annual Review of Political Science*, 11: 303–26.

Sirovátka, T. and Hora, O. (2012) 'The Czech Republic: activation, diversification and marginalisation', in J. Clasen and D. Clegg (eds) *Regulating the risk of unemployment*, Oxford: Oxford University Press, pp 255–77.

Streeck, W. and Thelen, C. (eds) (2005) *Beyond continuity: Institutional change in advanced political economies*, Oxford: Oxford University Press.

Úřad práce (2014) *Zpráva o činnosti Úřadu práce České republiky za rok 2013*, Prague: Ministry of Labour and Social Affairs.

Vládní návrh (2005) 'Vládní návrh zákona o pomoci o pomoci v hmotné nouzi (Proposal by Government of the Act on Assistance in Material Need)', last revision 31 March 2006. Available at: http://www.psp.cz/sqw/text/orig2.sqw?idd=14460 (accessed 8 January 2009).

Appendix

See Table 11.6.

Table 11.6: Summary of the changes to the policies for the unemployed, Czech Republic

Policy field	2009	2015	Year of change
Unemployment protection	Period covered (months): 5, for those under 50 years 8, for those 50+ years 11, for those 55+ years (insurance of 12 months required within last 24 months)	No change	
	Replacement rate: 65% first two months, 50% next two months, 45% remaining months, and for those who were dismissed due to misconduct from the first month (ceiling of 0.58 times the average wage)	45% for those who terminated contract without serious reasons (re-elected centre-right government)	2011
	Earnings up to half of minimum wage tolerated in temporary job for the entitlement to unemployment benefits	No earnings tolerated	2011
	Individual action plans obligatory (condition to be registered and to receive the unemployment/social assistance benefits after 5 months of unemployment)	No change	
ALMPs/PES governance	Decentralised structure (central–local)	Centralisation (shift of competences from local to regional and central level), staff reduction (re-elected centre-right government)	2011
	Relative low level/emphasis of ALMPs	Increasing scope/emphasis on ALMPs	2009/10
		Decreasing scope/emphasis on ALMPs (re-elected centre-right government)	2011/12
		Increasing scope/emphasis on ALMPs (caretaker government and centre-left government)	2013/15

(continued)

Table 11.6: Summary of the changes to the policies for the unemployed, Czech Republic (continued)

Policy field	2009	2015	Year of change
Employment protection legislation	Harmonised with the EU law in 2000 and 2004	Partial flexibilisation (general)	2011
	Strong in case of permanent contracts, weak in case of temporary contracts	Improvement of protection of agency workers and temporary workers	
		Severance pay based on duration of work contract	
Minimum income scheme and activation	Allowance for living (guarantees income at the level of the living or subsistence minimum)	No change	
	Supplement to housing costs cover the costs of housing		
	After 6 months, the recipients get only the allowance that guarantees the subsistence minimum, which is one third less than the living minimum		
	If they participate in public service programme (20–30 hours *per month*), they get the allowance up to the level of the living minimum, and if they work more than 30 hours, they get a bonus	The bonus was cancelled	2011
		New obligation for all unemployed after 2 months to participate in public service programme up to 20 hours per week	
		Refusal leading to exclusion from unemployment benefit rights or reduction of social assistance benefit rights (re-elected centre-right government)	
		The obligation to participate in public service programme for the unemployed after 2 months and requirement of 20 hours per week was cancelled by the Constitutional Court (only applicable to social assistance recipients as in 2009, but no bonus provided)	2012

TWELVE

Slovakia: perpetual austerity and growing emphasis on activation

Stefan Domonkos

Introduction

This chapter provides an overview of labour market policies in Slovakia from the beginning of the post-socialist transition to the recent period, characterised by growing pressure for fiscal stringency from the European Union (EU). It provides a historical overview and investigates the differences between the prevalent trends in labour market policies before and after 2010. The European Commission initiated an excessive deficit procedure (EDP) against Slovakia between 2010 and 2014. However, for a variety of reasons, the emphasis on fiscal discipline has been nothing new in the Slovak case. Consistent with this, the analysis finds little difference between labour market policies before and after 2010. Although the 2011 Reform Programme of the Slovak government (MFSR, 2011), drawn up by a centre-right coalition, includes plans for labour market flexibilisation, these have not been implemented by subsequent governments. In the meantime, needs-based support was reformed, mainly by the political Left, with the intention of motivating labour market participation, also using punitive measures. While EU-led 'austerity' may have played a role by reinforcing existing tendencies to contain spending on labour market policies, the role of domestic politics appears much more important.

The chapter focuses on four pivotal areas: unemployment protection, employment protection, active labour market policies (ALMPs) and needs-based income support. The first three of these are commonly recognised as key parts of a modern labour market policy mix. Needs-based income support includes predominantly unconditional social transfers and measures provided on the basis of material deprivation. Although the primary objective of needs-based support is the alleviation of poverty, in the Slovakian context, these policies are also employed as a pillar of labour market activation.

The study proceeds as follows. In the second section, the Slovak macroeconomic and macro-institutional context is presented. The third section traces the development of labour market policies from the early 1990s to recent times. The fourth section discusses the most important differences between pre- and post-2010 labour market reforms and evaluates the impact of the growing EU-wide pressure for budgetary stringency. In order to aid the reader, each section is divided into three periodic subsections: post-1989 transition; EU accession and early post-accession; and crisis and recovery.

Macroeconomic and macro-institutional context

Slovakia is one of those post-socialist countries that do not fit into any clear-cut welfare state regime defined in terms of a Western European welfare state typology. Nevertheless, its classification by Bohle and Greskovits (2007) as an embedded neoliberal market economy, relying on reasonably stable institutions and a more favourable economic legacy than former Soviet states, might help evaluate the Slovak welfare state. Indeed, some elements of the Slovak social security system, such as the strong link between past contributions and benefits, are remnants of the country's century-long Bismarckian tradition. Nevertheless, low benefits and the limited duration of entitlement in the case of unemployment protection represent significant deviations from the Continental-Bismarckian model. Most importantly, the country's social security system has undergone several significant changes in the past decade. These reforms have been adopted despite the threat of electoral 'punishment' by a public generally supportive of redistribution. Thus, the Slovak welfare state possesses most of the traits that Aidukaite (2009, 2011) associates with a distinctively post-socialist welfare regime, such as adherence to insurance-based social security, wide coverage, low benefits, an emphasis on deregulation in industrial relations and an erosion of the welfare state, but also a strong public preference for solidarity. This makes the country a good case for studying the development of labour market policies in post-socialist EU member states.

Post-1989 Slovak welfare policy has been significantly influenced by the country's vulnerable political and macroeconomic situation as it unfolded after the fall of the semi-authoritarian left-wing/nationalist Mečiar government in 1998. In contrast to its neighbours, Slovakia was a latecomer to European integration, internationally shamed for its poor performance with regard to democratisation and human rights (Mathernová and Renčko, 2006; Tudoroiu et al, 2009; Bohle and Greskovits, 2012). The Mečiar government's loss of credibility after the country's exclusion from the first round of EU accession negotiations led to the rise of a 'free-market liberal' coalition devoted to EU integration, foreign investors and limiting redistribution (Fisher et al, 2007; Bohle and Greskovits, 2012).

Mečiar's government was replaced in 1998 by a grand coalition of reformed left-wing, Christian Democrat and 'free-market liberal' parties led by Prime Minister Mikuláš Dzurinda from the centre-right Slovak Democratic Coalition (SDK). Subsequently, the 2002 elections gave rise to Dzurinda's second, ideologically more coherent, centre-right government, which carried out an overhaul of the Slovak tax and social security system, including the Labour Code. Confronted with growing unemployment and an acutely capital-poor economy, one of the leitmotifs of the reform programme adopted by the second Dzurinda government was the attraction of foreign direct investment (FDI). This objective was pursued successfully. Slovakia became home to one of Europe's most important automotive industry hubs (Frigant and Miollan, 2014). However, in accordance with the political rhetoric of those days, increasing competitiveness required a marketised social security system, reducing needs-based income maintenance programmes and the marginalisation of trade unions.

The second Dzurinda government also developed the first plans to join the euro area by 2009 (Government of the Slovak Republic, 2008) and decided to implement a partial shift from the country's mature state-run pay-as-you-go (PAYG) pension system to a mandatory fully funded retirement scheme similar to the one implemented in Chile (Drahokoupil and Domonkos, 2012). These proved to be particularly important long-term policy choices, influencing public finances well beyond the 2006 elections, which led to a left-wing shift in domestic politics.

The plan to adopt the euro by 2009 required considerable fiscal effort, combined with a need to limit monetary expansion. The introduction of mandatory funded pensions went hand in hand with significant transition costs, increasing the deficit of the old-age social security system (Drahokoupil and Domonkos, 2012).[1] Given these systemic reform choices (see Pierson, 1994), Slovak governments were left with limited fiscal space, even at times of high economic growth during 2005–08. Thus, in the early and mid-2000s, Slovakia not only joined the EU, but also rapidly adopted austere 'reform' policies in practically all significant social policy areas. Much of the 2002–06 reform package has successfully outlived its architects. It has also significantly influenced the policy trajectory of the left-leaning governments led by the Smer Party, in office between 2006 and 2010 and since 2012.

The system of employment and unemployment protection, ALMPs and the regulation of needs-based income support have also been significantly reformed in this period (Jurajda and Mathernová, 2004; Bohle and Greskovits, 2006). The increased importance of 'fiscal discipline' during the euro adoption process and the EDP between 2010 and 2014 left its mark on the quality of services provided by the Regional Offices of Labour, Social Affairs and Family (hereinafter, labour offices), as low spending on public services, including staffing at labour offices and ALMPs, constitutes a significant impediment to addressing many of the long-term problems of the Slovak labour market (Duell and Kureková, 2013). However, it should be noted that the Commission's assessment of the country's national reform programmes during the EDP did not include calls for more flexibilisation. In fact, the 2011 Commission assessment argues that 'the acute increase in unemployment experienced in 2009–10 does not point to excessive rigidity in the labour market during the crisis either' (European Commission, 2011: 10).

Nevertheless, in order to be able to evaluate the impact of concrete labour market policies, one must first investigate the particularities of the Slovak labour market. Similar to most state-socialist nations, unemployment was non-existent in Slovakia before 1989. The state-socialist regime formally guaranteed full employment, even at the cost of economic imbalances. Under these circumstances, unemployment protection and ALMPs remained underdeveloped. Following the implosion of the Eastern Bloc, a high unemployment rate has become typical in the Slovak economy. The first large increase in the number of unemployed took place in 1991, when the unemployment rate rose from about 1% to 4% in Czechia and almost 12% in Slovakia (Ham et al, 1995: 94). As can be seen in Figure 12.1, unemployment has remained above 10% for most of the post-socialist period, peaking at 19.2% in 2001. While the FDI-led economic upswing of the mid-2000s contributed to a significant decline in the unemployment rate, a more detailed look at the figures also shows that the country is suffering from deep structural imbalances that have not been sufficiently addressed.

As can be seen in Figure 12.1, long-term unemployment is particularly high. In 2015, more than 60% of all unemployed had been jobless for more than 12 consecutive months and approximately 45% for more than two years (MoLSAF, 2015). The high share of long-term unemployed is not merely a consequence of the crisis of the late

Figure 12.1: Total, youth and long-term unemployment rates in Slovakia, 1994–2015

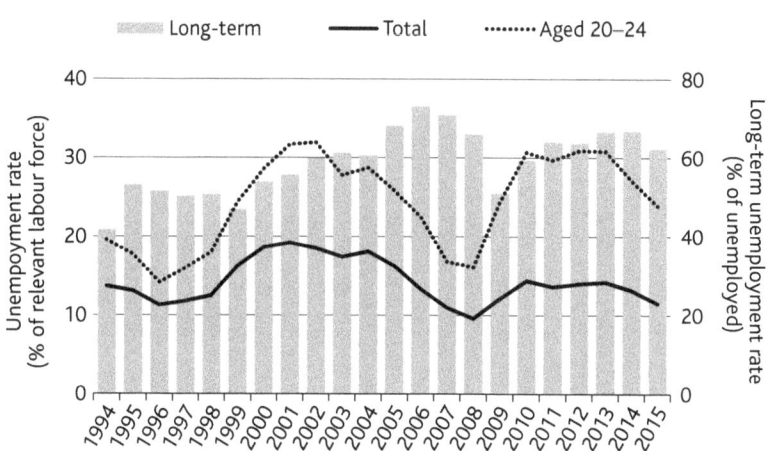

Note: Data derived from the Slovak Labour Force Survey (*Výberové zisťovanie pracovných síl*).
Source: Slovak Statistical Office – SLOVSTAT Database (available at http://www.statistics.sk/pls/elisw/vbd)

2000s. Their share in total unemployment has exceeded 50% for the past 15 years. Given the limited duration of unemployment protection, the long-term unemployed have to rely on the so-called 'benefit in material need' (BMN) and other needs-based benefits. Although governments on both the Left and Right have shown an awareness of the severity of long-term structural unemployment (Government of the Slovak Republic, 2010, 2012), the steps taken to address this phenomenon have been fairly limited. Long-term unemployment has thus remained a challenge even in 2015/16, when the country's unemployment rate has once again fallen to around 10%.

Besides long-term unemployment, high youth unemployment and large regional disparities are the two most important characteristics of the Slovak labour market. As Table 12.1 shows, some parts of Western Slovakia – especially the capital city Bratislava – enjoy low levels of unemployment. By contrast, in the economically less advanced eastern regions, unemployment rates have oscillated between 12% and 21% for the past decade. Long-term unemployment is also concentrated primarily in Central and Eastern Slovakia (Švecová and Rajčáková, 2014).

While youth unemployment represents a challenge, the share of young people not in education, employment or training (NEET) is lower than the data on joblessness alone would suggest. From a

Table 12.1: The economic environment and regional disparities in Slovakia, 2004–15

	2004	2005	2006	2007	2008	2009	2010	2011	2012	2013	2014	2015
Macroeconomic environment*												
Real per capita GDP growth[a]	5.3	6.4	8.5	10.8	5.7	-5.5	5.1	2.8	1.5	1.4	2.5	3.8
Government deficit[a]	-2.3	-2.9	-3.6	-1.9	-2.3	-7.9	-7.5	-4.1	-4.3	-2.7	-2.7	-2.7
Government debt[a]	40.6	33.9	30.8	29.9	28.2	36.0	40.8	43.3	52.4	55.0	53.9	52.5
Employment rate (cohort 20–64)[a]	63.5	64.5	66.0	67.2	68.8	66.4	64.6	65.0	65.1	65.0	65.9	67.7
National currency in ERM II	No	Yes[†]	Yes	Yes	Yes							
Excessive deficit procedure	No	No	No	No	No	No	Yes	Yes	Yes	Yes	Yes[‡]	No
Unemployment rate[§]												
National average[b]	13.1	11.4	9.4	8.0	8.4	12.7	12.5	13.6	14.4	13.5	12.3	10.6
Bratislava Region[b]	3.4	2.6	2.3	2.0	2.3	4.4	4.6	5.4	5.7	6.2	6.1	5.3
Western Slovakia[b]	10.8	8.6	6.6	5.4	5.7	10.2	9.9	10.8	11.6	10.9	9.7	8.15
Central Slovakia[b]	15.3	13.8	11.6	9.8	10.2	14.9	14.8	15.8	16.7	15.4	14.0	11.9
Eastern Slovakia[b]	18.2	16.6	14.4	12.5	13.2	17.8	17.3	18.9	20.1	18.3	16.7	15.0

Notes: * Government debt, deficit and gross domestic product (GDP) growth are given as percentages of GDP; employment rate is given as a percentage of total population aged 20–64; [†] since 28 November 2005; [‡] EDP closed on 20 June 2014; [§] percentages of the total labour force registered as job seekers at labour offices.

Sources: [a]Eurostat (see: http://ec.europa.eu/eurostat); [b] Slovak Statistical Office – Datacube database (http://datacube.statistics.sk/TM1Web/TM1WebLogin.aspx)

low of 16.1% in 2008, the share of young people aged 20–24 falling into the NEET category rose to about 20% throughout 2010–15 (Eurostat, 2015). These numbers, although still above the EU average, are considerably below the youth unemployment rate shown in Figure 12.1. Part of the explanation for this discrepancy is the broad availability of secondary and tertiary education opportunities. Due to the expansion of secondary and tertiary education, 'young people not in education' has become a specific subgroup where the risk of unemployment is indeed higher.

The Slovak labour market is also characterised by limited use of temporary and part-time contracts. According to estimates from the Slovak module of the European Working Conditions Survey (EWCS), almost 70% of workers in 2005 and 67% in 2010 were employed on the basis of a permanent full-time job based on an open-ended contract. The same figures for the EU15 stood at 53.5% and 55.5% in 2005 and 2010, respectively. The share of workers employed in atypical forms of employment has been below the average of the EU15 and reached approximately 30% and 33% in 2005 and 2010, respectively (see Baboš, 2013: 181). While further research is needed on the subject, limited redundancy costs in both atypical and typical labour contracts may be one of the reasons behind the relatively large share of permanent job contracts in Slovakia.

Labour market policies during the economic transition and beyond

Income protection for the unemployed

Post-1989 transition

Labour market policies, both passive and active, had to be created practically from scratch in post-1989 Czechoslovakia. The legislation that entered into force in January 1990 provided unemployment protection comparable in its set-up to Western European systems. Those paying contributions for at least 12 months in the previous three years were eligible for unemployment benefits. Full-time study, military service and childcare also counted for this qualifying period. The entitlement period was set at 12 months. Although the gross replacement rate was relatively high (between 60% and 90%), the maximum unemployment benefit was first determined at CZK2400 (approximately US$80), and later set at 1.5 and 1.8 times the minimum wage for a regular unemployed person and for an unemployed person in retraining, respectively. In summary, the first unemployment protection scheme of the new Czechoslovak market economy was characterised by broad coverage, a relatively long entitlement period and low benefits (Terrell and Munich, 1996).

After the country's social welfare system was confronted with the first large increase in unemployment in 1991, limitations on benefits, the entitlement period and eligibility were introduced. Benefit levels were moderately reduced and the entitlement period decreased from 12 to six months (Ham et al, 1995). Further restrictions came into force in 1993. Although entitlement to benefits was not linked to proving an active search for work, those who refused retraining or participation in public works programmes would lose their benefits (Terrell et al, 1996). While some of these measures were later abolished, it became clear that unemployment protection was a badly needed, but costly and sensitive, aspect of the Slovak welfare state. Loose eligibility criteria have been seen by some as a factor increasing the likelihood of 'free-riding' on the welfare system (eg Ham et al, 1995; Terrell et al, 1996; Terrell and Munich, 1996). Nevertheless, the country's turbulent transition clearly threatened a large part of the labour force with joblessness. In reaction to this, the 1995 amendment of the legislation introduced differentiated entitlement periods by age, granting preferential treatment to older job seekers (Terrell et al, 1996).

European Union accession and early post-accession

Cuts in the entitlement period and the tightening of eligibility criteria continued throughout the 1990s and 2000s. By the early 2000s, full-time study was no longer included in the qualifying period and the necessary insurance period for gaining access to benefits was increased to 24 months. At the same time, following the 2004 reform of the social security system, eligibility for unemployment benefits became independent of the reason for job termination. Until 2004, both termination by the employer for breach of labour discipline and termination by the employee without a serious reason had a negative impact on unemployment benefit. These reforms introduced stricter general conditions applicable to everyone and abolished penalties and exceptions related to individual reasons for unemployment.

Moreover, the standard entitlement period was set at six months for all age groups without exceptions for older workers. Access to benefits was further tightened. From 2004, social insurance contributions for at least 36 months in the past four years were needed to qualify for unemployment benefits and the preferential treatment of seasonal workers, present in the legislation since the early 1990s, was abolished. In addition, besides registering with a labour office, job seekers have been required since 2003 to demonstrate an active search for employment. This involves providing written evidence, every other week, that the job seeker has established contact with prospective employers. Failure to do so results in the loss of unemployment benefits (Gyarfášová et al, 2006). These changes happened while unemployment levels were reaching levels close to 20% (see Figure 12.1). Between the mid-1990s and mid-2000s, the share of people drawing unemployment benefits in the total number of registered job seekers declined from above 25% in 1997 to approximately 10% by 2007 (see Figure 12.2). While other circumstances might have played a role, the tightening of access to benefits was a major cause behind this trend.

The 'generosity' of unemployment benefits was affected less by the austerity measures applied in the late 1990s and early 2000s, although gross replacement rates were decreased to 50% of the assessment base by 2004. The new social security legislation introduced a more significant differentiation based on past contributions. High-income workers saw the replacement rates of their unemployment benefits increase between 2003 and 2004. While, until 2003, benefits were maximised at 1.5 times the minimum subsistence level, the maximum unemployment allowance was raised to approximately 1.5 times the

Figure 12.2: Unemployment benefit recipients as a percentage of registered unemployed, Slovakia, various years 1997–2015

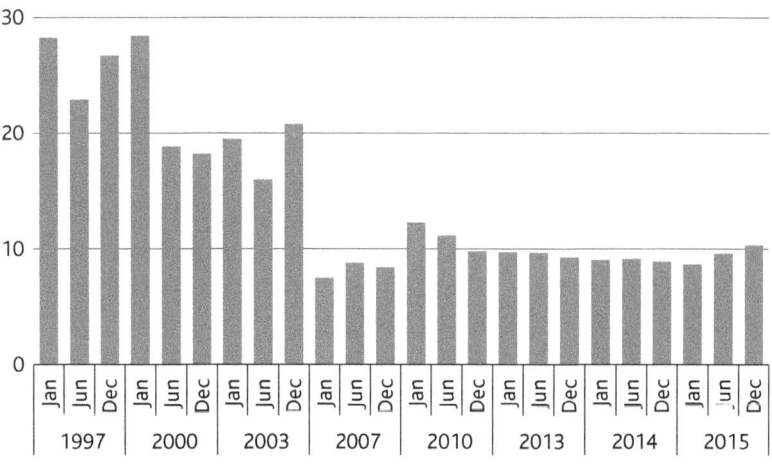

Sources: For 1997–2003: Central Office of Labour, Social Affairs and Family (see: http://www.upsvar.sk/statistiky/nezamestnanost-mesacne-statistiky.html?page_id=1254); for 2007–2015: Central Office of Labour, Social Affairs and Family and the Social Insurance Agency (see: http://www.socpoist.sk/647/1615s)

average wage in 2004, causing a threefold increase in the level of the maximum unemployment benefit. According to the Organisation for Economic Co-operation and Development (OECD, 2014), the net replacement rate of single childless individuals earning 150% of the national average wage increased from about 38% in 2003 to 66% in 2005. The post-2004 unemployment protection system, with its tightened eligibility criteria and increased maximum benefit levels, has thus benefited primarily higher-income individuals with a stable labour market position.

Crisis and recovery

Subsequent reforms carried out during the left-leaning Smer governments led to modest adjustments. With the exception of a short incumbency of a centre-right coalition between the summer of 2010 and April 2012, Smer has been continuously in government since 2006. First, since 2008, the maximum base for the calculation of unemployment insurance contributions has increased from approximately three to four times the average wage. In 2013, this was further raised to five times the average wage. The maximum benefit receivable remained approximately 1.5 times the average wage until 2012. In 2013, this was decreased to the average wage. Nevertheless, while these measures increased the compulsory payment wedge of high-earning workers and, at the same time, restricted maximum benefits, important loopholes were left open that allowed payroll tax avoidance (eg Kollárová, 2014).

Based on a law voted by Dzurinda's centre-right government but implemented by Smer, eligibility criteria were also made less stringent for workers on temporary contracts. Since September 2010, a Reform Act adopted by the Left and implemented by the centre-right, also loosened the general eligibility criterion to 24 months of insurance in the past three years. In addition, since 2013, the Social Security Code has been reformed in order to include people employed based on atypical contracts (so-called agreements on work performed outside an employment relationship) in regular old-age social security and unemployment protection. Some of these changes, such as the enrolment of atypical workers in the social security system and the decreased maximum unemployment benefit rate, may have been partly motivated by the policy of balancing the public budget.

While a comprehensive evaluation of the redistributive consequences of these measures is beyond the scope of this study, it may be concluded that the reforms in income protection for the unemployed after 2010 have led to improved coverage. Most of the restrictive measures have targeted high-earning individuals with a stable labour market position. After its reform in the early 2000s, the general unemployment protection scheme, which provided benefits closely commensurate with past contributions, has been gradually changed into a more redistributive system.

Employment protection

Post-1989 transition

In contrast to unemployment protection, employment protection was part of the Czechoslovak Labour Code already before 1989. In theory, employees were allowed to resign with or without stating a legitimate reason for resignation listed in the Labour Code. However, resignation without a reason would drastically increase the notice period. The employer's right to fire workers was considerably more restricted.

The new post-1989 regulation gave greater freedom to employers and employees alike, decreasing employment protection to a significant extent. Employers are allowed to fire workers to increase the efficiency of their organisation ('for economic reasons'), which provides considerable discretion in employment matters. Nevertheless, people on sickness and childcare leave are protected from job termination. For most of the 1990s, redundancy costs were kept fairly low. Employees were protected by a general notice period of two to three months and severance pay equal to two to three months of the employee's average wage. Notice-period wage and severance pay were provided independently from each other.

European Union accession and early post-accession

In the 2000s and 2010s, redundancy costs became an object of frequent changes. The reform package of the second Dzurinda government abolished the accumulation of notice-period wages and severance pay. The 2007 overhaul of the Labour Code under a left-leaning government reintroduced the general right to severance payments. Those working fewer than five years at their employer were entitled to two months' wages, while those working longer than five years were entitled to three months' wages, on top of their notice-period wages. In specific cases, such as job termination because of the employee's inability to carry out their work due to occupational health risks, the severance pay was increased to 10 times the average monthly wage.[2]

Taking into account a number of other amendments providing for a more equal treatment of contracted workers and core employees, it appears that the overall trend during the social-democratic government between 2006 and 2010 was a 'deflexibilisation' of the Labour Code. However, an important exception is the introduction of the so-called *flexikonto* in 2009, allowing for the more flexible organisation of working time through work-time accounts.

Crisis and recovery

The post-2010 development of employment protection legislation does not appear to point towards a prevailing trend in favour of or against greater flexibility. In line with the 2011 Reform Programme (MFSR, 2011), the Labour Code was liberalised to some extent during the 2010–12 centre-right government. The *flexikonto*, initially introduced as a temporary crisis-related measure, became an integral part of the Slovak Labour Code in 2011. The accumulation of notice-period wages and severance pay was again abolished, while a limitation of employers' liability in case of unlawful dismissal and a more flexible treatment of fixed-term contracts were introduced. Nevertheless, as Table 12.2 also shows, several of these changes, including those related

Table 12.2: Minimum notice period and severance pay according to the Slovak labour code, 2002–15

Year	Notice period/*severance pay*
2002–03	Two or three months depending on the reason for job termination/ two months' aw *(accumulation of npw and sp)*
2003–07	Two or three months depending on seniority/ two or three *months' aw depending on seniority (no accumulation of npw and sp)*
2007–11	Two or three months depending on seniority/ two or three *months' aw depending on seniority, 10 months' aw for specific occupational health-risk related job termination (accumulation of npw and sp)*
2011–13	Up to three months depending on seniority, reasons for job termination and contractual party terminating the work contract/ *severance derived from notice period (no accumulation of npw and sp), severance pay of 10 months' aw for specific occupational health-risk-related job termination*
2013–present	Up to three months depending on seniority, reasons for job termination and contractual party terminating the work contract/*up to five months depending on reason for job termination and seniority, 10 months' aw for specific occupational health-risk-related job termination (accumulation of npw and sp)*

Notes: aw = employee's average wage; npw = notice-period wage; sp = severance pay.
Sources: National legislation (see: www.slov-lex.sk)

to severance pay, were withdrawn shortly after the social-democratic Smer Party returned to power in 2012.

It appears that the alternation between left- and right-wing governments, rather than EU 'austerity', has been the key factor influencing the post-2010 development of employment protection legislation in Slovakia. Importantly, the European Commission did not criticise Slovakia for excessive rigidity in its employment protection legislation, leaving more space for domestic politics (see, eg, European Commission, 2011). While the economic crisis has had a negative impact on the Slovak labour market, these pressures have led to only limited changes towards flexibilisation, of which the introduction of the *flexikonto* is the most important example. The development of Slovak employment protection legislation clearly demonstrates the importance of the government of the day's ideological preferences. The left-leaning Smer Party has introduced several measures increasing the protection of employees through higher redundancy costs and the stricter regulation of various work contract types. Nevertheless, past experience shows that these policies can be easily reversed.

Active labour market policies

Post-1989 transition

ALMPs have been incorporated in the Slovak labour market policy framework since the early 1990s. The first post-1989 Labour Code already included several measures aimed at job creation and the retraining of job seekers (Ham et al, 1995). Most important among these have been the 'socially purposeful jobs' and the 'publicly useful jobs' schemes, both aimed at job creation. 'Socially purposeful jobs' covered job subsidisation in existing companies and support for start-ups for the unemployed. 'Publicly useful jobs' provided for placements within municipal services (Terrell and Munich, 1996). The share of spending on 'socially purposeful jobs' and 'publicly useful jobs' in total ALMP expenditure exceeded 80% throughout 1991–95, 'socially purposeful jobs' being the dominant measure (see Terrell et al, 1996: 258). In the same period, half of all ALMP participants were employed in 'socially purposeful jobs' (the same figure was between 22% and 26% for 'publicly useful jobs'). By contrast, retraining and graduate placement programmes played a considerably smaller role (Terrell et al, 1996). As Table 12.3 shows, ALMPs have gone through several important amendments since their initial introduction in the early 1990s. The Labour Code and the law governing the functioning of

Table 12.3: Selected active labour market policy instruments in the Slovak legislation, 1991–2015

Programme name	Period in force	Short description
Act 1/1991 Coll. on employment and Act 83/1991 Coll. on the powers of the Slovak authorities in the area of employment policy		
SPJs	1991–96	Jobs created by the private sector, based on a contract between the job provider and a labour office, to be filled by job seekers registered at a labour office.
PUJs	1991–96	Short-term jobs created by the public sector, based on a contract between the job provider and a labour office, to be filled by job seekers registered at a labour office.
Retraining	1991–ongoing	
programmes for graduates	1991–94 (merged into SPJs)	Subsidised practical training at a prospective employer and generic courses in a variety of areas.
Act 387/1996 Coll. on employment		
Subsidisation of existing jobs	1997–2003	Subsidies to be paid to employers in case of organisational changes leading to temporary underemployment in the enterprise.
Subsidised jobs for job seekers (including PUJs)	1997–2003	Subsidised jobs for job seekers and graduates, including the subsidisation of self-employment. Specific programmes for vulnerable groups, such as job seekers older than 50, the disabled (for example, protected workshops) and job seekers returning from maternity leave.
Large-scale job creation	1997–2003	Subsidies for large-scale investment projects creating several hundred jobs.
Retraining	1997–2003	
Graduate practice	2002–2003	Programme helping recent graduates to gain practical work experience.

(continued)

Table 12.3: Selected active labour market policy instruments in the Slovak legislation, 1991–2015 (continued)

Programme name	Period in force	Short description
Act 5/2004 Coll. on employment services		
Activation work programme	2004–ongoing	Mostly unqualified work for municipalities providing access to activation benefit (a component of needs-based income assistance).
Subsidisation of start-ups	2004–ongoing	Aimed at job seekers registered with a labour office taking up self-employment. Until 2013, support was claimable if a job seeker met all conditions stipulated by law. Since 2013, the support has been conditional on approval by a labour office.
Graduate practice	2004–ongoing	Programme helping recent graduates to gain practical work experience.
Financial support for commuters (and relocation)	2004–ongoing (2008–ongoing)	
Protected workshops	2004–ongoing	Enterprises with an increased share of disabled workers who could not find employment on the regular labour market.
Subsidisation of regional and local employment	2010–ongoing	Subsidy to cover part of the costs of employing disadvantaged job seekers. Subsidy may be received by municipalities and regions.
Subsidisation of employment in flood-protection programmes	2010–13	Subsidy to cover part of the costs of employing job seekers registered with the regional labour offices in flood-protection programmes. Subsidy may be received by municipalities and regions or public authorities responsible for flood protection.
Subsidisation of regional employment	2014–ongoing	Subsidy to cover part of the labour costs of municipalities and regions employing disadvantaged job seekers.
Subsidisation of subjects of social economy	2015–ongoing	A variety of entities (both self-employed and corporations) whose main purpose is to pursue a valid social objective. Subsidies are to be provided from EU funds and the state budget.

Notes: Coll= the collection of statute law; SPJs = socially purposeful jobs; PUJs = publicly useful jobs.
Sources: Terrel and Munich (1996); Terrell et al (1996); Uldrichova and Karpisek (1994) and national legislation (see: www.slov-lex.sk)

the labour offices have been thoroughly revised several times and, as part of these revisions, the system of ALMPs has also evolved.

Despite several changes throughout the 1990s and 2000s, the aforementioned main characteristics of Slovak ALMPs have remained largely unchanged. The emphasis has been on direct job creation and subsidised employment, while other measures have played a smaller role. As Figure 12.3 demonstrates, with the exception of a few years during the early transition, expenditure on ALMPs relative to gross domestic product (GDP) has remained below the level spent in more advanced EU member states. While ALMP expenditure typically approximates or exceeds 0.4% of GDP in Western European economies, Slovakia spends only around 0.2% of GDP on such measures (see OECD, 2015).

European Union accession and early post-accession

After 2004, finances from the European Social Fund became the key source of financing for ALMPs. Nevertheless, this change has not led to a significant improvement. In addition, the day-to-day administration of ALMPs at the regional labour offices has been adversely influenced by understaffing. Labour offices went through several rounds of downsizing in 2007 and 2011, when the number of their employees was decreased by approximately 14% and 9%, respectively. This decline

Figure 12.3: Expenditure on active labour market policies in Slovakia, Austria, France and Germany as a percentage of nominal GDP, 1991–2014

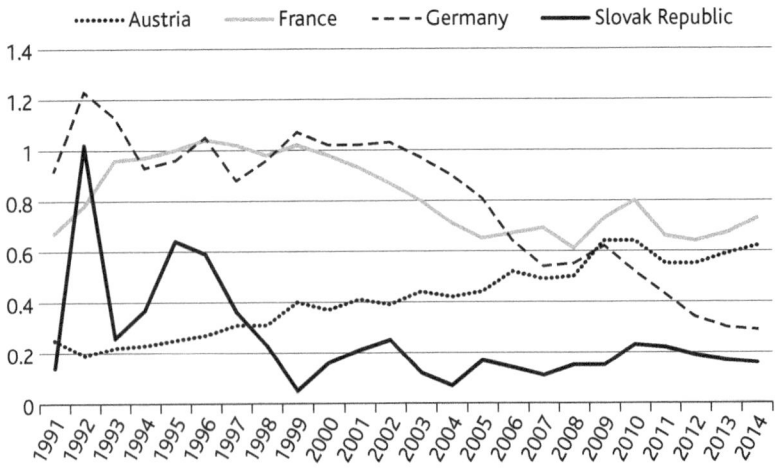

Note: Data refer to expenditure on policy measures 20–70 according to OECD methodology.
Source: OECD (see: stats.oecd.org)

in personnel and increasing unemployment have led to a major rise in the workload of consultants, which has remained an issue up to recent years (Duell and Kureková, 2013: 21–5). According to the 2015 National Reform Programme, the average caseload of first-contact consultants had reached 569 clients. The government realised that understaffing was a serious problem and intended to reduce the caseload to 226 throughout 2015 (MFSR, 2015: 33).

Probably the most important overhaul of ALMPs in the post-1989 period took place in 2004 under the second Dzurinda government. A significant shift towards 'workfare' was made by cutting needs-based income support and partly replacing it with the activation benefit payable for participation in the activation work programme.[3] At the same time, 'publicly useful jobs' were phased out entirely (Gyarfášová et al, 2006; Mýtna Kureková et al, 2013). Travel subsidies have also been introduced into the list of ALMPs.

The activation work programme subsequently became the most important ALMP until the late 2000s. As Figure 12.4 shows, direct job creation – namely, within the framework of the activation work programme – played the most important role among all ALMPs between 2004 and 2007. Nevertheless, as Mýtna Kureková et al (2013) note, activation is a hybrid policy instrument whose aim is not only to

Figure 12.4: Participation in active labour market policies in Slovakia, 2005–14 ('000)

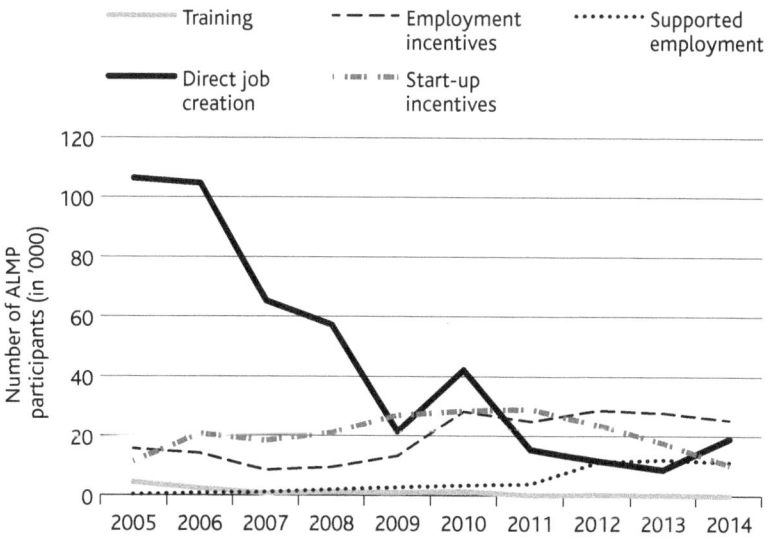

Source: Eurostat Labour Market Policy statistics (see: http://ec.europa.eu/eurostat/data/database)

integrate the long-term unemployed into the labour market, but also to provide a badly needed complement to the rather limited needs-based income support. In fact, the success of the programme as a tool of job-market (re)integration is debatable at best (eg Harvan, 2011).

In 2004, 88% of all ALMP participants took on activation work (for details, see Mýtna Kureková et al, 2013: 27). Although there has been a non-negligible decline in the relative and absolute number of activation work participants since the mid-2000s, the official Eurostat data overestimate the importance of this trend. Activation is partly organised through local labour offices and partly through municipalities. As the number of free positions offered by labour offices decreased, the number of positions available through the municipalities increased. As Mýtna Kureková et al (2013: 27) point out, the monthly number of activation benefits paid out has been stable at around 55,000 since 2010. Nevertheless, these empirical data still indicate a 50% decline in the number of activation work participants between 2004/05 and the early 2010s.

Crisis and recovery

Since the late 2000s, the government's focus has gradually shifted towards contributions to commuting to work, start-up incentives and social enterprises. Nevertheless, attempts by the 2006–10 left-leaning government to increase the importance of protected workshops and other social enterprises were jeopardised by the lack of transparency and subsequent fraud allegations associated with this policy instrument (eg Onuferová, 2010; Prušová, 2011). Following several scandals, support for the programme had been largely discontinued until recently.[4] In addition to job creation in social enterprises, the Fico government, and subsequently the centre-right incumbent between 2010 and 2012, attempted to combat rising joblessness during the crisis with the direct subsidisation of jobs in enterprises that temporarily closed down. These types of measures became neither a defining tendency in post-2010 ALMP policy nor a solution to the crisis in the labour market. Unemployment between 2007 and 2011 rose by 6.4 percentage points, reaching 14.4% by 2012.

A somewhat more successful shift in ALMPs concerned the targeting of vulnerable groups. After 2010, a number of measures were introduced in order to improve the labour market situation of young job seekers. As of 2013, individuals younger than 18 years of age were not entitled to activation benefit for activation work. This measure takes away a major disincentive to continuing education. Several new job-subsidisation schemes have been introduced with the specific aim of supporting the employment of people younger than 29 years of age who have been registered as job seekers for a longer period of time (three to six months, depending on the programme).

To summarise the most important aspects of the development of ALMPs, direct job creation has been the most commonly used active measure in Slovakia. Since the 2004 reform that de facto replaced a large part of needs-based income support with remuneration for participation in the activation work programme, an increasingly strong connection between the system of poverty relief and ALMPs can be observed. While many people are activated through such programmes, it is questionable whether these policies are of use for the long-term reintegration of the unemployed into the labour market. The most recent changes in ALMPs foster more concrete targeting of disadvantaged groups of job seekers. The draft of the 2015 National Reform Programme envisages further strengthening of policies aimed at tackling youth and long-term unemployment (MFSR, 2015).

Needs-based income support

Post-1989 transition

Needs-based income support has been provided to those whose household income has been below the minimum living standard ('životné minimum' [MLS]) (see Table 12.4). Residence in Slovakia and monthly household income below the minimum living standard are the main requirements to be fulfilled by BMN claimants. Movable and immovable assets, with the exception of one's permanent residence, are considered possible sources of income through sale and renting.

In absolute terms, needs-based income support has been very limited since the transition to a market economy. Reforms over the past two decades have also led to a gradual decline in the relative generosity of needs-based income support. Terrell et al (1996: 247) report that social assistance for a household of four could reach up to 2.5 times the minimum wage in the mid-1990s. In 2014, a similar family could receive needs-based benefits, comprising the BMN, housing allowance, activation and childcare benefits, amounting to approximately 1.2 times the minimum wage (approximately €390 per month), assuming the unlikely case that both parents receive an activation benefit (see Kusá, 2014: 6).

Table 12.4: Needs-based income support in Slovakia, 2004–15

	2004	2005	2006	2007	2008	2009	2010	2011	2012	2013	2014	2015
MLS for one-person household	139.7	152	152	165.3	170.3	178.9	185.2	185.4	189.8	194.6	198.1	198.1
BMN for one-person household	50.8	51.8	51.8	55.8	58.4	60.5	60.5	60.5	60.5	60.5	61.6	61.6
Activation allowance	49.8	56.4	56.4	63.1	63.1	63.1	63.1	63.1	63.1	63.1	63.1	63.1
Minimum wage*	201.8	215.8	229	252.3	268.9	295.5	307.7	317	327.2	337.7	352	380
Average wage	525.3	573.4	622.8	668.7	723	744.5	769	786	805	824	858	883

Notes: Values are given in euros rounded to first decimal; values for 2004–08 converted from Slovak koruna to euros using the official exchange rate of 1 euro = 30.126 SKK; *Values valid for low-skill routine jobs on 1 January of the given year.

Sources: MLS, BMN, activation allowance, minimum wage – national legislation (see: www.slov-lex.sk); average wage – Slovak Statistical Office, Slovstat database (see: http://www.statistics.sk/pls/elisw/vbd)

European Union accession and early post-accession

Social assistance to the poorest has been increasingly conditioned upon participation in ALMPs. The 2004 reform of the BMN significantly decreased the level of needs-based allowances and introduced the activation benefit that could be earned by members of households in material need who took on activation work or participated in education. The shift towards a system emphasising activation, mainly through the application of punitive measures, has been further strengthened since 2004. First, in 2008, the Smer-led left-wing/nationalist government increased the number of hours that people in material need may be required to work for the activation benefit from 40 hours per month to slightly above 80. In addition, as of 2014, a household's needs-based income support could be decreased by the sum of the BMN for each adult person who declined an offer to take up municipal work. As a result, at least some BMN recipients may be required to work up to 32 hours a month for their basic allowance.

Besides increased pressure on benefit recipients to participate in ALMPs, the level of the BMN and other allowances has also been left to erode over time. As shown in Table 12.4, the BMN is not adjusted on a regular basis by inflation or wage growth. By contrast, the minimum wage has increased rapidly in recent years.[5] This development appears to be independent of EU austerity or the ideology of the government, but the social-democratic Smer Party made increasing the minimum wage one of its main political messages for the 2016 general elections, thus perpetuating this trend set in the first half of the 2000s.[6]

Crisis and recovery

Nevertheless, alongside punitive measures, legislative changes since 2013 have also included enabling policies. Most important among these is the possibility to retain part of their social benefits by the long-term unemployed who have successfully re-entered the labour market. In 2014, a special allowance of approximately €63 per month was introduced. This could be drawn for six months by those long-term unemployed who found a job earning at least the minimum wage (but not more than three times the minimum wage) and whose household lost eligibility for the BMN. The eligibility period has been extended to 12 months since 2015. In addition, the long-term unemployed and their prospective employers are not required to enrol in social security for the first 12 months of employment if the gross salary of the newly employed worker does not exceed 67% of the average wage (MoLSAF,

2014, 2015). While this measure temporarily decreases labour costs, it also has a negative effect on the worker's pension, sickness and unemployment benefits.

The system of needs-based income support is being intensively reshaped to lure the long-term unemployed back into the regular labour market. While this tendency started well before 2010, it has been reinforced since then. The number of BMN recipients fell significantly throughout 2014 and 2015. While the average number of BMN recipients was almost 185,000 in 2013, it only reached 128,000 in 2015 (MoLSAF, 2013, 2015). This declining trend also continued throughout 2016 and the first half of 2017. It is beyond the scope of this study to assess whether it is the restrictive or the enabling measures that contributed more to this development. Moreover, since 2014, the Slovak labour market has been in a state of upswing, which has likely led to a further decrease in the number of BMN recipients.

In conclusion, needs-based social transfers have been weakened considerably over the past 20 years or so. While budgetary considerations have played an important role in these reform processes, they have been just as much the expression of an increasingly prevalent perception, shared by the political Left and Right, that people have to be motivated to return to the labour market. Most of the measures used to achieve this have been punitive, but a few enabling measures have also been implemented.

Conclusions: assessing the impact of EU austerity on labour market policies

Since 2010, there have been several significant changes in EU-level policies, fostering fiscal consolidation and focusing primarily on greater enforceability of the Stability and Growth Pact (SGP) (De la Porte and Heins, 2015). Taking into account the growing prominence of EU-led austerity since 2010, the main purpose of this study was to provide an overview of key trends in Slovak labour market policies, with an emphasis on differences between reforms that took place before and after 2010. As the availability of finances for a more generous welfare state has been missing both before and after 2010, the differences in labour market policies have also been rather limited between the two periods. Nevertheless, the overall picture of the past few years is one of austerity predominantly targeted at high-earning individuals with well-established social security rights, although some of the measures introduced also impacted the long-term unemployed. Table 12.5 compares the prevailing trends in the four policy areas before and after

Table 12.5: Summarising policy trajectories from the pre-accession to post-crisis European Union in Slovakia

	Pre-2010 period		2010 and onward	
	Pre-accession and early post-accession economic expansion; run-up to euro adoption		High unemployment and stalled growth until 2013; recovery since 2014; record low unemployment rate by early 2017	
	2002–06	2006–10	2010–12	2012–16
Incumbent	centre-right	left-wing/nationalist	centre-right/libertarian	left-wing
Unemployment protection	Retrenchment: Stricter eligibility rules, shorter duration, contribution–benefit link strengthened	Modest expansion: Moderately increased redistributiveness, loosened eligibility criteria for seasonal/temporary workers	Modest expansion: Moderately loosened general eligibility criteria	Expansion: Moderately increased redistributiveness, programme coverage increased to non-standard precarious labour contracts
Employment protection	Retrenchment: Accumulation of notice period and severance pay abolished	Expansion: Accumulation of notice period and severance pay reintroduced; larger severance pay (up to 10 times the monthly wage) introduced in specific cases; flexikonto introduced as temporary measure	Retrenchment: Accumulation of notice period and severance pay abolished; notice period shortened to 1 month for those employed at their employer for less than a year	Expansion: Accumulation of notice period and severance pay reintroduced; severance pay increased in selected cases
ALMPs	Retrenchment: Shift from PUJs (see Table 12.3) to activation work, subsidised commuting, (re)training; decline in funding and higher administrative burden (shift from budget financing to ESF)	Minor expansion: Introduction of a cap on the length of participation in activation works (18 months) contracted by labour offices; gradual decline in the number of activation work participants (see Figure 12.4); increased job subsidisation in order to combat crisis	Minor expansion: Public works programme on natural disaster prevention introduced	Expansion: Basic allowance for people in material need made conditional upon enrolment in activation work; targeted ALMPs at young workers; revival of the 'social enterprises' concept
Needs-based income support	Retrenchment: Radical cut in the amount of needs-based insurance, increments to the basic benefit made conditional upon participation in ALMPs	Stagnation: Moderate increase in the nominal amount of needs-based allowances; more stringent conditions for activation-benefit recipients	Stagnation: Very limited increase in the amounts of needs-based allowances; gradual erosion of the purchasing power of needs-based allowances	Retrenchment: Very limited nominal increase in the amounts of needs-based allowances; further erosion of the purchasing power of needs based allowances; basic allowance conditional upon enrolment in activation works programme

Note: A brief characterisation of the economic and political context, and examples of reforms adopted in the respective periods, is provided in italics.

2010, and during the four incumbencies that governed the country between 2002 and 2016. The expansionary policies in unemployment protection have gone hand in hand with a greater burden on high-income groups, while changes in ALMPs and needs-based income support have been to the detriment of labour-market outsiders and marginalised groups of society.

The EDP initiated against Slovakia between 2010 and 2014 required significant efforts to consolidate public finances. Nevertheless, the present analysis of labour market policies suggests that while fiscal limitations have had an impact, EU-wide pressure for fiscal discipline has not been among the most significant policy determinants. Slovakia's fiscal room to manoeuvre was limited well before 2010, mainly because of the difficulties of post-socialist economic transition, the adoption of the euro and the decision to partially privatise public pensions. Thus, in the Slovakian case, the onset of strict EU-led austerity has rather acted as a factor prolonging an existing trend.

Expenditure on ALMPs has stagnated at around 0.2% of GDP, both before and after 2010. No apparent trend is observable in the development of the number of ALMP participants. The most important parameters of unemployment income protection have not been changed. For an average-income worker, the gross and net replacement rate of unemployment benefits remained at 50% and approximately 65%, respectively, while the entitlement period was left at six months. Similarly, changes in employment protection have been fairly limited and influenced primarily by the ideological leaning of the government.

However, unemployment, as well as the likelihood of long-term unemployment, increased considerably during 2009–14. The unemployment protection system has not reacted to this new reality, leading to a hidden form of retrenchment. In the meantime, the maximum base for calculating social security contributions increased in 2008 and 2013, while the maximum unemployment benefit was decreased. Finally, the 2013 reform of the legislation provided for the enrolment of various categories of atypical workers in the social security system. The reluctance to address the problem of prolonged unemployment and the changes concerning contributions and benefits have been partly motivated by the need to raise more revenue and limit social security payments. However, the majority of these reforms put the burden of fiscal consolidation onto the shoulders of high-income individuals, partly sheltering low-income groups from cuts.

By contrast, reforms in the system of needs-based income maintenance, carried out with the declared objective of bringing people back into work, have been prevalently inimical towards the poor, especially the long-term unemployed. Slovakia has witnessed a gradual erosion of basic needs-based benefits and the introduction of new conditionalities for claimants. Most importantly, governments at both ends of the Left–Right axis have made efforts to link needs-based benefits to participation in ALMPs. Several enabling measures supporting (re)integration into the labour market have also been introduced. Among these, the right to draw benefits for the first few months of employment and payroll tax breaks are the most important. While a detailed causal analysis is beyond the scope of this study, the number of BMN recipients has declined significantly since 2014, which is probably a combined result of punitive and enabling measures and of a general improvement in the labour market situation.

The limits of Slovakia's public budget have significantly hampered the administrative capacity of labour offices. Labour offices were already understaffed before 2010 and their situation has become even more pressing since then. Despite rising unemployment, the government decided to decrease the number of labour office employees by approximately 10% in 2011. The high workload at the labour offices might also jeopardise efforts to increase the efficiency of ALMPs. While no significant reforms have been applied to tackle this weakness of the labour market policy system, the 2015 National Reform Programme acknowledged the problem and foresaw measures to decrease the workload of consultants in the labour offices. Taking into account the non-adjustment of unemployment protection legislation and the labour offices' staffing to match soaring unemployment rates, as well as the gradual erosion of basic income maintenance policies, it appears that policy drift (see Hacker, 2004) has been among the most important means of retrenchment in Slovakia in the past decade.

The EDP initiated against Slovakia in 2010 was concluded successfully in 2014. The end of the EDP, in combination with increased economic growth, might give more fiscal space to future governments. It remains a question for future research whether, and in what form, this opportunity will be used to improve the country's main labour market policies and the administrative capacity of the central and regional government.

Acknowledgement

This research has been financed in part by the Slovak Research and Development Agency (APVV), grant number APVV-14-0787, and by the Grant Agency of the Slovak Republic – VEGA, grant number 2/0158/18.

Notes

1. These transition costs result from the immediate decline in revenue once the state chooses to carry out such a transformation. While promises made to recent pensioners relying on the PAYG system cannot be (fully) avoided, much less revenue is collected from workers. The transition to funding is likely to lead to a decline in pensions payable from the PAYG system in the future, but it takes decades until the decrease in the annual public pension costs evens out the annual revenue lost due to the transition to funding (Simonovits, 2003; Ódor et al, 2004; Barr and Diamond, 2008).

2. The redundancy cost measures discussed refer to the legal minimum that employers are required to provide. Deviations that benefit employees can be agreed within the framework of individual contracts and collective agreements.

3. Only members of households in material need can receive the activation benefit. Each household member is entitled to the activation benefit if they improve their qualifications, are employed and earn above the minimum wage, or if they are long-term unemployed and participate in the activation work programme. The activation work programme requires job seekers to carry out 64 to 80 hours of work per month. The unemployed can also qualify for the activation benefit if they work 64 to 80 hours for a municipality or as volunteers. As of 2015, the monthly activation benefit amounted to €63.07. Participants in the activation work programme are not insured under the social security system.

4. A reform of the Labour Code in 2015 redefined the notion of social enterprise by establishing the 'subject of social economy'. Such enterprises, with a mainly social objective, will be eligible for grants and support via financial instruments from EU funds.

5. The minimum wage listed in Table 12.4 refers to the minimum wage applicable to employees working in routine jobs requiring low qualifications. The Slovakian minimum wage legislation recognises six different levels of difficulty of work. The minimum wage for more demanding jobs is higher. Those working in the most difficult roles as high-level professionals (category six) have a minimum wage equal to twice the minimum wage of low-skill routine workers. Nevertheless, this legislation is often circumvented by classifying employees in a category

with lower wages than the one that they belong to based on the nature of their job.

6. The 2016 elections gave rise to a broad coalition government, including Smer alongside several centre-right parties, which will most likely continue implementing a policy of steep increases of the minimum wage and restrictive measures targeted at BMN recipients. It should be noted that, with the exception of the libertarian Freedom and Solidarity Party (Sloboda a solidarita [SaS]), which advocates for the abolition of the minimum wage (Sloboda a solidarita, 2016), minimum wage increases have no significant opponent among political parties.

References

Aidukaite, J. (2009) 'Old welfare state theories and new welfare regimes in Eastern Europe: challenges and implications', *Communist and Post-Communist Studies*, 42(1): 23–39.

Aidukaite, J. (2011) 'Welfare reforms and socio-economic trends in the 10 new EU member states of Central and Eastern Europe', *Communist and Post-Communist Studies*, 44(3): 211–19.

Baboš, P. (2013) 'Pracovné podmienky v typických, netypických a veľmi netypických zamestnaniach na Slovensku: mapovacia štúdia' ['Work conditions in typical, atypical and very atypical employment in Slovakia: an exploratory study'], *Prognostické práce*, 5(3): 175–97.

Barr, N. and Diamond, P. (2008) *Reforming pensions: Principles and policy choices*, Oxford: Oxford University Press.

Bohle, D. and Greskovits, B. (2006) 'Capitalism without compromise: strong business and weak labour in Eastern Europe's new transnational industries', *Studies in Comparative International Development*, 41(1): 3–25.

Bohle, D. and Greskovits, B. (2007) 'Neoliberalism, embedded neoliberalism and neocorporatism: towards transnational capitalism in Central-Eastern Europe', *West European Politics*, 30(3): 443–66.

Bohle, D. and Greskovits, B. (2012) *Capitalist diversity on Europe's periphery*, Ithaca, NY: Cornell University Press.

De la Porte, C. and Heins, E. (2015) 'A new era of European integration? Governance of labour market and social policy since the sovereign debt crisis', *Comparative European Politics*, 13(1): 8–28.

Drahokoupil, J. and Domonkos, S. (2012) 'Averting the funding-gap crisis: East European pension reforms after 2008', *Global Social Policy*, 12(3): 283–99.

Duell, N. and Kureková, L. (2013) *Activating benefit in material need recipients in the Slovak Republic*, CELSI Research Report No. 3, Bratislava: CELSI.

European Commission (2011) 'Assessment of the 2011 national reform programme and stability programme for Slovakia', SEC (2011) 733 final. Available at: http://ec.europa.eu/europe2020/pdf/recommendations_2011/swp_slovakia_en.pdf (accessed 26 October 2016).

Eurostat (2015) 'Young people neither in employment nor in education (NEET rates)', (edat_lfse_20) time series. Available at: http://appsso.eurostat.ec.europa.eu/nui/show.do?dataset=edat_lfse_20&lang=en (accessed 26 October 2016).

Fisher, S., Gould, J. and Haughton, T. (2007) 'Slovakia's neoliberal turn', *Europe-Asia Studies*, 59(6): 977–98.

Frigant, V. and Miollan, S. (2014) 'The geographical restructuring of the European automobile industry in the 2000s', MPRA Paper No. 53509. Available at: http://mpra.ub.uni-muenchen.de/53509/1/MPRA_paper_53509.pdf (accessed 26 October 2016).

Government of the Slovak Republic (2008) *Národný plán zavedenia eura v Slovenskej republike (aktualizácia Apríl 2008)* [*National plan of the adoption of the Euro (update April 2008)*], Bratislava: National Bank of Slovakia. Available at: http://www.nbs.sk/_img/Documents/_PUBLIK_NBS_EURO/NP_SK_APRIL2008.pdf (accessed 26 October 2016).

Government of the Slovak Republic (2010) 'Manifesto of the government of the Slovak Republic 2010–2014'. Available at: http://www.vlada.gov.sk/data/files/2169_manifesto-entrans.pdf (accessed 26 October 2016).

Government of the Slovak Republic (2012) 'Manifesto of the government of the Slovak Republic – May 2012'. Available at: http://www.vlada.gov.sk/data/files/2169_manifesto-entrans.pdf (accessed 26 October 2016).

Gyarfášová, O., Brutovská, G., Filadelfiová, J., Sekulová, M., Gál, R. and Sirovátka, T. (2006) *Evaluácia sociálnej politiky zameranej na zníženie dlhodobej nezamestnanosti* [*The evaluation of social policies aimed at decreasing long-term unemployment*], Bratislava: IVO.

Hacker, J.S. (2004) 'Privatizing risk without privatizing the welfare state: the hidden politics of social policy retrenchment in the United States', *The American Political Science Review*, 98(2): 243–60.

Ham, J., Svejnar, J. and Terrell, K. (1995) 'Czech Republic and Slovakia', in S. Commander and F. Coricelli (eds) *Unemployment, restructuring and the labour market in Eastern Europe and Russia*, Washington, DC: World Bank, pp 91–146.

Harvan, P. (2011) *Hodnotenie efektívnosti a účinnosti výdavkov na aktívne politiky trhu práce na Slovensku* [*Evaluating the efficiency of expenditure on active labour market policies in Slovakia*], Economic Analysis, No. 22, Bratislava: Institute of Financial Policy – Ministry of Finance of the Slovak Republic. Available at: http://www.finance.gov.sk/Default.aspx?CatID=7837 (accessed 26 October 2016).

Jurajda, Š. and Mathernová, K. (2004) *How to overhaul the labour market: Political economy of recent Czech and Slovak reforms. Background paper prepared for the World Development Report 2005*, Washington, DC: World Bank. Available at: https://openknowledge.worldbank.org/handle/10986/9131 (accessed 26 October 2016).

Kollárová, Z. (2014) 'Sociálna poisťovňa sa chystá na zúčtovanie sociálnych odvodov' ['The social insurance agency is getting ready for the annual social-security contributions declaration'], Trend.sk, 1 May. Available at: http://www.etrend.sk/financie/socialna-poistovna-sa-chysta-na-zuctovanie-socialnych-odvodov.html (accessed 26 October 2016).

Kusá, Z. (2014) *European Minimum Income Network report: Slovak Republic: Analysis and road map for adequate and accessible minimum income schemes in EU member states*, Brussels: European Commission. Available at: https://eminnetwork.files.wordpress.com/2013/04/emin-slovakia-2014-en.pdf (accessed 25 July 2017).

Mathernová, K. and Renčko, J. (2006) 'Reformology: the case of Slovakia', *Orbis*, 50(4): 629–40.

MFSR (Ministry of Finance of the Slovak Republic) (2011) 'National reform programme of the Slovak Republic for 2011–2014'. Available at: http://www.finance.gov.sk/en/Components/CategoryDocuments/s_LoadDocument.aspx?categoryId=600&documentId=371(accessed 12 October 2017).

MFSR (2015) 'Národný Program Reforiem 2015' ['National reform programme 2015']. Available at: http://hsr.rokovania.sk/data/att/148388_subor.pdf (accessed 26 October 2016).

MoLSAF (Ministry of Labour, Social Affairs and Family) (2013) 'Správa o sociálnej situácii obyvateľstva Slovenskej republiky za rok 2013' ['Report on the social situation of the population of the Slovak Republic in 2013']. Available at: https://www.employment.gov.sk/files/slovensky/ministerstvo/analyticke-centrum/sprava-socialnej-situacii-obyvatelstva-za-rok-2013.pdf (accessed 26 October 2016).

MoLSAF (2014) 'Report on the social situation of the population of the Slovak Republic for 2014'. Available at: https://www.employment.gov.sk/files/slovensky/ministerstvo/analyticke-centrum/english-version_kvalita-tlac.pdf (accessed 26 October 2016).

MoLSAF (2015) 'Správa o sociálnej situácii obyvateľstva Slovenskej republiky za rok 2015' ['Report on the social situation of the population of the Slovak Republic in 2015']. Available at: https://www.employment.gov.sk/files/slovensky/ministerstvo/analyticke-centrum/sprava-socialnej-situacii-obyvatelstva-za-rok-2015.pdf (accessed 26 October 2016).

Mýtna Kureková, L., Salner, A. and Farenzenová, M. (2013) *Implementation of activation works in Slovakia. Evaluation and recommendations for policy change – Final report*, Bratislava: SGI. Available at: https://papers.ssrn.com/sol3/papers.cfm?abstract_id=2405808 (accessed 26 October 2016).

Ódor, Ľ., Antalicová, J., Krajčír, Z. and Novysedlák, V. (2004) *Vplyv dôchodkového sporenia na verejné financie a občanov* [*The impact of pension savings on public finance and the public*], Bratislava: Ministry of Finance – Institute of Financial Policy. Available at: http://www.finance.gov.sk/Default.aspx?CatID=3256 (accessed 26 October 2016).

OECD (Organisation for Economic Co-operation and Development) (2014) *Net replacement rates for six family types: Initial phase of unemployment*, Paris: OECD. Available at: http://webcache.googleusercontent.com/search?q=cache:-llNVSL44ksJ:www.oecd.org/els/benefits-and-wages-statistics.htm+&cd=1&hl=en&ct=clnk&gl=uk.

OECD (2015) *Public expenditure and participant stocks on LMP: Categories 20–70*, Paris: OECD. Available at: http://stats.oecd.org/Index.aspx?DataSetCode=LMPEXP (accessed 22 October 2016).

Onuferová, M. (2010) 'Prvý Tomanovej sociálny podnik skončil' ['Tomanová's first social enterprise has ended'], SME.sk, 13 January. Available at: http://ekonomika.sme.sk/c/5190545/prvy-tomanovej-socialny-podnik-skoncil.html (accessed 26 October 2016).

Pierson, P. (1994) *Dismantling the welfare state? Reagan, Thatcher and the politics of retrenchment*, New York, NY: Cambridge University Press.

Prušová, V. (2011) 'Polícia trestne stíha Tomanovej sociálne podniky' ['Police starts criminal investigation against Tomanová's social enterprises'], SME.sk, 18 November. Available at: http://ekonomika.sme.sk/c/6145603/policia-trestne-stiha-tomanovej-socialne-podniky.html (accessed 26 October 2016).

Simonovits, A. (2003) *Modeling pension systems*, Basingstoke: Palgrave.

Sloboda a solidarita (2016) 'Volebný program – parlamentné voľby 2016' ['Electoral programme – parliamentary elections 2016']. Available at: http://www.strana-sas.sk/program/file/4330/SaS_volebny_program.pdf (accessed 26 October 2016).

Švecová, A. and Rajčáková, E. (2014) 'Regionálne disparity v sociálno – ekonomickej úrovni regiónov Slovenska v rokoch 2001–2013' ['Regional disparities in the socio-economic level of Slovakian regions in 2001–2013'], in V. Lauko (ed) *Regionálne dimenzie Slovenska* [*Regional dimensions of Slovakia*], Bratislava: Comenius University, pp 256–94.

Terrell, K. and Munich, D. (1996) 'Evidence on the implementation and effectiveness of active and passive labour market policies in the Czech Republic', in OECD (ed) *OECD proceedings: Lessons from labour market policies in the transition countries*, Paris: OECD, pp 179–223.

Terrell, K., Lubyova, M. and Strapec, M. (1996) 'Evidence on the implementation and effectiveness of passive and active labour market policies in the Slovak Republic', in OECD (ed) *OECD proceedings: Lessons from labour market policies in the transition countries*, Paris: OECD, pp 227–65.

Tudoroiu, T., Horváth, P. and Hrušovský, M. (2009) 'Ultra-nationalism and geopolitical exceptionalism in Mečiar's Slovakia', *Problems of Post-Communism*, 56(4): 3–14.

Uldrichova, V. and Karpisek, Z. (1994) 'Labour market policy in the former Czech and Slovak Federal Republic', in T. Boeri (ed) *Unemployment in transition countries: Transient or persistent?*, Paris: OECD, pp 113–35.

THIRTEEN

Slovenian labour market policies under austerity: narrowing the gap between the well- and the less well-protected in the labour market?

Miroljub Ignjatović and Maša Filipovič Hrast

Introduction

The Slovenian welfare system is based on elements of a conservative-corporative welfare system, with compulsory social insurance systems and the state in a prominent role as provider of (universal) services, such as health, child care and education (Kolarič et al, 2009, 2011). In the 1990s, a fairly gradual approach to welfare system reform was adopted (Kolarič et al, 2009, 2011), which has continued until today. This gradualist approach is linked to the strong institutionalisation of social dialogue and relatively strong trade unions, the high coverage of collective agreements, and the prevalence of left-centrist parties in government over the past 25 years. Furthermore, as emphasised by Lavrač and Majcen (2006), Slovenia is one of the more developed countries in Central and Eastern Europe and thus could afford to take a gradual approach to structural reforms of the economy (eg privatisation). It thus opted for gradual reforms of the labour market, pension system, social welfare system and education system, keeping family policy intact, as well as social services such as childcare and elderly care (Kolarič et al, 2009, 2011; Filipovič Hrast and Rakar, 2017). However, the authors also warned that a potential negative side of this approach is the postponement of necessary structural reforms. Consequently, according to some authors (eg Guardiancich, 2011), although Slovenia has ensured social peace in this way, it may also be the reason that the crisis has hit Slovenia particularly hard.

The economic crisis, which led to high unemployment, stimulated several reforms of the labour market. In addition to the economic pressures, the Slovenian welfare state is also facing pressures from demographic ageing. These pressures are most evident in the poor sustainability of the pension system, but also in the labour market and its state of preparedness for an ageing workforce. One of the important reasons for the pension reform was the necessity to increase the activity rate among older age groups (55–64 years of age), which is among the lowest in the European Union (EU) (42.2% in the second quarter of 2016; see Eurostat, 2017).

In the next two sections, we present the major labour market policy changes, with emphasis on the period after 2010. These changes are also presented in relation to the retrenchment/expansion of policies, as well as the adoption of activation and flexicurity, as well as their consequences for the living standards of the most vulnerable groups. The chapter concludes with a discussion of the changes in, and limitations of the implementation of, activation and flexicurity in Slovenia.

Context and policy changes up to 2010

Over the past 25 years, the Slovenian labour market and economy have experienced two major economic crises: one in the early 1990s (related to the disintegration of Yugoslavia, transition from a socialist to a market economy and loss of markets in other Yugoslavian republics) and another in 2009 (related to the global economic and fiscal crisis). The two crises had a common effect, namely, a steep increase in unemployment (highest in 1993 and 2013; see Figure 13.1).

Figure 13.1: Number of unemployed registered with the employment service at the end of the year, Slovenia, 1967–2016

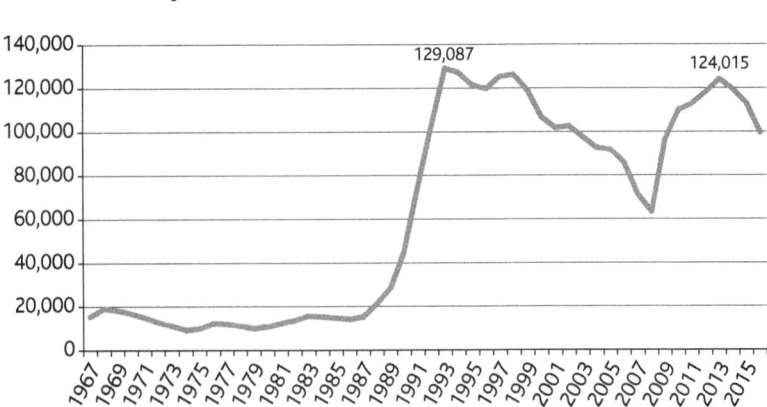

Source: ZRSZ (2017)

At the beginning of the first economic crisis, the Slovenian labour market was characterised by full employment, with almost the entire workforce in full-time permanent jobs. Despite the dramatic increase in unemployment in a very short period, the measures (changes in the pension and education systems, and various passive and active employment policy measures) were applied in a gradual manner. The use of predominantly passive employment policy measures (for Slovenia, relatively wide coverage of unemployment benefits and early retirement schemes) helped to maintain a relatively high social security level, although it soon became clear that it would be financially impossible to maintain it over the long term. Thus, both systems – the labour market and social security – were gradually subjected to fundamental changes.

There were several changes over the period 1990–2000 (Ignjatović et al, 2002: 211–12). First, the unemployment insurance system has become less insurance- and more social assistance-based, as well as less contribution- and more tax-financed. The duration of benefits has been shortened and the maximum payment decreased. The insurance scheme has become more redistributive, aiming at the provision of basic security rather than the maintenance of the same level of living conditions of those losing their jobs. Simultaneously, the share of unemployment benefit recipients in total registered unemployed started to fall (see Figure 13.2), thus providing a lower proportion of the registered unemployed with temporary social security.

Figure 13.2: Share of unemployment benefit recipients in total registered unemployed, Slovenia, 1991–2016

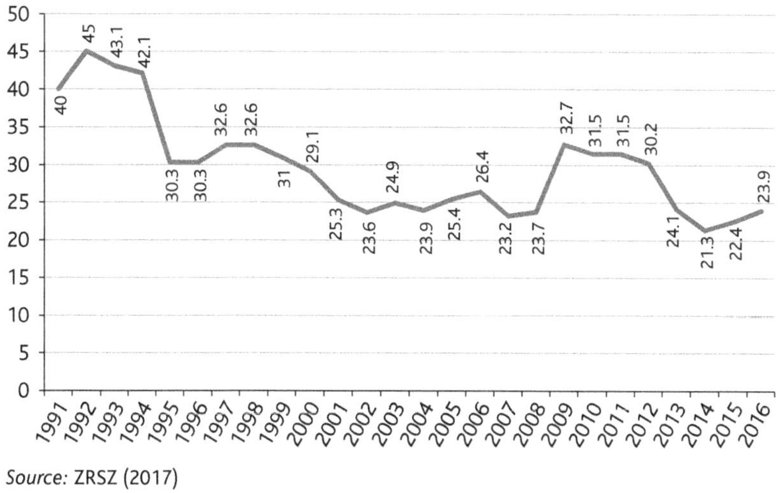

Source: ZRSZ (2017)

Second, the subsidiary nature of cash benefits was strongly emphasised. The aim of providing social security via employment came to the fore. The rights of workers became more closely related to their responsibilities. The payment of insurance contributions was by no means a sufficient condition for one to receive benefits. Compliance with a number of other rules (eg active job search) set by the state became necessary.

Third, there was increasing stress (at least in various legal and strategic documents) on active and activating measures as opposed to passive ones, which were also increasingly applied in an active way. A much higher level of individual activity was required. Employment policy programmes became more refined, more selective and more precisely focused on target groups. They became more concerned with costs and effectiveness. Increasing attention was paid to their side effects, monitoring and evaluation, despite the fact that the last two activities are still underdeveloped.

Furthermore, employment policy became increasingly individualised, that is, adjusted to the needs and particular situation of individuals. So-called tailor-made employment plans were implemented. Employment offices were expected to prepare employment plans in cooperation with the unemployed within a certain period (three months in the 1990s, falling to two months more recently) after registration. Unemployed people were supposed to participate in the preparation of a plan and sign it to confirm their responsibility to act accordingly. Certain job-seeking activities and/or enrolment in employment programmes were reviewed and reports made. Lastly, national employment policy was increasingly influenced by EU directives, recommendations and guidelines.

Even before the crisis, the trend in Slovenia was towards activation and the increasing conditionality of rights in the labour market and welfare policies (Kopač, 2005a, 2005b). The unemployment insurance scheme, which was laid down in the Employment and Unemployment Insurance Act until 2010 and later in the Labour Market Regulation Act, has been amended several times over the past 25 years. One of the most important changes was in 1998, when the activation principle was introduced (Kolarič et al, 2011), linking the rights of unemployed persons to their obligations more closely. The activation principle was further strengthened in 2006 when unemployment assistance (as part of the insurance scheme and financial assistance for the unemployed after the expiry of unemployment benefit) was abolished. Entitlement to unemployment benefit is conditional upon the preparedness of the unemployed person to actively seek work, accept job offers offered by employment counsellors at the Employment Service or participate in active labour market programmes. The requirements for receiving unemployment benefit have become more selective and demanding than in the past, despite also having some enabling elements. Moreover, not fulfilling the requirements could ultimately result in being removed from the register[1] and losing all benefits and access to unemployment measures.

Overall, during the past 25 years, the main structural problems affecting the Slovenian economy and labour market have remained the same: the relatively traditional structure of the economy, with slow transformation and a low share of companies oriented towards global markets; the relatively high social contributions and a high tax burden on wages (which led to the avoidance of payments of contributions, higher use of flexible employment contracts and even use of undeclared work); the persistence of structural unemployment (increasingly heightened by young university graduates failing to find a job in a slowly transforming economy); and a high share of long-term unemployment.

Another important labour market trend in Slovenia over the past 20 years has been the increasing segmentation and the widening gap between workers with secure permanent contracts and the increasing share of workers with flexible contracts, such as fixed-term or part-time contracts and student work (see Ignjatović, 2002, 2011; Kajzer, 2011; Kanjuo Mrčela and Ignjatović, 2015). These more flexible forms of employment have been increasingly used by employers to cut labour costs and increase flexibility. Younger people can most often be found in these more flexible and often more precarious forms of employment. For example, the share of young people (15–24 years of age) with fixed-term contracts among all employed young people is among the highest in Europe – 75.7% in the second quarter of 2016 (Eurostat, 2017).

Thus, during the past 15 years, the Slovenian labour market has experienced some structural changes (dualisation, segmentation and 'servicisation' of the labour market) and has become increasingly more flexible, with an increasing share of flexible forms of employment and work. Following the shares of the three most important forms of flexible employment (see Figure 13.3), we can observe their relatively even distribution in the second quarter of 2016 (fixed-term = 12.4%, part-time = 10.1% and self-employed = 11.6%). Simultaneously, Slovenian employers are also increasingly using other forms of flexible employment and work: agency and posted work, student work, civil contracts and (sometimes forced and bogus) self-employment. The

Figure 13.3: Level of flexible employment among persons in employment, Slovenia, 2007–16

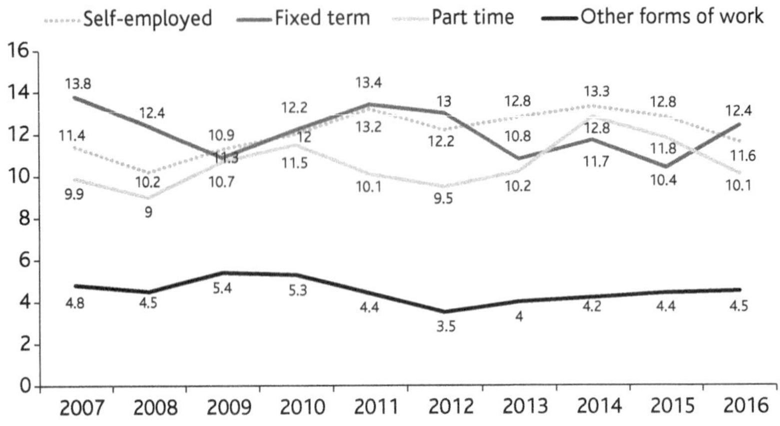

Year	Self-employed	Fixed term	Part time	Other forms of work
2007	11.4	10.2	13.8	4.8
2008	12.4	9	12.2	4.5
2009	10.9	10.7	11.3	5.4
2010	12	11.5	13.2	5.3
2011	13	10.1	13.4	4.4
2012	12.2	9.5	12.8	3.5
2013	10.8	10.2	13.3	4
2014	12.8	11.7	12.8	4.2
2015	11.8	10.4	12.8	4.4
2016	12.4	10.1	11.6	4.5

Source: SORS (2017b), Labour Force Survey (LFS) data, 2nd quarter

increasing flexibilisation of the Slovenian labour market has not been accompanied by adequate changes in the social security system.

Despite the problems facing an increasingly segmented labour market, until 2008, Slovenia was considered one of the most successful transition countries, with rapidly declining unemployment, very low poverty rates, low inequality and growing gross domestic product (GDP). This changed with the economic and financial crisis. GDP growth was relatively stable from the beginning of the 1990s until 2008, when it declined significantly (to −9.8% in the second quarter of 2009), and only recently (in 2014) has Slovenia again registered GDP growth. Thus, the real growth rate of GDP in 2009 was −7.8%, and in 2014, it was 2.6% (SORS, 2017a). At the same time, consolidated gross debt at year-end has been increasing dramatically since 2008, as well as net borrowing/deficit (see Figure 13.4).

In 2013, the European Council issued a recommendation to Slovenia to correct its excessive deficit by 2015. The main related problems are the recapitalisation of Slovenian banks (which happened in 2013, causing a spike in the deficit) and the insolvency of many Slovenian companies.

The negative impact of the 2008 financial and economic crisis was evident in the labour market, where there was rapid growth in the number of unemployed and the unemployment rate. This was accompanied by growing poverty rates and social exclusion. Despite these negative trends, inequality remained low, and in 2010, was one of the lowest in the EU27. The at-risk-of-poverty rate was

Figure 13.4: Consolidated gross debt and net borrowing/deficit at year-end, Slovenia, 2000–16 (% of GDP)

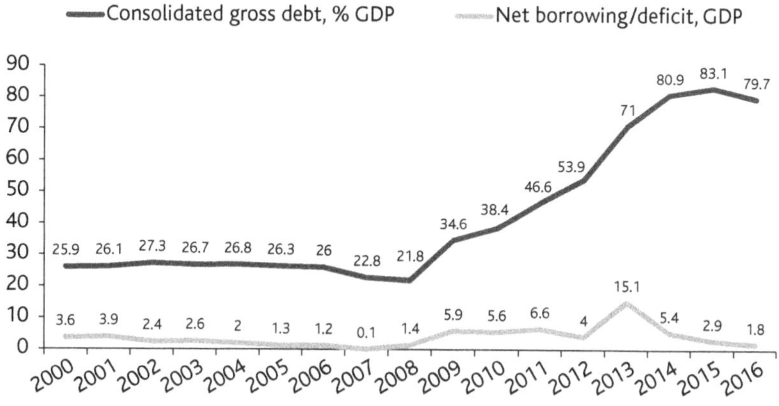
Consolidated gross debt, % GDP
Net borrowing/deficit, GDP
90
80
70
60
50
40
30
20
10
0
25.9 26.1 27.3 26.7 26.8 26.3 26 22.8 21.8 34.6 38.4 46.6 53.9 71 80.9 83.1 79.7
3.6 3.9 2.4 2.6 2 1.3 1.2 0.1 1.4 5.9 5.6 6.6 4 15.1 5.4 2.9 1.8
2000 2001 2002 2003 2004 2005 2006 2007 2008 2009 2010 2011 2012 2013 2014 2015 2016

Source: SORS (2017a)

12.7% in 2010, 14.5% in 2013 and 13.9% in 2016 (SORS, 2017c). Recognising the increasing vulnerability of the population, in 2009, the government introduced a special allowance for those most in need (Special Allowance for Socially Disadvantaged Persons Act).

Since the start of the crisis, there has been increasing pressure from some Slovenian policymakers and the economic sector to adopt more radical labour market reforms, including further flexibilisation of employment contracts. On the other hand, policymakers have been faced with an increasing number of unemployed and also increasingly numerous groups falling out of existing benefit and insurance schemes due to irregular employment patterns. The initial response of the government to the financial crisis was to absorb the shock and intervene in the labour market to reduce rising unemployment.

It adopted two temporary measures. The first was the Partially Subsidising Full-time Work for Part-time Workers Act. This Act aimed to ease the effects of the advancing financial crisis by providing assistance to employers if they decided to preserve their workforce by shortening working time (from 40 to 36 or even 32 hours per week) instead of laying them off. The Act was based on the principle that economic measures taken during the financial crisis should seek to ensure employment and maintain jobs, including incentives to shorten working time by partly subsidising full-time work. The second temporary measure was the Partial Reimbursement of Payment Compensation Act. The aim of the measure was also to preserve as many jobs as possible (up to 25,000) by introducing 'temporary waiting on the job' (temporary layoff) – workers on the waiting list were entitled to 85% of their normal wage (50% was covered by the state and 35% by the employer).

In 2009, approximately 4.8% of employed people were enrolled in these two schemes (Bednaš et al, 2011). Both measures, which were intended to preserve jobs, were actually used for buying time for the consolidation of enterprises and the preparation of new measures that would have a long-term influence on the labour market. According to some experts (IMAD, 2014), the wage response to the crisis was slow and delayed, partly also due to the changes in the wage system for public employees, implemented in 2008. The Act of Intervention Step because of Economic Crises 2010 limited the envisioned growth of public sector wages and limited increases in transfers and pensions (freezing indexation).

In general, the trend in employment policy over recent decades has been towards activation, but also increasing labour flexibility. Aware of the potential consequences of an increase in flexibility in the Slovenian labour market, the government that took office in 2008 sought to implement comprehensive flexicurity and activation in the labour market and social policies (see next section). Whether these changes meant retrenchment or expansion will be discussed.

Labour market policy developments and outcomes since 2010

Labour market policy measures since 2010 include the Minimum Wage Act 2010, the Labour Market Regulation Act 2010 (amended in 2013), the Employment Relationship Act 2013 and the Youth Guarantee scheme in 2014. The direction of labour market reforms in these policies will be discussed within the framework of the following contexts: flexicurity; the divide between 'insiders' and 'outsiders'; and the importance of activation principles. In addition to labour market policies, we will look at the austerity measures that have also introduced significant changes in the labour market (the Fiscal Balance Act 2012). Where relevant for the labour market situation and in relation to observed policy trends, we will also discuss accompanying social security reforms (the Financial Social Assistance Act 2010 and the Exercise of Rights to Public Funds Act 2010). A chronological overview of the reforms is presented in Figure 13.5.

Slovenian labour market policies under austerity

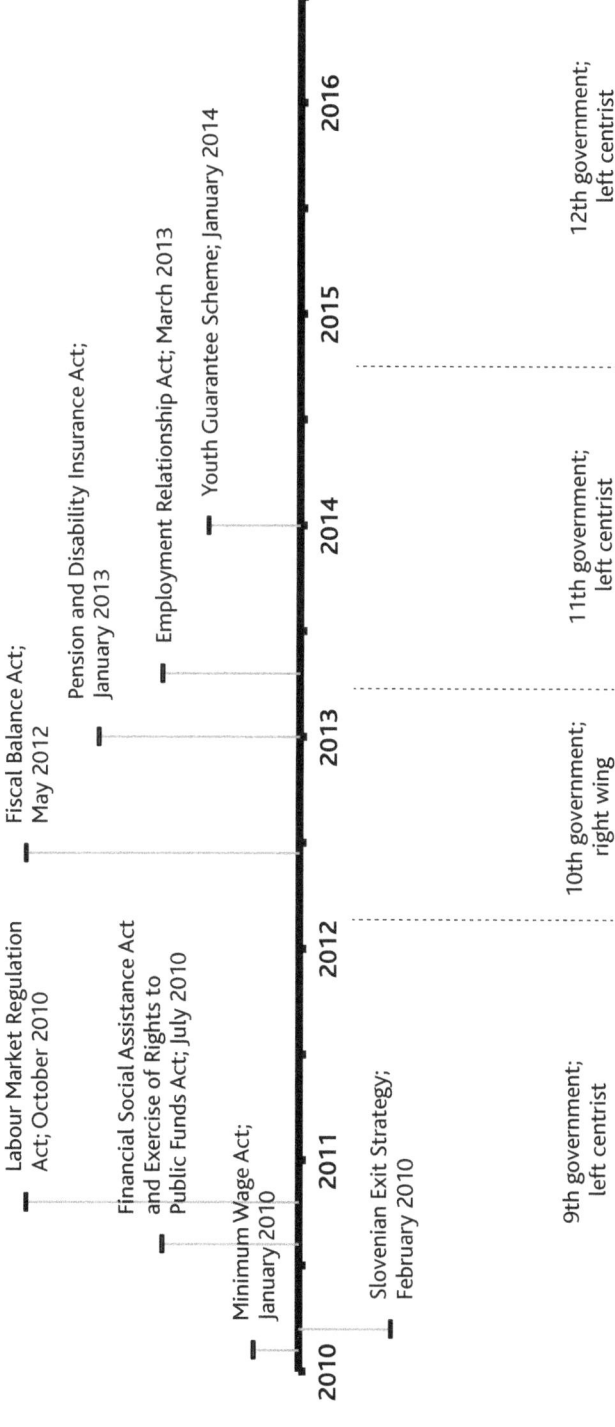

Figure 13.5: Chronological overview of the most important reforms, Slovenia, 2010–16

Income and employment protection policies since 2010

It is difficult to evaluate the whole corpus of policies on the linear axis of retrenchment or expansion. As Häusermann (2011) argues, the welfare reforms can be seen as particular packages and mixtures of policy instruments. Furthermore, when observing one particular policy, labelling it in only one way can be difficult. In the next section, we describe the labour market and related social policy changes after 2010, trying to identify the predominant direction of reforms.

Since 2010, the (centre-left) government has been determined to implement a comprehensive response to the challenges of the Slovenian economy and labour market (such as labour market segmentation, high youth unemployment rates, high shares of long-term unemployment and structural unemployment, increasing precarisation of the labour force, and decreasing social security of those in flexible forms of employment) and to introduce the flexicurity concept more decisively into the Slovenian labour market and social policies as a framework for a new social security approach. In early February 2010, the Slovenian government adopted the 'Slovenian Exit Strategy 2010–13' to serve as a framework (a combination of economic policy measures, structural changes and institutional adjustments) for future short-term and long-term strategic action to exit the economic crisis. Flexicurity was one of the main ideas on which the Exit Strategy was built, although the understanding of flexicurity among many Slovenian policymakers is questionable.[2] For many years, the official translation of flexicurity and its use in documents and speeches was '*prožna varnost*' (flexible security) and not '*varna prožnost*' (secure flexibility = flexicurity). The former translation of the term can be still found in legal documents and in different articles. Only recently (with the ninth government of Slovenia, whose Minister of Labour, Family and Social Affairs came from academia) did the concept finally come alive in its original form, in which flexicurity is understood as:

> a policy strategy that attempts, synchronically and in a deliberate way, to enhance the flexibility of labour markets, work organisation and labour relations on the one hand, and to enhance security – employment security and social security – notably for weaker groups in and outside the labour market on the other hand. (Wilthagen and Tros, 2004: 5)

One of the first actions directed towards increasing the security of workers, which can also be seen as the expansion of the 'industrial logic' or 'old' social policies that relate to income and job protection (see Häuserman, 2011), was the new Minimum Wage Act, which was adopted in January 2010. As the minimum wage (introduced in 1995) was very low before 2010, the new Act was adopted to allow workers on minimum wages to at least reach the poverty threshold. The new minimum wage has been fixed at €734.15 (gross minimum wage), which was 22.9% higher than previously. The introduction of the new Act caused a significant increase in the number of minimum wage recipients (from 16,277 in January 2010 to 39,858 in October of the same year). On the other hand, it did not significantly affect the increase of unemployment during 2010 (Kordež, 2015).

Several of the labour market policy changes also meant policy expansion, especially in addressing the new risks to the most vulnerable groups in the labour market, such as those on flexible short-term contracts, irregular employment patterns and students. The new Labour Market Regulation Act (LMRA) (adopted in 2010 and amended three times in 2013) has expanded the rights and benefits of the unemployed, as well as those employed on fixed-term contracts. It was a response to the too strict eligibility rules for unemployment benefits, thus expanding the circle of insured persons and people who are obliged to insure themselves against unemployment. The condition for receiving unemployment benefit has been expanded to nine months' service in the past 24 months (previously 12 months in 18 months). With that, the right to unemployment benefit was expanded, especially for young people, often with little professional experience, thereby increasing their social security. The Act also increased the minimum (€350) and maximum (three times the minimum) levels of unemployment benefit, as well as the amount of unemployment benefit in the first three months of receipt (80% of the worker's wage instead of 70%), and reduced the period for determining the basis of compensation to eight months (previously 12).

Furthermore, in an attempt to improve the financial situation of the unemployed and their employability, it offered them an opportunity to work (to a limited extent, for up to €200 a month) while retaining the right to unemployment benefit and introduced the option of partial unemployment at the start of a new job. In the case of part-time employment, a previously unemployed person retains the right to a proportion of unemployment benefit (a provision in line with the enabling principle of activation policies). The key purpose of the LMRA was thus to provide a more transparent system of social security, which would be effective in preventing social exclusion and poverty and in encouraging the integration of the unemployed and inactive into the labour market. This would provide the necessary support under flexicurity and address the unemployment trap.

In 2013, the LMRA (adopted in 2010) was further amended in order to increase flexibility in the labour market: (1) by allowing pensioners to perform temporary and occasional work; (2) by enabling workers to register with the Employment Service during the notice period; (3) by enabling broader access to unemployment benefits (with the possibility of obtaining the right to unemployment benefit for two months for unemployed persons under 30 years of age who were employed for at least six months in the past 24 months, as well as specific conditions for older workers, with extension [from one to two years] of the duration of the right to the payment of contributions for pension and disability insurance until retirement for older recipients of unemployment benefits); and (4) by further simplifying administrative procedures through abolishing the obligation to declare a vacancy to the Employment Service, which in its current form represents an unnecessary administrative burden for an employer and obscures what jobs are available.

Similar to the new LMRA, the new Employment Relationship Act (ERA-1) (adopted in March 2013) was part of a comprehensive labour market reform that aimed to establish the appropriate balance between the adequate protection of workers and the ability to effectively adapt to market conditions (MLFSA, 2013). The LMRA can be seen as an expansion of policies on income and job protection (for those on fixed-term contracts), with incentives for employment for an indefinite period, balancing this by decreasing the protection of the most protected workforce (older workers with special protection against dismissal). Therefore, it partly follows the welfare readjustment approach, which is linked with the expansion of new policies of activation and the retrenchment of old policies of income and job protection (see Häuserman, 2011). The starting point for the new Act was the need for relative equalisation of the statuses of employees in regular employment for an indefinite period of time in relation to those on fixed-term contracts or other forms of flexible employment in order to reduce segmentation in the labour market and high labour costs. It therefore means retrenchment of policies related to income and job protection for the most protected workforce ('insiders') in favour of the less protected part of the labour force ('outsiders'). However, this was achieved not with the expansion of new policy instruments of activation and needs-based social protection, but within existing old policies of income and job protection. Thus, the new ERA-1 reduced the notice period in the case of employment termination. The longest notice period for business reasons or for reasons of incapacity is shortened from 120 to 60 days. A longer notice period (80 days) applies only when the employee has completed 25 years of service with the same employer and if the collective agreement at the sectoral level does not specify a different notice period (but not less than 60 days). Such changes lowered employment protection legislation in the Slovenian labour market below the Organisation for Economic Co-operation and Development (OECD) average (IMAD, 2013).

In order to limit the usage of fixed-term contracts in the Slovenian labour market, the new ERA-1 further restricted the implementation of successive contracts of fixed-term employment for the same work, where continuous duration would be longer than two years (except in some explicitly determined cases). Furthermore, it proposed as a new solution establishing a right to severance pay in the event of the termination of fixed-term employment. On the other hand, this obligation is absent in the case of transition from a fixed-term contract to a permanent contract. As an additional incentive for reducing the share of fixed-term employment, there are certain exemptions from paying the employer's contribution for unemployment benefits in the first two years of employment for an indefinite period. On the other hand, the amount of this contribution in the case of a signed contract of employment for a fixed term is five times higher than the normal contribution. It also reduced the amount of severance pay in the event of termination of employment due to business reasons or due to incompetence.[3] Furthermore, it simplified the termination of employment and limited the protected category of workers.[4] We can therefore observe several changes that tried to improve the position of so-called 'outsiders' in the labour market at the expense of the most protected 'insiders'.

The new ERA-1 also introduced a quota for employers seeking to use agency workers. The Act provides that the number of posted workers at the employer should not exceed 25% of the workforce (based on all employees, permanent and fixed-term). This level is relatively high; relatively few employers have actually used a higher percentage of agency workers to date, which indicates further potential for workforce flexibilisation.

The new ERA-1 also tries to provide increased legal security for employees, especially with the intention of preventing legal abuses. In terms of practical prevention, especially regarding 'shell companies', the amendments to ERA-1 ensure more effective protection of workers' rights in cases of the transfer of a company or part of a company to a new employer. According to ERA-1, both the old and the new employer are liable for claims. In addition, the law provides that all rights attached to workers' seniority should take into account years of service with both employers.

These measures (especially those introduced by LMRA), which, for the most part, led towards policy expansion in favour of workers less protected in the labour market, have been heavily limited by the Fiscal Balance Act 2012, which introduced austerity measures. The Act and austerity measures were adopted by the centre-right government that ruled from February 2012 to March 2013. Motivated by a more neoliberal approach (influenced by budget constraints and European recommendations and signed agreements, such as the Euro Plus Pact), the introduced measures can be seen as a significant turn towards policy retrenchment. Among other things, the Act cut some benefits, thus reducing the social security of some vulnerable groups. It also reduced labour costs, affecting all employees in the public sector.[5] In addition, the measures also included, first, reducing the amount of unemployment benefit: unemployment benefit is paid in the amount of 80% of the worker's wage for the first three months and 60% for a further nine months. After this period, benefit is paid in the amount of 50% of the base wage. At the same time, the upper limit of unemployment benefit was reduced. Second, the measures also included abolishing compensation for sick leave for the unemployed.

Changes were also significant in other areas, such as social protection, which is highly relevant in the context of increasing vulnerability and high unemployment. Retrenchment of labour market policies with austerity measures was accompanied by retrenchment of social policies. In July 2010, a new Financial Social Assistance Act was adopted (and introduced on 1 January 2012). The new Act provides a gross minimum income of €288.81 for working-age individuals who are temporarily in a difficult social situation. This was €62 more than in the old Social Security Act and could therefore be seen as an expansion of welfare policies, but it is still inadequate, relatively and absolutely, to provide a significant improvement in the recipient's standard of living.[6]

The amendments to the Fiscal Balance Act (adopted in 2014, introduced on 1 February 2015) dealt with the position of the most flexible category of young people in the labour market, namely, student workers. Key changes in the new legislation were related to the inclusion of this type of work in the social security system and determining the minimum hourly rate. With the inclusion of student work in different forms of social insurance (pension, disability, health insurance and insurance for accidents at work and occupational diseases), the economic and social security of those involved in student work has been increased (following the principle of 'every job counts'), but, on the other hand, student work has become more expensive for employers. Nevertheless, this change in the treatment of student work will somewhat reduce the segmentation of the Slovenian labour market.

The outcome of policy changes (along with labour market developments) can be tracked through rising poverty rates and the decreasing shares of those receiving unemployment benefit. The proportion of people receiving unemployment benefit is low and has been decreasing steadily, falling from 45% in 1992 to only 20% in 2007. After that, the proportion started to rise again, along with unemployment, and remained at around 30% until 2012, when it started to fall again steeply, reaching 21.3% in December 2014 (see Figure 13.2).

Looking at the effects of policy changes in the context of increasing unemployment and poor national economic performance, the unemployed are evidently becoming increasingly vulnerable, although the most rapid increase in poverty rates happened before the crisis. Their poverty rate is almost three times higher than the poverty rate in the general population (see Figure 13.6). This can partly be linked to cuts/retrenchment and the demanding nature of the unemployment benefit system in the past (before the change in 2010), as well as

Figure 13.6: At-risk-of-poverty rates by labour market status (aged 18 years and more), Slovenia, 2005–16

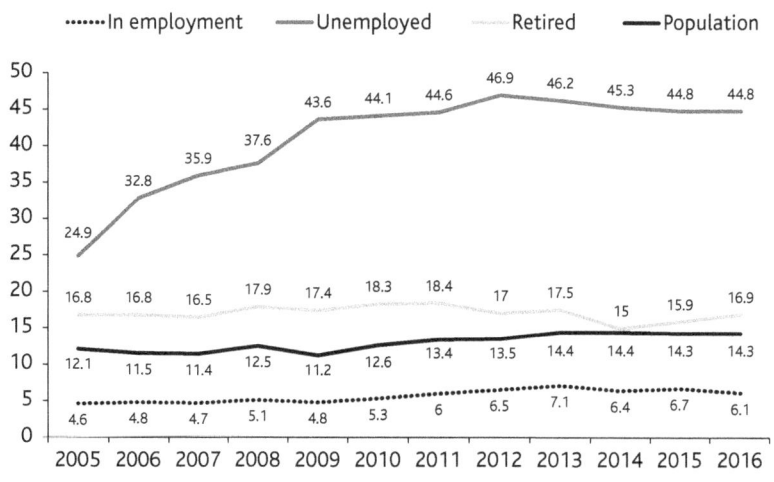

Source: SORS (2017c)

retrenchment evident in the social welfare system, which is vital for many unemployed people but has fallen victim to austerity measures, in common with many other European welfare states (see Vandenbroucke and Vleminckx, 2011; Hemerijck, 2013).

However, the difficult position on the labour market is also reflected in the increasing vulnerability of some groups of workers, especially the self-employed, but also higher at-risk-of-poverty rates among those in fixed-term employment and especially among part-timers (see Figure 13.7). These categories are often linked to one vulnerable group in particular, young people.

Policy developments regarding activation

In this section, we look at the changes in labour market policies from the perspective of the implementation of activation. Activation has been a popular framework for labour market reforms in the EU and is linked to conditions imposed on welfare recipients to be active, prepared to work or go into education or training. This introduces another important conditionality dimension (enabling as against demanding/punitive) to social and active labour market policy (ALMP) (Rueda, 2012).

The labour market policy reforms during 2010–15 follow this pattern. While expanding eligibility for unemployment benefit and introducing some new ALMP programmes (with more emphasis on career orientation), the conditionality not only for receiving unemployment benefits, but also for being on the register, also remained strict. The ultimate penalty for those failing to show activity through active job search or participation in different ALMP programmes is removal from the unemployment register. The main aim of the new LMRA 2010 was also to extend active labour market measures (eg career guidance, preparation for employment) to more beneficiaries (in addition to the unemployed, those who are in the process of losing their jobs). The new ERA-1 also emphasised activation principles (simultaneously promoting the enabling dimension), for example, it enables the integration of workers in the relevant active labour market measures during the notice period as the employer must allow such employees at least one working day a week free to respond to calls from the Employment Service for training and attending any job interviews.

A similar activation principle is evident in recent changes introduced in the social security system, included in the Financial Social Assistance Act 2010. The recipients of financial social assistance are able to increase its amount if they are deemed active (employed, participating

Slovenian labour market policies under austerity

Figure 13.7: In-work at-risk-of-poverty rates for some forms of employment in Slovenia by employment status, 2005–16

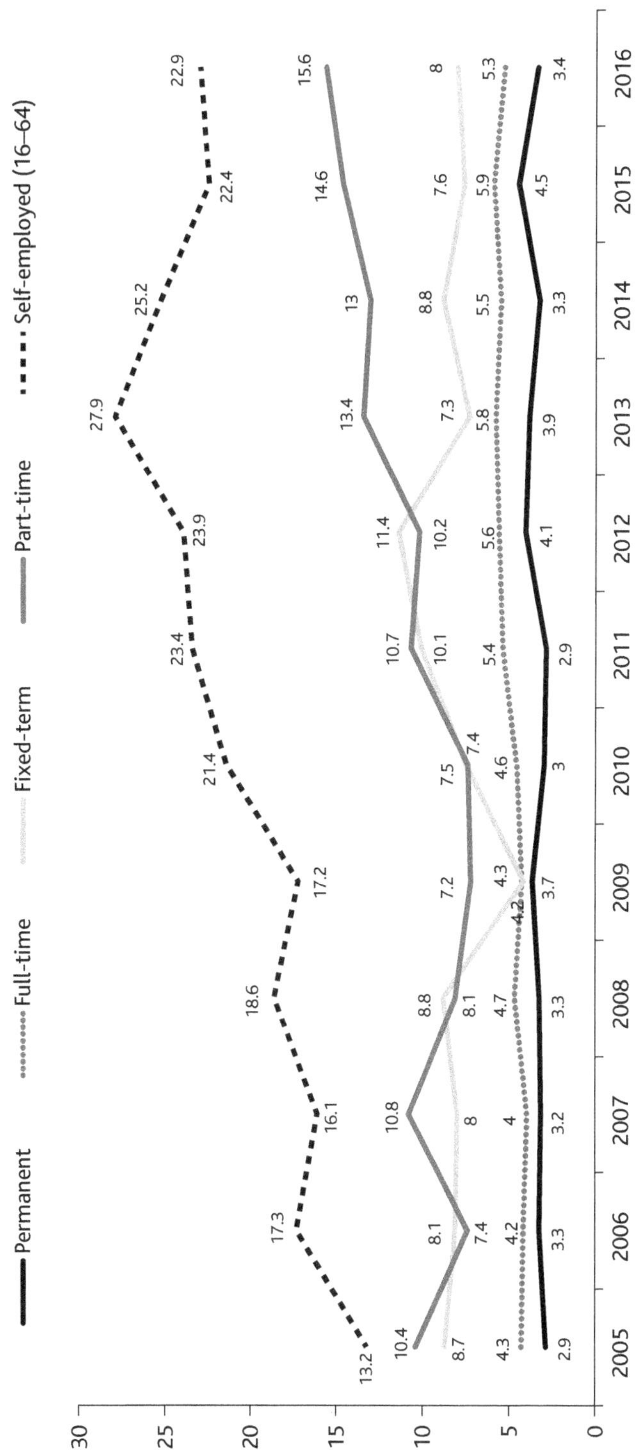

Source: Eurostat (2017); for self-employed, SORS (2017c)

in ALMP measures or psychosocial rehabilitation programmes aimed at increasing employability, performing voluntary work[7] and similar). However, the share of those receiving this increase is very low, at only 3% of all recipients of financial social assistance (Trbanc et al, 2015).

Special emphasis has been put on the activation of young people. As in many other European countries, the young have been one of the main victims of the crisis. The unemployment rate for 15–24 years olds was 9.3% just before the economic crisis (in the second quarter of 2008) and it rose to 12.4% in the second quarter of 2009. The latest data (LFS) for the second quarter of 2016 (14.0%) show further increases of the youth unemployment rate despite the measures taken in the previous period (SORS, 2017b). Despite some changes in the labour market policies already implemented, their vulnerable position on the labour market has not been sufficiently addressed. This was recognised and at the end of January 2014, the Ministry of Labour, Family, Social Affairs and Equal Opportunities adopted the 'Youth Guarantee Implementation Plan for 2014–15'. With the adoption of the Youth Guarantee, Slovenia guarantees to every young person between the ages of 15 and 29 years the offer of a job (including apprenticeships), on-the-job training, integration into formal education or an abbreviated form of institutional or practical training within four months of entry on to the unemployment register. The measures laid down in the document are arranged in four pillars:

1. First pillar (preventive measures): scholarships, forecasting labour market needs, practical training at the time of education, career orientation.
2. Second pillar (measures immediately after unemployment): preparation of an individual plan, counselling, integration into ALMPs, national vocational qualifications, project-based learning for young people.
3. Third pillar (after three months of unemployment): mentoring schemes, business consultancy, tax exemptions. The third pillar contains more targeted measures, ranging from in-depth counselling to further integration in ALMP measures to increase the employability of young unemployed persons.
4. Fourth pillar (after four months of unemployment): integration in additional ALMP measures, co-funding internships, public works and other things.

However, some measures easing activation can also be observed. For example, one of the most important changes in the new Financial

Social Assistance Act 2010 in relation to the previous Social Security Act is a slight relaxation of the obligation for social assistance recipients to accept any kind of work offered by employment counsellors.

Through the 1990s and into the 21st century, ALMPs have been important in Slovenia, although not as much as they are described in various documents. In practice, the share of Slovenian GDP spent on ALMPs is much lower than for passive policies. With the economic crisis and the increase in the number of unemployed, the difference between the shares in expenditure for passive measures and ALMPs only grew, especially between 2010 and 2012. However, from 2012 to 2014, there was a slight increase in expenditure on ALMPs, along with a significant decrease of expenditure for passive labour market policies, narrowing the gap between the two. This can partly be linked to a slight decrease in unemployment (see Figure 13.8).

Despite the significant emphasis on labour market restructuring and the principles of activation in policy documents, public expenditure on labour market policy in general, and for ALMPs in particular, has remained low in comparison with other EU countries and highly dependent on European Social Fund (ESF) funding as the majority of ALMP programmes are financed at 85% by the ESF. In 2012, Slovenia spent around 1.1% of GDP on labour market policies (the average for the EU28 in 2011 was 1.82%), while the share for ALMPs has been 0.18% of GDP, which is quite low in comparison with other European countries (the EU28 average in 2011 was 0.46%) (Eurostat, 2017).

Thus, in practice, there are divergent trends in Slovenian ALMPs. While the activation principle is one of the key elements of long-term reform, actual activation has insufficient funding and, in practice, has often been more demanding than enabling in the past. With the introduction of the aforementioned legal instruments, the situation changed somewhat. The newly introduced measures favour more enabling activation for different groups in the labour force and society (workers on hold, pensioners, the partly unemployed, persons receiving social benefits and young people included in the Youth Guarantee scheme). However, activation policies are still demanding in nature and, again due to financial restrictions, the enabling trends are overall relatively weak as a relatively small part of society actually benefits from them.

Evaluation of labour market conditions (IMAD, 2014) indicates that a further strengthening of ALMPs is vital, especially in-job training and the prevention of long-term unemployment. However, social investment strategies are productive only when a virtuous circle is created, linking social protection and social investment, which are

Labour market policies in the era of pervasive austerity

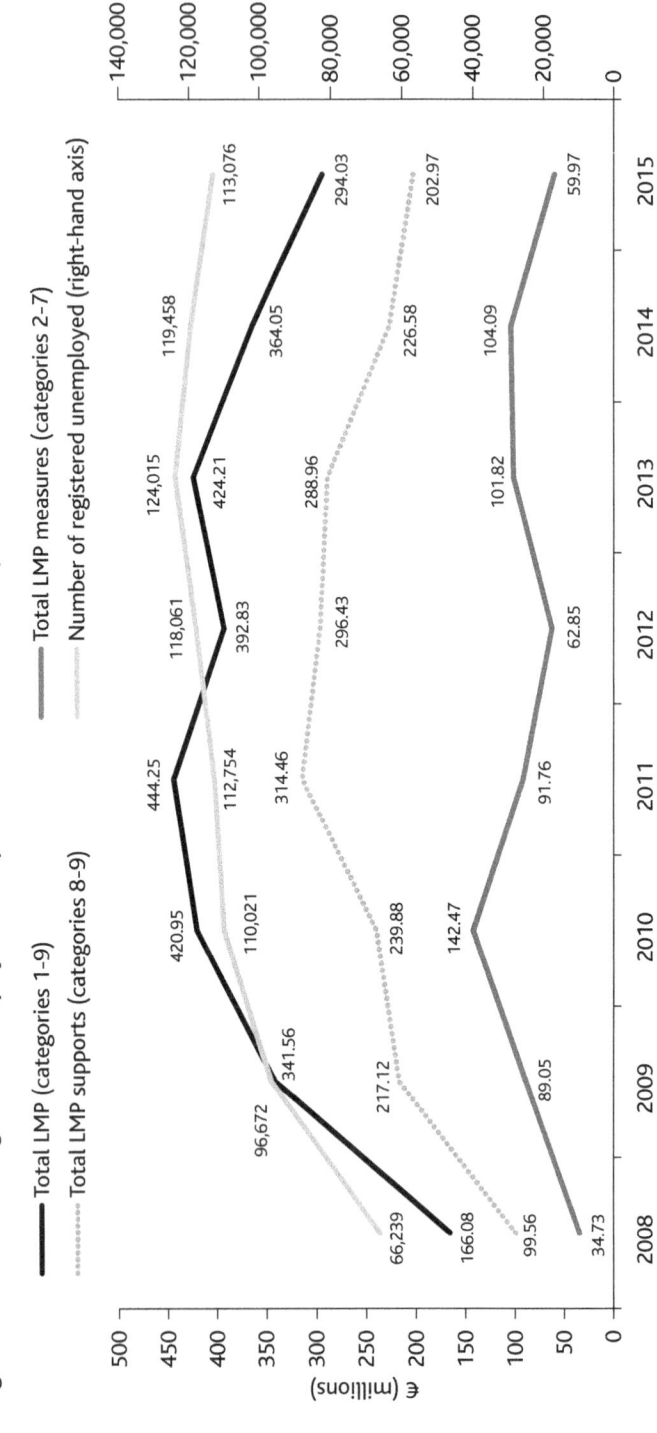

Figure 13.8: Number of registered unemployed and expenditure for labour market policies, Slovenia, 2008–15

Note: LMP = labour market policy.
Source: Eurostat (2017) and ZRSZ (2017)

then mutually reinforcing (Vandenbroucke and Vleminickx, 2011). In Slovenia, therefore, increasing the social protection of workers (in precarious forms of employment or unemployed) would be needed to further strengthen ALMPs.

Conclusion

At a general level, reforms adopted during 2010–15 seem to be in line with EU recommendations, with the aim of achieving full employment and productivity growth, which are key issues for the future economic growth of Slovenia and the EU. The objective of labour market changes seems to be to increase flexibility and to implement activation (and social investment) more fully, as well as to improve the position of the most vulnerable groups on the labour market (unemployed, employees with fixed-term contracts, student workers and irregular workers). However, on the other hand, there are still many questions related to the direction and quality of changes (reducing the rights of workers in standard forms of employment, prolonging working life and the further flexibilisation of the labour market leading to possible further segmentation). Such changes are not tackling some fundamental issues and limitations of the current Slovenian system, such as the precarisation of the workforce, low funding, rigid bureaucracy and so on. Last but not least, new amendments to the ERA adopted in March 2013 were the third amendment of the most important Labour Act over the past 15 years, which means that the social partners (especially employers and employees) do not have a stable environment in which labour standards are known and predictable.

Slovenia's unfavourable financial situation caused by the global economic crisis and austerity measures adopted in 2012 weakened household and state consumption and especially the performance of the public sector. In the case of state consumption, the austerity measures reduced funding for the implementation of many measures, at least for those related to ALMPs, and seriously obstructed attempts to increase their effectiveness. In relation to investments in education, research, innovation and ALMPs, the Slovenian reality is that they are more or less hostages to the Fiscal Balance Act and the overall poor financial situation. In the case of the public sector, very important systems (such as the health and education system) are experiencing major difficulties in maintaining the same quality of service due to the severe cuts in their financing.

Despite ample evidence of activation and also the extension of the rights of the more flexible part of the labour force, retrenchment has also been evident. The changes in labour regulations in 2014 reduced the employment protection legislation index for regular contracts, and the cuts (eg of unemployment benefits), along with the changes in the social security system, have affected the unemployed, who remain among the groups most at risk of poverty.

Implementation of flexicurity in Slovenia has proved to be fairly difficult. Some of the proposed measures were not welcomed, especially by trade unions and younger people (students), who feared drastic changes, such as a reduction of workers' rights and an increase of insecurity in society, as was evident in the rejection of the Mini Jobs Act to re-regulate student work and all other occasional and temporary forms of work on a new basis. Furthermore, the recent economic crisis only increased the gap and distrust between employers' and employees' representatives, which was reflected in the failure to sign a new social agreement after the last expired in 2009. Only in early 2015 did the majority of the social partners' representatives sign a new social agreement for 2015/16. Another obstacle to the more successful implementation of flexicurity was increasing political instability during the period of economic crisis. However, the major obstacle was, and still is, Slovenia's financial situation, which, regardless of the austerity measures, means that the security part of flexicurity cannot receive the emphasis it requires.

Notes

[1] For example, a person could be removed from the register under the following conditions: a person refuses to participate in the active labour market policy (ALMP) programme or violates the commitments made in the agreement on inclusion in the ALMP programme; a person refuses appropriate or suitable employment or does not seek to obtain employment in a job interview; or the person refuses to sign an employment plan.

[2] For many policymakers, this concept emphasised the further flexibilisation of the Slovenian labour market without improving the social security of those involved in flexible forms of employment.

[3] In the event of termination of employment due to business reasons or incompetence, the employee is entitled to severance pay in the amount of one fifth of the worker's wage if employed at the company for between one and 10 years, a quarter of the base wage for 10 to 20 years service and one third of the base wage for more than 20 years of service with the employer.

4. The new ERA-1 increases (gradually) the age of workers (from 55 years in 2013 to 58 years in 2017) who have special protection against dismissal. Thus, special protection against dismissal is intended for workers who meet the age requirement of 58 years or employees who do not otherwise meet the age requirement, but would qualify for retirement in five years or less.

5. In addition to a further freezing of wage indexation, promotions and limitations on performance bonuses, reductions in basic wages, holiday pay and other personal income of employees, and the elimination of the third and fourth quarter of wage disparities were implemented.

6. The last Minimum Cost of Living Study (MLFSA, 2009) identified the minimum cost of living in Slovenia at €562.02.

7. This was added in recent amendments in 2014.

References

Bednaš, M., Kajzer, A. and Hafner, M. (eds) (2011) *Ekonomski izzivi 2011*, Ljubljana: IMAD.

Eurostat (2017) 'Database'. Available at: http://ec.europa.eu/eurostat/data/database

Filipovič Hrast, M. and Rakar, T. (2017) 'The future of the Slovenian welfare state and challenges to solidarity', in: P. Taylor-Gooby, B. Leruth and H. Chung (eds) *After austerity: Welfare state transformation in Europe after the great recession*, Oxford: Oxford University Press, pp 115–35.

Guardiancich, I., (2011) 'Slovenian social policy in a consensual political system: the dilemmas of a delayed transition', in M. Sambolieva and S. Dohnert (eds) *Welfare states in transition. 20 years after the Yugoslav welfare model*, Sofia: Friedrich-Ebert-Stiftung, pp 310–44.

Häusermann, S. (2011) 'Post-industrial social policy reforms in continental Europe: what role for social partners?'. Available at: http://www.mwpweb.eu/1/22/resources/publication_955_1.pdf

Hemerijck, A. (2013) *Changing welfare states*, Oxford: Oxford University Press.

Ignjatović, M. (2002) *Družbene posledice povečanja prožnosti trga delovne sile* [*Social consequences of increasing flexibilisation of the labour market*], Fakulteta za družbene vede, Ljubljana: Znanstvena knjižnica.

Ignjatović, M. (2011) 'Slowenien: Konsolidierung oder Erosion des Arbeitsmarktes', in W. Reiter and K.H. Müller (eds) *Arbeitsmärkte und Sozialsysteme nach der Krize: strukturelle Veränderungen und politische Herausforderungen*, Wien: Echoraum, Bundesministerium für Arbeit, Soziales und Konsumentenschutz: cop. 2011, pp 91–7.

Ignjatović, M., Kopač, A., Svetlik, I. and Trbanc, M. (2002) 'Slovenia's navigation though a turbulent transition', in J. Goul Andersen, J. Clasen, W. Van Oorschot and K. Halvorsen (eds) *Europe's new state of welfare*, Bristol: The Policy Press.

IMAD (Institute for Macroeconomic Analysis and development) (2013) *Ekonomski izzivi 2013*, Ljubljana: IMAD.

IMAD (Institute for Macroeconomic Analysis and Development) (2014) 'Ekonomski izzivi 2014'. Available at: http://www.umar.gov.si/fileadmin/user_upload/publikacije/izzivi/2014/EI_2014_splet_nov.pdf

Kajzer, A. (2011) 'Vpliv gospodarske krize na trg dela v Sloveniji in izzivi za politiko trga dela', *IB revija*, 4: 13–21.

Kanjuo Mrčela, A. and Ignjatović, M. (2015) 'Od prožnosti do prekarnosti dela: stopnjevanje negativnih sprememb na začetku 21. Stoletja' ['From the flexibility to the precarity of work: intensification of negative changes at the beginning of the 21st century'], *Teorija in praksa*, 3: 350–79.

Kolarič, Z., Kopač, A. and Rakar, T. (2009) 'The Slovene welfare system: gradual reform instead of shock treatment', in K. Schubert, S. Hegelich and U. Bazant (eds) *The handbook of European welfare systems*, London and New York, NY: Routledge, pp 444–61.

Kolarič, Z., Kopač, A. and Rakar, T. (2011) 'Welfare states in transition. Development of the welfare system in Slovenia', in M. Sambolieva and S. Dohnert (eds) *Welfare states in transition. 20 years after the Yugoslav welfare model*, Sofia: Friedrich-Ebert-Stiftung, pp 288–309.

Kopač, A. (2005a) 'Od brezpogojne k pogojevani državi blaginje – spremembe znotraj koncepta državljanstva', *Družboslovne razprave*, 21(49/50): 51–64.

Kopač, A. (2005b) 'Aktivacija kot konvergentni in divergentni proces reforme države blaginje', *Teorija in praksa*, 424(6): 771–86.

Kordež, B. (2015) 'Ali zajamčene minimalne plače res ogrožajo delovna mesta?' ['Is the guaranteed minimum wage really a threat to jobs?']. Available at: https://damijan.org/2015/10/12/ali-zajamcene-minimalne-place-res-ogrozajo-delovna-mesta/

Lavrač, V. and Majcen, B. (2006) *Economic issues of Slovenia's accession to EU*, Working Paper No. 31, Ljubljana: IER.

MLFSA (Ministry of Labour, Family and Social Affairs) (2009) 'Ocena minimalnih življenjskih stroškov v letu 2009'. Available at: http://www.mddsz.gov.si/fileadmin/mddsz.gov.si/pageuploads/dokumenti__pdf/240709-tk-min_zivlj_stroski.pdf

MLFSA (2013) 'Employment Relationship Act'. Available at: http://www.pisrs.si/Pis.web/pregledPredpisa?id=ZAKO5944

Rueda, D. (2012) 'West European welfare states in times of crisis', in N. Bermeo and J. Pontusson (eds) *Coping with crisis*, New York: Russell Sage Foundation. Available at: http://users.ox.ac.uk/~polf0050/Rueda%20Sage%202012.pdf

SORS (Statistical Office of Republic of Slovenia) (2017a) 'SI-Stat data portal. gross domestic product'. Available at: http://pxweb.stat.si/pxweb/Dialog/statfile2.asp

SORS (2017b) 'SI-Stat data portal. Working age population by activity and activity rates, age groups, sex and cohesion regions, Slovenia, quarterly'. Available at: http://pxweb.stat.si/pxweb/Dialog/varval.asp?ma=0762003S&ti=&path=../Database/Dem_soc/07_trg_dela/02_07008_akt_preb_po_anketi/01_07620_akt_preb_ADS_cetrt/&lang=2

SORS (2017c) 'SI-Stat data portal. At-risk-of-poverty rate'. Available at: http://pxweb.stat.si/pxweb/Database/Dem_soc/08_zivljenjska_raven/08_silc_kazalniki_revsc/10_08672_stopnja_tveg_revcine/10_08672_stopnja_tveg_revcine.asp

Trbanc, M., Črnak Meglič, A., Dremelj, P., Smolej Jež, S., Narat, T., Kovač, N. and Kobal Tomc, B. (2015) *Socialni položaj v Sloveniji 2013–2014, končno poročilo*, Ljubljana: Inštitut Republike Slovenije za socialno varstvo.

Vandenbroucke, F. and Vleminckx, K. (2011) 'Disappointing poverty trends: is the social investment state to blame?', *Journal of European Social Policy*, 21(5): 450–71.

Wilthagen, T. and Tros, F.H. (2004) 'The concept of flexicurity: a new approach to regulating employment and labour markets', *Transfer, European Review of Labour and Research*, 10(2): 166–86. Available at: http://trs.sagepub.com/content/10/2/166.full.pdf+html

ZRSZ (Zavod Republike Slovenije za zaposlovanje) (2017) 'Number of registered unemployed'. Available at: http://www.ess.gov.si/trg_dela

Appendix

See Table 13.1.

Table 13.1: Summary of labour market policy changes in Slovenia

		2010	2016	Year of change and comments
Permanent contracts	Notice period	120 days	60 days	Change in 2013
	Severance pay	The basis for calculating severance pay is the average monthly wage received by the worker in the last three months before the cancellation of the contract. The amount was: • 1/5 of the basis if employed by the employer for more than one year to five years, for each year of work for the employer; • 1/4 of the basis if employed by the employer for a period of five to 15 years, for each year of work for the employer; • 1/3 of the basis if employed by the employer over 15 years, for each year of work for the employer.	The basis for calculating severance pay is the average monthly wage received by the worker in the last three months before the cancellation of the contract. The amount is: • 1/5 of the basis if employed by the employer for more than one year to ten years, for each year of work for the employer; • 1/4 of the basis if employed by the employer for a period of ten to 20 years, for each year of work for the employer; • 1/3 of the basis if employed by the employer over 20 years, for each year of work for the employer.	Change in 2013; reduced in 2013 in the event of termination of contract due to the business reasons
Fixed-term contracts	Right to severance pay	–	If the fixed-term employment contract is concluded for more than one year, the employee is entitled to a severance pay of 1/5 of the basic wage. The amount is increased for each month of work (1/5 of the base + 1/12 of 1/5 of the base for each month worked over one year).	Introduced in 2013

(continued)

Table 13.1: Summary of labour market policy changes in Slovenia (continued)

		2010	2016	Year of change and comments
Agency workers	Quota for employers seeking to use agency workers	–	Should not exceed 25% of the workforce in the organisation	Introduced in 2013
Student work	Minimum hourly rate	–	€4.53/h	Introduced in 2015
	Social insurance	–	Pension, disability, health insurance and insurance for accidents at work and occupational diseases	Introduced in 2015
EPL index (OECD)	Protection of permanent workers against individual and collective dismissals	2.65	2.16	Change in the beginning of 2014
LMP expenditure (total)	% GDP	1.192	0.763 in 2015	
ALMP expenditure	% GDP	0.393	0.156 in 2015	
Minimum wage		Increased from €597.43 in 2009 to €734.15 in 2010	€790.73	Change in 2010

(continued)

Table 13.1: Summary of labour market policy changes in Slovenia (continued)

		2010	2016	Year of change and comments
Unemployment benefit	Conditions	Before 2010, it was 12 months in 18 months	9 months in 24 months; 6 months in past 24 months for youth under 30 years of age	Change in 2010 Change in 2013
	Level	Increase to minimum €350 and maximum 3 × minimum (€1050)	Minimum €350 and max €892.50	Change in 2012 by Fiscal Balance Act
	Amount	80% of wage in the first three months and 70% for a further nine months (before 2010, it was 70% of average wage in first three months and 60% after first three months)	80% of wage in the first three months and 60% for a further nine months	Change in 2010 and revised in 2012 by Fiscal Balance Act
	Basis of compensation	12 months of person's average wage	8 months of person's average wage	
	Additional work for unemployed	Opportunity to have €200 additional income from occasional work without losing full UB		Introduced in 2010
Social assistance	Amount	€226.81, increased to €288.81 in 2012	€292.56	Yearly changes (increases)
	Work activity allowance	–	€ 81.91 (for 60–128 hours of work) to €163.76 (for more than 128 hours of work)	In case of being active (eg voluntary work) recipient can receive additional benefit, introduced in 2014

Note: All benefits are presented in gross amounts.

FOURTEEN

Conclusions

Sotiria Theodoropoulou

Introduction

This book has investigated whether and, if so, how the pattern of labour market reforms has been changing in Europe during the recent crisis and, in particular, following the shift in fiscal policy in Europe from an expansionary stance to austerity from 2009/10 onwards, whereby public expenditure has been cut and taxes risen in the midst of the biggest post-war recession experienced in the area. Prior to the crisis, labour market policies had again been under (financial) pressure due to structural changes affecting European economies. However, reforms aimed at cutting costs and increasing flexibility had been matched with the development of new policy instruments and approaches, such as activation and, in some cases, social investment, while there had also been calls, not necessarily translated into actions, for expanding the protection and rights of labour market 'outsiders', to reduce their differentiation from those of 'insiders'. The motivating premise behind this book has been that pressures for public spending cuts in a context of deep recession can alter the considerations that shape change in labour market policies as strong and self-reinforcing constraints are placed on both the supply (costs) and the demand for them. We have, therefore, sought to examine how these pressures for cuts have been distributed across 'old' and 'new' policy instruments, among insiders and outsiders, and across different activation instruments.

Eleven national case studies have been used, spanning member states with different welfare regimes and under different degrees of European Union (EU) pressures for fiscal austerity. An additional chapter placed labour market reforms undertaken between 1999 and 2012 across the EU within a wider context of structural reforms in several key areas (pensions, education, research and development, and the public sector). Starting from the assumption that structural reforms attempt to balance social protection and investment for growth objectives, this comparative chapter developed a typology of reform strategies and characterised structural reform patterns across Europe and over time between 1999 and 2012.

In this final chapter, quantitative and qualitative information is brought together in order to look at the bigger picture of reform patterns as it emerges. I also take a look at the evolution of labour market insecurity and examine whether there seems to be convergence or divergence in that respect. Although explaining the underlying drivers of these developments and the share of responsibility that can be attributed to fiscal austerity for the observed developments is beyond the scope of this book, I reflect on some questions for further research.

Overall, it appears that the 'welfare readjustment' and 'flexicurity' agendas are still the most common direction aimed for, at least on paper, within the group of countries examined in the book while there have also been cases where labour market policies changed in the direction of 'welfare protectionism' and of overall 'retrenchment'. Welfare readjustment and flexicurity have, however, resulted in more flexibility and activation and less security/protection overall. Budget pressures have been evident in most of the examined cases, although they have varied in severity. The trend towards activation has been strengthened, although the cuts in public spending per person wanting to work in that domain have meant that activation has been pursued more by means of incentives reinforcement than by means of more expensive 'enabling' programmes.

Changes in labour market policies

A bird's-eye view of labour market reforms since 2000

I first look at the number of reforms undertaken in each of the countries examined in this book, based on data collected by the European Commission in their Labour Market Reforms (LABREF) database. The policy areas that I look into are: active labour market policies, that is, public employment services, training, direct job-creation schemes, employment subsidies and special schemes for the disabled and for the young; unemployment benefits, with reported reforms covering the net replacement rate, the duration of unemployment benefit, their coverage and eligibility conditions, and the search and job-availability requirements; other welfare-related benefits, from social assistance to in-work benefits; and job protection for permanent and temporary contracts, as well as for collective dismissals (for more details on the database, see European Commission, 2014).

More specifically, I calculate an indicator on the 'reform effort', that is, the number of reforms undertaken in a particular policy domain during a certain period (European Commission, 2014) (see Table 14.1). Given that the information in the database starts from 2000 and runs up until 2014, I have divided the information into three periods: 2000–07 (before the crisis), 2008–09 (the first period of the crisis when there was a fiscal stimulus), and 2010–14 (the second period of the crisis when fiscal austerity began). As these periods are different in length, I divide the number of reforms undertaken in each period by the number of years to obtain a more comparable 'reform effort per year' indicator.[1]

The indicators calculated as laid out earlier suggest that in the vast majority of countries examined in the book, the reform effort per year accelerated once the crisis began and, in particular, from 2010 onwards. Exceptions to this are Germany and Sweden, both of which demonstrated higher reform effort per year during 2000–07. Moreover, with the exception of Italy and the Netherlands during 2010–14, the number of reforms in the domain of active labour market policies (ALMPs) was the highest, often by far, than in other labour market policy domains.

Indeed, as Figure 14.1 illustrates, there seems to be a fairly positive association between the extent of fiscal austerity pursued between 2010 and 2014, measured as the cumulative improvement in the structural fiscal balance of a government, excluding interest payments,[2] and labour market reform effort per year during that period, with a positive linear correlation coefficient of 0.5. However, this is driven by the presence of Greece in the sample, as the association becomes much weaker (0.3) once Greece is excluded. Instead, it is the association between the average annual growth rate of unemployed persons, which could be taken as a proxy of the problem load in the labour market, and the reform effort per year during the period 2010–14 that is stronger (correlation coefficient = 0.63) and fairly robust to the exclusion of Greece than that between fiscal effort and reform effort (correlation coefficient = 0.53) (see Figure 14.2).

I also provide here data on public expenditure on labour market interventions, more specifically, labour market services,[3] labour market policy measures (ie ALMPs) and labour market supports (ie financial support), per person wanting to work (see Figures 14.3–14.5, respectively) for the period between 1998 and 2015. Public expenditure on ALMPs per person wanting to work had clearly declined by 2015 in several of the countries where it was relatively high in the early 2000s, most notably, the Netherlands, Sweden and Germany, but also

Table 14.1: Reform effort per year, selected EU member states, 2000–14

Reform effort per year = number of reforms/number of years in period

Domain	ALMPs			EPL			Unemployment Benefits			Other welfare benefits			Total reform effort per year		
Country and period	2000–07	2008–09	2010–14	2000–07	2008–09	2010–14	2000–07	2008–09	2010–14	2000–07	2008–09	2010–14	2000–07	2008–09	2010–14
GR	1	5.5	5.8	0.75	0.5	4	0.25	1.5	1.4	0.25	2	0.8	2	10	12
IT	0.875	0.5	5.4	1	3	7.4	1.25	1	1.6	0.25	3	0.2	3	8	15
FR	2.625	4.5	3.4	0.625	1.5	2.6	0.875	4	1.2	0.625	1.5	0.4	5	12	8
DE	3.625	4	1.8	0.625	0	0.2	1.4	0	0	0.375	4	1.4	6	8	3
NL	1.875	2	2.2	0.125	0.5	2.8	1.125	0	0.6	1	1.5	1.6	4	4	7
SE	3.25	3	3.6	0.5	0	0.4	1.125	1	0.2	0.625	1	1	6	5	5
IE	1.5	6	3	0.5	0	0.6	0.25	1	1	0.75	0.5	3	3	8	8
UK	2	9.5	4.2	0.625	1	2.2	0	1	0.4	1.25	1.5	2.2	4	13	9
CZ	1.625	0.5	0.8	1.4	0	1.6	0.5	2	1.2	1.5	0.5	1.2	5	3	5
SK	0.625	1	2.6	1.125	0	2.8	0.75	0	0.4	0.25	2	1.8	3	3	8
SI	0.875	2.5	2	0.625	0	2.4	0	0	1.2	0	1.5	1	2	4	7

Notes: EPL = Employment Protection Legislation; ALMPs = Active Labour Market Policies.
Source: Own calculations using data from the European Commission LABREF database

Conclusions

Figure 14.1: Fiscal consolidation effort and labour market reform effort per year, selected European Union member states, 2010–14

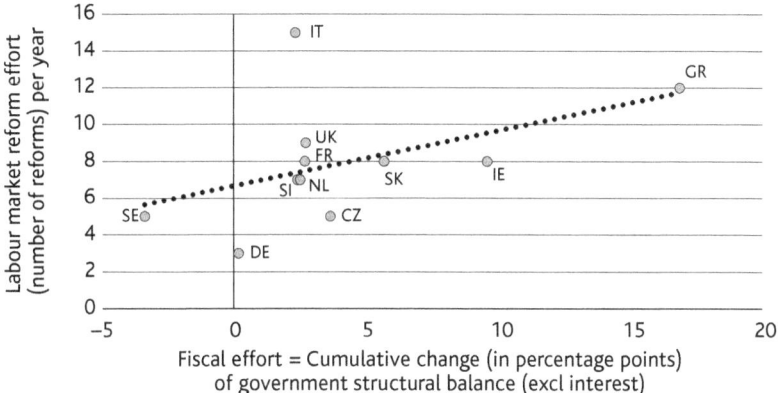

Source: Own calculations using data from the European Commission AMECO database (UBLGBP series) and LABREF database.

Figure 14.2: Labour market reform effort per year and average annual growth of unemployed, selected European Union member states, 2010–14

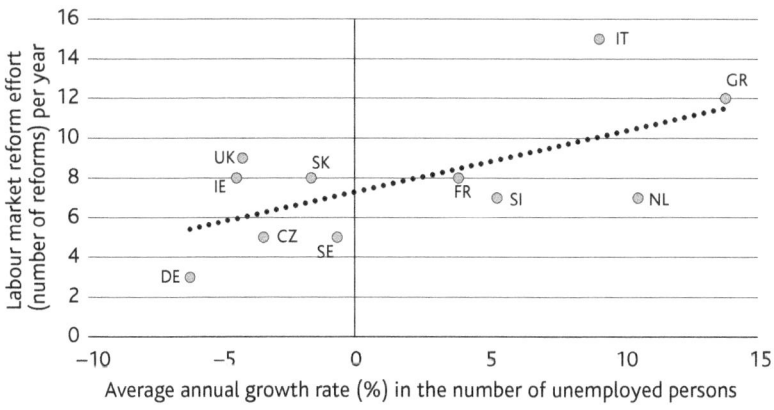

Source: Own calculations using data from the Eurostat Labour Force Survey (LFS) database (lfsa_ugan series) and the European Commission LABREF database.

Figure 14.3: Public expenditure in labour market services per person wanting to work, selected European Union member states, 1998–2015

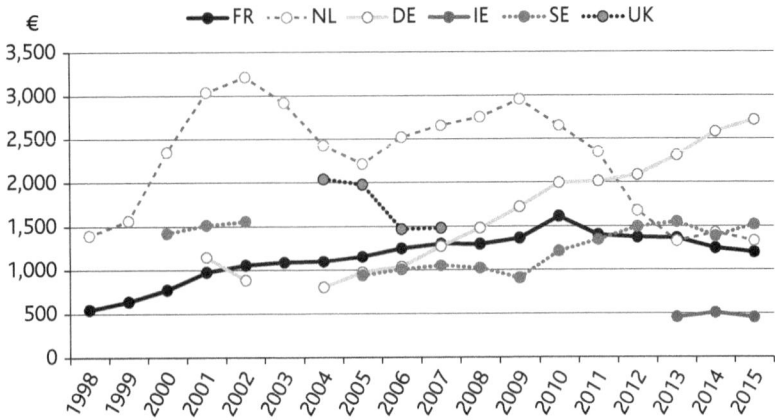

Source: Own calculations using European Commission (DG Empl) data (lmp_expsumm, lmp_partsumm and lmp_ind_actsup series)

Figure 14.4: Public expenditure in labour market policy measures per person wanting to work, selected European Union member states, 1998–2015

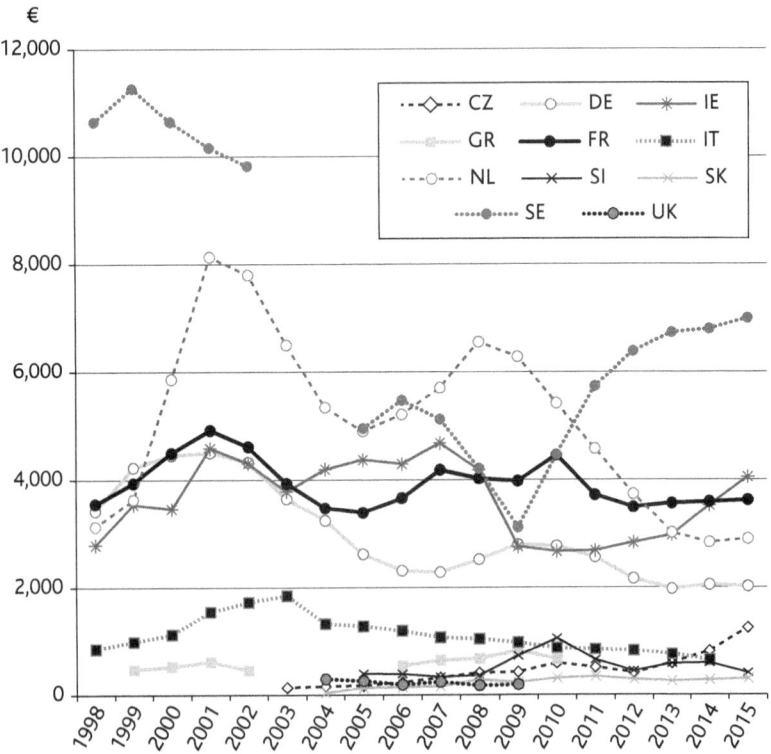

Source: Own calculations using European Commission (DG Empl) data (lmp_expsumm, lmp_partsumm and lmp_ind_actsup series)

Figure 14.5: Public expenditure in labour market (financial) support policies per person wanting to work, selected European Union member states, 1998–2015

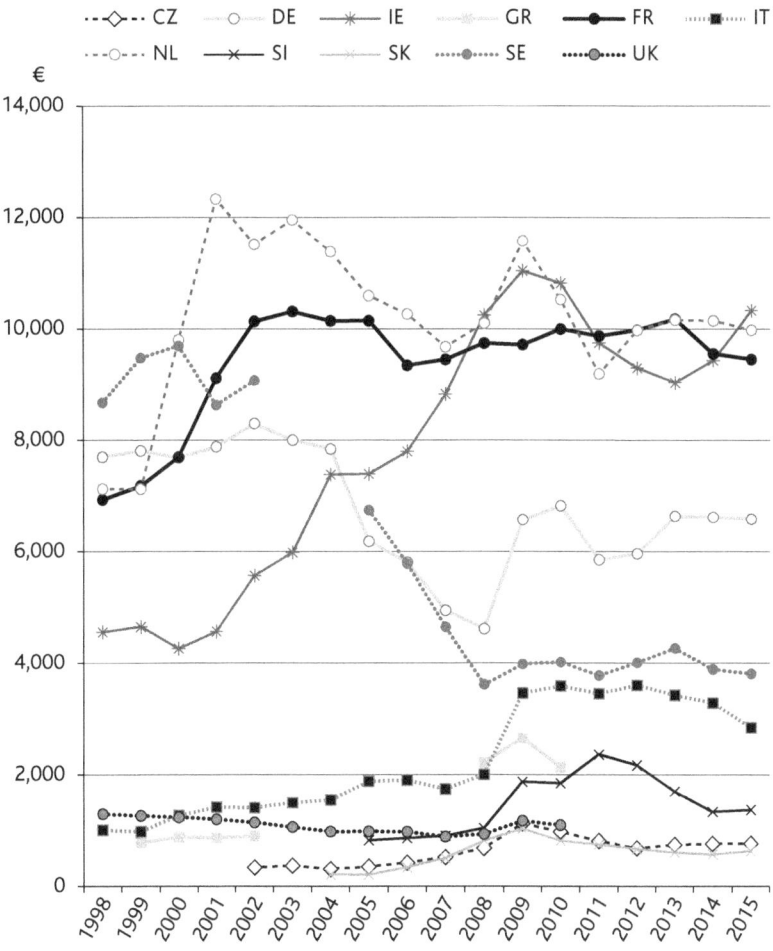

Source: Own calculations using European Commission (DG Empl) data (lmp_expsumm, lmp_partsumm and lmp_ind_actsup series)

in Italy, where it has traditionally not been high. This is a striking development insofar as the share of long-term unemployment in total unemployment had increased in all these countries bar Germany and the UK by 2015 (see Figure 14.6).

Although declining trends have also been evident in the public expenditure per person wanting to work for labour market financial support policies, there was invariably an increase in all examined countries during 2008–09, reflecting the expansionary fiscal efforts of governments across Europe to counter the effects of the global

Figure 14.6: Long-term unemployment as share of total unemployment, selected European Union member states, 2008, 2010, 2015

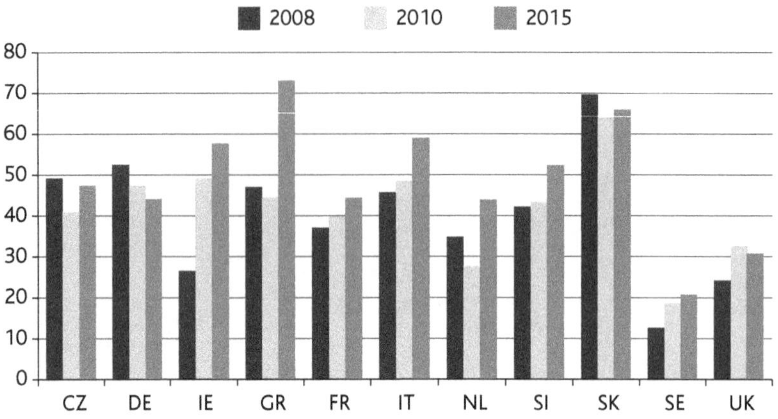

Source: Eurostat LFS database (lfsa_upgan series)

financial shock to their economies. However, starting in 2010, this common trend reversed to various extents.

The Netherlands and Ireland registered some of the steepest declines in public expenditure on financial support measures per person wanting to work, as did Slovenia. On the other hand, public expenditure on labour market policies as a share of gross domestic product (GDP) expanded in France, fully reversing the reductions of the years prior to the crisis.

As far as the balance of public spending across different types of labour market policies is concerned, financial support (unemployment benefits) still seem to absorb a higher share of spending than ALMPs or public services. Interestingly, however, the trends in public spending as a share of GDP have been declining in several cases, especially in countries that spent relatively high amounts in the late 1990s and early 2000s.

Evidence from the national case studies

To understand more on the direction of change, I now turn to the findings of the chapters. The empirical evidence provided by the country chapters confirms the diverse pattern of change both within and across labour market regimes, with retrenchment but also expansion taking place and allocated in different ways across functions and labour force groups. An exception to this has been the pair of the UK and Ireland (the countries of the 'liberal' regime), where, on balance, the authors have found that retrenchment has taken place, despite the marked shift of emphasis from passive to active instruments in Ireland. Overall, three broad patterns have been observed: retrenchment, 'welfare readjustment' and 'welfare protectionism' (cf Hausermann, 2012).

As far as activation policies are concerned, incentive reinforcement has been common in many of the examined countries. The targeting of ALMPs towards those at higher risk of long-term unemployment has also intensified, under budget pressures. Another common trend has been the replacement of social assistance schemes (ie 'needs-based' income support) covering the long-term unemployed, but also the young, single parents and disabled people, by mandatory participation in activation programmes, a trend that Heins and Bennett characterise in their chapter as a shift of focus from tackling unemployment to tackling 'worklessness', which is consistent with what Clasen and Clegg (2011) identify as the activation dimension in their 'triple integration' concept of policies regulating the risk of unemployment. While enabling instruments of activation have remained in place wherever they were previously available, the considerable incentive reinforcement that has taken place, coupled with the tightening of budgets for ALMPs, suggests that, on balance, changes in ALMPs after 2009/10 were weighed towards 'punitive' measures rather than towards 'enabling' ones, let alone those akin to social investment.

In Greece, a country with a highly segmented labour market and relatively low labour market 'reform effort' prior to the crisis, retrenchment was the dominant trend in spite of the unprecedented loss in GDP and massive increase in unemployment since 2008. Eligibility for unemployment benefits, both insurance-related and assistance, was extended to groups not previously covered, namely, the self-employed and those aged 20–44, while it was restricted for groups that were better covered before. The threshold for the income test of assistance benefits was increased. These changes present some elements of distributive recalibration. However, there was also retrenchment in the form of drift, caused by the lack of indexation/adjustment of benefit levels or income thresholds, the establishment of spending ceilings, and the failure to adapt eligibility rules to deteriorating circumstances and rising numbers of unemployed workers, especially the long-term unemployed, which more than counterbalanced the recalibration elements. Overall, as Matsaganis demonstrated in his chapter, there was a drop in the coverage rate of unemployment benefits during the crisis in spite of the stellar increase in unemployment.

Employment protection legislation became lighter for many (but not all) of those under permanent and those under temporary work contracts, while the rules governing the use of temporary work agencies were substantially relaxed. ALMPs, of questionable effectiveness in Greece prior to the crisis, did not go far beyond planning during the period of economic adjustment programmes and focused mostly on the Youth Guarantee and a public works programme for the long-term unemployed in jobless households. Flexibility increased in the Greek labour market thanks to deregulation, but clearly at the expense of security.

The magnitude of adjustment that Greece would have to undergo given its current account and budget deficits in 2010 could not have been anything other than painful since the financial flows that funded them dried up suddenly. Nevertheless, in his chapter, Matsaganis argues that the legacy of backwardness, neglect and lack of sophistication in Greek labour market policies, combined with the unwillingness (or inability?) of Greek domestic actors to constructively engage and puzzle for genuine and effective solutions, also bear responsibility for the patent failure of Greek labour market policies to rise to the challenges raised by the crisis and the massive increase in unemployment that it brought.

In Italy, Vesan and Pavolini have demonstrated that there was an important shift in the direction of reforms in the domains of employment protection legislation and unemployment benefits. There was substantial retrenchment in employment protection legislation for open-ended contracts, while the regulation of temporary contracts increased, marking a break with the pre-crisis period, when employment protection legislation liberalisation took place 'at the margin'. Important reforms took place in the domain of unemployment benefits during the crisis, in contrast with only incremental reforms since the mid-1990s. The old mobility allowance, which functioned as an unemployment benefit for people losing their jobs in collective dismissals, and the short-time working schemes were abolished or their use limited substantially in favour of financing new unemployment insurance and assistance benefits and active inclusion schemes. Italy followed, at least in normative terms, the trends towards activation. Still, expenditure on ALMPs and social investment remained limited (cf Beramendi et al, 2015), leading to an incomplete adjustment, as Vesan and Pavolini argued in their chapter, and a missing element that could increase security as a counterbalance to higher flexibility.

These changes have taken place against a context of chronically low growth in Italy, which preceded the crisis. Italy found itself in the shadow of the public debt crisis not so much because its budget deficits grew more than in other member states in the early years of the crisis, but rather due to its persistently high public debt to GDP ratio and the doubts over the health of several Italian banks. In that respect, the direction of reforms seems to be informed by a logic that perceived the crisis as a 'structural challenge' (Clasen et al, 2012). At the same time, welfare readjustment has not been complete, with the investment part clearly lagging, suggesting that there may be limits to how far this logic can drive reforms.

In France, policy changes from 2009 onwards continued along the path followed since the early 2000s, namely, the pursuit of '*flexicurité à la française*': while nominally aiming at increasing flexibility and improving security, the balance has clearly been in favour of flexibility, both internal and external. Retrenchment in the form of drift has taken place in public expenditure for income support for the unemployed and for ALMPs, but also in employment protection legislation. The balance of change in ALMPs has been on incentive enforcement, while subsidised contracts also increased. Reforms in unemployment income support and ALMPs also attempted to blur the distinction in rights between insiders and outsiders. However, this happened not by improving the position of outsiders, but rather by reducing the protection of insiders, thus presenting elements of 'subtractive recalibration' (Ferrera, 2012, cited in Ascoli et al, 2016).

Following the extensive Hartz I–IV reforms in the early 2000s, which went in the direction of 'welfare readjustment', labour market reforms in Germany since the shift of fiscal policy trends in Europe have not been as dramatic as in other cases. Germany's fiscal effort to consolidate its public finances was below the EU and Eurozone average, that is, it experienced less fiscal austerity than others. Nevertheless, the federal budget was rebalanced in line with the 'black zero' constitutional rule. Public expenditure on labour market services per person wanting to work increased quite steeply between 2010 and 2015 whereas it fell commensurably for other ALMPs (see Figures 14.3 and 14.4). Public expenditure on labour market (financial) support measures per person wanting to work fluctuated somewhat after 2010 but remained at the higher levels it reached following the fiscal stimulus of 2008/09.

Eichhorst and Hassel argued that the policy changes since 2009 demonstrate elements of 'welfare protectionism'. Changes in labour market policies have aimed at stabilising 'regular' employment. This mostly took the form of reducing competition from more flexible forms of employment that had been introduced in the 2000s through the Hartz I–IV reforms. Thus, temporary agency employment was re-regulated and a statutory minimum wage was introduced. At the same time, early retirement was reintroduced. Eichhorst and Hassel argue that German policies since the beginning of the crisis have been aimed at stimulating growth and expansion. Their point resonates with that of Clasen et al (2012), who attributed the motivation behind the German labour market policy responses in the early stages of the crisis to a logic of countering a 'demand shock'.

The Netherlands has been a pioneer of the 'flexicurity' approach in Europe since the 1990s. In the 1990s, eligibility for unemployment insurance benefits was increasingly extended to those under 'atypical' forms of employment (eg part-time, fixed-term contracts), whose numbers had grown following concurrent reforms in labour law that facilitated the use of these types of contracts. Moreover, spending on ALMPs had grown substantially since the 1990s in order to facilitate mobility across jobs as compensation for the increased flexibility from labour law reforms. As Hoogenboom argues, however, the evaluation of the effectiveness of ALMPs in the Netherlands prior to the 2008 crisis had been rather disappointing, initiating a debate on how to reform the paradigm followed hitherto. From 2008 onwards, pressures for fiscal adjustment eventually touched upon assistance benefits, a retrenchment that had been planned already before the crisis, and the ALMP budgets for the recipients of unemployment benefits (both insurance and assistance). Employment protection legislation was left intact. Moreover, a new active labour market paradigm seems to be emerging in the Netherlands. As Hoogenboom argues, the shift has gone from remedying skills deficiencies through education and training to accepting them and financially compensating them while getting people into jobs.

Sweden has been a special case in the book as it was the only country that was largely untouched by the crisis. Along with Estonia, they were the only two countries not to have been subjected to an excessive deficit procedure since 2008. The pattern of reforms that has been followed since the 1990s has decisively moved the country away from its universalist model of the past and towards a more dualised one. Davidsson has attributed this shift to the fiscal austerity pressures that Sweden faced at the time and an ideational change that followed it. Retrenchment in unemployment benefits, ALMPs and employment protection legislation took place well before the current crisis and its greatest burden invariably fell onto those in weaker positions, who became outsiders over time. During the period under consideration in this edited volume, Sweden was one of the very few countries in which public expenditure in labour market policy interventions per person wanting to work rose, while its reform effort was rather low. As Davidsson argues in his chapter, these developments were not sufficient to reverse the labour market policy trends since the 1990s.

In the period after 2010, which was also the year when Conservative or Conservative-led governments took over in the UK, there have been significant efforts to reduce the government structural budget balance. The UK economy was among the first to be hit by the international financial crisis in 2007 and suffered a deep downturn between 2007 and 2009. However, it has been recovering ever since and unlike Eurozone member states, the UK did not face any problems financing its public debt, although, like the vast majority of EU member states, the UK has been subject to an excessive deficit procedure. The main driver of fiscal austerity in Britain, however, has been the small-state agenda of the Conservative Party, which has been in power since 2010. Until the June 2017 elections, fiscal austerity was espoused by all three government parties as the 'responsible' course of action, against the views of most British academic economists (Wren-Lewis, 2016).

The UK labour market has been considered flexible and lightly regulated. Income support policies for the unemployed have been aiming more towards poverty alleviation than income replacement. Unemployment benefit and ALMPs had been closely intertwined since the late 1990s around a 'work-first' principle. Reforms since 2010 shifted the pattern of labour market policies further towards more flexibility and less protection. As Heins and Bennett argue in their chapter, since 2010, there has been a clear tendency for the aim of employment growth to take primacy over, rather than complement, social protection. Although British active labour market, training and human capital policies did incorporate some enabling elements, such as training, wage subsidies and job-creation options, they have been redefined as either work tests or an opportunity for employers to undercut existing employment protection legislation and the minimum wage since 2010. Any earlier tentative attempts to establish policies of social investment have been curtailed in a drive to reduce public deficits. Another notable example of retrenchment in the domain of employment protection legislation has been the introduction of zero-hour contracts, that is, contracts that do no state working hours. Overall, the evolution of labour market policies in the UK since 2010 point to clear retrenchment.

Ireland was one of the two countries examined in the book that received financial support by the EU and the International Monetary Fund (IMF). Like the UK, it was the impact of the global financial crisis on the Irish banking sector that pulled the Irish economy into the crisis early. Unlike the UK, however, Ireland did not have its own central bank to guarantee the continued servicing of its public debt once the Irish government started shoring up the banks operating in Irish territory, while the absence of a banking union in the EU/Eurozone made that burden very heavy. Employment declined continuously between 2008 and 2012 while outward migration re-emerged.

Prior to the crisis, Ireland's labour market policies were considered as overly focused on passively subsidising non-employment, as well as taking a passive approach to activation, making Ireland a relative 'laggard' in pro-employment policies. In the course of the crisis, under both national and EU pressures and tight budget constraints, there was retrenchment in income protection benefits for the unemployed. In ALMPs, entitlements were reduced and eligibility conditions were tightened. More generally, 'passive' protection was rolled back in favour of 'activation', with tougher incentives for the unemployed, in particular, the long-term unemployed, the young and single parents. The focus of ALMPs shifted from occupation to labour market integration and a mutual obligations model of employment services.

Overall, changes in Ireland have privileged an important shift towards activation in a labour market with low protections. The Irish labour market policy model has not yet 'settled' as changes are ongoing and as it is still possible that growth in the Irish economy and an improvement in public finances may ease financing constraints. As Dukelow points out, however, developments so far create concerns that rather than leading towards flexicurity, they are promoting a model of cost containment and labour precarity as part of a strategy for economic competitiveness, echoing the framework presented by Agostini and Natali in Chapter Two of the book.

In Czechia, as Sirovátka demonstrated, the emphasis of labour market policies since 2009 has been on public expenditure cuts, restricting access to benefits, increased conditionality and activation. The burden of retrenchment has mostly been borne by outsiders as eligibility criteria for unemployment benefits were tightened, while the benefit rates for the first two months of receipt were raised. The already low budget by EU standards on ALMPs has been further cut down, thus restricting the participation of unemployed workers in them. Moreover, minimum income/social assistance schemes started differentiating between 'deserving' and 'undeserving'/inactive recipients, restricting the entitlements of the latter. Activation policies for the recipients of minimum income shifted towards more workfare. Last but not least, changes in employment protection legislation somewhat improved the position of those employed under temporary contracts.

In Slovakia, the pattern of labour market reforms was not substantially different before and after 2010. As Domonkos explained, public funds for financing a more generous welfare state, including labour market policies, were heavily constrained even before 2010 due to the difficulties of post-socialist economic transition, the adoption of the euro and the decision to partially privatise public pensions. The coverage of unemployment insurance benefits expanded in favour of those formerly less well-protected and some retrenchment fell onto insiders.

Employment protection legislation has not been particularly restrictive in Slovakia and changes since the 2000s have been frequent and alternating in direction according to the partisan colour of the government in office. ALMPs have been increasingly targeting the more disadvantaged among the unemployed, including young job seekers. In fact, changes after 2010 have continued the trend established in 2004, which essentially replaced social assistance benefits with direct job-creation schemes to which benefit recipients had to participate. Thus, the emphasis of poverty relief policies for people of working age has increasingly been on their activation, with uncertain effects for their long-term integration into the labour market, while the level of social assistance benefits for working-age people fell steadily from the mid-1990s.

Slovenia's labour market policies after 2010 have had the nominal objective of implementing and enhancing flexicurity, following pressures in the years prior to that for more activation and labour flexibility. However, as Ignjatović and Filipovič Hrast show, under significant fiscal constraints due to the excessive deficit procedure, there have been budget limitations in implementing this approach. These limitations have taken the form of policy drift in areas such as income support for the unemployed and ALMPs. Retrenchment, especially in unemployment insurance, has mostly fallen on the shoulders of insiders, while eligibility was expanded for those working under atypical contracts. As in other member states, the conditionality of social assistance benefits on participation in ALMPs has increased, with the parallel reduction of benefit rates. While some enabling measures were also implemented, the coverage of social assistance benefit has fallen overall since 2014. Budget constraints have also created limitations for the effective functioning of employment services.

Trends in policy output

Overall, there seems to be diversity in the patterns of labour market policies across groups (regimes) of countries but also within them, a pattern that is also confirmed when looking into a broader selection of structural reforms in Chapter Two of the book (see Table 14.2).

Table 14.2: Summary of labour market policy developments, selected European Union member states, 2010–16

Country	Unemployment benefits			Needs-based benefits		
	Expansion/retrenchment	Increase in activation conditions - Punitive	Increase in activation conditions - Enabling	Expansion/retrenchment	Increase in activation conditions - Punitive	Increase in activation conditions - Enabling
GR	– for insiders	+ for self-employed		+ but subject to too tight rules and budget cap → very limited take-up		
IT	–			+		
FR	+ (establishment of 'portability' of unused entitlement	✓				
DE	+ (reintroduction of early retirement)			+		
NL				–	✓	
SE* (1990s–2000s)	– for all but by more for outsiders	✓		–		
IE	–		✓	+	✓	✓
UK	–			–	✓	
CZ	– + for the shorter-term unemployed	– for the unemployed for longer	✓	–	✓	
SK	– for insiders	+ for outsiders		–	✓	✓
SI	– for the better protected	✓		+		

Note: EPL = Employment Protection Legislation; ALMP = Active Labour Market Policies.

Conclusions

EPL		ALMPs			
Regular	Atypical	Expansion/ retrenchment	Punitive	Enabling	Overall balance in direction of change
−	−	+		✓ (targeted to the young and the long-term unemployed in jobless households)	Retrenchment
−		− until 2015; some + after 2015			Welfare readjustment
− (by more than for atypical)	+	+		+ especially for the young	Welfare readjustment/ flexicurity
	+			+	Welfare protectionism/welfare readjustment?
	+	−		−	Welfare protectionism
	−	−			Welfare protectionism
	−	−	−	−	Retrenchment
	−	−	✓ (workfare- see next)	✓ (workfare through placements in community work and work experience programmes	Retrenchment
−	+	−			Welfare protectionism
+/− (alternating)				✓ (several new ALMPs targeted at young job seekers)	Welfare readjustment
−	+	−			Welfare readjustment/ Flexicurity

It is thus not opportune to talk of convergence in labour market regimes. Pressures on public budgets, whether EU-imposed or self-inflicted, seem ubiquitous, although there is variation again depending on how deeply member states were drawn into the multiple economic crises that affected especially the Eurozone part of the EU. Activation has remained a common priority of reform or labour market policy configuration but budgetary pressures have meant that incentive reinforcement activation mechanisms have gained in importance.

Even where one can speak of similar trends of labour market policy change across countries with the same welfare state regime, the pressures under which reforms are undertaken can originate from different sources, thus allowing different degrees of freedom or implying different degrees of EU integration in labour market policymaking (De la Porte and Heins, 2015). This is not surprising: the increasing 'indirect' EU pressures on national welfare states (cf Leibried, 2010) through the process of fiscal policy coordination and, in some cases, through the conditionality attached to financial rescues have varied for reasons related to economic developments (eg membership or not of the euro, variable reliance on the external financing of domestic demand) prior to the crisis.

Overall, although diversity across regimes is preserved, labour market reforms after 2009/10 have led to or preserved the leaner and meaner labour market policies that were established prior to the crisis in the group of countries considered here. Even in countries such as Germany and Sweden, where reforms after 2010 were limited, there was no substantial reversal of reforms taken in the 2000–07 period or earlier.

Looking into a broader context of structural reforms, of which labour market reforms form a part, Agostini and Natali argue in their chapter that since the beginning of the crisis, there has been a diversified trend across welfare regimes in favour of following a 'low road' to competitiveness, with reduced spending and investment affecting predominantly labour market policies, pensions and education, while research and development (R&D) policies have been expanding or not contracting, with only exception the Nordic countries. Southern European countries have been following policies leading to less protection and less investment ('devaluation of social standards' strategy).

Increasing and divergent labour market insecurity

Labour market outcomes, such as employment, unemployment and wage inequality, depend on both demand- and supply-side factors, that is, among others, the labour market policies and institutions in place. Dolvik and Martin (2015) provide a detailed discussion of the ways in which demand- and supply-side forces can account for developments in these labour market outcomes since the crisis began. I focus instead on another labour market outcome, namely, labour market insecurity. The Organisation for Economic Co-operation and Development (OECD, 2014: 87) measures labour market insecurity as a dimension of the quality of work as the expected income loss associated with unemployment. This is particularly pertinent in the case of Europe, where the principle of flexicurity has been informing policy recommendations since the mid-2000s (Viebrock and Clasen, 2009). In the OECD's framework for measuring job quality, labour market insecurity is the one of three dimensions that is influenced by the labour market policy domains examined in this book. In practice, the indicator of labour market insecurity is measured as 'the uninsured average expected earnings' loss associated with unemployment as a share of previous earnings' (OECD, 2014: 103).

The indicator consists of two sub-indicators, namely, the risk of becoming unemployed and its expected cost in terms of previous income measured by the 'effective unemployment insurance'. In turn, the risk of becoming unemployed depends on the monthly probability of becoming unemployed and the expected average duration of unemployment. The strictness of employment protection legislation can affect both the risk of becoming unemployed and the expected average duration of unemployment: the stricter the employment protection legislation, the lower the flows into and out of unemployment, resulting in an ambiguous overall effect on the unemployment risk. At the same time, effective activation policies are more likely to reduce the expected average duration of unemployment for a given labour market slack.

Effective unemployment insurance combines the coverage and net replacement rates of unemployment insurance and assistance recipients and benefits. To calculate net replacement rates, family, social assistance and housing benefits are taken into account. In that respect, the generosity of unemployment benefit systems in terms of benefit level, duration of entitlement and, ultimately, the coverage of unemployed workers that they achieve, other things being equal, mitigates labour market insecurity as measured by the OECD. In terms of the 'flexicurity' agenda, increases in labour market insecurity suggest that increases in flexibility through employment protection legislation reforms have not been balanced sufficiently by income and activation support, given also the labour demand conditions.

Examining OECD data for the period of 2007, 2010 and 2013[4] for our countries (see Figures 14.5–14.7), one can see that there have been large *cross-country* variations in labour market insecurity, reflecting the different configurations of labour market policies and the different unemployment performances. Labour market insecurity was higher in 2013 compared to 2007 in all the countries examined in the book except Germany. In most cases, the largest increase in labour market insecurity took place between 2007 and 2010 and then stabilised in many of them between 2010 and 2013, while it also fell in Ireland, Slovakia and the UK. Dispersion in labour market insecurity within our group increased even between 2010 and 2013, although its increase was considerably smaller if Greece, arguably an outlier, is excluded from the calculation. During the austerity period, labour market insecurity increased by most in Greece (by 77%), Italy (by 72%) and the Netherlands (where it doubled), with the unemployment risk again being the driving force. Labour market insecurity increased by 4% in Sweden and by 31% in Czechia, driven mostly by the cuts in the generosity of unemployment insurance benefits rather than increases in the unemployment risk.

Looking at the components of labour market insecurity, the risk of unemployment was also higher in 2013 than in 2007 in all countries except Germany. Between 2010 and 2013, the unemployment risk fell in several countries, namely, Czechia, Slovakia, Ireland, Sweden

Figure 14.7: Evolution of the OECD labour market insecurity indicator (% of previous earnings), selected European Union member states, 2007, 2010 and 2013

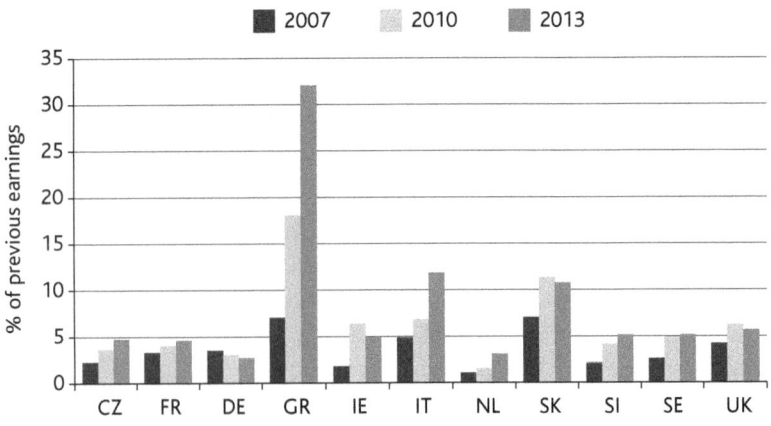

Note: Labour market insecurity = average expected monetary loss associated with becoming unemployed, as a share of previous earnings.

Source: OECD Job Quality statistics; own calculations

Conclusions

and the UK. Disparities in unemployment risk have increased since 2007, but if Greece is excluded from the calculation, disparity within the group fell, although unemployment risk remained as high as in 2010 on average.

Effective unemployment insurance declined between 2010 and 2013 rather than between 2007 and 2010, when, on average, it remained virtually stable in our group. Interestingly, the decline in the group's average of effective insurance is larger if Greece is excluded from the calculation. On the other hand, disparity across the countries examined was reduced both between 2007 and 2010 and between 2010 and 2013, suggesting that the countries in our group converged towards lower effective unemployment insurance. The only member state where effective unemployment insurance rose between 2010 and 2013 was the UK, whereas it remained stable in France.

Overall, we can say that policies have failed to reverse the increase in labour market insecurity since the beginning of the crisis, given the rise in unemployment. After 2010, the decline in effective unemployment insurance seems to have been the main driver of this failure while the unemployment risk remained, on average, stable. Disparities in labour market insecurity rose throughout this period.

Figure 14.8: Evolution of the OECD unemployment risk indicator (% of time), selected European Union member states, 2007, 2010 and 2013

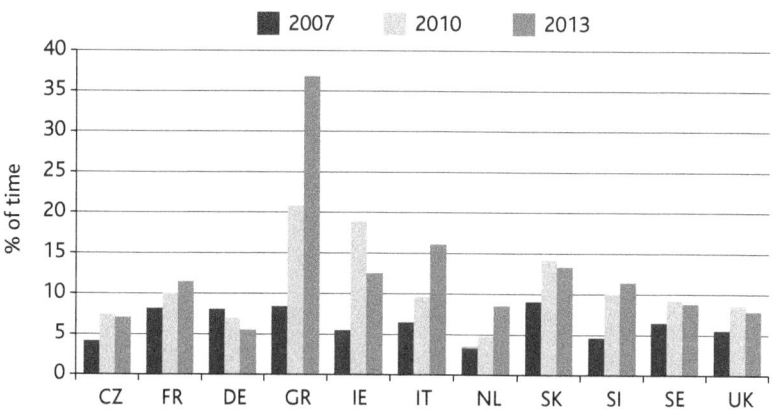

Note: Unemployment risk = proportion of time a working person can expect to spend on average in unemployment.

Source: OECD Job Quality statistics; own calculations

Figure 14.9: Evolution of the OECD effective unemployment insurance indicator (% of earnings), selected European Union member states, 2007, 2010 and 2013

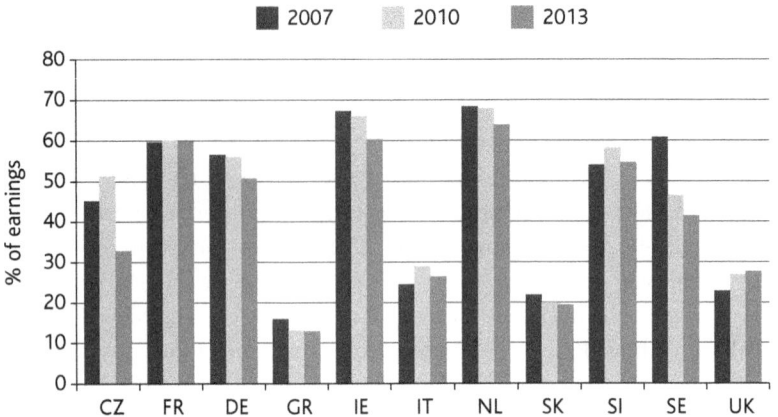

Note: Effective unemployment insurance = the share of earnings that employed workers can reasonably expect to retain during their eventual unemployment spell on average.
Source: OECD Job Quality statistics; own calculations

Concluding remarks

The findings of this book suggest that the broad directions of labour market policy change that were observed in the era of 'permanent austerity' prior to the recent crisis have not been fundamentally altered since the shift of fiscal policies in Europe towards austerity in 2010. Common principles such as activation, welfare readjustment and flexicurity still seem to be guiding labour market reforms to varying extents in several member states. Dualisation and welfare protectionism trends have also been evident and reinforced in certain member states. Fiscal austerity seems to have been borne particularly heavily in certain countries that either had to seek international financial support for their public debt and banks (Greece and Ireland) or were led by governments with an unwavering 'small state' agenda (UK), leading to retrenchment in their labour market policies. Diversity across and within labour market regimes has been observed rather than convergence.

The empirical analysis of the book also suggests that even in those countries where we can observe change guided by flexicurity or 'welfare readjustment' intentions, reforms have been taking place under tight budget constraints and cheaper approaches to implementing these directions have been privileged, while reforms in employment protection legislation have, in general, led to lower overall protection even if the gap between insiders and outsiders has been narrowed. Even in countries where pressures for cost containment have not been high, previous changes towards 'leaner and meaner' labour market policies have not been significantly reversed (eg Germany and Sweden). Although further research is required in order to identify the precise effects of labour market policies (and combinations thereof) on labour market insecurity and its components, the evidence presented in this chapter suggests that the labour market policies since 2010 have largely failed to reverse the increase in labour market insecurity since 2007, in the context of the deepest post-war recession and a very prolonged recovery that increased the risk of unemployment, while effective insurance against unemployment has declined in all but two countries. Not only has labour market insecurity grown on average, but disparities in its incidence have also grown across member states (as have disparities in employment and unemployment).

At the time of writing, fiscal policies in Europe have become less restrictive overall, although by no means stimulating despite calls from international organisations such as the OECD and the IMF for a more expansionary stance, and recovery in output growth appears to be slowly gaining strength. However, employment creation has been relatively weak, while there are concerns about the quality of jobs that are created (ECB, 2016): they tend to be insecure and allowing for fewer hours of employment than often desired, resulting overall in 'hidden unemployment' even though the headcount of those in employment has been rising. At the same time, public debt to GDP ratios are still too high for comfort and are only slowly declining. What this means is that the pressures identified in the introduction of the book on the demand for and supply of labour market policies are still in place, if somewhat weaker. This is why the patterns of change identified in this book are still a 'work in progress' and will require further research.

It is an open question whether the trends of reduced protection will be reversed once pressures on public budgets ease. For one, given the 'bad equilibrium' of low growth, high unemployment, zero interest rates and the overly restrictive overall fiscal policy stance that the EU and, in particular, large parts of the euro area have been caught in, reducing public debt to levels that would allow some latitude in fiscal policy will likely take a long time. For another, it is not clear whether the observed trends towards more labour market flexibility, activation by means of incentive reinforcement and less security are circumstantial or will be locked in as part of the 'low-road' growth strategies of member states who cannot afford to spend on enhancing labour market security, further reinforcing the divergence in labour market outcomes that is observed. This is an ominous prospect for the EU and particularly the Economic and Mentary Union (EMU) given the recent rise of Euro-sceptic parties across Europe and of labour market insecurity (Halikiopoulou and Vlandas, 2015). EU policymakers, among others, seem to have changed their discourse from the promotion of 'flexicurity' to the pursuit of flexibility and resilience (Canton et al, 2014), the latter being essentially a variant of flexibility. While labour market policies remain a national competence, the indirect pressures from the EU and especially the EMU have increased substantially, not just through budget constraints, but also through greater adjustment pressures on labour markets. The way in which the two policy levels interact in shaping labour market policy changes will also have to be further researched given the observed disparities across member states.

Notes

[1] The 'reform effort per year' is arguably a crude indicator as the effects of labour market reforms have been shown to depend on the context in which they are undertaken and often the interactions among them.

[2] Positive cumulative change in the structural balance indicates stronger effort for consolidation, that is, the reduction of deficits. Under conditions of recession, this is more fiscal austerity.

[3] Public expenditure on labour market services per person wanting to work could only be calculated for a very limited number of countries due mostly to a lack of data on the number of participants and participation rates per 100 persons wanting to work in these programmes, from which the persons wanting to work could be deduced.

[4] Data from the OECD Job Quality Database.

References

Ascoli, U., Guillen, A.M., Leon, M. and Pavolini, E. (2016) 'From austerity to permanent strain? European Union and welfare state reform in Italy and Spain', in C. De La Porte and E. Heins (eds) *The sovereign debt crisis, the EU and welfare state reform*, Basingstoke: Palgrave Macmillan.

Beramendi, P., Hausermann, S., Kitschelt, H. and Kriesi, H. (2015) 'Conclusion: advanced capitalism in crisis', in P. Beramendi, S. Hausermann, H. Kitschelt and H. Kriesi (eds) *The politics of advanced capitalism*, Cambridge: Cambridge University Press.

Canton, E., Grilo, I., Monteagudo, J., Pierini, F. and Turrini, A. (2014) 'The role of structural reform for adjustment and growth', DG Ecfin Economic Brief, Brussels.

Clasen, J. and Clegg, D. (2011) 'Unemployment protection and labour market change in Europe: towards "triple integration"?', in J. Clasen and D. Clegg (eds) *Regulating the risk of unemployment: National adaptations to post-industrial labour markets in Europe*, Oxford: Oxford University Press.

Clasen, J., Clegg, D. and Kvist, J. (2012) *European labour market policies in (the) crisis*, ETUI Working Paper 2012.12, Brussels: ETUI.

De la Porte, C. and Heins, E. (2015) 'A new era of European Integration? Governance of labour market and social policy since the sovereign debt crisis', *Comparative European Politics*, 13(1): 1–21.

Dolvik, J.E. and Martin, A. (eds) (2015) *European social models from crisis to crisis: Employment and inequality in the era of monetary integration*, Oxford: Oxford University Press.

ECB (European Central Bank) (2016) Recent wage trends in the Euro area, ECB Economic Bulletin-Box 2, Issue 3/2016, Frankfurt: ECB.

European Commission (2014) *Coverage and structure of the labour market reform (LABREF) database*, Reference Guide, Brussels: European Commission.

Ferrera, M. (2012) 'Verso un welfare piu europeo? Conclusione', in M. Ferrera, V. Fargion and M. Jessoula (eds) *Alle radicie del welfare all'italiana*, Venice: Marsilio.

Halikiopoulou, D. and Vlandas, T. (2015) 'Risks, costs and labour markets: explaining cross-national patterns of Far-Right party success in European Parliament elections', *Journal of Common Market Studies*, 54: 636–55.

Hausermann, S. (2012) 'The politics of old and new social policies', in G. Bonoli and D. Natali (eds) *The Politics of the 'New' Welfare State*, Oxford: Oxford University Press, pp 111–32.

Leibfried, S. (2010) 'Social policy: left to the judges and the markets?', in H. Wallace, M.A. Pollack and A.R. Young (eds) *Policy-making in the European Union*, Oxford: Oxford University Press, pp 253–83.

OECD (Organisation for Economic Co-operation and Development) (2014) *How good is your job? Measuring and assessing job quality*, Employment Outlook, Paris: OECD Publishing.

Viebrock, E. and Clasen, J. (2009) 'Flexicurity and welfare reform: a review', *Socio-economic Review*, 7: 305–31.

Wren-Lewis, S. (2016) 'A general theory of austerity', BSG-WP-2016/014, May, Blavatnik School of Government-University of Oxford.

Index

A

ageing populations   26, 132, 310
agency work   125–6, 314, 321, 335, 347
Agostini, C.   19, 22, 23, 25, 27, 29, 350, 354
Aidukaite, J.   278
Albertini, M.   83
Alesina, A.   18
ALMPs (active labour market policies) *see also specific policies*
  overview of   7, 41, 51–2
  conclusions on   338, 339–40, 344, 345, 355, 358
  Czechia   131, 258–62, 264, 266–7, 270, 275, 276, 350
  Denmark   184
  France   97–8, 102–4, 109, 131, 347
  Germany   117, 118, 128–32, 137–8, 347
  Greece   51–6, 131
  Ireland   197–8, 200–1, 202–3, 205, 206, 209–16, 219, 350
  Italy   73, 74, 75, 79, 83, 86, 131, 339, 346
  Netherlands   131, 141–2, 146, 149–51, 152, 158–9, 160–1, 162–5, 339, 348
  Portugal   131
  Slovakia   131, 280, 289–95, 297, 299, 300, 351
  Slovenia   131, 312–13, 316, 324–9, 335, 351
  Southern European countries   29
  summary of trends in   352–3, 354
  Sweden   24, 131, 170, 171, 179, 181–2, 184–7, 189, 190, 348
  types of   3–4
  UK   131, 233–5, 239, 240–2, 245, 349
Amlinger, M.   128
Amsterdam Institute for Advanced Labour Studies (AIAS)   62
Anglo-Saxon countries   8, 21–4, 38–41 *see also* Ireland; UK
anti-poverty measures   30, 87 n8, 103, 117, 128–9, 201, 228, 244, 349, 351 *see also* income support; social assistance; unemployment benefits
Antonopoulos, R.   55, 56
Anxo, D.   170
Appelbaum, E.   2
apprenticeships   54, 103, 133–4, 136–7, 237–8, 245
Arbetsförmedlingen   181
Armingeon, K.   8
Arni, P.   128
Ascoli, U.   347
atypical employment   4, 5, 27, 81, 95, 104, 106, 283, 286, 300, 315, 348, 351 *see also* fixed-term contracts; precarious employment; self-employment; temporary employment; zero-hours contracts
Austria   26, 54, 181, 182, 292
Autor, D.   186

B

Baboš, P.   283
Baccaro, L.   17
Baethge, M.   134
Ball, L.   7
banking systems   93, 143, 198, 226, 244, 314, 349
Bannink, D.   151
Barbier, J.-C.   110
Barnes, L.   226
Baumol, W.J.   2
Bednaš, M.   316
Belgium   26, 52, 126, 164 n1
Bengtsson, M.   184
Bennett, H.   233, 234, 345, 349

Beramendi, P. 8, 346
Bergmark, Å 182
Berton, F. 74, 77
Blanchard, O.J. 7, 49
Boeri, T. 61, 84
Bohle, D. 9, 19, 30, 31, 278, 279, 280
Boisson-Cohen, M. 17, 27
Bonoli, G. 2, 3, 4, 5, 9, 74, 141, 162, 184, 186, 201, 209, 240, 242, 246
Borghi, V. 216
Bowen, W.G. 2
Brenke, K. 128
Brinkley, I. 232
Bruckmeier, K. 119
Busemeyer, M.R. 133, 134

C

Canton, E. 18, 360
Card, D. 51, 55
carers, support for 209, 211, 240
Carlin, W. 27
Castel, R. 96
Central and Eastern Europe (CEE) 8, 9, 17, 28–30 *see also* Czechia; Slovakia; Slovenia
Charpy, C. 102
childcare 83–4, 129, 206, 254
children, dependent 47, 48, 78, 129, 205, 258
Chkalova, K. 154
Christopoulou, R. 61
Chung, H. 189
civil service jobs *see* public sector employment
Claessen, J. 154
Clasen, J. 6, 9, 50, 60–1, 76, 96, 101, 102, 110, 141, 147, 151, 206, 209, 229, 230, 231, 235, 239, 240, 262, 345, 347, 348, 355
Clegg, D. 9, 96, 97, 101, 102, 103, 110, 141, 147, 151, 206, 209, 227, 230, 234, 236, 345
collective agreements 27, 76, 80, 106, 107–8, 125–6, 127, 171, 172–7, 208, 231, 246, 263, 309, 321
Colomb, F. 98
common currency area *see* Eurozone
community work programmes 55–6, 216, 234, 236 *see also* public service/public works
competitiveness 19–20, 27, 28–30, 208, 279
compulsoriness in benefit provision 119, 147, 210, 215, 216, 231, 233–7, 243, 269, 345
conditionality 26
 Czechia 257, 266, 267, 270, 350
 France 97
 Italy 75, 82
 Slovakia 284–5, 297, 301
 Slovenia 312–13, 324, 351
 Sweden 181–2, 187
 UK 234, 235, 240, 242, 243, 244
Continental European countries 8, 17, 26–8, 38–41 *see also* France; Germany
Coquet, B. 54
cost containment 29, 31, 359
 Continental European countries 27
 Czechia 259, 269, 270
 France 96, 97, 102
 Ireland 198, 204, 219, 350
 Sweden 186
Cronert, A. 191 n8
Crouch, C. 226
Czechia 253–76
 ALMPs (active labour market policies) 131, 258–62, 264, 266–7, 270, 275, 276, 350
 conclusions on 350
 employment protection legislation (EPL) 262–3, 270, 275, 276, 350
 labour market insecurity 356–7
 long-term unemployed 255, 257, 265–7, 344
 minimum wages 126, 258
 public expenditure in labour market policy measures 342–3
 reform effort per year 340–3
 structural reforms (SRs) 28–30
 summary of policy trends on 352–3
 unemployment 121, 255, 256, 261–2, 341, 356
 unemployment benefits 256–8, 266–7, 269, 270, 275, 350

Index

unemployment insurance 358

D

Daniel, C. 96
Dar, A. 233, 235
Davidsson, J.B. 9, 18, 98, 170, 171, 174, 175, 178, 179, 348
De Beer, P. 141, 159
De Groot, N. 154
De la Porte, C. 298, 354
De Mets, P. 49
debt (government) 29, 44, 228, 244, 255, 256, 282, 314, 315, 347, 349, 358, 359
Deeming, C. 239, 240, 242
DeGrauwe, P. 10 n3
Degryse, C. 17
Dekker, F. 151
demographic trends 21, 115, 121–2, 310 *see also* ageing populations; older workers; youth unemployment
Den Butter, F. 144, 145
Denmark 24, 25, 50, 184
dependent children 47, 48, 78, 129, 205, 258
deregulation of labour market 6, 19, 25, 59, 61, 117, 125, 137–8, 156–7, 173, 174, 175–6, 190, 278, 346
Dingeldey, I. 181
direct work schemes 200, 209–10, 212, 214, 257, 260, 293, 351
disability welfare 30, 345
  Czechia 266
  Ireland 201, 202, 204–5, 209, 211, 218
  Netherlands 152, 155, 158, 160, 161, 163
  UK 230, 239, 240, 242, 244
dismissal rules
  Czechia 262, 263, 270
  France 98–9, 105, 109
  Germany 119
  Greece 56–7, 66–8
  Italy 74, 76, 77, 78, 80, 81, 82, 83, 84, 85
  Netherlands 151–2, 155, 159
  Slovakia 287
  Slovenia 321
  Sweden 172, 174, 175
  UK 232

Doherty, M. 208
Dolado, J.J. 54
Dolvik, J.E. 355
Dølvik, E. 18, 19, 24, 25, 26
Domonkos, S. 350
Doorley, J. 211
Drahokoupil, J. 279
drift, policy 4, 9, 99, 109, 230, 301, 345, 347, 351
dualisation of labour markets 358
  see also insiders; outsiders
  Continental European countries 27
  France 95, 96–9, 106, 107, 108–11
  Greece 61
  Ireland 197
  Italy 84
  Slovenia 313
  Southern European countries 28
  Sweden 170, 171, 190, 348
Duell, N. 280, 293
Dukelow, F. 198, 202, 350

E

early retirement 30, 123–4, 132–3, 311, 347
Ebbinghaus, B. 117, 118
Economic and Monetary Union (EMU) 5, 7, 8, 17, 29, 115, 145, 256, 360
economic growth 18–20, 27, 30
  France 92
  Germany 348
  Ireland 21, 199
  Italy 346–7
  Netherlands 143
  Slovakia 282
  Slovenia 314
  UK 226, 227
education 3, 20 *see also* training
  Anglo-Saxon countries 22, 23, 39
  Continental European countries 27, 28, 39
  Greece 53
  Ireland 23, 211, 213, 216–18
  Italy 79, 86
  Netherlands 146, 149, 163, 348
  Nordic countries 24, 25, 26, 39
  Slovakia 283
  Slovenia 329

Southern European countries 29, 30, 39
Sweden 187
UK 22, 236, 237–8
Visegrad countries 31, 32, 39
Eichhorst, W. 16, 92, 117, 118, 119, 122, 187, 347
Elbaum, M. 104
Emmenegger, P. 5, 170, 171, 172, 175
employment assistance measures 3–4, 9, 95, 97, 141, 162 *see also* employment services
employment protection legislation (EPL) *see also* dismissal rules; redundancy procedures
overview of 3, 41
conclusions on 340, 355, 358–9
Czechia 262–3, 270, 275, 276, 350
France 98–9, 104–8, 347
Germany 119–20, 123–4, 125
Greece 44, 56–60, 346
Ireland 206–9, 211, 219, 350
Italy 74, 76, 77, 78, 80, 81, 82, 85, 346
Netherlands 151–2, 155, 159, 348
Slovakia 280, 287–9, 299, 351
Slovenia 319, 321–2, 330, 335
and structural reforms (SRs) 19
summary of policy trends on 352–3
Sweden 172–7, 188, 348
UK 230–3, 243–4, 245, 246, 349
employment services 74, 86, 102, 118, 130, 233, 292–3, 301, 312, 351
EMU (Economic and Monetary Union) 5, 7, 8, 17, 29, 115, 145, 256, 360
enterprise, support for 209, 211, 212, 214 *see also* start-up incentives
Erhel, C. 97
Erixon, L. 170
Esping-Andersen, G. 5, 9, 225
Estonia 126, 348
Europe 2020 strategy 6
European Central Bank (ECB) 44, 84, 198

European Commission
assessment of Greece 59
employment protection legislation (EPL) 289
excessive deficit procedure 91, 92–3, 255–6, 277, 300, 301, 314, 349, 351
and flexicurity 60
internships 211
Labour Market Reforms (LABREF) database 59, 338
Stability and Growth Pact 86, 91, 92–3, 115, 298
Task Force for Greece 52, 54, 55
on tax 199
unemployment benefits 45
Youth Guarantee initiative 54, 83, 185, 216, 316, 326, 346
European Employment Strategy (EES) 6, 50, 52
European Qualifications Framework 134
European Semester process 202
European Social Charter 256
European Social Fund (ESF) 50, 51, 52, 54, 83, 258–9, 327
European Union
ALMPs (active labour market policies) 50
and Czechia 255
and the El Khomri law (France) 107
as international supervisor of Greece 44
and labour market flexibility 360
and sovereign debt crises 7
structural funds in Greece 55
in the Troika 44, 198, 349
and the UK 225
Euro Plus Pact 322
Eurostat 22, 25, 28, 31, 38–41
Eurozone 29, 93, 116, 184, 279, 347, 354, 359
expansion 1, 5–6, 9, 25, 29, 344–5, 352–3
Germany 27, 116, 123, 125, 127
Greece 49, 54, 66–8
Ireland 202, 217
Italy 81, 82, 83
Slovakia 283, 299
Slovenia 319, 320, 322, 329
Sweden 170

Index

UK 244, 245
Eydoux, A. 98

F

Falkner, G. 263
family benefits 205
Farnsworth, K. 226, 227
Felgueroso, F. 54
Ferrera, M. 73
Filipovič Hrast, M. 309, 351
Finland 24, 25, 26, 181
Finn, D. 233
Fisher, S. 279
Fishwick, T. 236
fixed-term contracts
  France 94–5, 104, 105, 106
  Germany 122
  Greece 44, 56–7
  Italy 74, 75, 78, 81, 84
  Slovenia 313, 314, 319, 320, 321, 324, 325, 334
  Sweden 172–3, 176
flat-rate benefits 117, 178, 182, 197, 229, 239
flexicurity 5–6, 6, 338, 353, 355, 358, 360
  France 92, 105–8, 109–10, 347
  Germany 117
  Greece 50, 52, 60–1
  Ireland 60–1
  Italy 80
  Netherlands 147, 148, 156–7, 348
  Slovenia 316, 318–20, 330, 351
Fontaine, F. 95
foreign direct investment (FDI) 21, 199, 279, 280
Foster, S. 237
France 91–114
  ALMPs (active labour market policies) 97–8, 102–4, 109, 131, 292, 347
  conclusions on 347
  employment protection legislation (EPL) 98–9, 104–8, 347
  labour market insecurity 356
  long-term unemployed 99, 100, 109, 344
  minimum wages 126
  public expenditure in labour market policy measures 342–3, 344

reform effort per year 340–3
structural reforms (SRs) 26–8
summary of policy trends on 352–3
unemployment 93–4, 95, 99, 103, 109, 121, 341
unemployment benefits 95, 96–108, 178, 347
unemployment insurance 96, 101–2, 107, 357, 358
Freud, D. 243
Freyssinet, J. 93, 96, 100, 101, 102, 105, 106, 110
Frigant, V. 279

G

Gallie, D. 73, 256
Garibaldi, P. 61, 84
Gautié, J. 100, 105
generosity levels of benefits 80, 86, 129, 133, 169, 182, 285, 295, 355–6
Germany 115–39
  ALMPs (active labour market policies) 117, 118, 128–32, 137–8, 292, 347
  conclusions on 347–8, 359
  employment protection legislation (EPL) 119–20, 123–4, 125
  labour market insecurity 356–7
  long-term unemployed 117, 118, 127, 130, 344
  minimum wages 119, 123–4, 126–8, 347
  overview of structural reforms 27
  public expenditure in labour market policy measures 342–3, 347
  reform effort per year 339, 340–3
  structural reforms (SRs) 26–8
  summary of policy trends on 352–3
  unemployment 116, 120, 121, 128, 130, 341, 343, 356
  unemployment benefits 117, 178, 181
  unemployment insurance 117–18, 358
Gingerich, D. 17
globalisation 17, 115

367

Glynn, I. 200
Goerne, A. 236
Greece 43–68
 ALMPs (active labour market policies) 51–6, 131
 conclusions on 345–6, 357
 employment protection legislation (EPL) 44, 56–60, 346
 labour market insecurity 356–7
 long-term unemployed 46, 47–8, 49, 50, 344
 minimum wages 47, 59, 61, 126
 public expenditure in labour market policy measures 342–3
 reform effort per year 339, 340–3
 structural reforms (SRs) 28–30
 summary of policy trends on 352–3
 unemployment 43–4, 52–4, 55–6, 121, 339, 341, 345
 unemployment benefits 45–50, 345
 unemployment insurance 45–7, 49, 50
Green-Pedersen, C. 85
Gregg, P. 243
Greskovits, B. 9, 19, 30, 31, 278, 279, 280
Griggs, J. 233, 239
Grubb, D. 201, 204, 206, 215
Gualmini, E. 73
Gustafsson, S. 172
Gyarfášová, O. 285, 293

H

Hacker, J.S. 4, 9, 99, 301
Halikiopoulou, D. 360
Hall, P. 16, 17, 27, 225, 254
Ham, J. 280, 284, 289
Hamskär, I. 172
Harari, D. 236
Hassel, A. 16, 17, 118, 122, 347
Häusermann, S. 4, 5, 6, 20, 69, 81, 83, 116, 156, 201, 318, 319, 320, 345
health care 22, 30, 107, 160, 255–6, 268, 329
Heins, E. 298, 345, 349, 354 *see also* Viebrock, E.
Hemerijck, A. 2, 17, 156, 324
Heyes, J. 60–1

high road 17, 20, 24
Hills, J. 229, 230
Hodgson, A. 238
Hohendanner, C. 119, 122
Hoogenboom, M. 141, 149, 151, 157, 162, 348
Hora, O. 267
Houston, E. 19
Howell, C. 17
human capital
 and ALMPs 3
 Italy 81
 and pensions 18
 recalibration 17
 UK 235–8, 240, 242, 243, 349
Hungary 28–30, 31, 126

I

Ignjatović, M. 311, 313, 351
illness benefits *see* sickness insurance/benefits
Immervoll, H. 201
incentive reinforcement measures 3–4, 9, 109, 141, 162, 209, 345, 354, 359
income protection 25, 170, 171, 177–83, 188, 283–7, 318–24, 350 *see also* minimum income schemes
income support 4, 7, 44, 45–50, 84, 96–102, 108, 117, 228–30, 347, 349, 351 *see also* needs-based social protection policies; social assistance; unemployment benefits
industrial relations *see* collective agreements; employment protection legislation (EPL); trade unions
industrial-logic social policies 81, 82, 83, 116, 156, 162, 225, 228, 246, 319
inequality 24, 110, 117
inflation 230, 255, 265
information and communication technologies 3, 32
in-kind benefits 265, 267
insiders 5, 6, 7, 9, 337, 359 *see also* dualisation of labour markets
 Czechia 256, 258, 262, 267, 268, 270
 France 101, 110, 347

Index

Germany   133
Greece   61
Italy   69, 74, 81
Slovakia   351
Slovenia   318, 320, 321, 351
Sweden   171, 177, 180, 190
UK   228, 230, 244, 246
institutionalism   253–4, 269, 270
intellectual property   32
International Labour Office (ILO)   56, 60
International Monetary Fund (IMF)   44, 49, 55, 59, 198, 349, 359
internships   211, 214, 216
inter-professional agreements   104, 105
involuntary part-time work   60, 94, 204, 359
involuntary temporary work   60, 71–2, 94–5, 101
in-work benefits   102, 129–30, 205, 239
in-work poverty   4, 129, 325
Ioannidou, A.   53
Ireland   197–224
   ALMPs (active labour market policies)   197–8, 200–1, 202–3, 205, 206, 209–16, 219, 350
   conclusions on   349–50
   employment protection legislation (EPL)   206–9, 211, 219, 350
   flexicurity   60–1
   labour market insecurity   356–7
   long-term unemployed   200, 205, 210, 215, 218, 219, 344
   minimum wages   126, 208
   overview of structural reforms   21–4
   public expenditure in labour market policy measures   342–3, 344
   reform effort per year   340–3
   structural reforms (SRs)   21–4
   summary of policy trends on   352–3
   unemployment   197, 199–200, 202, 341, 350, 356
   unemployment benefits   181, 202–5, 207, 209–16, 350
   unemployment insurance   358
Italy   69–90

ALMPs (active labour market policies)   73, 74, 75, 79, 83, 86, 131, 339, 346
conclusions on   346–7
employment protection legislation (EPL)   74, 76, 77, 78, 80, 81, 82, 85, 346
labour market insecurity   356–7
long-term unemployed   344
public expenditure in labour market policy measures   342–3
reform effort per year   340–3
structural reforms (SRs)   28–30
summary of policy trends on   352–3
unemployment   69, 71–3, 121, 341, 343
unemployment benefits   73–4, 75, 76, 77, 78–9, 80, 82, 83, 85–6, 346
unemployment insurance   73–4, 75, 77, 83, 85–6, 358
Iversen, T.   2, 5, 170, 171

J

Jansen, M.   54
Jansson, O.   24, 25
Jessop, B.   20
Jessoula, M.   10 n2
job coaching   161, 162
job creation schemes
   conclusions on   359
   Czechia   260, 261
   France   97, 99, 100, 104
   Germany   118
   Greece   51, 59
   Ireland   198, 209
   Netherlands   156, 161
   Slovakia   289, 290, 292, 295, 351
   UK   233, 235, 349
job mobility   142, 151, 171
job protection programmes   147, 151–2, 158, 162, 171, 172–7, 226, 244, 320, 321
joblessness/worklessness   43, 45, 242, 281, 284, 294, 345 *see also* unemployment
job-placement services   74, 86, 102, 118, 130, 233, 292–3, 301, 312, 351
Jurajda, Š   280

369

K

Karlsson, N. 177
Karpisek, Z. 291
Kazepov, Y. 75, 83, 86, 87
Kelly, E. 211
Kjellberg, A. 176, 180
Kluve, J. 51, 55
Knotz, C. 181
Kolarič, Z. 309, 312
Konle-Seidl, R. 92, 187
Kopač, A. 312
Kordež, B. 319
Kornelakis, A. 61
Kotrusová, M. 269
Krugman, P. 7
Kureková, L. 280, 293
Kusá, Z. 295
Kvist, J. 110, 240

L

Lanning, T. 238
Lartigot-Hervier, L. 102
Latvia 126
Lavrač, V. 309
Le Cacheux, J. 28, 98
Leibried, S. 354
Leigh, D. 7
Lenihan, B. 204
Leon, M. 83
liberal welfare state regimes 225, 244, 345 *see also* Ireland; UK
life-cycle perspectives 70
Lindberg, H. 177
Lindsay, C. 242
Lithuania 126
Lødemel, I. 209
Loftus, C. 204, 209
lone parents *see* single parents
long-term unemployed 343, 344, 345
   Czechia 255, 257, 265–7, 344
   France 99, 100, 109
   Germany 117, 118, 127, 130
   Greece 46, 47–8, 49, 50
   Ireland 200, 205, 210, 215, 218, 219
   Netherlands 152, 163–4
   Slovakia 280–1, 295, 297, 298, 301
   Slovenia 313, 318
   UK 229, 233, 235
low road 17, 19, 20, 29, 354, 359–60
low-skilled work 2, 103, 104, 125, 176, 186, 187, 199–200
low-wage workers 118, 119, 127, 128, 133, 156, 157, 162, 208, 231, 258
Luxembourg 26, 126

M

Mabbett, D. 10 n3
Majcen, B. 309
Malherbert, E. 95
Malik, S. 231
Mallone, G. 79
mandatory elements *see* compulsoriness in benefit provision
manufacturing jobs 1, 3, 120, 121–2, 125, 154
marketisation of employment services 198, 215–16, 219, 234, 254, 259
Martin, A. 18, 19, 355
Martin, J.P. 201, 215
Mathernová, K. 278, 280
Matsaganis, M. 4, 46, 53, 61, 345–6
Mayhew, K. 22, 24
McGauran, A.M. 217
McGuinness, F. 233, 235
McGuinness, S. 201, 215
McKinsey 53
McKnight, A. 233, 234
means-tested benefits 47–8, 78, 96, 117, 147, 182–3, 197, 205–6, 229, 230, 239
Meikle, J. 231
Memorandum of Understanding (MoU) 22, 29, 54, 55, 58, 202
middle-class workers 142, 179
middle-income workers 100, 156, 157, 162
mid-siders 10 n2
migration 31, 200
Millberg, W. 19
Milner, S. 95, 103, 107
mini-jobs 118, 119, 128, 129, 330
minimum income schemes
   Czechia 259, 261, 264–7, 276, 350
   France 102

Germany   129
Ireland   205–6
Italy   80
Slovakia   295
Slovenia   322
Sweden   182–3
minimum wages
  Belgium   126
  Czechia   126, 258
  Estonia   126
  France   126
  Germany   119, 123–4, 126–8, 347
  Greece   47, 59, 61, 126
  Hungary   126
  Ireland   126, 208
  Latvia   126
  Lithuania   126
  Luxembourg   126
  Netherlands   126, 152
  Poland   126
  Portugal   126
  Romania   126
  Slovakia   126, 295, 296, 297
  Slovenia   126, 316, 319, 335
  Spain   126
  UK   126, 232, 237, 243, 349
  US   126
Miollan, S.   279
Mirza-Davies, J.   234, 237, 238
Mitrakos, T.   53
mobility allowances   58, 73, 76, 77, 81–2
Möller, J.   122
Monastiriotis, V.   61
Moreira, A.   209
Morel, N.   20, 240
Munich, D.   284, 289, 291
Murphy, M.P.   201, 204, 206, 209, 211, 217, 218
mutual obligations model   216, 219, 350
Mýtna Kureková, L.   293–4

N

Naczyk, M.   170, 171
Natali, D.   2, 4, 9, 350, 354
needs-based social protection policies
  conclusions on   345
  Germany   116
  Ireland   205–6

Italy   81, 83
overview of structural reforms   4
Slovakia   277, 280, 281, 294, 295–8, 299, 300–1
Slovenia   320
summary of trends in   352–3
UK   229, 239–40, 245
Nelson, K.   182
net replacement rate (NRR)
  Anglo-Saxon countries   23, 38
  conclusions on   355
  Continental European countries   38
  Czechia   258, 265
  Ireland   201
  Nordic countries   24, 26, 38
  Slovakia   285
  Southern European countries   29, 38
  and structural reforms (SRs)   21
  Sweden   178, 179, 180, 183
  Visegrad countries   31, 38
Netherlands   141–68
  ALMPs (active labour market policies)   131, 141–2, 146, 149–51, 152, 158–9, 160–1, 162–5, 339, 348
  conclusions on   348
  employment protection legislation (EPL)   151–2, 155, 159, 348
  labour market insecurity   356–7
  long-term unemployed   152, 163–4, 344
  minimum wages   126, 152
  public expenditure in labour market policy measures   342–3, 344
  reform effort per year   340–3
  structural reforms (SRs)   26–8
  summary of policy trends on   352–3
  unemployment   121, 144–5, 146–53, 341
  unemployment benefits   146, 348
  unemployment insurance   141, 142, 145, 146–9, 150–1, 154, 155, 160–1, 162, 163, 358
New Public Management   216
new social risks   1–4, 20, 29
Nieuweboer, J.   154
Niklasson, H.   170

non-standard employment
 44, 60, 117, 118 *see also*
 atypical employment; fixed-
 term contracts; temporary
 employment
Nordic countries *see also* Sweden
 ALMPs (active labour market
  policies) 184–6
 anti-cyclical reform path 18
 divergence of socio-economic and
  labour policies 17
 overview of structural reforms 8,
  24–6, 38–41
 recalibration 17
 retrenchment 18
 social investment 17
 summary of policy trends on 354
not-for-profit sector 218
Nycander, S. 172, 175

O

OECD (Organisation for Economic
 Co-operation and Development)
 ALMPs (active labour market
  policies) 50, 186
 calls for more expansionary stance
  359
 deregulation of labour market 6
 employment protection legislation
  (EPL) 59, 74, 206
 measure of labour market
  insecurity 355
 mutual obligations model 216
 recommendations for labour
  market deregulation 6
 unemployment benefits 45, 178
older workers 70, 71, 72, 94, 97,
 104, 132, 172, 284, 290, 310,
 320
one-parent households *see* single
 parents
Open Method of Coordination
 50, 201
open-ended contracts 78, 81, 85,
 346
O'Rorke, G. 209
O'Sullivan, M. 204
outsiders 5, 6, 7, 9, 337, 359 *see
 also* dualisation of labour markets
 Czechia 258, 262, 268, 269,
  270, 350
 France 97, 101, 102, 110, 347

Greece 61
Italy 69
Slovakia 300
Slovenia 318, 320, 321
Sweden 171, 177, 180, 187, 190
UK 230, 239, 244

P

Palier, B. 17, 27, 95, 96, 98, 103,
 170, 254
Palme, J. 191 n8
Papadimitriou, D. 44, 52
Park, A. 243
partial unemployment 101, 105,
 110, 319
part-time employment 204, 359
 Czechia 257, 258
 France 94, 104, 107
 Germany 117, 118, 119, 128,
  129
 Greece 59
 involuntary part-time work 60,
  94, 204, 359
 Ireland 200, 204, 205, 206, 209,
  214
 mini-jobs 118, 119, 128, 129,
  330
 Netherlands 147, 148, 151, 154,
  159–60
 Slovakia 283
 Slovenia 313, 314, 315, 319,
  324, 325
 Sweden 174
passive labour market policies 19,
 24, 41, 75, 179, 215, 219, 311,
 312, 327, 345, 350
path dependency 189, 253–4, 269,
 270
Paugam, S. 73, 256
Pavolini, E. 29, 83, 346–7
Paz-Fuchs, A. 242
Peck, J. 242
Pennycook, M. 232
pensions 18, 20, 21, 24, 26, 27–8,
 29, 30–2, 38
 Czechia 255–6, 268
 Germany 133
 Ireland 202, 204–5
 Italy 86
 Slovakia 279, 298, 351
 UK 23, 230
Perez, S. 28–30

Index

Phillips, L. 231
Pierson, P. 1, 4
Pina, Á 208
Pochet, P. 17
Poland 28–30, 31, 86, 126
Polanyi, K. 19
Polder model 156
populism 141
portability of rights 105
Portugal 28–30, 59, 121, 126, 131
post-industrial logic of social policies 81, 82, 83, 151, 163, 225, 246
poverty reduction measures 30, 87 n8, 103, 117, 128–9, 201, 228, 244, 323, 325, 330, 349, 351 *see also* income support; social assistance; unemployment benefits
precarious employment 61–2, 78, 95, 141–2, 160, 198, 200, 204, 211, 232, 313, 318, 329, 350 *see also* fixed-term contracts; temporary employment; zero-hours contracts
private contractors for work services 198, 215–16, 219, 234, 254, 259, 261
private unemployment insurance 177, 179, 180, 183, 190, 230
public sector employment 23–4, 25, 26, 28, 30, 31, 58, 61–2, 97, 149, 171, 210, 280, 289, 290, 292
public sector spending (on administration) 20, 22, 23–4, 25, 26, 27, 28, 29, 30, 31, 40, 93, 280
public service/public works 55–6, 257, 266, 267–8, 269, 346
Pullan, L. 232
punitive versus enabling policies 187, 242, 297–8, 301, 313, 324, 327, 345, 352–3 *see also* sanctions

Q

quality of jobs 60

R

race to the bottom 15, 16–17, 32
Rajčáková, E. 281
Rakar, T. 309

Ranci, C. 83, 86, 87
readaptation policies 100
real wages 52, 105, 255
recalibration 6, 17, 110, 345, 347
rechargeable rights 101–2, 106
redundancy procedures 58, 106, 175–6, 230, 231, 244, 258, 262, 283, 287, 288, 321, 334 *see also* dismissal rules
Regan, A. 21
Renčko, J. 278
re-regulation 125, 126, 137, 347
research and development (R&D) 20, 22, 23, 25, 26, 27, 28, 29, 30, 31, 32, 40, 41, 354
resilience 360
retirement age 23, 146
retrenchment 5–6, 8, 9, 17, 21, 29–30, 30–1, 338, 344–5, 352–3
  Czechia 259, 350
  France 93, 97, 99, 109, 347
  Germany 116, 125, 129, 137
  Greece 345
  Ireland 197, 202
  Italy 82, 83, 84, 87, 346
  Netherlands 146, 159, 161–2
  Slovakia 299, 300, 301, 351
  Slovenia 318, 320, 322, 324, 329–30, 351
  Sweden 187, 189, 190, 348
  UK 243, 244, 245, 349
Rhodes, M. 28–30
risk re-categorisation 9, 206, 209
Rogers, S. 210
Romania 126
Ross, G. 28, 98
Rubio, E. 18
Rueda, D. 5, 324

S

Sacchi, S. 74, 75, 76, 84
sanctions 177, 181, 183, 204, 210, 216, 234, 239, 240, 241–2, 244, 257, 268, 269, 270, 313
Saxonberg, S. 253
Scarpetta, L. 201
Schelke, W. 10 n3
Schettkat, R. 2
Schiller, C. 118
Schmid, G. 19
Schmidt, V.A. 254
Schroeder, W. 18

Schweiger, C. 17, 31
seasonal workers 46, 284–5
segmentation, labour market 56–7, 60–1, 101, 122
selective investment 20, 24, 27, 32, 33, 34
self-employment
  Germany 118, 128
  Greece 46, 49, 50, 345
  Ireland 209
  Netherlands 141–2, 159–60
  Slovenia 313, 314, 324
  UK 226–7, 232
  Visegrad countries 31
service sector
  Germany 118, 119, 127
  mini-jobs 119
  Netherlands 151
  Slovenia 313
  Sweden 170, 171, 180
  tertiarisation of employment 2
  UK 238
short-time working schemes 27, 55, 76, 76–9, 83, 86, 101, 105, 116, 120–1, 122, 190, 261, 346
sickness insurance/benefits 160, 170, 201, 202, 203, 204–5, 227, 298, 322 *see also* disability welfare
Sinfield, A. 229
single parents 129, 201, 205, 206, 207, 209, 211, 218, 219, 234, 239, 240, 345
Sirovátka, T. 267, 350
skills 53–4, 118, 121–2, 130, 142, 171, 184, 186–7, 199–200, 236, 237, 238, 348 *see also* education; training
Slater, T. 229, 233
Slovakia 277–307
  ALMPs (active labour market policies) 131, 280, 289–95, 297, 299, 300, 351
  conclusions on 350–1
  employment protection legislation (EPL) 280, 287–9, 299, 351
  labour market insecurity 356–7
  long-term unemployed 280–1, 295, 297, 298, 301, 344
  minimum wages 126, 295, 296, 297

public expenditure in labour market policy measures 342–3
reform effort per year 340–3
structural reforms (SRs) 28–30
summary of policy trends on 352–3
unemployment 121, 279, 280–1, 282, 284, 285, 341, 356
unemployment benefits 280, 283–7, 299
unemployment insurance 286, 351, 358
Slovenia 309–36
  ALMPs (active labour market policies) 131, 312–13, 316, 324–9, 335, 351
  conclusions on 351
  employment protection legislation (EPL) 319, 321–2, 330, 335
  labour market insecurity 356
  long-term unemployed 313, 318, 344
  minimum wages 126, 316, 319, 335
  public expenditure in labour market policy measures 342–3, 344
  reform effort per year 340–3
  summary of policy trends on 352–3
  unemployment 121, 309, 310–11, 314, 319, 327, 328, 341
  unemployment benefits 311–12, 319, 320, 321, 322, 323, 324, 336, 351
  unemployment insurance 311, 312–13, 319, 351, 358
small firms 53, 74, 174
Smyth, P. 239, 240, 242
social assistance 26, 345
  Czechia 257, 259, 261, 264–5, 267, 350
  France 96, 100, 102, 103
  Germany 117, 118, 119, 129
  Ireland 197
  Italy 74, 78, 80, 82
  Netherlands 142, 145, 147, 148, 149–50, 151, 155, 158, 161, 162, 163, 348
  Slovakia 295–8, 299, 351
  Slovenia 311, 314, 315, 322, 324–6, 327, 336, 351

Sweden 169, 182–3
UK 23
social insurance 77, 182, 197, 261, 268, 309
social investment 4, 17, 20, 24, 345
Italy 81, 83–4, 86–7, 346
Slovenia 327–9
UK 235, 237, 240, 242, 243, 246, 349
vocational training as 4
versus workfare 34
social partnerships 202, 208, 269, 329, 330
social protection *see also* needs-based social protection policies
atypical careers/contracts 4
Continental European countries 28
Greece 43, 44
Ireland 200–2, 205–6, 209, 218
Italy 85
Nordic countries 26
Slovenia 322, 327–9
Southern European countries 28
and structural reforms (SRs) 19
UK 240, 242, 349
social standards devaluation 19, 20, 21, 22, 25, 29, 31, 32, 33, 34, 41, 354
social standards improvement 19, 20, 21, 27, 31–2, 32, 33, 41, 354
socio-economic protectionism 20, 27–8, 32, 33
Soskice, D. 16, 225
Southern European countries 8, 17, 28–30, 38–41, 354 *see also* Greece; Italy
sovereign debt crises 7, 29, 44, 69, 77, 80, 198
Spain 28–30, 126
Spermann, A. 126, 130
Spours, K. 238
start-up incentives 99, 118, 130, 289, 291, 293, 294
Stegmaier, J. 119
Streeck, W. 4, 17, 254
structural reforms (SRs) 15–41
student loans 146
student work 313, 322–3, 330, 335
subsidised employment contracts
Czechia 257, 260
France 95, 97, 103, 106, 110
Ireland 209–10, 214
Netherlands 149, 152, 161, 162, 164
Slovakia 289, 290, 291, 292, 294–5
Slovenia 315
Sweden 187
UK 233, 235
subsistence minimums 264–5, 266
Švecová, A. 281
Sweden 169–95
ALMPs (active labour market policies) 131
conclusions on 348–9, 359
employment protection legislation (EPL) 172–7, 188, 348
labour market insecurity 356–7
long-term unemployed 344
public expenditure in labour market policy measures 342–3
reform effort per year 339, 340–3
structural reforms (SRs) 24–6
summary of policy trends on 352–3
unemployment 121, 169, 171, 173, 177, 184, 186–7, 189, 341, 356
unemployment benefits 170, 177–81, 188, 189
unemployment insurance 176, 190, 358

T

tax 21, 22, 26, 31, 119, 146, 170, 199, 228, 230, 268, 286, 301, 311, 313
technological change 32, 186
temporary employment
Czechia 258, 263, 350
France 94–5, 101, 104, 105, 109, 110
Germany 117, 118, 122, 125–6, 347
Greece 44, 56–7, 59, 346
involuntary temporary work 60, 71–2, 94–5, 101
Ireland 208
Italy 71–2, 74–5, 80, 346
Netherlands 147, 151, 159–60

Slovakia   283
Slovenia   313, 314, 330
Sweden   25, 170, 173, 174, 175, 176, 187
UK   231–2, 236
Visegrad countries   31
Terrell, K.   284, 289, 291, 295
Teulings, V.   149
Thelen, K.   4, 20, 95, 98, 133, 134, 170, 254
Theodoropoulou, S.   7, 61
Thewissen, S.   189
Tobsch, V.   122
trade unions *see also* collective agreements
  Czechia   262
  France   96, 97, 98, 103, 106
  Germany   125–6, 127, 128, 133
  Greece   61, 62
  Ireland   202
  Italy   74
  Netherlands   141–2, 159, 162
  Nordic countries   25
  Slovakia   279
  Slovenia   309, 330
  Sweden   170, 172–7, 190
  UK   246
training *see also* apprenticeships; education; internships
  Continental European countries   27
  France   95, 97, 99, 100, 103, 106
  Germany   118, 121, 123–4, 130, 133–7
  Greece   53–4, 55, 66
  Ireland   200, 210, 216–18
  Italy   72, 81
  Netherlands   149, 154, 163, 348
  Slovakia   289, 290, 293
  Slovenia   326, 327
  Sweden   184–7
  UK   233, 234, 235–8, 243, 245, 246, 349
travel subsidies   291, 293, 294
Trbanc, M.   326
tribunals   231
Troika of lenders   44, 55, 58, 61, 198, 202, 209, 217, 349
Trommel, W.   149
Tros, F.H.   318
Tudoroiu, T.   278
Tuschizer, C.   98

U

UK   225–51
  ALMPs (active labour market policies)   131
  conclusions on   349
  employment protection legislation (EPL)   230–3, 243–4, 245, 246, 349
  labour market insecurity   356–7
  long-term unemployed   229, 233, 235, 344
  minimum wages   126, 232, 237, 243, 349
  overview of structural reforms   21–4
  public expenditure in labour market policy measures   342–3
  reform effort per year   340–3
  structural reforms (SRs)   21–4
  summary of policy trends on   352–3
  unemployment   121, 226, 243, 341, 343
  unemployment benefits   181, 228–30, 239–40, 243, 245
  unemployment insurance   229–30, 239, 357, 358
Uldrichova, V.   291
underemployment   197, 204 *see also* involuntary part-time work; partial unemployment
unemployment (rates of) *see also* long-term unemployed; youth unemployment
  conclusions on   341, 355–7
  Czechia   121, 255, 256, 261–2, 341, 356
  France   93–4, 95, 99, 103, 109, 121
  Germany   116, 120, 121, 128, 130, 356
  Greece   43–4, 52–4, 55–6, 121, 345
  Ireland   197, 199–200, 202, 350, 356
  Italy   69, 71–3, 121
  Netherlands   121, 144–5, 146–53
  partial unemployment   101, 105, 110, 319
  Slovakia   121, 279, 280–1, 282, 284, 285, 356

376

Slovenia 121, 309, 310–11, 314, 319, 327, 328
Southern European countries 30
Sweden 121, 169, 171, 173, 177, 184, 186–7, 189, 356
UK 121, 226, 243
unemployment assistance
 Greece 47–8, 49–50
 Italy 73–4, 83, 86
unemployment benefits 3, 340, 344, 352–3
 Czechia 256–8, 266–7, 269, 270, 275, 350
 France 95, 96–108, 347
 Germany 117
 Greece 45–50, 345
 Ireland 202–5, 207, 209–16, 350
 Italy 73–4, 75, 76, 77, 78–9, 80, 82, 83, 85–6, 346
 Netherlands 146, 348
 Slovakia 280, 283–7, 299
 Slovenia 311–12, 319, 320, 321, 322, 323, 324, 336, 351
 Sweden 170, 177–81, 188, 189
 UK 228–30, 239–40, 243, 245
unemployment insurance 355–6, 357–8, 359
 Czechia 358
 France 96, 101–2, 107, 357, 358
 Germany 117–18, 358
 Greece 45–7, 49, 50
 Ireland 358
 Italy 73–4, 75, 77, 83, 85–6, 358
 Netherlands 141, 142, 145, 146–9, 150–1, 154, 155, 160–1, 162, 163, 358
 private unemployment insurance 177, 179, 180, 183, 190, 230
 Slovakia 286, 351, 358
 Slovenia 311, 312–13, 319, 351, 358
 Sweden 176, 190, 358
 UK 229–30, 239, 357, 358
universal welfare model 170–1, 189, 348
US 126, 226

V

Van Berkel, R. 216
Van Bottenburg, M. 157
Van der Veen, R. 149
Van Gerven, M. 149, 150
Van Gestel, N. 150
Vandenbroucke, F. 324, 329
Veliziotis, M. 60
Venn, D. 231
Verschraegen, G. 52
Vesan, P. 74, 75, 79, 84, 346–7
Viebrock, E. 50, 60–1, 355
Visegrad countries 15, 30–2, 38–41 *see also* Central and Eastern Europe (CEE)
Visser, J. 62, 156
Vlandas, T. 360
Vleminickx, K. 324, 326
vocational training 3, 4, 27, 53, 54, 55, 100, 123–4, 133–7, 217–18, 256, 260
Vom Berge, P. 128
Voskeritsian, H. 61

W

wage bargaining *see* collective agreements
wage subsidies 4, 51, 54, 118, 161, 162, 164, 349
Weaver, K. 4
welfare dependency 209, 239, 246, 268
welfare protectionism 6, 116, 125–38, 338, 345, 347–8, 353, 358
welfare readjustment 6, 69, 81, 86, 116, 320, 338, 345, 347, 353, 358
Whitson, C. 208
Wickham Jones, M. 22
Wiggan, J. 215, 239, 242
Willmann, C. 102
Wilthagen, T. 318
women 3, 70–1, 79, 95
work experience programmes 130, 237, 260, 261
work-family reconciliation 52, 79, 83
workfare 20, 34, 210, 235, 242, 243, 245, 266–7, 269, 270, 293, 350
work first approaches 215, 235, 240–2, 349
working poor 4, 129, 325
working time regulation 108, 120–1, 190, 232, 262, 288

worklessness/joblessness 43, 45, 242, 281, 284, 294, 345 *see also* unemployment
Wren, A. 2, 3, 5, 171, 226
Wren-Lewis, S. 7, 349

Y

Young Person's Guarantee (UK) 235–6
Youth Guarantee initiative (European Commission) 54, 83, 185, 216, 316, 326, 346
youth unemployment
  Czechia 264, 267
  France 93–4, 100, 103, 104, 110
  Greece 52–4, 345
  Ireland 200, 216, 219
  Italy 70–1
  Netherlands 145, 148, 153–4
  Slovakia 281, 283, 294–5, 351
  Slovenia 313, 318, 319, 326
  UK 235–6, 237

Z

Zartaloudis, S. 52
Zeitlin, J. 50
zero-hours contracts 160, 232, 349